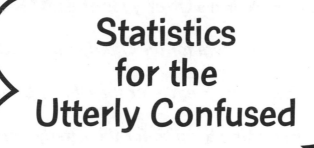

Statistics
for the
Utterly Confused

Second Edition

Other books in the **Utterly Confused** Series include:

Algebra for the Utterly Confused

Beginning French for the Utterly Confused

Beginning Spanish for the Utterly Confused

Calculus for the Utterly Confused

English Grammar for the Utterly Confused

Physics for the Utterly Confused

Test Taking Strategies and Study Skills for the Utterly Confused

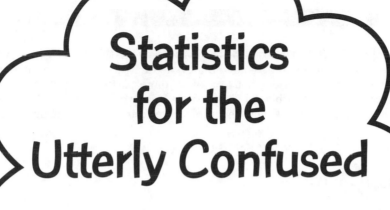

Statistics for the Utterly Confused

Second Edition

Lloyd R. Jaisingh

McGraw-Hill

New York   Chicago   San Francisco   Lisbon   London
Madrid   Mexico City   Milan   New Delhi   San Juan
Seoul   Singapore   Sydney   Toronto

The McGraw·Hill Companies

1 2 3 4 5 6 7 8 9 0   FGR/FGR   0 9 8 7 6 5

ISBN 0-07-146193-0

McGraw-Hill books are available at special quantity discounts to use as premiums and sales promotions, or for use in corporate training programs. For more information, please write to the Director of Special Sales, Professional Publishing, McGraw-Hill, Two Penn Plaza, New York, NY 10121-2298. Or contact your local bookstore.

Information contained in this work has been obtained by The McGraw-Hill Companies, Inc. ("McGraw-Hill") from sources believed to be reliable. However, neither McGraw-Hill nor its authors guarantee accuracy or completeness of any information published herein, and neither McGraw-Hill nor its authors shall be responsible for any errors, omissions, or damages arising out of use of this information. This work is published with the understanding that McGraw-Hill and its authors are supplying information but are not attempting to render engineering or other professional services. If such services are required, the assistance of an appropriate professional should be sought.

Further help with statistics can be found at the author's Web site: http://people. morehead-st.edu/fs/l.jaisin/

 This book is printed on recycled, acid-free paper containing a minimum of 50% recycled, de-inked fiber.

Library of Congress Cataloging-in-Publication Data

Jaisingh, Lloyd R.
    Statistics for the utterly confused / by Lloyd R. Jaisingh.—2nd ed.
        p. cm.
    Includes index.
    ISBN 0-07-146193-0 (acid-free paper)
    1. Statistics—Study and teaching.   I. Title.

QA276.18.J35 2006
519.5—dc22   2005024677

Dedication

This book is dedicated to my wife, Pam, for her tolerance, support, and love. Also, to my son Nathan, for all his love and appreciation, and to the memory of my mother, Mary, father, Solomon, and brother, Leslie, for all their nurturing, dedication, inspiration, and love.

Acknowledgments

I would like to thank my colleague Dan Seth for his suggestions, which were incorporated into the second edition of the text. Also, I would like to thank the very capable staff at McGraw-Hill, especially Editorial Assistant Adrinda Kelly and Senior Editing Supervisor Janice Race, for their tremendous help. In addition, I would like to express appreciation to my editor, Barbara Gilson, for having the faith in me to do the second editon of this book. I thank her for her support and will forever be grateful.

Contents

Contents

Contents

Preface

The main goal of this book is to present basic concepts in elementary statistics and to illustrate how to tackle some of the most common problems encountered in any elementary, noncalculus statistics course.

Statistics is a frightful subject for most students. This book provides a friendly, logical, step-by-step approach to any introductory college-level noncalculus statistics course to help students overcome this barrier. It is designed such that it can be used as the main text for AP statistics and by college students enrolled in any elementary noncalculus course. It is also ideal for the nontraditional student who is returning to school and needs to review or who needs a nontechnical reference book on the subject of statistics. In addition, professionals who need a quick reference guide may use this book. The book is written for nonstatisticians and can be used by students in all disciplines. The book takes a direct approach to the learning of concepts so that the reader does not have to wade through pages and pages of unnecessary information. Such an approach offers the student an effortless way to understand statistical concepts and, as such, furnishes him or her with a better chance at doing well in a noncalculus statistics course. In addition, this approach to presenting statistical concepts eases the stress of students who are enrolled in noncalculus statistics courses or who are reviewing before returning to college.

The "Test Yourself" section at the end of each chapter allows students to build confidence by working problems related to relevant concepts. Nonthreatening explanations of terms and symbols rather than definitions are given throughout the book. Examples are taken from a wide variety of disciplines that emphasize the concepts and are to the point.

It is the honest desire of the author that this book will help students to have a better understanding of concepts in elementary statistics. It is also the sincere hope of the author that this book will help students to lessen the stress brought about by the subject of statistics.

Lloyd R. Jaisingh
Morehead State University

Technology Integration

Because of the rapid changes in technology, the study of elementary statistics has undergone significant changes. Our teaching methods must be redesigned to accommodate and incorporate technology and to help students investigate, discover, and understand the needed concepts. In the "Technology Corner" sections of the book, the MINITAB software and the TI–83/84 calculators are used to illustrate how to alleviate much of the computational drudgery and manipulation within the text, enabling students to concentrate on the discovery, application, and reinforcement of the concepts. Keep in mind that the "Technology Corner" is not intended as a tutorial guide to the technology. It is anticipated that use of the technology will encourage students to discover and further clarify key concepts within elementary statistics in a relaxed environment. In addition, other technologies may apply, such as the SPSS, Microsoft EXCEL, etc.

Organization of the Text

This book is arranged into 15 chapters. These chapters cover a wide range of topics found in any elementary statistics course. The material is such that it can be used as a stand-alone text or along with any of the traditional texts. The book is divided into three main themes or parts. Part I deals with the descriptive nature of statistics, Part II deals with probability concepts, and Part III deals with statistical inference. The "Technology Corner" sections illustrate how the MINITAB software and the TI-83/84 calculator can be used to overcome some of the math anxiety and number crunching. Each chapter ends with a "Test Yourself" section, where students can attempt true/false, fill-in-the- blanks, or multiple-choice questions.

PART I

Descriptive
Statistics

CHAPTER 1

Graphical Displays

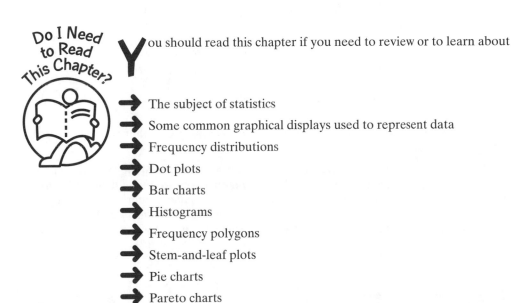

Do I Need to Read This Chapter?

You should read this chapter if you need to review or to learn about

➡ The subject of statistics

➡ Some common graphical displays used to represent data

➡ Frequency distributions

➡ Dot plots

➡ Bar charts

➡ Histograms

➡ Frequency polygons

➡ Stem-and-leaf plots

➡ Pie charts

➡ Pareto charts

In later chapters you will be introduced to other graphical displays, and you will recognize that these graphical displays can be combined with other measures to describe the data distribution.

1-1   Introduction

For us to have an understanding of what the subject of **statistics** is all about, we need to introduce some terminology. First, we will explain what we mean by the subject of statistics.

Explanation of the term—statistics: Statistics is the science of collecting, organizing, summarizing, analyzing, and making inferences from data.

    The subject of statistics is divided into two broad areas that incorporate the collecting, organizing, summarizing, analyzing, and making inferences from data. These categories are **descriptive statistics** and **inferential statistics**. These classifications are shown in **Figure 1-1**.

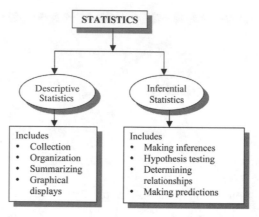

Figure 1-1:   Breakdown of the subject of statistics

    In order to obtain information, **data** are collected from variables used to describe an event.

Explanation of the term—data: Data are the values or measurements that variables describing an event can assume.

    Variables whose values are determined by chance are called **random variables**. There are two types of variables: **qualitative variables** and **quantitative variables**. Qualitative variables are nonnumeric in nature. Quantitative variables can assume numeric values and can be classified into two groups: **discrete variables** and **continuous variables**. A collection of values is called a **data set**, and each value is called a **data value**. **Figure 1-2** shows these relationships.

Figure 1-2:   Breakdown of the types of variables

Explanation of the term—quantitative data: **Quantitative data** are data values that are numeric. For example, the heights of female basketball players are quantitative data values.

Explanation of the term—qualitative data: **Qualitative data** are data values that can be placed into distinct categories according to some characteristic or attribute. For example, the eye color of your parents is classified as qualitative data.

Explanation of the term—discrete variables: **Discrete variables** are variables that assume values that can be counted. For example, the number of days it rained in your neighborhood for the month of March is a discrete variable.

Explanation of the term—continuous variables: **Continuous variables** are variables that can assume all values between any two given values. For example, the time it takes for you to do your Christmas shopping is a continuous variable.

In order for statisticians to do any analysis, data must be collected. One of the things statisticians may want to do is to make some inference on or general statement about a characteristic of a **population**. Sometimes it is impractical or too expensive to collect data from an entire population. In such instances, the statistician may select a representative portion of the population, called a **sample**. This is depicted in **Figure 1-3**.

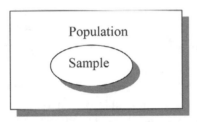

Figure 1-3: The relationship between sample and population

Explanation of the term—population: A **population** consists of all subjects that are being studied. For example, we may be interested in studying the distribution of ACT math scores of freshmen at a particular college campus. In this case, the population will be the ACT math scores of all the freshmen at that particular campus.

Explanation of the term—sample: A **sample** is a subset of a population. For example, if we were interested in studying the distribution of students on a given campus who will vote for a particular candidate for president of the student government, we may call every twenty-fifth student from a list. The sample will consist of the group of students who responded to the call.

Explanation of the term—census: A **census** is a sample of an entire population. For example, we may be interested in the distribution of the total flight times for a fleet of airplanes over a one-year period. If we collect total flight times for all the planes over the one-year period, then this set of data will constitute a census of total flight time values.

Both populations and samples have characteristics that are associated with them. These are called **parameters** and **statistics**, respectively.

Explanation of the term—parameter: A **parameter** is a characteristic or a fact of a population. For example, we may be interested in studying the distribution of the selling price of stocks for Fortune 500 companies on the last day of trading on Wall Street for the year. If the average stock price for these companies is $60, then this will be the value of the population average for the year or it will represent the value of a parameter. This is so because the population in this case constitutes all the Fortune 500 companies.

Explanation of the term—statistic: A **statistic** is a characteristic or a fact of a sample. For example, we may be interested in studying the distribution of the heights of female students at a college campus. If the average height of female students in a statistics class is five feet, then this will be the value of the sample average if we consider this group of students to be a sample. This is so because the sample in this case constitutes all female students in the class.

Since parameters are descriptions of a population, a population can have many parameters. Similarly, a sample can have many statistics. These associations are shown in **Figure 1-4**.

Figure 1-4: The difference between parameters and statistics

When selecting a sample, statisticians would like to select values in such a way that there is no inherent bias. One way of doing this is by selecting a **random sample**.

Explanation of the term—random sample: A **random sample** of a particular size is a sample selected in such a way that each group of the same size has an equal chance of being selected. For example, in a lottery game in which six numbers are selected, this will be a random sample of size six, since each group of size six will have an equal chance of being selected.

Quick Tip

There are other types of samples that will not be discussed in this text. These include systematic, stratified, cluster, and convenience samples.

1-2   Frequency Distributions

In this section we will deal with **frequency distributions**.

Explanation of the term—frequency distribution: A **frequency distribution** is an organization of raw data into tabular form using classes (or intervals) and frequencies.

The types of frequency distributions that will be considered in this section are **categorical, ungrouped**, and **grouped** frequency distributions.

Explanation of the term—frequency count: The **frequency** or **frequency count** for a data value is the number of times the value occurs in the data set.

Categorical or Qualitative Frequency Distributions

Explanation of the term—categorical frequency distributions: Categorical frequency distributions represent data that can be placed in specific categories, such as gender, hair color, or religious affiliation.

Example 1-1: The blood types of 25 blood donors are given below. Summarize the data using a frequency distribution.

AB	B	A	O	B
O	B	O	A	O
B	O	B	B	B
A	O	AB	AB	O
A	B	AB	O	A

Solution: We will represent the blood types as classes and the number of occurrences for each blood type as frequencies. The frequency table (distribution) in **Table 1-1** summarizes the data.

Table 1-1: Frequency Table for Example 1-1

CLASS (BLOOD TYPE)	FREQUENCY f
A	5
B	8
O	8
AB	4
Total	25

Quantitative Frequency Distributions—Ungrouped

Explanation of the term—ungrouped frequency distribution: An **ungrouped frequency distribution** simply lists the data values with the corresponding number of times or frequency count with which each value occurs.

Example 1-2: The following data represent the number of defective products observed each day over a 25-day period for a manufacturing process. Summarize the information with an ungrouped frequency distribution.

DAY	1	2	3	4	5	6	7	8	9	10	11	12	13
Defects	10	10	6	12	6	9	16	20	11	10	11	11	9

DAY	14	15	16	17	18	19	20	21	22	23	24	25
Defects	12	11	7	10	11	14	21	12	6	10	11	6

Solution: The ungrouped frequency distribution for the number of defects is shown in **Table 1-2**.

Table 1-2: Frequency Table for Example 1-2

CLASS (DEFECTS)	FREQUENCY f
6	4
7	1
9	2
10	5
11	6
12	3
14	1
16	1
20	1
21	1
Total	25

Quick Tip

Sometimes frequency distributions are displayed with the relative frequencies as well.

Explanation of the term—relative frequency: The **relative frequency** for any class is obtained by dividing the frequency for that class by the total number of observations.

$$\text{Relative frequency} = \frac{\text{frequency for class}}{\text{total number of observations}}$$

The frequency distribution in **Table 1-3** uses the data in **Example 1-2** and displays the relative frequencies as well as the corresponding percentages.

Table 1-3: Frequency Distribution Along with Relative Frequencies and Corresponding Percentages for Example 1-2

CLASS (DEFECTS)	FREQUENCY f	RELATIVE FREQUENCY	PERCENTAGE %
6	4	$^4/_{25} = 0.16$	16
7	1	$^1/_{25} = 0.04$	4
9	2	$^2/_{25} = 0.08$	8
10	5	$^5/_{25} = 0.20$	20
11	6	$^6/_{25} = 0.24$	24
12	3	$^3/_{25} = 0.12$	12
14	1	$^1/_{25} = 0.04$	4
16	1	$^1/_{25} = 0.04$	4
20	1	$^1/_{25} = 0.04$	4
21	1	$^1/_{25} = 0.04$	4
Total	25	1	100

Quick Tip

Sometimes, frequency distributions are displayed with the *cumulative frequencies* and *cumulative relative frequencies* as well.

Explanation of the term—cumulative frequency: The **cumulative frequency** for a specific value in a frequency table is the sum of the frequencies for all values at or below the given value.

Explanation of the term—cumulative relative frequency: The **cumulative relative frequency** for a specific value in a frequency table is the sum of the relative frequencies for all values at or below the given value.

Note: The explanations given for the cumulative frequency and cumulative relative frequency assume that the values (or classes) are arranged in ascending order from top to bottom.

The frequency distribution in **Table 1-4** uses the data in **Example 1-2** and also displays the cumulative frequencies and the cumulative relative frequencies.

Table 1-4: Frequency Distribution Along with Relative Frequencies, Cumulative Frequencies, and Cumulative Relative Frequencies for Example 1-2

CLASS (DEFECTS)	FREQUENCY	RELATIVE FREQUENCY	CUMULATIVE FREQUENCY	CUMULATIVE RELATIVE FREQUENCY
6	4	0.16	4	0.16
7	1	0.04	5	0.20
9	2	0.08	7	0.28
10	5	0.20	12	0.48
11	6	0.24	18	0.72
12	3	0.12	21	0.84
14	1	0.04	22	0.88
16	1	0.04	23	0.92
20	1	0.04	24	0.96
21	1	0.04	25	1.00

Quantitative Frequency Distributions—Grouped

Here we will discuss the idea of **grouped frequency distributions**.

Explanation of the term—grouped frequency distribution: A **grouped frequency distribution** is obtained by constructing classes (or intervals) for the data and then listing the corresponding number of values (frequency count) in each interval.

Quick Tip

There are several procedures that one can use to construct a grouped frequency distribution. However, because of the many statistical software packages available today, it is not necessary to try to construct such distributions using pencil and paper. Later in the chapter we will encounter a graphical display called a *histogram.* We will see that one can construct grouped frequency distributions directly from these graphical displays.

Quick Tip

A frequency distribution should have a minimum of 5 and a maximum of 20 classes. For small data sets, one could use between 5 and 10 classes. For large data sets, one can use up to 20 classes.

Example 1-3: The weights of 30 female students majoring in biology on a college campus are given below. Summarize the information with a frequency distribution using seven classes.

143	151	136	127	132	132	126	138	119	104
113	90	126	123	121	133	104	99	112	129
107	139	122	137	112	121	140	134	133	123

Solution: A histogram with seven classes is given in **Figure 1-5**. Further discussion about the histogram as a graphical display is given later in the chapter.

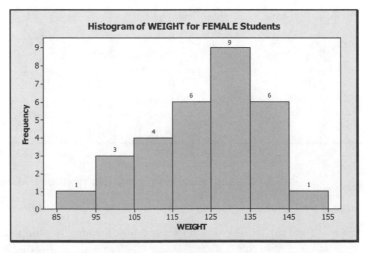

Figure 1-5: Histogram for the weight information in Example 1-3

One can extract the information from **Figure 1-5** to help in constructing a group frequency distribution. The frequency count for each class is given at the top of the vertical bars. A grouped frequency distribution for the data using seven classes is presented in **Table 1-5**. Observe, for instance, that the upper limit value for the first class and the lower limit value for the second class have the same value of 95. The value of 95 cannot be included in both classes, so the convention that will be used here is that **the upper limit of each class is not included in the interval of values**; only the lower limit values are included in the interval. Thus, the value of 95 is only included in the interval of values for the second class. In addition, the relative frequency for each class is presented as well as the percentage equivalent.

Table 1-5: Grouped frequency Distribution for Example 1-3

CLASS (WEIGHTS)	FREQUENCY	RELATIVE FREQUENCY	PERCENTAGE %
85–95	1	0.033	3.3
95–105	3	0.100	10.0
105–115	4	0.133	13.3
115–125	6	0.200	20.0
125–135	9	0.300	30.0
135–145	6	0.200	20.0
145–155	1	0.033	3.3
Total	30	≈1	≈100

Note: The **class width** for this frequency distribution is 10. It is obtained by subtracting the lower class limit for any class from the lower class limit for the next class. For the third class, the class limit = 115 – 105 = 10.

Quick Tip

In the group frequency distribution, observe that the relative frequency column did not add up to exactly 1, and the percentage column did not add up to exactly 100 percent. This is due to rounding of the relative frequency values to three decimal places.

1-3   Dot Plots

Explanation of the term—dot plot: A **dot plot** is a plot that displays a dot for each value in a data set along a number line. If there are multiple occurrences for a specific value, then the dots will be stacked vertically.

Example 1-4: Construct a dot plot for the information given in **Example 1-2.**

Solution: Figure 1-6 shows the dot plot for the data set. Observe that since there are multiple occurrences of specific observations, the dots are stacked vertically. The number of dots represents the frequency count for a specific value. For instance, the value of 11 occurred six times because there are six dots stacked above the value of 11.

Figure 1-6: Dot plot for Example 1-2

1-4   Bar Charts or Bar Graphs

Explanation of the term—bar chart (graph): A **bar chart** or **bar graph** is a graph that uses vertical or horizontal bars to represent the frequencies of a category in a data set.

Quick Tip

A bar chart (graph) is a valuable presentation tool because it is effective at reinforcing differences in magnitude. Bar charts permit the visual comparison of data by displaying the magnitude of each category as a horizontal or vertical bar. Bar charts are useful when the data set has categories (for example, hair color, gender, etc.) and data values that are qualitative in nature. Note that the bars are separated equally from each other.

Example 1-5: A sample of 300 college students was asked to indicate their favorite soft drink. The survey results are shown in **Table 1-6**. Display the information using a bar chart.

Table 1-6: Frequency Distribution for Example 1-6

SOFT DRINK	NUMBER OF STUDENTS
Pepsi-Cola	92
Coca-Cola	78
Dr. Pepper	48
7-Up	42
Others	40

Solution: Observe that these are categorical or qualitative data. The vertical bar chart for this information is shown in **Figure 1-7**. The number at the top of each category represents the number of values (frequencies) for that specific group (soft drink).

A horizontal bar chart for the same soft drink information is shown in **Figure 1-8**.

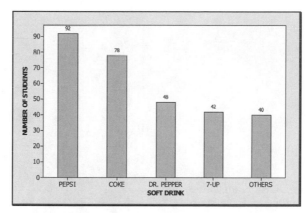

Figure 1-7: Vertical bar chart for Example 1-5

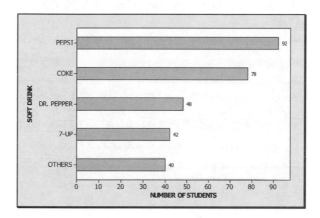

Figure 1-8: Horizontal bar chart for Example 1-5

1-5   Histograms

Explanation of the term—histogram: A **histogram** is a graphical display of a frequency or a relative frequency distribution that uses classes and vertical bars (rectangles) of various heights to represent the frequencies.

Quick Tip

Histograms are useful when the data values are quantitative. A histogram gives an estimate of the shape of the distribution of the population from which the sample was taken.

Example 1-6: Display the data in **Example 1-3** with a histogram using eight classes.

Solution: A histogram with eight classes for the data is shown in **Figure 1-9**.

Figure 1-9: Histogram with eight classes for data in Example 1-3

The histogram shows the frequency count for each class and with each class having a width of eight.

Quick Tip

Observe from the histogram in Figure 1-9 that there is a frequency count of 1 for the interval 88–96, a frequency count of 3 for the interval 104–112, etc. From this information we can construct a grouped frequency distribution swith eight classes similar to Example 1-3.

Quick Tip

If the relative frequencies (percents) are plotted along the vertical axis to produce a relative frequency (percent) histogram, the shape of the resulting histogram will be the same as that of a histogram in which the frequencies were plotted along the vertical axis. This is true because the relative frequencies are obtained by dividing the frequency values by the total number of values in the data set.

Figure 1-10 shows the histogram for the data given in **Example 1-3** with the percents (relative frequencies expressed as percents) plotted along the vertical axis. Observe that the shape of the histogram in **Figure 1-10** is identical to that displayed in **Figure 1-9**.

Figure 1-10: Histogram with eight classes for data in Example 1-3 with percents (relative frequencies expressed as percents) displayed along the vertical axis.

1-6   Frequency Polygons

Explanation of the term—frequency polygon: A **frequency polygon** is a graph that displays the data using lines to connect points plotted for the frequencies. The frequencies represent the heights of the vertical bars in the histograms.

Note: A frequency polygon provides an estimate of the shape of the distribution of the population.

Example 1-7: Display a frequency polygon for the data in **Example 1-3**.

Solution: The display given in **Figure 1-11** shows the frequency polygon superimposed on the histogram for **Example 1-6**.

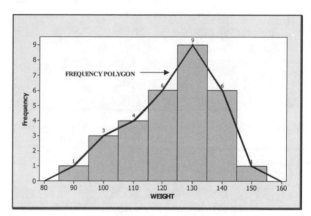

Figure 1-11: Frequency polygon superimposed on the histogram for the data in Example 1-3

Quick Tip

Observe that the distribution is mound shaped, with more of the values to the left of the peak. If this were a truly representative sample from the population, then one would expect that the distribution of the population of weights would have a similar shape. Also, observe that the line segments pass through the midpoints at the top of the rectangles and that the polygon is "tied down" to the horizontal axis at both ends. The points where the polygon is tied down correspond to the midpoints of the classes with zero frequency. In this case, the midpoints are 80 and 160. Midpoints of classes are called *class marks* or *class midpoints*.

1-7   Stem-and-Leaf Displays or Plots

Explanation of the term—stem-and-leaf plot: A **stem-and-leaf plot** is a data plot that uses part of a data value as the **stem** to form groups or classes and part of the data value as the **leaf**. A stem-and-leaf plot has an advantage over a grouped frequency distribution because a stem-and-leaf plot retains the actual data by showing them in graphic form.

The next example will illustrate how a stem-and-leaf plot is constructed.

Example 1-8: Consider the following values: 96, 98, 107, 110, and 112.

(a) Use the unit digit values as the leaves.

Solution: The data, with the stem and leaves, are shown in **Table 1-7**.

The corresponding stem-and-leaf plot is shown in **Table 1-8**.

(b) Use the unit and tens digits as the leaves.

Solution: The data, with the stem and leaves, are shown in **Table 1-9**.

The corresponding stem-and-leaf plot is shown in **Table 1-10**.

Table 1-7: Stems and Leaves for the Data in Example 1-8 with the Unit Digit as the Leaves

DATA	STEM	LEAF
96	09	6
98	09	8
107	10	7
110	11	0
112	11	2

Table 1-8: Stem-and-Leaf Plot with the Units Digit as the Leaves for Example 1-8

STEM	LEAVES
09	6 8
10	7
11	0 2

Table 1-9: Stems and Leaves for the Data in Example 1-8 with the Unit and Tens Digits as the Leaves

DATA	STEM	LEAVES
96	0	96
98	0	98
107	1	07
110	1	10
112	1	12

Table 1-10: Stem-and-Leaf Plot with the Unit and Tens Digits as the Leaves for Example 1-8

STEM	LEAVES
0	96 98
1	07 10 12

Example 1-9: A sample of the number of admissions to a psychiatric ward at a local hospital during the full phases of the moon is given below. Display the data using a stem-and-leaf plot with the leaves represented by the unit digits.

22	21	31	20	25	21	32	26	43	30	27
30	27	36	28	33	38	35	19	30	34	41
13	16	18	41	43						

Solution: The stem-and-leaf display for the data is given in **Table 1-11**.

Table 1-11: Stem-and-Leaf Display for Example 1-9

STEM	LEAVES
1	3 6 8 9
2	0 1 1 2 5 6 7 7 8
3	0 0 0 1 2 3 4 5 6 8
4	1 1 3 3

1-8 Time-Series Graphs

Data collected over a period of time can be displayed using a **time-series graph**.

Explanation of the term—time-series graph: A **time-series graph** displays data that are observed over a given period of time. From the graph, one can analyze the behavior of the data over time.

Example 1-10: The data given are the number of hurricanes to strike the mainland United States each decade from 1900 to 1999. Display this information using a time-series graph.

DECADE	1	2	3	4	5	6	7	8	9	10
Number	15	20	15	17	23	18	15	12	16	14

Note: Decade 1 corresponds to the years 1900 to 1909, decade 2 corresponds to the years 1910 to 1919, and decade 10 corresponds to the years 1990 to 1999.

Solution: The time-series plot for the data is shown in **Figure 1-12**.

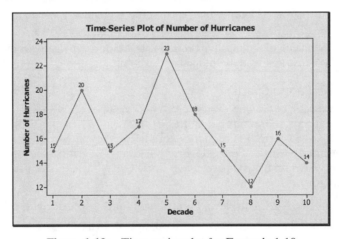

Figure 1-12:   Time-series plot for Example 1-10

Observe from the graph that the highest total number of hurricanes occurred during the fifth decade (1940–1949), and the smallest total number occurred during the eight decade (1970–1979).

1-9 Pie Graphs or Pie Charts

Explanation of the term—pie graph (chart): A **pie graph** or **pie chart** is a circle that is divided into slices according to the percentage of the data values in each category.

A pie chart allows us to observe the proportions of sectors relative to the entire data set. It can be used to display qualitative data as well as quantitative data. However, categorical or qualitative data readily lend themselves to this type of graphical display because of the inherent categories in the data set.

Example 1-11: Present a pie chart for the blood-type data given in **Example 1-1**.

Solution: The pie chart for the data is presented in **Figure 1-13**.

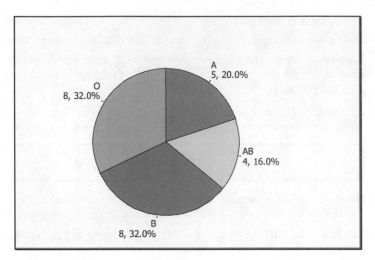

Figure 1-13: Pie chart for the blood-type data in Example 1-1

Each slice of the pie chart represents a blood-type category with its frequency count and the corresponding percentage for the count.

1-10 Pareto Charts

Explanation of the term—Pareto chart: A **Pareto chart** is a type of bar chart in which the horizontal axis represents categories of interest. When the bars are ordered from largest to smallest in terms of frequency counts for the categories, a Pareto chart can help you to determine which of the categories make up the critical few and which are the insignificant many. A cumulative percentage line helps you to judge the added contribution of each category.

Example 1-12: Display a Pareto chart for the soft-drink data in **Example 1-5**.

Solution: The Pareto chart for the data is shown in **Figure 1-14**.

Figure 1-14: Pareto chart for the data in Example 1-5

Observe that the categories have been ordered from the highest frequency to the lowest frequency.

Technology Corner

Calculators and Computer Software Packages

Statistical calculations usually involve large data sets that cannot be analyzed efficiently using pencil and paper. Modern technology eases this challenge through calculators and computers that can handle large numbers of arithmetic calculations. Most scientific calculators on the market today have features that make statistical computations easy. Many specialized statistical software packages have features that perform quite sophisticated analyses of data.

Calculators are portable and relatively inexpensive. However, calculators have the drawback of not being able to deal with large amounts of data. There are many different types of calculators on the market today, so you should research their features before you purchase one. Once you purchase one, in order to get familiar with its statistical features, you will need to consult the owner's manual for the calculator and practice using the appropriate keys. Specialized statistical software packages usually are more expensive than handheld calculators. These packages, however, can handle large amounts of data and usually perform a wider array of statistical calculations. Further, it is much easier to insert screen outputs from the software directly into word-processing documents. Also, it is relatively easy to transport data and analyses of data through electronic mail and other forms of electronic devices. For the more modern calculators, screen outputs can be imported into word-processing documents as well. The graphical features of statistical software packages usually are superior to the graphical features of calculators.

✓ All the preceding graphical displays can be constructed with many of the software packages on the market today. As a matter of fact, all the graphs in this chapter were constructed using the MINITAB for Windows software. A few other examples of software packages that can aid in the construction of the graphs in this chapter are Microsoft EXCEL, SAS, and SPSS for Windows.

True/False Questions

1. A statistic is a characteristic of a population.
2. A parameter is a characteristic of a population.
3. Discrete data are data values that are measured over a continuous interval.
4. Continuous data are data that are measured over a given interval.
5. The amount of rainfall in your state for last month is an example of discrete data.
6. The number of days it rained where you live during last month is an example of discrete data.
7. Statistics is the science of collecting and graphically displaying numerical data.
8. The subject of statistics can be broadly divided into two areas: descriptive statistics and inferential statistics.
9. A sample is the set of all possible data values for a given subject under consideration.
10. Descriptive statistics involves the collection, organization, summarization, and graphic presentation of data relating to some population or sample under study.

11. The subject of statistics is concerned with collecting, organizing, summarizing, analyzing, and making inferences from data.
12. A population is a set of all possible values for a given subject under consideration.
13. Inferential statistics involves making predictions or decisions about a sample from a population of values.
14. The frequency of a measurement is the number of times that measurement was observed.
15. The lower class limit for a given class is the smallest possible data value for that class.
16. The class mark for a class is the average of the upper and lower class limits for the given class.
17. The cumulative frequency of a class is the total of all class frequencies up to but not including the frequency of the present class.
18. The relative frequency for a given class is the total of all class frequencies below the class divided by the total number of entries.
19. The class midpoint for a class is computed from (upper limit − lower limit)/2, where the upper and lower limits are for the given class.
20. A frequency histogram and a relative frequency histogram for the same (grouped) frequency distribution always will have the same shape.
21. A frequency polygon for a set of data is obtained by connecting the class marks on the histogram displaying the set of data.
22. The choice of a single item from a group is called random if every item in the group has the same chance of being selected as any other item.
23. The class mark of a class is the midpoint between the lower limit of one class and the upper limit of the next class.
24. A population is part of a sample.
25. In stem-and-leaf displays, the trailing digits (digits to the right) are called the leaves.
26. The sum of the relative frequencies in a relative frequency distribution always should equal 1.
27. A population refers to the entire set of data values for a subject under consideration; a sample is a subset of the population.
28. A census is a sample of an entire population.
29. A histogram can be used to display qualitative data.
30. The relative frequency for a given class in a grouped frequency distribution is obtained by dividing the frequency for the class by the total frequency for the distribution.

Completion Questions

1. A (parameter, statistic) _____ is a characteristic of the population.
2. A (parameter, statistic) _____ is a characteristic of the sample.
3. A sample of an entire population is called a (sample, population, census) _____.
4. Data that are counting numbers are called (discrete, continuous) _____ data.
5. Data that are measured over an interval are called (discrete, continuous) _____ data.
6. Drawing conclusions about a population from a sample is classified as (descriptive, inferential) _____ statistics.
7. (Descriptive, Inferential) _____ statistics is concerned with making predictions about an entire population based on information from a sample that was appropriately chosen from the population.

8. (Descriptive, Inferential) _____ statistics involves the collection, organization, summarization, and presentation of data.

9. A set of all possible data values for a subject under consideration is called a (sample, population) _____.

10. Class marks are the (lower limits, midpoints, upper limits) _____ of each class.

11. A subset of a population is called a (census, sample, small population) _____.

12. The lower class limit is the (smallest, largest) _____ possible data value for a class.

13. The (relative frequency, frequency, cumulative frequency) _____ is the number of occurrences of a measurement or data value.

14. The shape of the frequency distribution and the relative frequency distribution always will be (the same, different, skewed) _____.

15. Name three graphical methods by which you can display a set of data:
    (a) _____; (b) _____; (c) _____.

16. The (relative, cumulative) _____ frequency of a class is the total of all class frequencies below and including the present class when the data values in the classes are arranged in ascending order.

17. Data such as gender, eye color, ethnicity, etc., are classified as (quantitative, qualitative) _____ data.

18. The class mark of a class is defined to be the (average, minimum, maximum) _____ of the upper and lower limits of the class.

19. In a histogram there are no (gaps, values) _____ between each class represented.

20. A pie chart or pie graph can be used to display (qualitative, quantitative, both types of) _____ data.

21. In a stem-and-leaf plot, the trailing digits are called the (leaves, stems) _____ of the plot, and the leading digits are called the (leaves, stems) _____ of the plot.

22. The choice of a single item from the group is called (random, biased) _____ if every item from a group has the same chance of being selected as any other item.

23. When constructing a frequency distribution for a small data set, it is wise to use (5 to 20 classes, 5 to 15 classes, 5 to 10 classes) _____.

24. When quantitative data are displayed graphically, one can use a (bar chart, histogram) _____ to create such a display.

25. When using a data value in constructing a stem-and-leaf display (only part of the, the actual) _____ data value is used in the display.

Multiple-Choice Questions

1. The section of statistics that involves the collection, organization, summarization, and presentation of data relating to some population or sample is
    (a) inferential statistics.
    (b) descriptive statistics.
    (c) an example of a frequency distribution.
    (d) the study of statistics.

2. A subset of a population selected to help make inferences on a population is called
   (a) a population.
   (b) inferential statistics.
   (c) a census.
   (d) a sample.

3. A set of all possible data values for a subject under consideration is called
   (a) descriptive statistics.
   (b) a sample.
   (c) a population.
   (d) statistics.

4. The number of occurrences of a data value is called
   (a) the class limits.
   (b) the frequency.
   (c) the cumulative frequency.
   (d) the relative frequency.

5. A large collection of quantitative data may be condensed by
   (a) constructing classes.
   (b) computing class marks.
   (c) computing class limits.
   (d) constructing a group frequency distribution.

6. When constructing a frequency distribution for a small data set, it is wise to use
   (a) 5 to 20 classes.
   (b) 5 to 15 classes.
   (c) 5 to 10 classes.
   (d) fewer than 10 classes.

7. When constructing a frequency distribution for large data sets, it is wise to use
   (a) 5 to 20 classes.
   (b) 5 to 15 classes.
   (c) 5 to 10 classes.
   (d) fewer than 10 classes.

8. When straight-line segments are connected through the midpoints at the top of the rectangles of a histogram with the two ends "tied down" to the horizontal axis, the resulting graph is called
   (a) a bar chart.
   (b) a pie chart.
   (c) a frequency polygon.
   (d) a frequency distribution.

9. A questionnaire concerning satisfaction with the financial aid office on a campus was mailed to a random selection of 50 students on a university campus. This group of students in this survey is an example of a
   (a) statistic.
   (b) parameter.

(c) population.

(d) sample.

The following information relates to Questions 10 to 15:

The Love Your Lawn lawn care company is interested in the distribution of lawns in a certain subdivision with respect to size (square feet) of the lawn. The following table shows the distribution of the size of the lawns in hundreds of square feet.

SIZE OF LAWN (IN 100 SQUARE FEET)	NUMBER OF LAWNS
10–15	2
15–20	12
20–25	27
25–30	19
30–35	6
35–40	3

10. The class mark for the class 25–30 is

(a) 24.5.

(b) 29.5.

(c) 4.

(d) 27.5.

11. The relative frequency for the class 15–20 is

(a) 0.2029.

(b) 0.0290.

(c) 0.1739.

(d) 0.4058.

12. The lower class limit for the class 35–40 is

(a) 34.5.

(b) 35.

(c) 37.

(d) 39.5.

13. The upper class limit for the class 20–25 is

(a) 24.5.

(b) 25.

(c) 24.

(d) 22.

14. The cumulative frequency for the class 25–30 is

(a) 41.

(b) 9.

(c) 19.

(d) 60.

15. The cumulative relative frequency for the class 30–35 is

(a) 0.8696.

(b) 0.0870.

(c) 0.1304.

(d) 0.9565.

16. The graphical display with the relative frequencies along the vertical axis for quantitative data is
    (a) the pie chart.
    (b) the bar chart.
    (c) the histogram.
    (d) all the above.

17. The cumulative relative frequency for a given class is defined to be
    (a) the proportion of values preceding the given class.
    (b) the proportion of values smaller than and including the given class when the classes are in ascending order of magnitude.
    (c) the proportion of values for the given class.
    (d) the proportion of values below the given class.

18. A property of a frequency polygon is that
    (a) a histogram is always needed in the construction of the polygon.
    (b) the polygon is made up of line segments.
    (c) the end points of the polygon need not be tied down to the horizontal axis at both ends.
    (d) the polygon can be constructed on a pie chart.

19. If you are given that the total number of observed values in a group frequency distribution is 50 and the frequency of a given class 25–30 is 10, as well as that the cumulative frequencies of all classes with smaller values than this given class is 40, then the cumulative frequency for this class is
    (a) 10.
    (b) 50.
    (c) 40.
    (d) 30.

20. If a class for a frequency distribution for a sample of 50 has a frequency of 5, the cumulative relative frequency for this class
    (a) is 0.1000.
    (b) is 0.9000.
    (c) is 0.1111.
    (d) cannot be determined from the given information.

21. If the first five classes of a frequency distribution have a cumulative frequency of 50 from a sample of 58, the sixth and last class must have a frequency count of
    (a) 58.
    (b) 50.
    (c) 7.
    (d) 8.

The following information relates to Questions 22 to 28. *Hint:* Read the exam scores distribution from smallest value to largest value.

The following table shows the distribution of scores on a final elementary statistics examination for a large section of students.

CLASSES FOR EXAM SCORES	NUMBER OF STUDENTS
90 and over	5
80–90	12
70–80	40
60–70	18
50–60	13
40–50	6
Under 40	6

22. The class width is
    (a) 9.
    (b) 10.
    (c) 7.
    (d) 1.

23. The class mark for the class 40–50 is
    (a) 39.5.
    (b) 49.5.
    (c) 45.
    (d) 9.

24. The relative frequency for the class 80–90 is
    (a) 0.1700.
    (b) 0.0500.
    (c) 0.8300.
    (d) 0.1200.

25. The lower class limit for the class 50–60 is
    (a) 49.5.
    (b) 50.
    (c) 59.
    (d) 59.5.

26. The upper class limit for the class 70–80 is
    (a) 69.5.
    (b) 70.
    (c) 80.
    (d) 79.5.

27. The cumulative frequency for the class 60–70 is
    (a) 18.
    (b) 57.

(c) 43.

(d) 12.

28. The cumulative relative frequency for the class 50–60 is
   (a) 0.8800.
   (b) 0.1300.
   (c) 0.7500.
   (d) 0.2500.

29. Can a frequency distribution have overlapping classes?
   (a) Sometimes
   (b) No
   (c) Yes
   (d) All the above

30. Organizing observed data into tabular form in which classes and frequencies are used is called
   (a) a bar chart.
   (b) a pie chart.
   (c) a frequency distribution.
   (d) a frequency polygon.

31. Examine the following stem-and-leaf diagram:
   1 | 0 3
   2 | 2 2 4
   3 | 1 2 3 3 3
   4 | 1 1 2 2 2 2 5 6
   5 | 3 3 5 6
   6 | 2 4
   7 | 3

   The number that occurred the most is
   (a) 2.
   (b) 42.
   (c) 33.
   (d) 3.

32. Which of the following does not pertain to descriptive statistics?
   (a) Summarizing quantitative data
   (b) Collecting quantitative data
   (c) Making generalizations about a population from a sample of quantitative data
   (d) Graphical presentation of quantitative data

33. It was reported from a survey that 48 percent of the population will vote for the current president instead of the leading opposing candidate. This is an example of
   (a) a population.
   (b) a sample.

(c) inferential statistics.

(d) descriptive statistics.

34. The following time-series graph displays the divorce rate in the United States (per 1000 people) from 1900 to 2001. The graph displays

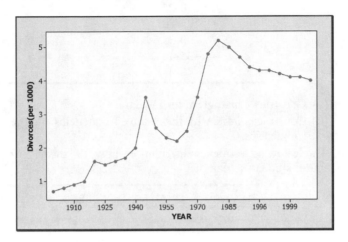

(a) a downward trend in the divorce rate.

(b) an upward trend in the divorce rate.

(c) a uniform divorce rate.

(d) none of the above.

35. Refer to the graph in **Question 34**. Which year had the highest divorce rate?

(a) 1945

(b) 1960

(c) 2001

(d) 1980

Further Exercises

If possible, you can use any technology available to help you solve the following questions.

1. The at-rest pulse rates for 16 athletes at a meet are

   67   57   56   57   58   56   54   64   53   54   54   55   57   68   60   58

   (a) Construct a relative frequency distribution for this data set using classes 50–55, 55–60, and so on.

   (b) Construct a histogram for this set of data using part (a).

2. The speeds (in mph) of 16 cars on a highway were observed to be

   58   56   60   57   52   54   54   59   63   54   53   54   58   56   57   67

   (a) Construct a relative frequency distribution for this data set using classes 52–55, 55–58, and so on.

   (b) Construct a stem-and-leaf plot for the data set.

3. The starting incomes for mathematics majors at a particular university was recorded for five years and are summarized in the following table:

STARTING SALARY (IN $1000)	FREQUENCY
20–25	3
25–30	5
30–35	10
35–40	6
40–45	1

(a) Construct a histogram for the data.
(b) Construct a table with the relative frequencies and the cumulative relative frequencies.

4. The following frequency distribution shows the distances traveled (in miles) by 30 commuter students to campus.

DISTANCE (IN MILES)	FREQUENCY
35–40	8
40–45	13
45–50	6
50–55	3

For the class 40–45, find the following:
(a) lower class limit
(b) upper class limit
(c) class width
(d) class mark
(e) cumulative frequency
(f) relative frequency
(g) cumulative relative frequency

5. In a random sample of 100 adults, the following data display their marital status. Display the data using a bar chart.

MARITAL STATUS	FREQUENCY
Married	50
Single	18
Divorced	27
Widowed	5

ANSWER KEY
True/False Questions

1. F   2. T   3. F   4. T   5. F   6. T   7. F   8. T   9. F   10. T   11. T   12. T
13. F   14. T   15. T   16. T   17. F   18. F   19. F   20. T   21. T   22. T   23. F   24. F
25. T   26. T   27. T   28. T   29. F   30. T

Completion Questions

    1. parameter   2. statistic   3. census   4. discrete   5. continuous   6. inferential
    7. inferential   8. descriptive   9. population   10. midpoints   11. sample
    12. smallest   13. frequency   14. the same   15. bar chart, histogram, pie chart,
frequency polygon, stem-and-leaf plot   16. cumulative   17. qualitative
    18. average   19. gaps   20. both types   21. leaves, stems   22. random
    23. 5 to 10 classes   24. histogram   25. the actual

Multiple-Choice Questions

    1. (b)   2. (d)   3. (c)   4. (b)   5. (d)   6. (c)   7. (a)   8. (c)   9. (d)
    10. (d)   11. (c)   12. (b)   13. (b)   14. (d)   15. (d)   16. (c)   17. (b)   18. (b)
    19. (b)   20. (d)   21. (d)   22. (b)   23. (c)   24. (d)   25. (b)   26. (c)   27. (c)
    28. (d)   29. (b)   30. (c)   31. (b)   32. (c)   33. (c)   34. (b)   35. (d)

Further Exercises

    1. (a) and (b). Relative frequencies are 4/16, 8/16, 2/16, and 2/16 for the classes 50–55,
       55–60, 60–65, and 65–70, respectively.

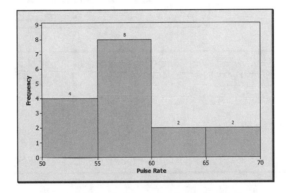

    2. (a) From the histogram for the respective classes, the relative frequencies are 6/16,
       4/16, 4/16, 1/16, 0/16, and 1/16.

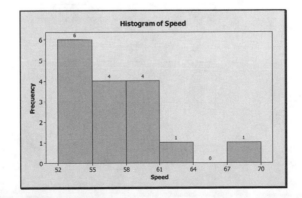

(b) The following is the stem-and-leaf plot:

```
5 | 2 3
5 | 4 4 4 4
5 | 6 6 7 7
5 | 8 8 9
6 | 0
6 | 3
```

3. (a)

(b)

SALARY	FREQUENCY	CUMULATIVE FREQUENCY	RELATIVE FREQUENCY (%)	CUMULATIVE RELATIVE FREQUENCY(%)
10–15	3	3	11.54	11.54
15–20	5	8	19.23	30.77
20–25	10	18	38.46	69.23
25–30	7	25	26.92	96.15
30–35	1	26	3.85	100.00

4. (a) 40; (b) 45; (c) 5; (d) 42.5; (e) 21; (f) 0.4333 or 43.33 percent; (g) 0.7 or 70 percent.

5. Bar chart for the data:

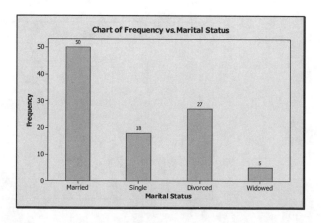

CHAPTER 2

Numerical Measures of Central Tendency

Do I Need to Read This Chapter?

You should read this chapter if you need to review or you need to learn about

➜ Numerical values that measure central tendencies of a numerical data set for a single variable (such as the height of females, ACT math scores, distance you live from your workplace, etc.)

➜ How to compute these measures and investigate their properties

You will recognize that these measures deal with only one property of the data set: the centralness. Thus you will need to combine these measures with other properties of the data set in order to fully describe it. Other properties for single-variable data will be investigated in later chapters.

Get Started

A measure of central tendency for a collection of data values is a number that is meant to convey the idea of centralness for the data set. The most commonly used measures of central tendency are the mean, the median, and the mode. These measures are discussed in this chapter.

2-1   The Mean

Explanation of the term—mean: The **mean** of a set of numerical values is the average (arithmetic) of the set of values.

Thus the mean for a set of numerical values is obtained by adding the values and dividing this sum by the number of numerical values which are in the data set.

Note: In computing the mean, the numerical values can be population values or sample values. Hence we can compute the mean for either a population or sample.

Explanation of the term—population mean: If the values are from an entire population, then the mean of the values is called a **population mean**. It is usually denoted by μ (read as "mu").

Explanation of the term—sample mean: If the values are from a sample, then the mean of the values is called a **sample mean**. It is denoted by $\bar{x}$ (read as "x bar").

Example 2-1: What is the mean for the following sample values?

$3, 8, 6, 14, 0, -4, 0, 12, -7, 0, -10$

Solution: The sample mean is obtained as

$$\bar{x} = \frac{3 + 8 + 6 + 14 + 0 + (-4) + 0 + 12 + (-7) + 0 + (-10)}{11} = 2$$

That is, the value of the sample mean is 2.

Quick Tip

The word *mean* or *average* is used in everyday conversation and has come to represent a typical value or the center of a set of values. Because of this, the mean is called a *measure of central tendency.*

Question: Why do we use the mean as a measure of the center of a set of values?

The following discussion will give an insight into this question. First, **Figure 2-1** shows a plot of the data points with the location of the sample mean.

Figure 2-1: Plot of data values for Example 2-1

Next, we compute the deviation from the sample mean for each value in the data set. That is, we compute $(x - \bar{x})$ for each value x. These deviations are given in **Table 2-1**.

Table 2-1: Deviations from the Mean for Values in Example 2-1

DATA	DEVIATIONS
3	1
8	6
6	4
14	12
0	−2
−4	−6
0	−2
12	10
−7	−9
0	−2
−10	−12

Next, a plot of the deviations from the sample mean is displayed in **Figure 2-2**.

When the deviations from the left and the right of the sample means are added, disregarding the sign of the values, we see that when the "balancing point" is the sample mean, then these sums will be equal in absolute values. Here in **Example 2-1** the sum of the deviations to the right of the mean is 33. The sum of the deviations to the left of the mean is −33. However, we use the absolute value of these negative deviations. That is, we use +33. This is depicted in **Figure 2-3**.

Thus *the mean is that central point where the sum of the negative deviations (absolute value) from the mean and the sum of the positive deviations from the mean are equal. This is why the mean is considered a measure of central tendency.*

Figure 2-2: Deviations from the sample mean for Example 2-1

Figure 2-3: Balanced deviations

The next example shows us how to find the mean of a set of values when the data are summarized in an ungrouped frequency table.

Example 2-2: Find the mean for the following ungrouped frequency table and express the answer to four decimal places.

Solution: Observe that the value of 20 has a frequency count of 2, so the total or sum can be written as 20 + 20 or 2 × 20. We can do the same for each value and its corresponding frequency count. The total number of values in the table is 15, which is the sum of the frequency values. Thus we can compute the mean for the frequency distribution as

VALUES (x)	FREQUENCY (f)
20	2
29	4
30	4
39	3
44	2

$$\bar{x} = \frac{2 \times 20 + 4 \times 29 + 4 \times 30 + 3 \times 39 + 2 \times 44}{2 + 4 + 4 + 3 + 2} = 32.0667$$

2-2   The Median

The next measure of central tendency we will consider is the median.

Explanation of the term—median: The **median** of a numerical data set is a numerical value in the middle when the data set is arranged in order.

Example 2-3: What is the median for the following sample values?

3, 8, 6, 14, 0, −4, 2, 12, −7, −1, −10

Solution: First of all, we need to arrange the data set in order. The ordered set is as follows:

$$-10, -7, -4, -1, 0, 2, 3, 6, 8, 12, 14$$

$\uparrow$

6th

Since the number of values is **odd**, the median will be the middle value in the ordered set. Thus the median will be found in the sixth position because we have a total of 11 values. That is, the value of median is 2.

Question: Why does the middle number in an ordered data set measure central tendency?

The following discussion will give an insight to this question. **Figure 2-4** shows a plot of the data points with the location of the sample median.

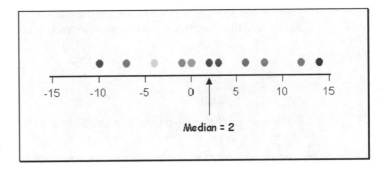

Figure 2-4: Plot of data points for Example 2-3

A list of the values that are **above** the median or **below** the median is given in **Table 2-2**.

Table 2-2: List of Values That Are Above or Below the Median for Example 2-3

DATA	DEVIATIONS	DATA	DEVIATIONS
3	Above	2	Neither
8	Above	12	Above
6	Above	−7	Below
14	Above	−1	Below
0	Below	−10	Below
−4	Below		

When the values from above and below the median are pooled together, we see that if the "balancing point" is the sample median, then the number of values above the median balances (equals) the number of values below the median. This is depicted in **Figure 2-5**.

Figure 2-5: Median as a balancing point for data values in Example 2-3

Observe that there are the same number of values above the median as there are below the median. This is why the median is considered as a measure of central tendency.

Example 2-4: Find the median for the ages of the following eight college students:

23   19   32   25   26   22   24   20

Solution: First, the values need to be placed in order. The ordered array is

19   20   22   23   24   25   26   32

Since this is an even number of ages, the median will be the average of the two middle numbers. Since the two middle numbers are located in the fourth and fifth positions, the median

$$= \frac{23 + 24}{2} = 23.5.$$

2-3   The Mode

Explanation of the term—mode: The **mode** of a numerical data set is the most frequently occurring value in the data set.

Quick Tips

- If all the elements in a data set have the same frequency of occurrence, then the data set is said to have *no mode*.
- If a data set has only one value that occurs more frequently than the rest of the values, then the data set is said to be *unimodal*.
- If two elements of a data set are tied for the highest frequency of occurrence, then the data set is said to be *bimodal*.

Example 2-5: What is the mode for the following sample values?

3   5   1   4   2   9   6   10

Solution: We see from **Figure 2-6** that each value occurs with a frequency of one. Thus the data set has **no mode**.

Figure 2-6: Plot of data values for Example 2-5

Example 2-6: What is the mode for the following sample values?

3   5   1   4   2   9   6   10   5   3   4   3   9   3   6   1

Solution: **Figure 2-7** shows a plot of the data values.

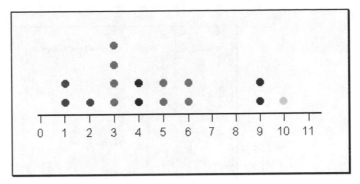

Figure 2-7: Plot of data values for Example 2-6

Observe that the value of 3 occurs with the highest frequency. Thus the value of the mode is 3, and this data set is **unimodal**.

Example 2-7: What is the mode for the following sample values?

6 10 5 3 4 3 9 3 6 1 6

Solution: **Figure 2-8** shows a plot of the data values.

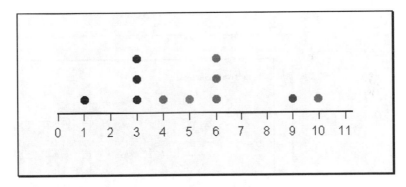

Figure 2-8: Plot of data values for Example 2-7

Observe that the value of 3 and the value of 6 occur with the highest but equal frequency. Thus the values of the mode are 3 and 6, and this data set is **bimodal**.

2-4   Shapes (Skewness)

The three most important shapes of frequency distributions are positively skewed, symmetrical, and negatively skewed.

Positively Skewed Distribution

In a positively skewed distribution, most of the data values fall to the left of the mean, and the "tail" of the distribution is to the right. In addition, the mean is to the right of the median, and the mode is to the left of the median. These properties are depicted in **Figure 2-9**.

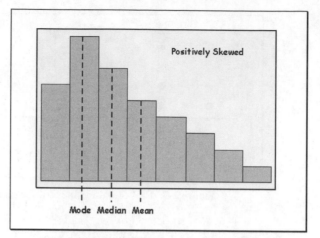

Figure 2-9: Positively skewed distribution

Negatively Skewed Distribution

In a negatively skewed distribution, most of the data values fall to the right of the mean, and the "tail" of the distribution is to the left. In addition, the mean is to the left of the median, and the mode is to the right of the median. These properties are depicted in **Figure 2-10**.

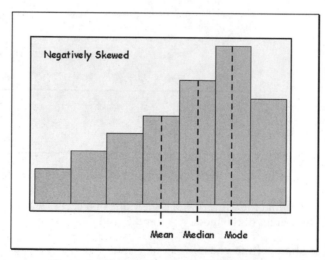

Figure 2-10: Negatively skewed distribution

Symmetrical Distribution

In a symmetrical distribution, the data values are evenly distributed on both sides of the mean. Also, when the distribution is unimodal, the mean, median, and mode are all equal to one another and are located at the center of the distribution. These properties are depicted in **Figure 2-11**.

Figure 2-11: Symmetric distribution

Technology Corner

All the concepts discussed in this chapter can be illustrated through most statistical software packages. All scientific and graphical calculators will aid directly in the computations. In addition, some of the newer calculators, such as the TI-83/84 model, will allow you to compute the mean and the median directly. If you own a calculator, you should consult the manual to determine what statistical features are included.

Illustration: **Figure 2-12** shows the descriptive statistics computed by the EXCEL software. **Figure 2-13** shows the 1- Var Stats (descriptive statistics) computed by the TI-83/84 calculator. The data used, in both cases, were from **Example 2-3**. Observe that EXCEL has given the value of the mean to nine decimal places, whereas the TI–83/84 calculator also gives the value to nine decimal places. The median using both technologies is 2. Observe that the mode is not displayed in either figure. You would have to use other features of the technologies to obtain the value of the mode. There are other descriptive statistics in the outputs that we will encounter later in this text.

Descriptive Statistics: Values

Mean	2.090909091	Standard Deviation	7.555852638	Minimum	-10
Standard Error	2.278175288	Sample Variance	57.09090909	Maximum	14
Median	2	Kurtosis	-0.741280579	Sum	23
Mode	#N/A	Skewness	0.041165485	Count	11
		Range	24		

Figure 2-12: EXCEL descriptive statistics output for Example 2-3

```
1-Var Stats
x̄=2.090909091
Σx=23
Σx²=619
Sx=7.555852638
σx=7.20422282
↓n=11
```

```
1-Var Stats
↑n=11
minX=-10
Q₁=-4
Med=2
Q₃=8
maxX=14
```

Figure 2-13: TI-83/84 1-Var Stats output for Example 2-3

Quick Tips

- Unlike the median and the mode, the mean is sensitive to a change in any of the values of the data set.
- If the same constant is added (subtracted) to each value in the data set, the mean of the data set will increase (decrease) by the same amount of the constant.
- If each value in the data set is multiplied by the same constant, the mean of the data set also will be multiplied by that constant.

The three most commonly used measures of central tendency for numeric data are the

✓ Mean

✓ Median

✓ Mode

Care always should be taken when using these measures of central tendency. They should be used appropriately and not used in a misleading manner. For instance, the median will be a more appropriate measure of central tendency than the mean when there are outlying values in the data set.

True/False Questions

1. The mean of a set of data always will divide the data set such that 50 percent of the values lie above the mean and 50 percent lie below the mean.
2. The mode is a measure of variability.
3. The median of a set of data values is that value that occurs with the highest frequency.
4. The mean is not necessarily equal to the median in a symmetrical distribution.
5. Of the mean, the median, and the mode of any numerical data set, the mean is most influenced by an outlying value in the data set.
6. If the number of observations in a data set is even, the median cannot be found accurately but rather is approximated.

7. A data set with more than one mode is said to be bimodal.
8. The sum of the deviations from the mean for any numerical data set is always zero.
9. For a negatively skewed distribution, the longer tail is to the right of the mean for the distribution.
10. For a positively skewed distribution, the mode is less than the median, and the median is less than the mean for the distribution.
11. The mean of a numerical data set could divide the data set such that at most 50 percent of the values lie above the mean and at most 50 percent lie below the mean.
12. For a negatively skewed distribution, the mean is greater than the median.

Completion Questions

1. If the number of measurements in a numerical data set is odd, the median is the (middle, average of the two middle) _____ value(s) when the data set is ordered from the smallest value to the largest value.
2. If the number of measurements in a numerical data set is even, the median is the _____ of the two _____ values when the data set is ordered from the smallest value to the largest value.
3. The (mean, median, mode) _____ for a set of data is the value in the data set that occurs most frequently.
4. Two measures of central tendency for a numerical set of data values are the _____ and the _____.
5. For a symmetrical distribution of numerical values, the mean, mode, and median are all (equal to, different from) _____ one another.
6. For a negatively skewed distribution, the mean is (smaller, greater) _____ than the median and the mode for the distribution.
7. For a positively skewed distribution, the longer tail of the distribution is to the (right, left)_____ of the distribution.
8. For a positively skewed distribution, the median is (smaller, greater) _____ than the mode for the distribution.
9. For a negatively skewed distribution, the median is (smaller, greater) _____ than the mode for the distribution.
10. For a positively skewed distribution, the mode is (smaller, greater) _____ than the mean for the distribution.
11. Given a set of numerical values with mean = 10, median = 7, and mode = 4, the distribution is (negatively, positively) _____ skewed.
12. Given a set of numerical values with mean = 5, median = 7, and mode = 9, the distribution is (negatively, positively) _____ skewed.

Multiple-Choice Questions

1. A student has seven statistics books open in front of him. The page numbers are as follows: 231, 423, 521, 139, 347, 400, 345. The median for this set of numbers is
   (a) 139.
   (b) 347.

   (c) 346.
   (d) 373.5.

2. A cyclist recorded the number of miles per day she cycled for five days. The recordings
    were as follows: 13, 10, 12, 10, 11. The mean (average) number of miles she cycled per
    day was
    (a) 13.
    (b) 11.
    (c) 10.
    (d) 11.2.

3. An instructor recorded the following quiz scores (out of a possible 10 points) for the 12
    students who were present for her Friday afternoon statistics class. The scores were 7,
    4, 4, 7, 2, 9, 10, 6, 7, 3, 8, 5. The mode for this set of scores is
    (a) 9.5.
    (b) 7.
    (c) 6.
    (d) 3.

4. A statement is made that more students are purchasing graphing calculators than any
    other type of calculator. Which measure is being used here?
    (a) Mean
    (b) Median
    (c) Mode
    (d) None of the above

5. Which of the following is not a measure of central tendency?
    (a) Mode
    (b) Variability
    (c) Median
    (d) Mean

Use the following frequency distribution for Questions 6 to 8:

VALUES (x)	FREQUENCY (f)
20	2
29	4
30	4
39	3
44	2

6. The mean of the distribution is
    (a) 32.4.
    (b) 30.
    (c) 39.
    (d) 32.07.

7. The median of the distribution is
   (a) 4.
   (b) 30.
   (c) 29.5.
   (d) 34.5.

8. The mode of the distribution is
   (a) 29.
   (b) 30.
   (c) 29 and 30.
   (d) none of the above.

9. Examine the following data set:
   12 32 45 14 24 31

   The total deviation from the mean for the data values is
   (a) 0.
   (b) 26.3333.
   (c) 29.5.
   (d) 12.

10. The most frequently occurring value in a data set is called the
    (a) spread.
    (b) mode.
    (c) skewness.
    (d) maximum value.

11. A single numerical value used to describe a characteristic of a sample data sct, such as the sample median, is referred to as a
    (a) sample parameter.
    (b) sample median.
    (c) population parameter.
    (d) sample statistic.

12. Which of the following is true for a positively skewed distribution?
    (a) Mode = median = mean
    (b) Mean < median < mode
    (c) Mode < median < mean
    (d) Median < mode < mean

13. Which of the following would be affected the most if there is an extremely large value in the data set?
    (a) The mode
    (b) The median
    (c) The frequency
    (d) The mean

14. If the number of values in a data set is even, and the numbers are ordered from the smallest value to the largest value, then

(a) the median cannot be found.
(b) the median is the average of the two middle numbers.
(c) the median, mode, and mean are equal.
(d) none of the above answers is correct.

15. What type of distribution is described by the following information?
    Mean = 5.5   Median = 5.3   Mode = 4.4

    (a) Negatively skewed
    (b) Symmetrical
    (c) Bimodal
    (d) Positively skewed

16. What type of distribution is described by the following information?
    Mean = 56   Median = 58.1   Mode = 63

    (a) Negatively skewed
    (b) Symmetrical
    (c) Bimodal
    (d) Positively skewed

17. The mean of a set of numerical data is the value that represents
    (a) the middle value of the data set.
    (b) the most frequently observed value.
    (c) the average of the squared deviations of the values from the mean of the data
         set.
    (d) the arithmetic average of the data set.

18. The median of an ordered set of data is the value that represents
    (a) the middle or the approximate middle value of the data set.
    (b) the most frequently observed value in the data set.
    (c) the average of the squared deviations of the values from the mean of the data set.
    (d) the arithmetic average of the data set.

19. Examine the following data set:
    4 3 7 7 8 7 4 8 6

    What is the mean value for this data set?

    (a) 4
    (b) 5
    (c) 6
    (d) 7

20. Examine the following data set:
    3 2 7 7 8 7 3 8 5

    What is the median value for this data set?

    (a) 5
    (b) 6
    (c) 7
    (d) 8

21. Examine the following data set:
    4 5 7 7 8 6 5 8 7

    What is the mode for this data set?

    (a) 4
    (b) 5
    (c) 6
    (d) 7

22. A sample of 10 students was asked by their instructor to record the number of hours they spent studying for a given exam from the time the exam was announced in class. The following data values were the recorded number of hours:
    12   15   8   9   14   8   17   14   8   15

    The median number of hours spent studying for this sample is

    (a) 10.
    (b) 11.
    (c) 12.
    (d) 13.

23. The numbers of minutes spent in the computer lab by 20 students working on a project are given below:

    Number of minutes

    30 | 0 2 5 5 6 6 6 8
    40 | 0 2 2 5 7 9
    50 | 0 1 3 5
    60 | 1 3

    The median for this data set is

    (a) 400.
    (b) 402.
    (c) 405.
    (d) 407.

24. The numbers of minutes spent in the computer lab by 20 students working on a project are given below:

    Number of minutes

    30 | 0 2 5 5 6 6 6 8
    40 | 0 2 2 5 7 9
    50 | 0 1 3 5
    60 | 1 3

    The mode for this data set is

    (a) 305.
    (b) 402.
    (c) 306.
    (d) 300.

25. The numbers of minutes spent in the computer lab by 20 students working on a project are given below:

    Number of minutes

    30 | 0 2 5 5 6 6 6 8
    40 | 0 2 2 5 7 9
    50 | 0 1 3 5
    60 | 1 3

    The mean for this data set is
    (a) 306.0.
    (b) 402.0.
    (c) 403.8.
    (d) 450.0.

26. A set of exam scores are given below:

    Exam scores

    4 | 5 6 8
    5 | 3 4 5 6 9
    6 | 2 3 5 6 6 9 9
    7 | 0 1 1 3 3 4 5 5 5 7 8
    8 | 1 2 3 6 9
    9 | 3 5 7 8

    The mode for this data set is
    (a) 75.
    (b) 78.
    (c) 45.
    (d) 98.

27. Which of the following is true for a negatively skewed distribution?
    (a) Mode = median = mean
    (b) Mean < median < mode
    (c) Mode < median < mean
    (d) Median < mode < mean

28. Examine the following data set:
    4   5   7   7   8   6   5   8   7   9   8   6   4
    What is the mode or modes for this data set?
    (a) 4
    (b) 7
    (c) 8
    (d) 7 and 8

29. Examine the following data set:
    14   15   17   17   18   16   15   18   17   19   18   16   14
    This data set can be appropriately characterized as
    (a) unimodal.
    (b) bimodal.

(c) multimodal.

(d) all the answers are correct.

30. What type of distribution could be described by the following information?
    Mean = 56   Median = 56.0001   Mode = 55.999

    (a) Approximately negatively skewed

    (b) Approximately symmetrical

    (c) Approximately positively skewed

    (d) All of the above answers are correct

Further Exercises

If possible, you could use any technology to help solve the following questions.

1. The at-rest pulse rates for 16 athletes at a meet are

   67 57 56 57 58 56 54 64 53 54 54 55 57 68 60 58

   (a) Find the mean, median, and mode for this set of data.

   (b) Construct a dot plot for the data in part (a).

   (c) From the statistics computed in part (a) and the dot plot in part (b), how would you describe the data set?

2. The speeds (mph) of 16 cars on a highway were observed to be

   58 56 60 57 52 54 54 59 63 54 53 54 58 56 57 67

   (a) Find the mean, median, and mode for this set of data.

   (b) Construct a dot plot for the data in part (a).

   (c) From the statistics computed in part (a) and the dot plot in part (b), how would you describe the data set?

3. Estimate the mean for the following frequency distribution. *Hint:* Use the class marks as the actual observed values in each class.

CLASS	FREQUENCY
10–15	2
15–20	4
20–25	4
25–30	3
30–35	2

4. (a) Find the mean, median, and mode for the following examination scores.

   Exam scores

   4|5 6 8
   5|3 4 5 6 9
   6|2 3 5 6 6 9 9
   7|0 1 1 3 3 4 5 5 5 7 8
   8|1 2 3 6 9
   9|3 5 7 8

(b) From the shape of the stem-and-leaf plot and the statistics computed in part (a), how would you describe the data set?

5. The following frequency distribution shows the scores for the exit examination for statistics majors at a four-year college for a given year.

98 75 85 97 80 87 97 60 83 90

(a) Find the mean, median, and mode for this set of data.
(b) Construct a dot plot for the data in part (a).
(c) From the statistics computed in part (a) and the dot plot in part (b), how would you describe the data set?

6. The starting incomes for mathematics majors at a particular university was recorded for five years and are summarized in the following table:

STARTING SALARY (IN $1000)	FREQUENCY
10–15	3
15–20	5
20–25	10
25–30	7
30–35	1

(a) Construct a histogram for the data.
(b) How would you describe the shape of the distribution?
(c) Compute an approximate value for the mean by using the class mark values.

7. The numbers of 30-second radio advertising spots purchased by each of the 25 members of a local restaurant association last year are given below:

Number of minutes

1|1 1 2 3 3 3 4 5 6 7
2|3 4 4 5 6 6
3|1 1 2 2 2 3
4|0 0 1

(a) Find the mean, median and mode for the distribution.
(b) Construct a projection graph for the data set.
(c) Describe the shape of the distribution from the projection graph.

ANSWER KEY
True/False Questions

1. F 2. F 3. F 4. F 5. T 6. T 7. F 8. T 9. F 10. T 11. T 12. F

Completion Questions

1. middle 2. average, middle 3. mode 4. mean, median, mode (any two)
5. equal to 6. smaller 7. right 8. greater
9. smaller 10. smaller 11. positively 12. negatively

Multiple-Choice Questions

1. (b)   2. (d)   3. (b)   4. (c)   5. (b)   6. (d)   7. (b)   8. (c)   9. (a)   10. (b)
11. (d)   12. (c)   13. (d)   14. (b)   15. (d)   16. (a)   17. (d)   18. (a)   19. (c)   20. (c)
21. (d)   22. (d)   23. (b)   24. (c)   25. (c)   26. (a)   27. (b)   28. (d)   29. (b)   30. (b)

Further Exercises

1. (a) mean = 58;   median = 57;   mode = 54 and 57.

   (b)

   (c) bimodal

2. (a) mean = 57; median = 56.5; mode = 54.

   (b)

   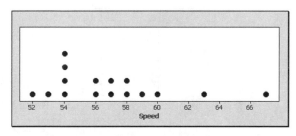

   (c) unimodal;   positively (right) skewed.

3. Estimated mean = 22.1667

4. (a) mean = 71.2; median = 71;   mode = 75

   (b) approximately symmetrical.

5. (a) mean = 85.2; median = 86;   mode = 97

   (b)

   (c) unimodal;   negatively (left) skewed.

6. (a)

   (b) approximately symmetrical
   (c) approximate mean value = 22.1154

7. (a) mean = 23.8;   median = 24;   mode = 13 and 32
   (b)

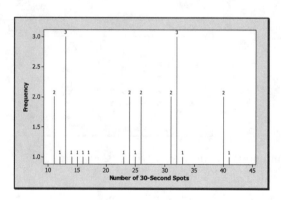

   (c) bimodal

CHAPTER 3

Numerical Measures of Variability

Do I Need to Read This Chapter?

You should read this chapter if you need to review or to learn about

➜ Numerical values that measure spread or variability of a numerical data set
➜ How to compute these measures and investigate some of their properties

You will recognize that these measures deal with only one property of the data set: the spread or variability. Thus you will need to combine these measures with other properties of the data set in order to fully describe it. Other properties for a single variable data will be investigated in future chapters.

Get Started

A measure of variability for a collection of data values is a number that is meant to convey the idea of spread for the data set. The most commonly used measures of variability for sample data are the range, the interquartile range, the mean absolute deviation, the variance or standard deviation, and the coefficient of variation. These measures are discussed in this chapter.

3-1   The Range

Explanation of the term—range: The **range** of a set of numerical values is the difference between the largest and smallest values in a data set.

This definition is true for a sample as well as for a finite population of numerical values.

$$\text{Range} = R = \text{largest value} - \text{smallest value}$$

Example 3-1: What is the range for the following sample of numerical values?

3   8   6   14   0   −4   0   12   −7   0   −10

Solution: We can arrange the data values in order so as to obtain the smallest and the largest values in the data set. The ordered set is as follows:

−10   −7   −4   0   0   0   3   6   8   12   14

Thus the sample range = $R = 14 - (-10) = 24$.

Question: **Why does subtracting the smallest value from the largest value in a data set measure spread?**

The following will give an insight to this question. **Figure 3-1** shows a plot of the data points with the locations of the end points. The range measures the distance between the largest and the smallest values and, as such, gives an idea of the spread of the data set.

Figure 3-1: Plot of data values for Example 3-1

Quick Tips

- The range does not use the concept of deviations. It is affected by outliers (large or small values relative to the rest of the data set) and does not use all the information in the data set except the largest and smallest values. As such, it is not a very useful measure of variation.
- We can only compute the range for numerical data sets.

Example 3-2: What is the range for the following sample values?

996   1014   1000   997   1001   1002   999   995   990

Solution: We can arrange the data values so as to obtain the smallest and the largest values in the data set. The ordered set is as follows:

990   995   996   997   999   1000   1001   1002   1014

Thus the sample range $= R = 1014 - 990 = 24$.

The range here is also 24, same as in **Example 3-1**. Note that no information about the values between the extreme data points is involved in the computation. You also should note that outlying values in the data set will influence the value of the range.

Example 3-3: What is the range for the following sample values?

9   1014   1000   997   1001   1002   999   995   990

Solution: We can arrange the data values so as to obtain the smallest and the largest values in the data set. The ordered set is as follows:

9   995   996   997   999   1000   1001   1002   1014

Thus the sample range $= R = 1014 - 9 = 1005$.

Here the value of the range is affected significantly by the outlying value of 9. This value is significantly smaller than the rest of the values in the data set and has caused the range of the data set to be wider.

3-2   The Interquartile Range

A measure of spread that is not influenced by any extreme values (outliers) in the data set but still preserves the idea of a range is the **interquartile range**.

Explanation of the term—interquartile range: The **interquartile range** measures the spread of the middle 50 percent of an ordered data set.

One procedure used in finding the interquartile range is as follows:

Step 1: Order the data set from the smallest value to the largest value.
Step 2: Find the median of the ordered set. Denote this by Q_2.
Step 3: Find the median of the first 50 percent of the data set. The median in step 2 is not included for this portion of the data set. Let this value be denoted by Q_1.
Step 4: Find the median of the second 50 percent of the data set. The median in step 2 is not included for this portion of the data set. Let this value be denoted by Q_3.
Step 5: The interquartile range,

$$IQR = Q_3 - Q_1$$

Figure 3-2 depicts the idea of the interquartile range.

Figure 3-2: General interquartile range

Example 3-4: The following scores for a statistics 10-point quiz were reported. What is the value of the interquartile range for this data set?

4 7 8 9 6 8 0 9 9 9 0 0 7 10 9 8 5 7 9

Solution: First, let us arrange the data in order from the smallest value to the largest value. This is given next.

0 0 0 4 5 6 7 7 7 8 8 8 9 9 9 9 9 9 10

From this array, the median $Q_2 = 8$. Next, the median for the first and second 50 percent of the values, excluding the median, are 5 and 9, respectively.

0 0 0 4 5 6 7 7 7 8 8 8 9 9 9 9 9 9 10

Q_1 Q_2 Q_3

Thus the interquartile range = IQR = $9 - 5 = 4$. That is, the middle 50 percent of the quiz scores spans a 4-point range.

3-3   The Mean Absolute Deviation

The **mean absolute deviation** uses deviations of the data values from the mean in its computation.

Explanation of the term—mean absolute deviation (MAD): The **MAD** is the average of the absolute deviation values from the mean. That is, the deviations of the data values from the mean are first computed, then absolute (positive) values for these deviations are obtained, and then the average of these positive values is calculated.

Generally, if there are n data values in the sample, with x representing the individual values and $\bar{x}$ being the sample mean, then the mean absolute deviation is defined as the average of the absolute deviations from the mean and is given by

$$\text{MAD} = \frac{\Sigma|x - \bar{x}|}{n}$$

The formula says that you subtract the mean from each data value and take the absolute value of the result; then you add up these values and divide by the sample size.

Example 3-5: What is the MAD for the following sample values?

3 8 6 12 0 −4 10

Solution: First of all, the sample mean $\bar{x} = 5$. (Verify.)

Next, we will construct a table to aid in the computations. **Table 3-1** shows the actual data values, the values for the deviations from the mean, and the absolute values for these deviations.

Table 3-1: Deviations and Absolute Deviations for Example 3-5

DATA VALUES (X)	DEVIATIONS $(x - \bar{x})$	ABSOLUTE DEVIATIONS $(x - \bar{x})$
3	-2	2
8	3	3
6	1	1
12	7	7
0	-5	5
-4	-9	9
10	5	5
Total	0	32

Thus, from **Table 3-1**, the MAD $= \dfrac{32}{7} = 4.57$. That is, the average (absolute) distance of these sample values from the mean is 4.57. **Figure 3-3** displays the values of the absolute deviations, the mean, and the MAD.

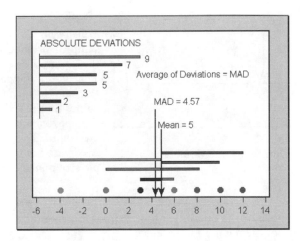

Figure 3-3: Display of absolute deviations for Example 3-5

Observe, for instance, that the absolute deviation of 9 will contribute the most to the total deviation. As a matter of fact, the deviations will contribute to the total in proportion to the size of the deviation. It is desirable to define a variability measure in which each data value contributes in proportion to its distance from the mean, as in the case with the mean absolute deviation.

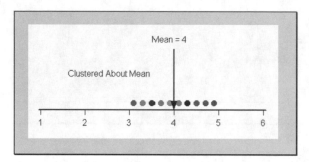

Figure 3-4: Data with small variability

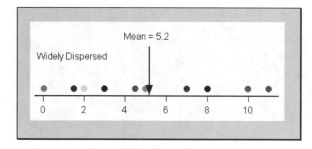

Figure 3-5: Data with large variability

3-4   The Variance and Standard Deviation

The variance and the standard deviation are the most common and useful measures of variability. These two measures provide information about how the data vary about the mean.

If the data are clustered around the mean, then the variance and the standard deviation will be somewhat small. There is small variability when data values are clustered about the mean, as shown in **Figure 3-4**.

If, however, the data are widely scattered about the mean, the variance and the standard deviation will be somewhat large. There is large variability when data values are widely scattered about the mean, as shown in **Figure 3-5**.

Explanation of the term—sample variance: The **sample variance** is an approximate average of the squared deviations from the sample mean. That is, the deviations of the data values from the sample mean are first computed, then the values for these deviations are squared, and then the **approximate** average of these square values are found. The average is approximate because we divide not by the sample size but by the **sample size minus one**.

Note:

1. We divide by the quantity $n - 1$ in order to make the sample variance an **unbiased estimator** of the population variance.

2. An estimator is unbiased if its average value is equal to the parameter it is estimating. For example, the sample mean $\bar{x}$ is an unbiased estimator of the population mean μ. That is, if we take all possible samples of a fixed size and find the means of these samples, then the average of all these sample means will be equal to the population mean.

3. The sample variance uses the squares of the deviations from the mean because this will eliminate the effect of the signs (as was also the case when we used the absolute value of the deviations in computing the MAD).

Generally, if there are n data values in the sample, with x representing the data values and $\bar{x}$ representing the sample mean, then the variance of the set of sample values is given by

$$\text{Sample variance} = s^2 = \frac{\Sigma(x - \bar{x})^2}{n - 1}$$

The formula says that you subtract the mean from each data value and square the differences, then you add these values, and then you divide by the sample size minus one.

- -

Quick Tip

Do not let the formula frighten you. We will build a table to help compute the variance.

- -

Example 3-6: What is the variance for the following sample values?

3   8   6   14   0   11

Solution: First of all, we need to compute the sample mean:

$$\bar{x} = \frac{3 + 8 + 6 + 14 + 0 + 11}{6} = \frac{42}{6} = 7$$

Next, we will build a table to help in the computations. **Table 3-2** displays the data values, the deviations from the sample mean, and the square deviations.

Table 3-2: Table Used in Helping to Compute the Sample Variance for Example 3-6

DATA	DEVIATIONS $(x - \bar{x})$	SQUARED DEVIATIONS $(x - \bar{x})^2$
3	$3 - 7 = -4$	$(-4)^2 = 16$
8	$8 - 7 = 1$	$(1)^2 = 1$
6	$6 - 7 = -1$	$(-1)^2 = 1$
14	$14 - 7 = 7$	$(7)^2 = 49$
0	$0 - 7 = -7$	$(-7)^2 = 49$
11	$11 - 7 = 4$	$(4)^2 = 16$
Total	0	132

This table illustrates why we square the deviations. As the second column shows, the sum of the deviations is zero. Squaring the deviations yields a positive value.

From the table, $\Sigma(x - \bar{x})^2 = 132$. Thus the sample variance is

$$s^2 = \frac{\Sigma(x - \bar{x})^2}{n - 1} = \frac{132}{6 - 1} = \frac{132}{5} = 26.4$$

This variance is somewhat large relative to the size of the data values. This can be observed from **Figure 3-6**, which shows that the data values are very much spread out about the mean value of 7.

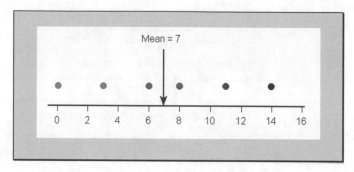

Figure 3-6: Plot of data values for Example 3-6

Explanation of the term—sample standard deviation: The **sample standard deviation** is the positive square root of the sample variance. It is given by

$$\text{Sample standard deviation} = s = +\sqrt{s^2} = \sqrt{\frac{\Sigma(x - \bar{x})^2}{n - 1}}$$

Note: The positive square root of the variance has the same unit as the variable. Since the variance is a square of the variable unit, taking the square root returns the original unit.

Example 3-7: What is the sample standard deviation for the sample data in **Example 3-6**?
Solution: The sample standard deviation is $s = \sqrt{26.4} = 5.14$.

Example 3-8: What is the MAD for the sample data in **Example 3-6**?
Solution: The sum of the absolute deviations $= 4 + 1 + 1 + 7 + 7 + 4 = 24$. Thus the MAD $= \dfrac{24}{6} = 4$. This value can be used as a rough estimate for the value of the standard deviation.

Quick Tips

• The sample standard deviation is approximately equal to the average distance (MAD) of the observations from their mean.

• If all the observations have the same value, the sample standard deviation will be zero. That is, there is no variability in the data set.

• The variance (standard deviation) is influenced by outliers (very small or very large values) in the data set.

• The unit for the standard deviation is the same as that for the raw data, so it is preferable to use the standard deviation instead of the variance as a measure of variability.

Explanation of the term—population variance: The **population variance** is the average of the squared deviations from the population mean. That is, the deviations of the data values from the population mean are first computed, then the values for these deviations are squared, and then the average of these square values is found. The average will be exact because we divide by the population size.

Generally, if there are N data values in the population, with x representing the data values and μ being the population mean, then the population variance, denoted by σ^2 (read as "sigma squared") is given by

$$\text{Population variance} = \sigma^2 = \frac{\Sigma(x - \mu)^2}{N}$$

This formula says that you subtract the population mean from each data value and square the result; then you add up these values and divide by the population size.

Explanation of the term—population standard deviation: The **population standard deviation** is the positive square root of the population variance. It is given by

$$\text{Population standard deviation} = \sigma = |\sqrt{\sigma^2} = \sqrt{\frac{(x - \mu)^2}{N}}$$

where the Greek letter σ (read as "sigma") is used to represent the population standard deviation. Observe that σ^2 represents the population variance.

Note: Recall that sample values are obtained from a population. Thus the sample mean and the sample variance (standard deviation) will estimate the population mean and the population variance (standard deviation), respectively. Also observe that the population variance will be the average of the squared deviations from the population mean because we divide by the population size N.

3-5 The Coefficient of Variation

The coefficient of variation (CV) allows us to compare the variation between two (or more) different variables.

Explanation of the term—sample coefficient of variation: The **sample coefficient of variation** is defined to be the sample standard deviation divided by the sample mean of the data set. Usually, the result is expressed as a percentage:

$$\text{Sample CV} = \frac{s}{\bar{x}} \times 100\%$$

Note: The sample coefficient of variation standardizes the variation by dividing it by the sample mean. The coefficient of variation has no units because the standard deviation and the mean have the same units, and thus the units cancel each other. Because of this property, we can use this measure to compare variations for different variables with different units.

Example 3-8: The mean number of parking tickets issued in a neighborhood over a four-month period was 90, and the standard deviation was 5. The average revenue generated from the tickets was $5400, and the standard deviation was $775. Compare the variations of the two variables.

Solution: CV (number of tickets) $= \dfrac{5}{90} \times 100\% = 5.56\%$

CV (number revenues) $= \dfrac{775}{5400} \times 100\% = 14.35\%$

Since the CV is larger for the revenues, there is more variability in the recorded revenues than in the number of tickets issued.

Explanation of the term—population coefficient of variation: The **population coefficient of variation** is defined to be the population standard deviation σ divided by the population mean μ. Again, the result is usually expressed as a percentage:

$$\text{Population CV} = \frac{\sigma}{\mu} \times 100\%$$

Note: Again, the population coefficient of variation standardizes the variation by dividing it by the population mean. Thus the coefficient of variation has no units, and so we can use this measure to compare variations for different population variables with different units.

3-6   The Empirical Rule

Knowing the value of the mean and the value of the standard deviation for a data set can provide a great deal of information about that data set. In particular, if the data set has a single mound and is symmetrical ("bell-shaped"), then one can generalize some properties of the distribution. One such generalization is called the **empirical rule**.

Empirical Rule

The empirical rule gives some general statements relating the mean and the standard deviation of a bell-shaped distribution. It relates the mean to one standard deviation, two standard deviations, and three standard deviations. Without loss of generality, we will use a symmetrical distribution with a mean of zero and a standard deviation of one to discuss the empirical rule.

One-Sigma Rule: Approximately 68 percent of the data values should lie within one standard deviation of the mean. This is illustrated in **Figure 3-7**.

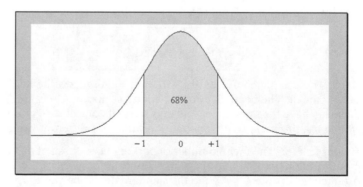

Figure 3-7: One-sigma rule

Thus one can expect a deviation of more than one sigma from the mean to occur once in every three observations. This is true because approximately 33 percent $\approx \frac{1}{3}$ of the values are outside one standard deviation from the mean.

Two-Sigma Rule: Approximately 95 percent of the data values should lie within two standard deviations of the mean. This is illustrated in **Figure 3-8**.

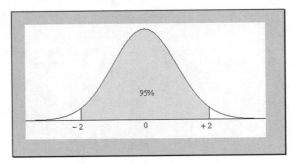

Figure 3-8: Two-sigma rule

Thus one can expect a deviation of more than two sigma from the mean to occur once in every 20 observations. This is true because approximately 5 percent $= \frac{1}{20}$ of the values are outside two standard deviations from the mean.

Three-Sigma Rule: Approximately 99.7 percent of the data values should lie within three standard deviations of the mean. This is illustrated in **Figure 3-9**.

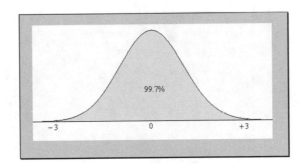

Figure 3-9: Three-sigma rule

Thus one can expect a deviation of more than three sigma from the mean to occur once in every 333 observations. This is true because approximately 0.3 percent $\approx \frac{1}{333}$ of the values are outside three standard deviations from the mean.

Example 3-9: A group of Internet stocks had an average cost per share of $46.20 with a standard deviation of $10.11. If the distribution of the data is bell-shaped, what interval will contain approximately 95 percent of the stock prices?

Solution: Using the two-sigma rule, 95 percent of the data will be included in the interval $46.20 $\pm$ 2 $\times$ $10.11 = $46.20 $\pm$ $20.22. The lower limit of the interval is

$46.20 − $20.22 = $25.98, and the upper limit of the interval is $46.20 + $20.22 = $66.42. Thus 95 percent of the stock prices should fall between $25.98 and $66.42.

3-7   Skewness

In Chapter 2 we discussed the idea of symmetrical, right-skewed, and left-skewed distributions. **Figures 3-10, 3-11**, and **3-12** further illustrate these shapes.

Figure 3-10: Symmetrical distribution

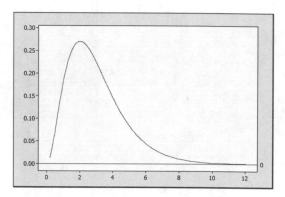

Figure 3-11: Right or positively skewed distribution

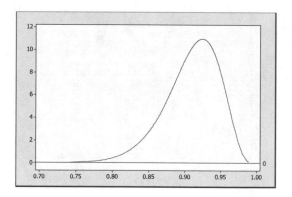

Figure 3-12: Left or negatively skewed distribution

Recall that in a symmetrical distribution the mean, median, and mode are all equal. For a right-skewed distribution, the mode is less than the median is less than the mean. For a left-skewed distribution, the mean is less than the median is less than the mode.

There are several formulas that one can use to compute the skewness for a distribution of numerical values. The simplest, developed by Karl Pearson, one of the great contributors to the science of statistics, is based on a relationship between the mean, median, and standard deviation. This measure is often called **Pearson's coefficient of skewness**.

Pearson's Coefficient of Skewness

The Pearson's coefficient of skewness, denoted by sk, is computed from the following formula:

$$sk = \frac{3(\bar{x}-median)}{s}$$

Example 3-10: The information for a data set are as follows: mean = 10.28, median = 9.45, and standard deviation = 4.61. Compute Pearson's coefficient of skewness.

Solution: Based on the information given, sk = 3(10.28 − 9.45)/4.61 = 0.54.

Observe that this value is positive. Hence the distribution of values will display a longer tail to the right.

Quick Tips

- The Pearson's coefficient of skewness can range from −3 to +3.
- Pearson also developed the formula to compute the coefficient of variation.

Technology Corner

All the measures of variability discussed in this chapter can be computed directly or indirectly with most statistical software packages. Most scientific calculators will compute the variance or standard deviation for both samples and population. However, only the newer calculators with extensive statistical capabilities, such as the TI-83/84, will compute all of these measures directly or indirectly. If you own a calculator, you need to consult the manual to determine what statistical features are included.

Illustration: **Figure 3-13** shows the descriptive statistics computed by the MINITAB software. **Figure 3-14** shows the 1-Var Stats (descriptive statistics) computed by the TI-83/84 calculator. The data used in both cases were from **Example 2-3**. Observe that MINITAB has given the value of the standard deviation (StDev) to two decimal places, whereas the TI-83/84 calculator gives the value of the standard deviation (Sx) to nine decimal places.

Descriptive Statistics: Eg2-3

Variable	Total Count	Mean	SE Mean	TrMean	StDev	Variance	CoefVar	Sum
Eg2-3	11	2.09	2.28	2.11	7.56	57.09	361.37	23.00

Variable	Minimum	Q1	Median	Q3	Maximum	Range	IQR	Skewness
Eg2-3	-10.00	-4.00	2.00	8.00	14.00	24.00	12.00	0.04

Figure 3-13: MINITAB descriptive statistics output for Example 2-3

```
1-Var Stats
x̄=2.090909091
Σx=23
Σx²=619
Sx=7.555852638
σx=7.20422282
↓n=11
```

```
1-Var Stats
↑n=11
 minX=-10
 Q₁=-4
 Med=2
 Q₃=8
 maxX=14
```

Figure 3-14: TI-83/84 1-Var Stats output for Example 2-3

Squaring the standard deviation will give the sample variance. The range can be obtained by subtracting the minimum value from the maximum value. Also, the interquartile range can be obtained by subtracting Q_1 from Q_3, which is displayed in both figures. One can use other features of the technologies to illustrate other concepts discussed in this chapter, as well as for other computations.

Quick Tip

Unlike the interquartile range, the range, the mean absolute deviation, and the variance (standard deviation) are all sensitive to outlying very small or very large) values.

The most commonly used measures of variation for numeric data are the
✓ Range
✓ Interquartile range
✓ Mean absolute deviation
✓ Variance or standard deviation
✓ Coefficient of variation
✓ Skewness

Care always should be taken when using these measures of variation.

Test Yourself

True/False Questions

1. The mean absolute deviation of a set of data always divides the data set in such a way that 50 percent of the values lie above the mean and 50 percent lie below the mean.
2. The median is a measure of variability.
3. The range of a set of data values is the largest value in the data set.
4. If the standard deviation for a data set is large, then the data set is less dispersed.

5. The standard deviation of a data set can be positive or negative.
6. Of a set of numerical data values, 50 percent will lie between one standard deviation from the mean of the data set.
7. In an ordered data set of numerical values, the median of the upper 50 percent of the data set corresponds to a numerical value such that 75 percent of the values are below it.
8. The sum of the absolute deviations from the mean of a data set is always equal to 0.
9. The empirical rule states that exactly 95 percent of a data set will lie within two standard deviations of the mean.
10. The unit for the variance of a data set is the square of the unit for the variable associated with the data set.
11. The interquartile range is the average of the medians of the lower and upper 50 percent of an ordered data set.
12. The standard deviation is the square of the variance.
13. The mean absolute deviation is a measure of variability.
14. On a statistics exam, Joe's score was at the median for the lower 50 percent of the scores, and John's score was at the median of the upper 50 percent the scores. Thus we can say that John's score was twice that of Joe's score.
15. The mean value of a data set corresponds to half the value of the range.
16. Of the range, the interquartile range, and the variance of a data set, the interquartile range is most influenced by an outlying value in the data set.
17. The middle 50 percent of an ordered set of data values constitutes the interquartile range.
18. Quantities that describe populations are called parameters, and quantities that describe samples are called statistics.
19. For a bell-shaped distribution, the range of the values is approximately equal to length of values within three standard deviations of the mean.
20. The coefficient of variation can be used to compare the variability of data sets that have different units.
21. A data set can have more than one measure of variability.
22. The empirical rule applies to all sets of data.
23. The value of the mean absolute deviation represents the number of standard deviations above or below the mean of the data set.
24. The sum of the absolute deviations from the mean for any data set may equal to 0.
25. The range is not influenced by an outlying value in a data set.

Completion Questions

1. The range of a set of data values is the difference between the (largest, smallest) value _____ and the (largest, smallest) _____ value.
2. The mean absolute deviation always will be a (positive, negative) _____ number.
3. The sum of the deviations from the mean in a data set always will be (negative, positive, zero) _____.
4. The coefficient of variation can be used to compare the (centralness, variability) _____ of data sets.
5. The interquartile range is the middle (25, 50, 75) _____ percent of the ordered data values.

6. The smaller the value of the standard deviation of a data set, the smaller is the amount of (range, variability, MAD) _____ in the data set.

7. According to the empirical rule, approximately (68, 95, 99.7) _____ percent of the values in a data set will lie within three standard deviations of the (mean, median, mode) _____ if the data set is bell-shaped.

8. The standard deviation of a data set has the same (value, unit) _____ as the variable from which the data was obtained.

9. The mean absolute deviation for a data set measures the (average, median) _____ distance of the values in the set from the mean.

10. It is preferred to use the (range, standard deviation) _____ rather than the variance because it has the same unit as the variable for the data.

11. Two measures of variability are the _____ and the _____.

12. When computing the mean absolute deviation and the variance, measurements are deviated from the (mean, median, standard deviation) _____ in the computations.

13. If two sets of data values are compared with different means, the larger (median, mean, mode, coefficient of variation) _____ indicates a larger dispersion about the (mean, variance) _____.

14. If a measurement in a data set is below the mean value of that set, then the deviation from the mean will be (positive, negative) _____.

15. For a bell curve distribution, approximately (68, 95, 99.7) _____ percent of the data values will lie within one standard deviation of the mean.

Multiple-Choice Questions

1. A sample of 10 students was asked by the instructor to record the number of hours each spent studying for a given exam from the time the exam was announced in class. The following data values were the recorded number of hours:

   12   15   8   9   14   8   17   14   8   15

   The variance for the number of hours spent studying for this sample is
   (a) 10.000.
   (b) 9.0000.
   (c) 3.4641.
   (d) approximately 12.

2. The numbers of minutes spent in the computer lab by 20 students working on a project are given below:

   Number of minutes
   30 | 0 2 5 5 6 6 6 8
   40 | 0 2 2 5 7 9
   50 | 0 1 3 5
   60 | 1 3

   The range for this data set is
   (a) 300.
   (b) 303.

(c) 603.

(d) 600.

3. The numbers of minutes spent in the computer lab by a sample of 20 students working on a project are given below:

Number of minutes

30 | 0 2 5 5 6 6 6 8
40 | 0 2 2 5 7 9
50 | 0 1 3 5
60 | 1 3

The standard deviation for this data set is

(a) 101.6.

(b) 403.8.

(c) 306.0.

(d) 500.5.

4. The price increases on five stocks were $7, $1, $8, $4, and $5. The standard deviation for these price increases is

(a) 2.3.

(b) 2.7.

(c) 3.2.

(d) 4.1.

5. Which of the following is not affected by an extreme value in a data set?

(a) The mean absolute deviation

(b) The median

(c) The range

(d) The standard deviation

6. Given the following sample values, what is the sample variance?

15   20   40   25   35

(a) 9.27

(b) 86.0

(c) 10.37

(d) 107.5

7. Which of the following is the crudest measure of dispersion?

(a) The mean absolute deviation

(b) The variance

(c) The mode

(d) The range

8. Which of the following is not a measure of central tendency?

(a) Mean

(b) Median

(c) The third quartile Q_3

(d) Mode

9. Examine the following data set:

   12   32   45   14   24   31

   The total deviation from the mean for the data values is
   (a) 0.
   (b) 26.3333.
   (c) 29.5.
   (d) 12.

10. Given that a sample is approximately bell-shaped with a mean of 60 and a standard deviation of 3, the approximate percentage of data values that is expected to fall between 54 and 66 is
    (a) 75 percent.
    (b) 95 percent.
    (c) 68 percent.
    (d) 99.7 percent.

11. Examine the following frequency distribution for a set of sample values.

VALUES (x)	FREQUENCY (f)
20	2
29	4
30	4
39	3
44	2

   The variance of the distribution is
   (a) 32.07.
   (b) 30.
   (c) 7.44.
   (d) 55.35.

12. Which of the following is a measure of variation?
    (a) Standard deviation
    (b) Midrange
    (c) Mode
    (d) Median

13. The following values are the ages of a sample of 15 students in a statistics class:

    18   21   25   21   28   23   21   19   24   26   21   24   18   27   23

    The standard deviation for this set of data is
    (a) 9.
    (b) 9.6857.
    (c) 21.
    (d) 3.1122.

14. An instructor recorded the following quiz scores (out of a possible 10 points) for the 12 students present. The scores were

    7   4   4   7   2   9   10   6   7   3   8   5

The interquartile range for this set of scores is
(a) 7.5.
(b) 6.5.
(c) 8.
(d) 3.5.

15. A statement is made that the average distance from the mean in a set of data values is 10. Which measure is being used here?
    (a) The range
    (b) The interquartile range
    (c) The mean absolute deviation
    (d) The standard deviation

16. Which of the following is not a measure of dispersion?
    (a) Interquartile range
    (b) Range
    (c) Median
    (d) Coefficient of variation

17. For the given sample data set 8, 12, 15, 20, 11, 5, 21, 0, what is the value of the coefficient of variation?
    (a) 62.52 percent
    (b) 11.5 percent
    (c) 7.19 percent
    (d) 159.9 percent

18. Which of the following statements is correct?
    (a) Two sets of numbers with completely different means and standard deviations may have the same coefficient of variation.
    (b) The most frequently used measure of variation is the standard deviation.
    (c) The range is a crude measure of dispersion because it only involves the smallest and the largest values in a data set.
    (d) All the above statements are correct.

19. Given that a sample is approximately bell-shaped with a mean of 25 and a standard deviation of 2, the approximate percentage of data values that is expected to fall between 19 and 31 is
    (a) 75 percent.
    (b) 95 percent.
    (c) 68 percent.
    (d) 99.7 percent.

20. The interquartile range in an ordered data set is the difference between
    (a) the median for the entire data set and the median for the lower 50 percent of the data set.
    (b) the median for the upper 50 percent of the data set and the median for the entire data set.
    (c) the median for the upper 50 percent and the median for the lower 50 percent of the data set.
    (d) the maximum value and the minimum value.

21. A single numerical value used to describe a characteristic of a sample data set, such as the sample median, is referred to as a
    (a) sample parameter.
    (b) sample median.
    (c) population parameter.
    (d) sample statistic.

22. The standard deviation always will be larger than the mean absolute deviation because
    (a) absolute values are not computed for the standard deviation.
    (b) the standard deviation is the square root of the variance.
    (c) the larger values in the data set receive stronger emphasis when squared.
    (d) of none of the above.

23. Which of the following is not a property of the standard deviation?
    (a) It is affected by extreme values in a data set.
    (b) It is the most widely used measure of spread.
    (c) It uses all the values in the data set in its computation.
    (d) It is always a positive number.

24. For which of the following is the coefficient of variation the smallest?
    (a) $\bar{x} = 10$ and $s = 2$
    (b) $\bar{x} = 14$ and $s = 3$
    (c) $\bar{x} = 30$ and $s = 5$
    (d) $\bar{x} = 39$ and $s = 8$

25. If a distribution has zero variance, which of the following is true?
    (a) All the values are positive.
    (b) All the values are negative.
    (c) The number of positive values and the number of negative values are equal.
    (d) All the values are equal to each other.

26. The following are given for a set of values:
    I. The values range from 40 to 95.
    II. The median value is 79.
    III. Twenty-five percent of the values are less than or equal to a value of 62.
    IV. Seventy-five percent of the values are less than or equal to 90.

    From this information, the interquartile range for the data set is
    (a) 55.
    (b) 28.
    (c) 50.
    (d) 33.

27. A sample of 10 students was asked by the instructor to record the number of hours each spent studying for a given exam from the time the exam was announced in class. The following data values were the recorded number of hours:

    12   15   8   9   14   8   17   14   8   15

    The mean absolute deviation for the number of hours spent studying for this sample is
    (a) 3.0.
    (b) 1.41.

(c) 1.33.

(d) 2.5.

28. The mean number of days it rained in January for a 10-year period on a college campus was 9 with a standard deviation of 3. The average amount of rainfall during that same 10-year period on the same campus was 8 inches with a standard deviation of 3 inches. Which variable has the higher relative variation?

(a) Neither

(b) Number of days it rained

(c) Amount of rainfall

(d) Number of days it rained but not the amount of rainfall

29. If we would like to compare the relative variation among three variables, the most appropriate statistics to use would be the

(a) variances of the three variables.

(b) ranges of the three variables.

(c) interquartile ranges of the three variables.

(d) coefficient of variations of the three variables.

30. The empirical rule usually can be applied to

(a) any distribution.

(b) only discrete distribution.

(c) only continuous distribution.

(d) any bell-shaped distribution.

31. Following are the earnings per share for a sample of 20 software companies for the year 2005. The earnings per share, in dollars, are given below:

15.60   1.20   0.40   0.15   0.10   1.50   3.20   3.50   6.36   8.90

12.59   3.35   0.09   10.15   13.99   7.00   17.25   14.55   9.00   16.00

The coefficient of skewness using Pearson's estimate is

(a) −0.2780.

(b) +0.2780.

(c) −0.0927.

(d) +0.0927.

32. The skewness of any symmetrical distribution always will be

(a) positive.

(b) negative.

(c) equal to zero.

(d) approximately zero.

33. In order to compute the Pearson's measurement of skewness of any distribution, we can compute it by knowing

(a) only the mean and standard deviation.

(b) only the median and standard deviation.

(c) only the mean and the median.

(d) only the mean, median and standard deviation.

34. Which is the most common type of distributions observed?

(a) Negatively skewed distributions

(b) Positively skewed distributions

(c) Symmetrical distributions

(d) All the above have an equal chance of being observed

35. The following data represent the time, in minutes, it takes a college professor to get to work for a sample of 15 days:

32 32 23 25 33 34 25 30 31 38 32 35 39 42 40

The coefficient of skewness using Pearson's estimate is

(a) +0.3929.

(b) −0.3929.

(c) +0.1310.

(d) −0.1310.

Further Exercises

If possible you could use any technology help to solve the following questions.

1. The at-rest pulse rates for a sample of 16 athletes at a meet are

67 57 56 57 58 56 54 64 53 54 54 55 57 68 60 58

Find the range, interquartile range, mean absolute deviation, variance, standard deviation, coefficient of variation, and Pearson's coefficient of skewness for this set of data.

2. The speeds (mph) of a sample of 16 cars on a highway were observed to be

58 56 60 57 52 54 54 59 63 54 53 54 58 56 57 67

Find the range, interquartile range, mean absolute deviation, variance, standard deviation, coefficient of variation, and Pearson's coefficient of skewness for this set of data.

3. **Estimate** the range, interquartile range, mean absolute deviation, variance, standard deviation, coefficient of variation, and Pearson's coefficient of skewness for the following frequency distribution. Recall that you can use the class marks (average of the lower and upper class limits for each class) for the intervals to approximate the observed values in the distribution.

CLASS	FREQUENCY
10–15	2
15–20	4
20–25	4
25–30	3
30–35	2

4. Find the range, interquartile range, mean absolute deviation, variance, standard deviation, coefficient of variation, and Pearson's coefficient of skewness for the following examination scores.

Exam scores

4 | 5 6 8
5 | 3 4 5 6 9
6 | 2 3 5 6 6 9 9
7 | 0 1 1 3 3 4 5 5 5 7 8

8|1 2 3 6 9
9|3 5 7 8

5. The following frequency distribution shows the scores for the exit examination for statistics majors at a four-year college for a given year:

98   75   85   97   80   87   97   60   83   90

Find the range, interquartile range, mean absolute deviation, variance, standard deviation, coefficient of variation, and Pearson's coefficient of skewness for this set of data.

6. The starting incomes for mathematics majors at a particular university were recorded for five years and are summarized in the following table:

STARTING SALARY (IN $1000)	FREQUENCY
10–15	3
15–20	5
20–25	10
25–30	7
30–35	1

Estimate the range, interquartile range, mean absolute deviation, variance, standard deviation, coefficient of variation, and Pearson's coefficient of skewness for this frequency distribution. Recall that you can use the class marks (average of the lower and upper class limits for each class) for the intervals to approximate the observed values in the distribution.

7. The number of minutes spent in the computer lab by 20 students working on a project are given in the following stem-and-leaf plot:

Number of minutes

30|0 2 5 5 6 6 6 8
40|0 2 2 5 7 9
50|0 1 3 5
60|1 3

Find the range, interquartile range, mean absolute deviation, variance, standard deviation, coefficient of variation, and Pearson's coefficient of skewness for this set of data.

8. The following frequency distribution shows the distances traveled (in miles) by 30 commuter students to campus:

DISTANCE (IN MILES)	FREQUENCY
35–40	8
40–45	13
45–50	6
50–55	3

Estimate the range, interquartile range, mean absolute deviation, variance, standard deviation, coefficient of variation, and Pearson's coefficient of skewness for this frequency distribution. Recall that you can use the class marks (average of the lower and upper class limits for each class) for the intervals to approximate the observed values in the distribution.

ANSWER KEY
True/False Questions

1. F   2. F   3. F   4. F   5. F   6. F   7. T   8. F   9. F   10. T   11. F   12. F
13. T   14. F   15. F   16. F   17. T   18. T   19. T   20. T   21. T   22. F   23. F   24. T
25. F.

Completion Questions

1. largest, smallest   2. positive   3. zero   4. variability   5. 50   6. variability   7. 99.7%, mean   8. unit   9. average   10. standard deviation   11. range, interquartile range, mean absolute deviation, variance, standard deviation, coefficient of variation (any two)   12. mean   13. coefficient of variation, mean   14. negative   15. 68

Multiple-Choice Questions

1. (d)   2. (b)   3. (a)   4. (b)   5. (b)   6. (d)   7. (d)   8. (c)   9. (a)
10. (b)   11. (d)   12. (a)   13. (d)   14. (d)   15. (c)   16. (c)   17. (a)   18. (d)
19. (d)   20. (c)   21. (d)   22. (c)   23. (b)   24. (c)   25. (d)   26. (b)   27. (a)
28. (c)   29. (d)   30. (d)   31. (b)   32. (c)   33. (d)   34. (b)   35. (a)

Further Exercises

1. range = 15; interquartile range IQR = 5.25; mean absolute deviation MAD = 3.375; variance s^2 = 20.93; standard deviation s = 4.58; coefficient of variation CV = 7.89; Pearson's coefficient of skewness sk = 0.655.

2. range = 15; interquartile range IQR = 2.875; mean absolute deviation MAD = 3.375; variance s^2 = 15.33; standard deviation s = 3.916; coefficient of variation CV = 6.87; Pearson's coefficient of skewness sk = 0.383.

3. range = 20; interquartile range IQR = 10; mean absolute deviation MAD = 5.0667; variance s^2 = 40.95; standard deviation s = 6.4; coefficient of variation CV = 28.87; Pearson's coefficient of skewness sk = −0.1547.

4. range = 53; interquartile range IQR = 19; mean absolute deviation MAD = 11.0629; variance s^2 = 201.05; standard deviation s = 14.18; coefficient of variation CV = 19.91; Pearson's coefficient of skewness sk = 0.0423.

5. range = 38; interquartile range IQR = 18.25; mean absolute deviation MAD = 8.6; variance s^2 = 137.73; standard deviation s = 11.74; coefficient of variation CV = 13.77; Pearson's coefficient of skewness sk = −0.2044.

6. range = 20; interquartile range IQR = 10; mean absolute deviation MAD = 3.9941; variance s^2 = 27.85; standard deviation s = 5.28; coefficient of variation CV = 23.86; Pearson's coefficient of skewness sk = −0.2159.

7. range = 303; interquartile range IQR = 194.8; mean absolute deviation MAD = 79.98; variance s^2 = 10312.9; standard deviation s = 101.6; coefficient of variation CV = 25.15; Pearson's coefficient of skewness sk = 0.0531.

8. range = 15; interquartile range IQR = 10; mean absolute deviation MAD = 3.6; variance s^2 = 21.954; standard deviation s = 4.686; coefficient of variation CV = 10.85; Pearson's coefficient of skewness sk = 0.4270.

CHAPTER 4

Numerical Measures of Position

You should read this chapter if you need to review or to learn about

→ Numerical values that measure location or position of a data value in a numerical data set

→ How to compute these measures and investigate some of their properties

You will recognize that these measures deal with only one property of the data set: the location or position. Thus you will need to combine these measures with other properties of the data set in order to fully describe it. Other properties for single-variable data will be investigated in future chapters.

Get Started

A measure of location or position for a collection of data values is a number that is meant to convey the idea of the relative position of a data value in the data set. The most commonly used measures of location are the *z* score or standard score and percentiles. These measures are discussed in this chapter, as are some special percentiles.

4-1   The *z* Score or Standard Score

Explanation of the term—*z* score: The *z* **score** for a sample value in a data set is obtained by subtracting the mean of the data set from the value and dividing the result by the standard deviation of the data set. Basically, the *z* score tells us how many standard deviations a specific value is above or below the mean value of the data set.

If we let x represent the sample value, $\bar{x}$ the sample mean, and s the sample standard deviation, then the *z* score can be computed from the following formula:

$$z \text{ score} = \frac{x - \bar{x}}{s}$$

The corresponding *z* score for a population value x is given by

$$z \text{ score} = \frac{x - \mu}{\sigma}$$

where μ represents the population mean, and σ represents the population standard deviation.

Quick Tips

- The *z* score is the number of standard deviations the data value falls above (positive *z* score) or below (negative *z* score) the mean for the data set.
- The *z* score is affected by an outlying value in the data set because the outlier (very small or very large value) directly affects the value of the mean and the standard deviation.

Example 4-1: What is the *z* score for the value of 14 in the following sample data set?

3   8   6   14   4   12   7   10

Solution: First, compute the sample mean and the sample standard deviation. The sample mean $\bar{x} = 8$, and the sample standard deviation $s = 3.8173$. Verify that these values are correct. Thus the *z* score is

$$z \text{ score} = \frac{14 - 8}{3.8173} = 1.5718 \approx 1.57$$

Thus the data value of 14 is located 1.57 standard deviations **above** the mean of 8 because the *z* score is **positive**.

Question: Why does a *z* score measure relative position?

The following discussion, using the information for **Example 4-1**, will give an insight to this question. **Figure 4-1** shows a plot of the data points with the location of the mean and the data value of 14. The distance between the mean of 8 and the value of 14 is **1.57 × standard deviation = 5.99 ≈ 6.** Observe that if we add the mean of 8 to this value, we will get 8 + 6 = 14, the data value. Thus this shows that the value of 14 is located 1.57 standard deviations **above** the mean. That is, the *z* score gives us an idea of how far away the data value is from the mean, and so it gives us an idea of the position of the data value relative to the mean.

Figure 4-1: Plot of data points for Example 4-1

Example 4-2: What is the z score for the value of 97 in the following sample data set?

96   99   94   101   96   104   103   97   109   101

Solution: First, compute the sample mean and the sample standard deviation. The sample mean $\bar{x} = 100$, and the sample standard deviation $s = 4.5461$. Verify that these values are correct. Thus the z score is

$$z \text{ score} = \frac{97 - 100}{4.5461} = -0.6599$$

Thus the data value of 97 is located 0.6599 standard deviation **below** the mean of 100 because the z score is **negative**.

   Figure 4-2 shows a plot of the data points for **Example 4-2** with the location of the mean and the data value of 97. The distance between the mean of 100 and the data value of 97 is **0.6599 × standard deviation = 2.9999 ≈ 3.** Observe that if we subtract the value of 3 from the mean of 100, we get a value of 97, the data value. Thus this shows that the value of 97 is located 0.6599 standard deviation **below** the mean. That is, the z score again gives us an idea of how far away the data value is from the mean, and so it gives us an idea of the position of the data value relative to the mean.

Figure 4-2: Plot of data points for Example 4-2

4-2   Percentiles

Explanation of the term—percentiles: **Percentiles** are numerical values that divide an ordered data set into 100 groups of values with at most 1 percent of the data values in each group.

When we discuss percentiles, we generally present the discussion through the kth percentile. The kth percentile for an ordered array of data is a numerical value P_k (say) such that at most k percent of the data values are smaller than P_k, and at most $(100 - k)$ percent of the data values are larger than P_k. The idea of the kth percentile is illustrated in **Figure 4-3**.

Figure 4-3: Illustration of the kth percentile

Example 4-3: Display the 98th percentile pictorially.

Solution: **Figure 4-4** displays the idea of the 98th percentile P_{98}. Here, at most 98 percent of the data values will be smaller than P_{98}, and at most 2 percent will be larger than P_{98}.

Figure 4-4: Pictorial representation of the 98th percentile

Percentile Corresponding to a Given Data Value

The percentile corresponding to a given data value, say, x, in a set is obtained by using the following formula:

$$\text{Percentile} = \frac{\text{number of values below } x + 0.5}{\text{number of values in data set}} \times 100\%$$

Example 4-4: The shoe sizes, in whole numbers, for a sample of 12 male students in a statistics class were as follows:

13   11   10   13   11   10   8   12   9   9   8   9

What is the percentile rank for a shoe size of 12?

Solution: First, we need to arrange the values from smallest to largest. This ordered set is given below:

8   8   9   9   9   10   10   11   11   12   13   13

Observe that the number of values below 12 is 9, and the total number of values in the data set is 12. Thus, using the formula, the corresponding percentile is

$$\frac{(9+0.5)}{12} \times 100\% = 79.17\%$$

That is, the value of 12 corresponds to approximately the 79th percentile.

Example 4-5: What is the percentile rank for a shoe size of 10 for the information in **Example 4-4**?

Solution: The ordered set from **Example 4-4** is repeated next:

8   8   9   9   9   10   10   11   11   12   13   13

Observe that the number of values below 10 is 5, and the total number of values is 12. Thus, using the formula, the corresponding percentile is

$$\frac{(5+0.5)}{12)} \times 100\% = 45.83\%$$

That is, the value of 10 corresponds to approximately the 46th percentile.

Procedure for Finding a Data Value for a General Percentile P_k

Assume that we want to determine what data value falls at some general percentile P_k. The following steps will enable you to find a general percentile P_k for a data set:

Step 1: Order the data set from smallest to the largest.

Step 2: Compute the position c of the percentile:

$$c = \frac{n \times k}{100}$$

where n = sample size

k = the required percentile

Step 3(a): If c **is not** a whole number, round up to the next whole number. Locate this position in the ordered set. The value in this location is the required percentile.

Step 3(b): If c **is** a whole number, find the average of the values in the c and $c + 1$ positions in the ordered set. The average value will be the required percentile.

Example 4-6: The data given below represent the total medals for 17 countries for the 2004 Athens Olympic Games. Find the 65th percentile for the data set.

49   37   48   33   32   30   30   27   23   17   19   16   22   19   12   15   10

Solution: First, we need to arrange the data set in order. The ordered set is

10   12   15   16   17   19   19   22   23   27   30   30   32   33   37   48   49

Next, compute the position of the percentile. Here, $n = 17$, and $k = 65$. Thus $c = (17 \times 65)/100 = 11.05$, so we need to round up to 12. Thus the 65th percentile will be located at the twelfth position in the ordered set. The twelfth value corresponds to the value of 30. Hence $P_{65} = 30$.

Question: Why does a percentile measure relative position?

The following discussion, using the information for **Example 4-6**, will give an insight into this question. **Figure 4-5** shows a plot of the data points with the location of the 65th percentile value of 30. This number is the cutoff point where at most, 65 percent of the data values are smaller than the percentile value of 30, and at most, 35 percent of the data values are larger than the percentile value of 30. Thus this shows that the percentile value of 30 is a measure of location. That is, the percentile gives us an idea of the relative position of a value in an ordered data set.

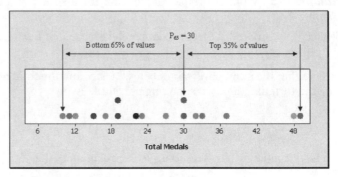

Figure 4-5: Plot to aid in answering the question, Why does a percentile measure relative position?

Example 4-7: Find the 25th percentile for the following data set:

6   12   18   12   13   8   13   11   10   16   13   11   10   10   2   14

Solution: First, we need to arrange the data set in order. The ordered set is

2   6   8   10   10   10   11   11   12   12   13   13   13   14   16   18

Next, compute the position of the percentile. Here, $n = 16$, and $k = 25$. Thus $c = (16 \times 25)/100 = 4$. Thus the 25th percentile will be the average of the values located at the fourth and the fifth positions in the ordered set. The fourth value corresponds to the value of 10, and the fifth value corresponds to the value of 10 as well. Hence $P_{25} = (10 + 10)/2 = 10$.

Special Percentiles: Deciles and Quartiles

Deciles and quartiles are special percentiles. Deciles divide an ordered data set into 10 equal parts, and quartiles divide it into four equal parts.

We usually denote the deciles by $D_1, D_2, \ldots, D_9$ and quartiles by $Q_1, Q_2,$ and Q_3. This is depicted in **Figures 4-6** and **4-7**, respectively. In the case of **Figure 4-6**, there is at most 10 percent of the values in each group. In the case of **Figure 4-7**, there is at most 25 percent of the values in each group.

Figure 4-6: Pictorial representation of deciles

Figure 4-7: Pictorial representation of quartiles

Quick Tips

- There are nine deciles and three quartiles.
- Q_1 is usually referred to as the *first quartile*, Q_2 as the *second quartile*, and Q_3 as the *third quartile*.
- $P_{50} = D_5 = Q_2$ = median. That is, the 50th percentile, the 5th decile, the 2nd quartile, and the median are all equal to one another.
- Finding deciles and quartiles is equivalent to finding the equivalent percentiles.

Outliers

Recall that an outlier is an extremely small or extremely large data value when compared with the rest of the data values. The following procedure allows us to check whether a given value in a data set can be classified as an outlier.

Procedure to Check for Outliers

The following steps will allow us to check whether a given value in a data set can be classified as an outlier.

Step 1: Arrange the data in order from smallest to largest.

Step 2: Determine the first quartile Q_1 and the third quartile Q_3. Recall that $Q_1 = P_{25}$ and $Q_3 = P_{75}$.

Step 3: Find the interquartile range (IQR) by computing $Q_3 - Q_1$.

Step 4: Compute $Q_1 - 1.5 \times$ IQR and $Q_3 + 1.5 \times$ IQR.

Step 5: Let x be the data value that is being checked to determine whether it is an outlier.

(a) If the value of x is smaller than $Q_1 - 1.5 \times$ IQR, then x is an outlier.

(b) If the value of x is larger than $Q_3 + 1.5 \times$ IQR, then x is an outlier.

Example 4-8: The data below represent the top 20 countries with total Olympic medals—including the United States, which had 103 medals —for the 2004 Athens Olympic Games. Determine whether the number of medals won by the United States is an outlier relative to the rest of the other 19 countries.

103 63 92 49 37 48 33 32 30 30 27 23 17 19 16 22 19 12 15 12

Solution: First, we need to arrange the data set in order. The ordered set is

12 12 15 16 17 19 19 22 23 27 30 30 32 33 37 48 49 63 92 103

Next, we need to determine the first and the third quartiles. That is, we need to determine P_{25} and P_{75}. Verify that $Q_1 = P_{25} = 18$ and $Q_3 = P_{75} = 42.5$. Thus the IQR = 42.5 − 18 = 24.5. From these computations, $Q_1 − 1.5 \times \text{IQR} = 18 − 1.5 \times 24.5 = −18.75$, and $Q_3 + 1.5 \times \text{IQR} = 42.5 + 1.5 \times 24.5 = 54.75$. Since 103 > 54.75, the value of 103 is an outlier relative to the rest of the values in the data set, based on the criterion presented in this section. That is, the number of medals won by the United States is an outlier relative to the numbers won by the other 19 countries for the 2004 Athens Olympic Games.

4-3 Box Plots

Explanation of the term—box plot: A **box plot** is a graphical display that involves a five-number summary of a distribution of values consisting of the minimum value, the lower quartile, the median, the upper quartile, and the maximum value.

A horizontal box plot is constructed by drawing a box between the quartiles Q_1 and Q_3. That is, a box is drawn to indicate the middle 50 percent of the data values. Horizontal lines then are drawn from the middle of the sides of the box to the minimum and maximum values. These horizontal lines are called **whiskers**. A vertical line inside the box marks the median. Outliers are usually indicated by a dot or an asterisk.

Example 4-9: Display the data for **Example 4-8** by a box plot.

Solution: The box plot for the data in **Example 4-8** is shown in **Figure 4-8**. Observe that the numbers of medals obtained by the United States and Russia are indicated by an asterisk. This box plot was generated by MINITAB, and the software indicates an outlying value by an asterisk.

Figure 4-8: Box plot for data in Example 4-8

By observing a box plot, important information concerning the distribution of the data set can be obtained. A summary of the potential information is given next.

Quick Tip

The vertical sides of a horizontal box plot are sometimes called *hinges*.

Information That Can Be Obtained from a Box Plot

- If the median is close to the center of the box, the distribution of the data values will be approximately symmetrical.
- If the median is to the left of the center of the box, the distribution of the data values will be positively skewed.
- If the median is to the right of the center of the box, the distribution of the data values will be negatively skewed.
- If the whiskers are approximately the same length, the distribution of the data values will be approximately symmetrical.
- If the right whisker is longer than the left whisker, the distribution of the data values will be positively skewed.
- If the left whisker is longer than the right whisker, the distribution of the data values will be negatively skewed.

Figure 4-9 shows box plots that display these characteristics.

Figure 4-9: Box plots with different characteristics

Example 4-10: Given the following information, determine whether the distribution is negatively skewed, symmetrical, or positively skewed.

(a) Minimum value = 25, Q_1 = 30, Q_2 = 33, Q_3 = 52, maximum value = 70.

(b) Minimum value = 10, Q_1 = 25, Q_2 = 45, Q_3 = 65, maximum value = 80.

(c) Minimum value = 5, Q_1 = 40, Q_2 = 55, Q_3 = 60, maximum value = 65.

Solution: (a) Observe that length of the left whisker = 30 − 25 = 5, and the right whisker = 70 − 52 = 18. Also, the median is only 33 − 30 = 3 units from Q_1 and 52 − 33 = 19 units from Q_3. From this information we can conclude that the distribution is skewed to the right, or positively skewed. The box plot for this information is shown in **Figure 4-10**.

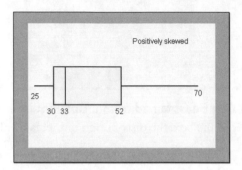

Figure 4-10: Box plot for Example 4-10(a)

(b) Observe that length of the left whisker = 25 − 10 = 15, and the right whisker = 80 − 65 = 15. Also, the median is only 45 − 25 = 20 units from Q_1 and 65 − 45 = 20 units from Q_3. From this information we can conclude that the distribution is symmetrical. The box plot for this information is shown in **Figure 4-11**.

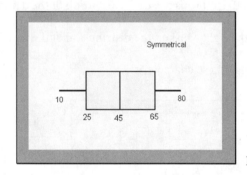

Figure 4-11: Box plot for Example 4-10(b)

(c) Observe that length of the left whisker = 40 − 5 = 35, and the right whisker = 65 − 60 = 5. Also, the median is only 55 − 40 = 15 units from Q_1 and 60 − 55 = 5 units from Q_3. From this information we can conclude that the distribution is skewed to the left, or negatively skewed. The box plot for this information is shown in **Figure 4-12**.

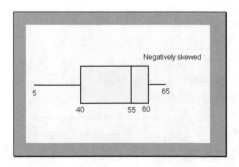

Figure 4-12: Box plot for Example 4-10(c)

Technology Corner

Usually only the first, second (median), and third quartiles can be computed directly with most statistical software packages. Box plots can be displayed by most statistical software packages. Most scientific calculators will not compute the measures of position discussed in this chapter. However, the newer calculators with extensive statistical capabilities, such as the TI-83/84, will compute the quartiles directly. All other percentiles and z scores will have to be computed using the formula or procedures discussed in the chapter when using statistical software or calculators. If you own a calculator, you should consult the manual to determine what statistical features are included.

Illustration: Figure 4-13 shows the descriptive statistics computed by the MINITAB software. **Figure 4-14** shows the 1-Var Stats (descriptive statistics) computed by the TI-83/84 calculator. The data used in both cases was from **Example 4-8**. Observe that MINITAB has given the value of the first, second (median), and the third quartiles. These values are also given by the TI-83/84 calculator. Note from the MINITAB output that the value for $Q_1 = 17.5$ and $Q_3 = 45.25$, as opposed to the TI-83/84, where $Q_1 = 18$ and $Q_3 = 42.5$. It is obvious that these two technologies are using different procedures to compute these percentiles. **You should be cautioned here to be vigilant about these differences in technologies**. One can use other features of the technologies to illustrate other concepts discussed in this chapter.

```
Descriptive Statistics: Number of Medals

                 Total
Variable         Count    Mean    SE Mean    StDev    Variance   CoefVar   Minimum
Number of Medals    20   34.70      5.70     25.48      649.17     73.43     11.00


Variable           Q1    Median      Q3    Maximum     Range      IQR
Number of Medals  17.50   28.50    45.25    103.00     92.00     27.75
```

Figure 4-13: MINITAB descriptive statistics output for Example 4-8

Figure 4-14: TI-83/84 1-Var Stats output for Example 4-8

Quick Tip

The *z* score is sensitive to outlying values. A large outlier may affect the upper percentiles. A small outlier may affect the lower percentiles.

The most commonly used measures of position for numeric data are the

✓ *z* score

✓ Percentiles

✓ Quartiles (special percentiles)

Care always should be taken when using these measures of position.

True/False Questions

1. If a student's exam score corresponds to a negative *z* score, then the student has a score that is less than the mean of the set of exam scores.
2. At most 50 percent of a set of data values lie between the first and third quartiles of the data set.
3. The third decile corresponds to the 70th percentile.
4. The midrange is the average of the first and third quartiles.
5. On a statistics exam, Joe's score was at the 30th percentile, and John's score was at the 60th percentile; thus we can say that John's score was twice that of Joe's score.
6. The 50th percentile of a data set corresponds to the mean value of the data set.
7. At most 50 percent of an ordered set of data values lie below the first quartile and above the third quartile.
8. For a symmetrical distribution, exactly 50 percent of the values are below the second quartile, and exactly 50 percent of the values are above the second quartile.
9. The *z* score associated with a data value represents the number of standard deviations that the value lies above or below the mean of the data set.
10. There are 100 percentiles in a data set.
11. In finding percentiles, it is not necessary to first order the data values.
12. If the 75th percentile for scores on a 100-point exam is 75, and the percentile position number *c* had to be rounded up to a whole number, then a student's score that ranks at the 75th percentile is equal to 75.
13. The 50th percentile is the same as the median.
14. The 9th decile is the same as the 90th percentile.
15. There are four quartiles in any data set.
16. An outlier does not affect the value of the median in a data set.
17. A box plot for a data set can be constructed if one knows the minimum value, the first quartile, the second quartile, the third quartile, and the maximum value of the data set.
18. If the right whisker is significantly longer than the left whisker on a box plot, then the distribution is skewed to the right.
19. In a box plot, if the median is to the right of the center of the box, the distribution of the data values will be positively skewed.

20. In a box plot, if the median is close to the center of the box, the distribution of the data values will be approximately symmetrical.
21. There are 10 deciles in a data set.
22. The following is given: minimum value = 20, $Q_1 = 25$, $Q_2 = 30$, $Q_3 - 35$, and maximum value = 40. From this information we can conclude that the distribution of values from which this information was obtained is symmetrical.
23. A z score always indicates the number of standard deviations a data value is above the mean.
24. z scores can be obtained only for sample values.
25. A large outlying value in a data set may affect the value of the 99th percentile.

Completion Questions

1. The z value associated with a measurement x represents the number of (percentiles, standard deviations) _____ that x lies above the mean or below the mean.

2. The first quartile is that value at or below which (25, 50, 75) _____ percent of all data entries in the ordered data set fall.

3. Two measures of position are _____ and _____.

4. If a measurement in a data set is below the mean value of that set, then the z value will be (positive, negative) _____.

5. Two special types of percentiles are _____ and _____.

6. There are (two, three, four) _____ quartiles in any data set.

7. The seventh decile corresponds to the (30th, 70th) _____ percentile.

8. There are (99, 100) _____ percentiles in any data set.

9. If the left whisker is significantly longer than the right whisker on a box plot, then the distribution is skewed to the (right, left) _____.

10. In a box plot, if the median is close to the (left edge, center, right edge) _____ of the box, the distribution of the data values will be approximately symmetrical.

11. The 50th percentile, the median, and the second quartile are all _____ to one another.

12. There are (nine, ten) _____ deciles in a data set.

13. In finding a z score for a given data value, if the z score is zero, then the data value and the mean are (different, equal) _____.

14. The third quartile corresponds to the (25th, 30th, 75th) _____ percentile.

15. In finding percentiles, it is first necessary to _____ the data values from smallest to largest.

16. A given data value is considered an outlier if it is (greater, less) _____ than Q_3 + 1.5 × IQR based on the procedure presented in this chapter.

17. A given data value is considered an outlier if it is (greater, less) _____ than Q_1 − 1.5 × IQR based on the procedure presented in this chapter.

18. When finding a data value for a given percentile, if the computed position number c is a whole number, then the required percentile will be the _____ of the values in the c and the $(c + 1)$ positions.

19. When finding a data value for a given percentile, if the computed position number c is not a whole number, then the position value will be obtained by rounding this value (up, down) _____ to the next whole number.

20. List three of the five numbers used in constructing a box plot.
_____

Multiple-Choice Questions

1. A student has seven statistics books open in front of him. The page numbers are as follows: 231, 423, 521, 139, 347, 400, 345. The second quartile for this set of numbers is
    (a) 231.
    (b) 347.
    (c) 330.
    (d) 423.

2. A cyclist recorded the number of miles per day she cycled for five days. The recordings were as follows: 13, 10, 12, 10, 11. The 50th percentile for the number of miles she cycled per day is
    (a) 12.5.
    (b) 11.
    (c) 10.
    (d) 11.5.

3. An instructor recorded the following quiz scores (out of a possible 10 points) for the 12 students present. The scores were 7, 4, 4, 7, 2, 9, 10, 6, 7, 3, 8, and 5. The 25th percentile for this set of scores is
    (a) 4.
    (b) 6.
    (c) 6.5.
    (d) 7.5.

4. An instructor recorded the following quiz scores (out of a possible 10 points) for the 12 students present. The scores were 7, 4, 4, 7, 2, 9, 10, 6, 7, 3, 8, and 5. The sixth decile for this set of scores is
    (a) 9.
    (b) 7.5.
    (c) 6.5.
    (d) 7.

5. The following values are the ages of 15 students in a statistics class:
    18   21   25   21   28   23   21   19   24   26   21   24   18   27   23

    The value of the first quartile for this set of data is
    (a) 25.
    (b) 23.
    (c) 21.
    (d) 22.5.

6. Which of the following is not a measure of position?

(a) First quartile
(b) Median
(c) Fourth decile
(d) Mean

7. A final statistics exam had a mean of 70 and a variance of 25. If Bruce made an 80 on his exam, what is his z score?
   (a) -2
   (b) 10
   (c) 0.4
   (d) 2

8. When it is necessary to determine whether an observation from a set of data falls in the upper 25 percent or lower 75 percent of the ordered data set, which measure should be used?
   (a) Third quartile
   (b) Mean
   (c) First quartile
   (d) Seventieth percentile

9. For the data set 38, 42, 45, 50, 41, 35, 51, 29, the value corresponding to the lower hinge (left vertical side) in a horizontal box plot would be equal to
   (a) 43.5.
   (b) 36.5.
   (c) 41.5.
   (d) 47.5.

10. For the data set 8, 12, 15, 20, 11, 5, 21, 0, what is the value of the seventh decile?
    (a) 6.5
    (b) 11.5
    (c) 17.5
    (d) 15

11. The following values are the ages of 15 students in a statistics class:

    18 21 25 21 28 23 21 19 24 26 21 24 18 27 23

    The percentile rank of 25 would be

    (a) 20th.
    (b) approximately 77th.
    (c) 80th.
    (d) 75th.

12. Which of the following is a measure of position?
    (a) Standard deviation
    (b) Box plots
    (c) Mode
    (d) Quartile

13. Examine the following frequency distribution:

VALUE	FREQUENCY
20	2
29	4
30	4
39	3
44	2

The 77th percentile of the distribution is
(a) 29.
(b) 30.
(c) 39.
(d) 32.

14. Given that a sample is approximately bell-shaped with a mean of 60 and a standard deviation of 3, the approximate value for the 98th percentile for this distribution is
(a) 63.
(b) 66.
(c) 69.
(d) 57.

15. Given that a sample is approximately bell-shaped with a mean of 60 and a standard deviation of 3, the approximate value for the 16th percentile for this distribution is
(a) 54.
(b) 66.
(c) 63.
(d) 57.

16. Examine the following data set:

12   32   45   14   24   31

The value of the interquartile range is
(a) 14.
(b) 32.
(c) 27.5.
(d) 18.

17. If a sample has a mean of 100 and a standard deviation of 6, what is the value in the data set that corresponds to a z score of 2?
(a) 88
(b) 94
(c) 92
(d) 112

18. The 50th percentile is the same as the
(a) mode.
(b) mean.
(c) median.
(d) midrange.

19. The vertical sides on a horizontal box plot are located at
    (a) the minimum value and first quartile of the data set.
    (b) the minimum value and the maximum value of the data set.
    (c) the third quartile and the maximum value of the data set.
    (d) the first quartile and the third quartile of the data set.

20. The interquartile range is the difference between
    (a) the second quartile and the first quartile.
    (b) the third quartile and the second quartile.
    (c) the third quartile and the first quartile.
    (d) the maximum value and the minimum value.

21. For a bell-shaped distribution, the most frequently occurring value in a data set will be the
    (a) third quartile.
    (b) interquartile range.
    (c) second quartile.
    (d) first quartile.

22. Which of the following may be affected the most if there is an extremely large value in a data set?
    (a) The first quartile
    (b) The second quartile
    (c) The third quartile
    (d) The 99th percentile

23. If the number of values in any data set is even, then
    (a) the second quartile cannot be found.
    (b) the second quartile will be the average of two numbers.
    (c) the interquartile range will be half the length between the minimum value and the median.
    (d) the second quartile will be twice the first quartile.

24. The 75th percentile of a data set is equivalent to
    (a) the seventh decile of the data set.
    (b) the first quartile of the data set.
    (c) the second quartile of the data set.
    (d) the third quartile of the data set.

25. Examine the following frequency distribution:

VALUE	FREQUENCY
20	2
29	4
30	4
39	3
44	2

The second quartile of the distribution is

(a) 29.

(b) 30.

(c) 39.

(d) 29.5.

26. In a box plot, if the median is to the left of the center of the box, then the distribution of the data values will be

(a) positively skewed.

(b) negatively skewed.

(c) symmetrical.

(d) bell-shaped.

27. In a box plot, if the left whisker is longer than the right whisker, the distribution of the data values will be

(a) positively skewed.

(b) negatively skewed.

(c) symmetrical.

(d) uniform.

28. The following information for a data set is given: minimum value = 105, Q_1 = 140, Q_2 = 155, Q_3 = 160, and maximum value = 165. From this information, the distribution is

(a) symmetrical.

(b) positively skewed.

(c) negatively skewed.

(d) bell-shaped.

29. The number of deciles in a data set is

(a) 10.

(b) 12.

(c) 99.

(d) 9.

30. A data value is considered to be an outlier if

(a) it lies between $-1.5 \times$ IQR and $+1.5 \times$ IQR.

(b) it lies between $Q_1 - 1.5 \times$ IQR and $Q_3 + 1.5 \times$ IQR.

(c) it lies between Q_1 and Q_3.

(d) if it is smaller than $Q_1 - 1.5 \times$ IQR or larger than $Q_3 + 1.5 \times$ IQR.

31. The numbers of minutes spent in the computer lab by 20 students working on a project are given below:

Number of minutes

30 | 0 2 5 5 6 6 6 8
40 | 0 2 2 5 7 9
50 | 0 1 3 5
60 | 1 3

The first quartile for this data set is

(a) 402.

(b) 306.

(c) 500.

(d) 403.5.

32. The numbers of minutes spent in the computer lab by 20 students working on a project are given in the following stem-and-leaf plot:

Number of minutes

30 | 0 2 5 5 6 6 6 8

40 | 0 2 2 5 7 9

50 | 0 1 3 5

60 | 1 3

The interquartile range for this data set is

(a) 306.

(b) 402.

(c) 500.5.

(d) 194.5.

33. In the 2004 Athens Summer Olympic Games, the following were the top 20 total number of gold medals earned by the different countries:

35   32   27   17   14   16   11   10   9   9   9   9   8   8   6   5   4   3   3   3

What is the percentile ranking for the value of 10?

(a) 20.0

(b) 37.5

(c) 30.0

(d) 35.0

34. The number of students entering a university cafeteria during a random selected hour was observed. Following are the numbers for 20 different randomly selected hours during a week of final examinations when the cafeteria was open for business.

141   100   94   88   79   74   72   71   55   54   52   41   35   34   33   31   29   28   28   23

What is the value of the first quartile for this set of values?

(a) 118.0

(b) 31.50

(c) 77.75

(d) 46.25

35. The number of students entering a university cafeteria during a random selected hour was observed. Following are the numbers for 20 different randomly selected hours during a week of final examinations when the cafeteria was open for business.

141   100   94   88   79   74   72   71   55   54   52   41   35   34   33   31   29   28   28   23

What is the value of the second quartile for this set of values?

(a) 53.00

(b) 31.50

(c) 77.75

(d) 46.25

36. The number of students entering a university cafeteria during a random selected hour was observed. Following are the numbers for 20 different randomly selected hours during a week of final examinations when the cafeteria was open for business.

141   100   94   88   79   74   72   71   55   54   52   41   35   34   33   31   29
28   28   23

What is the value of the third quartile for this set of values?

(a) 53.00
(b) 31.50
(c) 77.75
(d) 46.25

37. The number of students entering a university cafeteria during a random selected hour was observed. Following are the numbers for 20 different randomly selected hours during a week of final examinations when the cafeteria was open for business.

141   100   94   88   79   74   72   71   55   54   52   41   35   34   33   31   29
28   28   23

What is the value of the interquartile range for this set of values?

(a) 53.00
(b) 31.50
(c) 77.75
(d) 46.25

38. In a box plot, if the right whisker is longer than the left whisker, the distribution of the data values will be

(a) positively skewed.
(b) negatively skewed.
(c) symmetrical.
(d) uniform.

39. The following information for a data set is given: minimum value = 130, Q_1 = 140, Q_2 = 145, Q_3 = 160, and maximum value = 195. From this information, the distribution is

(a) symmetrical.
(b) positively skewed.
(c) negatively skewed.
(d) bell-shaped.

40. Given that a sample is approximately bell-shaped with a mean of 50 and a standard deviation of 5, the value for the 84th percentile for this distribution is

(a) 45.
(b) 55.
(c) 60.
(d) 65.

41. Given that the z score for a given value in a data set is zero, then this value must be
(a) above the mean.
(b) below the mean.

(c) same as the mean.

(d) equal to zero.

Further Exercises

If possible you could use any technology to help solve the following questions.

1. The at-rest pulse rates for 16 athletes at a track meet are

   67 57 56 57 58 56 54 64 53 54 54 55 57 68 60 58

   Find the quartiles, interquartile range, deciles, 47th percentile, and 88th percentile for this set of data. Display the data using a horizontal box plot, and label with the computed five-number summary information. Based on the box plot, how would you describe the shape of the distribution.

2. The speeds (mph) of 16 cars on a highway were observed to be

   58 56 60 57 52 54 54 59 63 54 53 54 58 56 57 67

   Find the quartiles, interquartile range, deciles, 33rd percentile, 66th percentile, and 99th percentile for this set of data. Display the data using a horizontal box plot, and label with the computed five-number summary information. Based on the box plot, how would you describe the shape of the distribution.

3. **Estimate** the quartiles, interquartile range, deciles, 11th percentile, 22nd percentile, 44th percentile, 66th percentile, and 88th percentile for the following frequency distribution. Display the data using a box plot, and label with the computed five-number summary information. Based on the box plot, how would you describe the shape of the distribution. Recall that you can use the class marks for the intervals to approximate the observed values in the distribution.

CLASS	FREQUENCY
10–15	2
15–20	4
20–25	4
25–30	3
30–35	2

4. Find the quartiles, interquartile range, deciles, 12th percentile, 24th percentile, 36th percentile, 48th percentile, 60th percentile, 72nd percentile, 84th percentile, and 96th percentile for the following examination scores. Display the data using a box plot. Based on the box plot, how would you describe the shape of the distribution.

   Exam scores

   4 | 5 6 8
   5 | 3 4 5 6 9
   6 | 2 3 5 6 6 9 9
   7 | 0 1 1 3 3 4 5 5 5 7 8
   8 | 1 2 3 6 9
   9 | 3 5 7 8

5. The following frequency distribution shows the scores for the exit examination for statistics majors at a four-year college for a given year:

   98 75 85 97 80 87 97 60 83 90

   Find the quartiles and interquartile range for this set of data. Display the data using a box plot. Based on the box plot, how would you describe the shape of the distribution.

6. The starting incomes for mathematics majors at a particular university were recorded for five years and are summarized in the following table:

STARTING SALARY (IN $1000)	FREQUENCY
10–15	3
15–20	5
20–25	10
25–30	7
30–35	1

   Estimate the quartiles, interquartile range, 33rd percentile, 66th percentile, and 99th percentile for this set of data. Display the data using a box plot. Based on the box plot, how would you describe the shape of the distribution. Recall that you can use the class marks for the intervals to approximate the observed values in the distribution.

7. The number of minutes spent in the computer lab by 20 students working on a project are given below:

   Number of minutes

   30 | 0 2 5 5 6 6 6 8
   40 | 0 2 2 5 7 9
   50 | 0 1 3 5
   60 | 1 3

   Find the quartiles, interquartile range, deciles, 33rd percentile, 66th percentile, and 99th percentile for this set of data. Display the data using a box plot. Based on the box plot, how would you describe the shape of the distribution.

8. The following frequency distribution shows the distances traveled (in miles) by 30 commuter students to campus.

DISTANCE (IN MILES)	FREQUENCY
35–40	8
40–45	13
45–50	6
50–55	3

   Estimate the quartiles and interquartile range for this set of data. Display the data using a box plot. Based on the box plot, how would you describe the shape of the distribution. Recall that you can use the class marks for the intervals to approximate the observed values in the distribution.

ANSWER KEY
True/False Questions

1. T 2. T 3. F 4. F 5. F 6. F 7. T 8. T 9. T 10. F 11. F 12. T
13. T 14. T 15. F 16. T 17. T 18. T 19. F 20. T 21. F 22. T 23. F 24. F
25. T.

Completion Questions

1. standard deviations 2. twenty-five (25) 3. z scores, percentiles 4. negative
5. deciles, quartiles 6. three (3) 7. seventieth (70th) 8. ninety-nine (99) 9. left
10. center 11. equal 12. nine (9) 13. equal 14. seventy-fifth (75th) 15. order
16. greater 17. less 18. average 19. up 20. minimum value; first quartile (Q_1) or
the 25th percentile P_{25}; median or second quartile (Q_2) or the 50th percentile P_{50}; third
quartile (Q_3) or the 75th percentile P_{75}; maximum value.

Multiple-Choice Questions

1. (b) 2. (b) 3. (a) 4. (d) 5. (c) 6. (d) 7. (d) 8. (a) 9. (b)
10. (d) 11. (b) 12. (d) 13. (c) 14. (b) 15. (d) 16. (d) 17. (d) 18. (c)
19. (d) 20. (c) 21. (c) 22. (d) 23. (b) 24. (d) 25. (b) 26. (a) 27. (b)
28. (c) 29. (d) 30. (d) 31. (b) 32. (d) 33. (b) 34. (b) 35. (a) 36. (c)
37. (d) 38. (a) 39. (b) 40. (b) 41. (c)

Further Exercises

1. $Q_1 = 54.25$; $Q_2 = 57$; $Q_3 = 59.5$; IQR $= 5.25$; $D_1 = 54$; $D_2 = 54$; $D_3 - 55$; $D_4 = 56$; $D_5 = 57$; $D_6 = 57$; $D_7 = 58$; $D_8 = 60$; $D_9 = 67$; $P_{47} = 57$; $P_{88} = 65.5$. Horizontal box plot. Right or positively skewed with one outlying value.

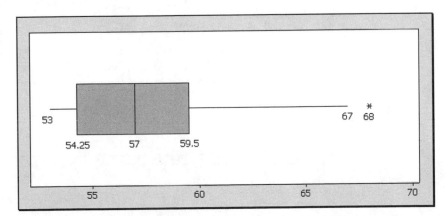

2. $Q_1 = 54$; $Q_2 = 57$; $Q_3 = 59.75$; IQR $= 5.75$; $D_1 = 53$; $D_2 = 54$; $D_3 = 54$; $D_4 = 56$; $D_5 = 57$; $D_6 = 58$; $D_7 = 59$; $D_8 = 60$; $D_9 = 64$; $P_{33} = 56$; $P_{66} = 58$; $P_{99} = 67$. Horizontal box plot. Right or positively skewed.

3. $Q_1 = 17.5$; $Q_2 = 22.5$; $Q_3 = 27.5$; IQR $= 10$; $D_1 = 12.5$; $D_2 = 17.5$; $D_3 = 17.5$; $D_4 = 20$; $D_5 = 22.5$; $D_6 = 22.5$; $D_7 = 27.5$; $D_8 = 27.5$; $D_9 = 32.5$; $P_{11} = 12.5$; $P_{22} = 17.5$; $P_{44} = 22.5$; $P_{66} = 22.5$; $P_{88} = 32.5$. Horizontal box plot. Symmetrical.

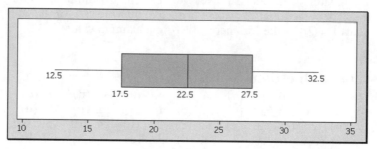

4. $Q_1 = 62$; $Q_2 = 71$; $Q_3 = 81.5$; IQR $= 19$; $D_1 = 53$; $D_2 = 57.5$; $D_3 = 65$; $D_4 = 69$; $D_5 = 71$; $D_6 = 74.5$; $D_7 = 77$; $D_8 = 82.5$; $D_9 = 93$; $P_{12} = 54$; $P_{24} = 62$; $P_{36} = 66$; $P_{48} = 71$; $P_{60} = 74.5$; $P_{72} = 78$; $P_{84} = 86$; $P_{96} = 97$. Horizontal box plot. Symmetrical.

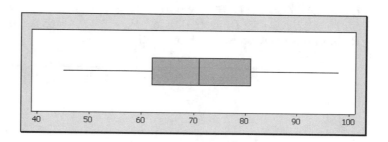

5. $Q_1 = 78.75$; $Q_2 = 86$; $Q_3 = 97$; IQR $= 18.25$. Horizontal box plot. Left or negatively skewed.

6. $Q_1 = 17.5$; $Q_2 = 22.5$; $Q_3 = 27.5$; IQR = 10; $P_{33} = 22.5$; $P_{66} = 22.5$; $P_{99} = 32.5$. Horizontal box plot. Symmetrical distribution.

7. $Q_1 = 306$; $Q_2 = 402$; $Q_3 = 500.8$; IQR = 194.8; $D_1 = 303.5$; $D_2 = 305.5$; $D_3 = 306$; $D_4 = 354$; $D_5 = 402$; $D_6 = 406$; $D_7 = 454.5$; $D_8 = 502$; $D_9 = 553$; $P_{33} = 306$; $P_{66} = 409$; $P_{99} = 603$. Horizontal box plot. Right or positively skewed.

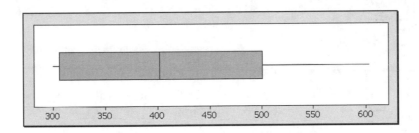

8. $Q_1 = 37.5$; $Q_2 = 42.5$; $Q_3 = 47.5$; IQR = 10. Horizontal box plot. Right or positively skewed.

CHAPTER 5

Exploring Bivariate Data

Y ou should read this chapter if you need to review or need to learn about

→ Graphical displays used to study the relationship between two variables

→ The correlation coefficient as a numerical measure of the strength of the relationship between two variables

→ Least-squares regression as a method for modeling the linear relationship between two variables

So far you have dealt with single-variable (univariate) data. However, this chapter will introduce you to bivariate (two-variable) data. That is, you will be dealing with data that are associated with two variables. You will study the idea of association through graphical displays, as well as through correlation analysis. In addition, you will study how to model the relationship between the two variables through regression analysis.

Get Started

The most common graphical display used to study the association between two variables is called a *scatter plot*. A measure of association for bivariate data is a number that is meant to convey the idea of the strength of the relationship between the two variables. The most commonly used measure of association is called the *correlation coefficient*. In addition, *regression analysis* will allow us to propose a mathematical model for the association. We can use such models to make predictions for one variable given a value of the other variable. We will, however, restrict the discussions to linear models. Concepts relating to these topics are discussed in this chapter.

5-1   Scatter Plots

In simple correlation and regression studies, data are collected on two quantitative variables to determine whether a relationship exists between the two variables.

Example 5-1: The bivariate data given in **Table 5-1** relate the high temperature (°F) reached on a given day and the number of cans of soft drink sold from a particular vending machine in front of a grocery store. Data were collected for 21 different days.

Table 5-1: High Temperature and Soft Drink Sales Data for Example 5-1

TEMP.	QUANTITY	TEMP.	QUANTITY	TEMP.	QUANTITY
70	30	98	59	90	53
75	37	72	33	95	56
80	40	77	36	98	62
90	52	75	38	91	51
93	57	80	45	99	63
82	42	84	47	86	48
87	46	88	49	78	41

We would like to study graphically the association between the temperature and the number of cans of soft drink sold.

To graphically analyze the data, we can display the data on a two-dimensional graph. We can plot the **number of cans of soft drink** along the vertical axis and the **temperature** along the horizontal axis. Such plots are called **scatter plots**. The variable along the vertical axis is called the **dependent variable**, and the variable along the horizontal axis is called the **independent variable**.

Notation: We will let y represent the dependent variable, and we will let x represent the independent variable.

Explanation of the term—scatter plot: A **scatter plot** is a graph of the ordered pairs (x, y) of values for the independent variable x and the dependent variable y.

Observe that the number of cans of soft drink sold from the machine is a *function* of the temperature. Thus, in **Example 5-1**, the dependent variable will be the number of cans of soft drink sold, and the independent variable will be the temperature.

Quick Tip

In a scatter plot, we let the values of the dependent variable be along the vertical (y) axis, and the values of the independent variable are along the horizontal (x) axis.

Solution: The scatter plot for **Example 5-1** is displayed in **Figure 5-1**.

Figure 5-1: Scatter plot for data in Example 5-1

We can observe from the plot that the number of cans of soft drink sold increases as the temperature increases and that there seems to be a linear trend for this association.

5-2 Looking for Patterns in the Data

Detecting an association or a relationship for bivariate data starts with a scatter plot. When examining a scatter plot, one should try to answer the following:

- Is there a straight-line pattern or association?
- Does the pattern or association slope upward or slope downward?
- Are the plotted values tightly clustered together in the pattern or widely separated?
- Are there noticeable deviations from the pattern?

Quick Tips

- Two variables are said to be *positively related* if larger values of one variable tend to be associated with larger values of the other.
- Two variables are said to be *negatively related* if larger values of one variable tend to be associated with smaller values of the other.

The scatter plots presented in **Figures 5-2** through **5-7** display different patterns. In **Figure 5-2**, the variables are positively related because larger values of the dependent variable are associated with larger values of the independent variable, and vice versa. The values are on a straight line, and therefore, one can say that there is a **perfect positive association** between the variables. Perfect association rarely occurs when sample data are collected.

Figure 5-2: Perfect positive association

Figure 5-3 shows variables that are negatively related because larger values of the dependent variable are associated with smaller values of the independent variable, and vice versa. The values are on a straight line, and therefore, one can say that there is a **perfect negative association** between the variables. Again, perfect association rarely occurs with sample data.

Figure 5-3: Perfect negative association

Figure 5-4 shows variables that are positively related. The values are not on a straight line but are somewhat closely packed together in a linear manner, so one can say that there is a very strong positive association between the variables.

Figure 5-4: Very strong positive association

Figure 5-5 shows variables that are negatively related. The values are not on a straight line but are relatively closely packed together in a somewhat linear pattern, so one can say that there is a very strong negative association between the variables.

Figure 5-5: Very strong negative association

Figure 5-6 does not show any noticeable pattern. The values are scattered around, so one can say that there is very little association between the variables.

Figure 5-6: No association

Figure 5-7 does not show any noticeable linear pattern. The scatter plot displays a non-linear or curvilinear relationship. We will not study such relationships in this text but will only concentrate on linear relationships between two variables.

Figure 5-7: Nonlinear association

5-3 Correlation

So far you have seen how a scatter plot can provide a visual image of the association between two variables. Here we will discuss a numerical measure of the linear association between two variables called the **Pearson product moment correlation coefficient** or simply the **correlation coefficient**.

Explanation of the term—correlation: **Correlation** is a statistical association or relationship between two variables.

Explanation of the term—sample correlation coefficient: The **sample correlation coefficient** measures the strength and direction of a linear relationship between two variables using sample data. The sample correlation coefficient is denoted by the letter r and is computed from the following equation:

$$r = \frac{n(\Sigma xy)-(\Sigma x)(\Sigma y)}{\sqrt{[n(\Sigma x^2)-(\Sigma x)^2]\times[n(\Sigma y^2)-(\Sigma y)^2]}}$$

where n is the number of (x, y) data pairs.

Note: This is only one way to compute the value of the correlation coefficient. There are several other ways to find the value of r that will not be discussed in this text.

Example 5-2: Compute the correlation coefficient for the following set of sample observations for the independent variable x and the dependent variable y.

x	8	4	5	−1	1	2	6
y	−2	2	1	6	4	3	−1

Solution: The formula may look intimidating, but we can construct a table, as shown in **Table 5-2**, to help with the computations. We can use a table such as **Table 5-2** to obtain the different sums in the formula.

Table 5-2: Table to Help with the Computation of r

x	y	$x \cdot y$	x^2	y^2
8	−2	−16	64	4
4	2	8	16	4
5	1	5	25	1
−1	6	−6	1	36
1	4	4	1	16
2	3	6	4	9
6	−1	−6	36	1
$\Sigma x = 25$	$\Sigma y = 13$	$\Sigma x \cdot y = -5$	$\Sigma x^2 = 147$	$\Sigma y^2 = 71$

Using the values from **Table 5-2** and substituting into the formula, we obtain

$$r = \frac{7(-5)-(25)(13)}{\sqrt{[7(147)-(25)^2]\times[7(71)-(13)^2]}} = -0.989$$

Following is a summary of the properties of the correlation coefficient.

Properties of the Correlation Coefficient

- The range of the correlation coefficient is from −1 to +1.
- If there is a perfect positive linear relationship between the variables, the value of r will be equal to +1. See **Figure 5-2**.
- If there is a perfect negative linear relationship between the variables, the value of r will be equal to −1. See **Figure 5-3**.
- If there is a strong positive linear relationship between the variables, the value of r will be close to +1. See **Figure 5-4**.

- If there is a strong negative linear relationship between the variables, the value of *r* will be close to −1. See **Figure 5-5**.
- If there is little or no linear relationship between the variables, the value of *r* will be close to 0. See **Figure 5-6**.

Figure 5-8 gives an idea about the range of the correlation coefficient *r*.

Figure 5-8: Range of the correlation coefficient *r*

Following are some general guidelines in interpreting the value of the correlation coefficient.

Interpretation of the Correlation Coefficients—General Rule of Thumb

- $-1 \leq r \leq -0.8 \Rightarrow$ strong negative linear relationship; $+0.8 \leq r \leq +1 \Rightarrow$ strong positive linear relationship.
- $-0.79 \leq r \leq -0.6 \Rightarrow$ moderately high negative linear relationship; $+0.6 \leq r \leq +0.79 \Rightarrow$ moderately high positive linear relationship.
- $-0.59 \leq r \leq -0.4 \Rightarrow$ moderate negative linear relationship; $+0.4 \leq r \leq +0.59 \Rightarrow$ moderate positive linear relationship.
- $-0.39 \leq r \leq -0.2 \Rightarrow$ low negative linear relationship; $+0.2 \leq r \leq +0.39 \Rightarrow$ low positive linear relationship.
- $-0.19 \leq r \leq +0.19 \Rightarrow$ little or no linear relationship.

Explanation of the term—population correlation coefficient: The **population correlation coefficient** measures the strength and direction of a relationship between two variables using population data values. The population correlation coefficient is denoted by the Greek letter ρ (read as "rho") and is computed by using all possible pairs of data values (*x, y*) taken from the population.

The same formula that is used to compute the sample correlation coefficient is employed, except that all possible pairs of values (*x, y*) from the population are now used.

Quick Tip

One always should examine the scatter plot and not just rely on the value of the linear correlation coefficient. This measure will not detect curvilinear or other types of complex relationships. That is, there may be a nonlinear relationship between two variables even though the linear correlation is close to zero.

Pearson correlation coefficient = 0.421

X axis

Figure 5-9: Association with small linear correlation but with strong nonlinear association

Figure 5-9 illustrates an example in which the linear relationship between the two variables is small (0.421); however, as one can see from the graph, there is strong nonlinear relationship between the variables. We will not study nonlinear relationships in this text because of their complexity at this level.

5-4   Correlation and Causation

It is important to understand the nature of the relationship between the independent variable x and the dependent variable y. Listed below are some possibilities that one should consider.

- There may be a direct cause-and-effect relationship between the two variables. For example, x may cause y. To illustrate, lack of water causes dehydration, intensive exercise causes thirst, heat causes ice cream to melt, etc.

- There may be a reverse cause-and-effect relationship between the two variables. For example, y causes x. To illustrate, one may believe that bad grades may be caused by absences, but one should not fail to also consider the fact that bad grades may cause absences.

- The relationship may be due to chance or coincidence. To illustrate, one may find a relationship between the number of suicides and the increase in the sale of bagels. One can only conclude that any association between these two variables must be due to chance.

- The relationship may be due to confounding. That is, the relationship may be due to the interrelationships among several variables.

Figure 5-10 shows the distinction between association and causation. For example, a large correlation (negative or positive) does not imply causation. Suppose that a high correlation is observed between the weekly sales of hot chocolate and the number of skiing accidents. One can reasonably conclude that hot chocolate sales could not cause skiers to have accidents while skiing and that more skiing accidents could not cause an increase in the sale of hot chocolate. Since the two variables are not actually related, what could explain such a relationship? The apparent relationship between the two variables may be caused by a third variable. In this case, the variables may be related to the weather conditions during the winter months.

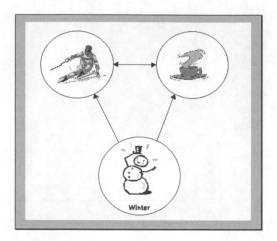

Figure 5-10: Correlation and causation

5-5　Least-Squares Regression Line

In investigating the relationship between two variables, the first thing one should do is to prepare a scatter plot after the data are collected. From the plot, one can observe any pattern of association. If the linear correlation coefficient is reasonably large (positive or negative), the next step would be to develop a model for the relationship. One of the purposes for the model is to help in making predictions. We will use the broad area of regression analysis to help determine this model.

Explanation of the term—regression analysis: **Regression analysis** is a broad area in statistics that enables us to find the line that best describes the relationship between two variables. We usually refer to this line as the **line of best fit**.

Line of Best Fit

The scatter plot in **Figure 5-11** shows two possible straight lines that may be used to model the data. The question is, Which of these lines best represents the association between the two variables?

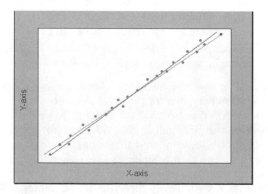

Figure 5-11: Line of best fit

Regression analysis allows us to determine which of the two lines best represents the relationship. From algebra, the equation of a straight line usually is given by $y = mx + b$, where m is the slope of the line, and b is the y intercept. In elementary statistics, the equation of the regression line is usually written as $\hat{y} = ax + b$, where a is the slope, b is the y intercept, and $\hat{y}$ is read as "y-hat," and it gives the predicted y value for a given x value. Least-squares analysis allows us to determine values for a and b such that the equation of the regression line best represents the relationship between the two variables by minimizing the error sum of squares—that is, by minimizing $\Sigma(y - \hat{y})^2$, where $(y - \hat{y})$ is the error for a given y value. This regression line is usually called the **line of best fit.** We usually refer to this type of regression analysis as **simple regression analysis** because we are only dealing with straight-line models involving one independent variable. The equations that one can use to compute the values for a and b are

$$a = \frac{n(\Sigma xy) - (\Sigma x)(\Sigma y)}{n(\Sigma x^2) - (\Sigma x)^2}$$

$$b = \frac{(\Sigma y)(\Sigma x^2) - (\Sigma x)(\Sigma xy)}{n(\Sigma x^2) - (\Sigma x)^2}$$

Other forms of the equations are possible and may be given by other authors.

Example 5-3: Determine the equation for the line of best fit for the following information where the independent variable is x and the dependent variable is y.

x	8	4	5	-1
y	-2	0	2	6

Solution: The formulas may look intimidating, but we can construct a table, as shown below, to help with the computations.

x	y	$x \cdot y$	x^2	y^2
8	-2	-16	64	4
4	0	0	16	0
5	2	10	25	4
-1	6	-6	1	36
$\Sigma x = 16$	$\Sigma y = 6$	$\Sigma x \cdot y = -12$	$\Sigma x^2 = 106$	$\Sigma y^2 = 44$

Thus, from this table, we have that $n = 4$, $\Sigma x = 16$, $\Sigma y = 6$, $\Sigma xy = -12$, $\Sigma x^2 = 106$, and $\Sigma y^2 = 44$. Substituting into the formulas above gives, to three decimal places,

$$a = \frac{(4)(-12) - (16)(6)}{4(106) - (16)^2} = -0.857 \quad \text{and} \quad b = \frac{(6)(106) - (16)(-12)}{4(106) - (16)^2} = 4.929$$

Thus, the line of best fit will be given by $\hat{y} = -0.857x + 4.929$. The line of best fit is superimposed on the scatter plot, as shown in **Figure 5-12**. Observe that the slope of the line is negative.

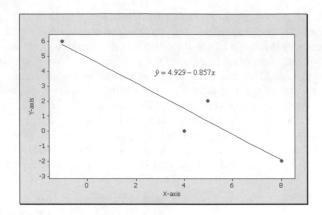

Figure 5-12: Display of the line of best fit for Example 5-3

Example 5-4: Interpret the value for the slope from **Example 5-3**.

Solution: Recall that the equation for the line of best fit was $\hat{y} = -0.857x + 4.929$, and so the slope is -0.857. We can interpret this value as saying that for 1 unit *increase* in the x (independent variable) value, there will be a *decrease* (because of the negative value) of 0.857 units in the y (dependent variable) value.

Example 5-5: Predict the value of y when $x = 4$ for the regression model in **Example 5-3**.

Solution: All one needs to do is to substitute $x = 4$ in the equation for the line of best fit and compute. Thus, $\hat{y} = -0.857 \times 4 + 4.929 = 1.501$. That is, the predicted value of y is 1.501 when the independent value $x = 4$. Note that the ordered pair (4, 1.501) will be a point located on the line of best fit. Observe that the value of 4 lies in the experimental range for the x values.

Quick Tip

When using the line of best fit to make predictions, care must be taken to use independent values that are within the range of the observed independent variable. Using values outside the range of observed independent values may lead to incorrect predictions because we do not know how the model is behaving outside this range. The model reflects the behavior of the association between the two variables only within the range of observed values.

5-6   The Coefficient of Determination

The **coefficient of determination** is a measure that allows us to determine how certain one can be in making predictions with the line of best fit.

Explanation of the term—coefficient of determination: The **coefficient of determination** measures the proportion of the variability in the dependent variable (y variable) that is explained by the regression model through the independent variable (x variable).

Properties of the Coefficient of Determination

- The coefficient of determination is obtained by squaring the value of the correlation coefficient and sometimes is expressed as a percentage.
- The symbol used to denote the coefficient of determination is R^2.
- Note that $0 \le R^2 \le 1$ or, equivalently $0 \le R^2 \le 100$ percent.
- R^2 values close to 1 or 100 percent would imply that the model is explaining most of the variation in the dependent variable and may be a very useful model.
- R^2 values close to 0 or 0 percent would imply that the model is explaining little of the variation in the dependent variable and may not be a useful model.

Example 5-6: What is the value of the coefficient of determination for the model in **Example 5-3**.

Solution: Using the information in **Example 5-3**, we can compute the correlation coefficient using the formula. Thus

$$r = \frac{4(-12)-(16)(6)}{\sqrt{[4(106)-(16)^2]\times[4(44)-(6)^2]}} = -0.939$$

Thus, the coefficient of determination $R^2 = (-0.939)^2 = 0.882$, or 88.2 percent. That is, the regression model can explain about 88.2 percent of the variation in the y values. This would be a reasonable model to use for prediction because of the large R^2 value.

5-7 Residual Plots

Residuals are just errors. In particular, a **residual** is the difference between an actual observed y value and the corresponding predicted y value. Thus the error for any observation is given by

$$\text{Residual} = \text{error} = (\text{observed} - \text{predicted}) = (y - \hat{y})$$

Plots of residuals may display patterns that would give some idea about the appropriateness of the model. If the functional form of the regression model is incorrect, the residual plots constructed by using the model often will display a pattern. The pattern then can be used to propose a more appropriate model.

The residual plot shown in **Figure 5-13** displays a linear pattern. Such a residual plot would imply that a linear model is the appropriate model for predicting the dependent y values.

Figure 5-13: Linear residual plot

The residual plot shown in **Figure 5-14** displays a nonlinear pattern. If a linear model were used to generate these residuals, this would imply that a nonlinear model is the appropriate model for predicting *y* instead of the linear model.

It is possible to have other curved patterns when residuals are plotted. However, if a linear model is used to generate the residuals, one should reevaluate the model and adjust for the curvature.

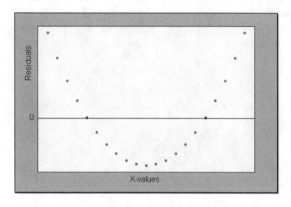

Figure 5-14: Nonlinear residual plot

5-8   Outliers and Influential Points

A value that is well separated from the rest of the data set is called an **outlier**. With respect to the line of best fit, an outlier is a an observation with a large absolute residual value. That is, an outlier will fall far from the regression line and will not follow the pattern of the linear relationship expressed by the line of best fit. In **Chapter 4** we discussed how to test to determine whether a value in single-variable data sets can be considered to be an outlier. An observation that causes the values of the slope and the intercept in the line of best fit to be considerably different from what they would be if the observation were removed from the data set is said to be **influential**.

Consider the the scatter plot in **Figure 5-15**. We will use it to discuss the concept of an outlier and an influential point in the context of regression.

Figure 5-15: Plot illustrating outliers and influential points

Observations 1 and 2 can be considered as outliers. Observation 1 is an outlier with respect to its y value but not with respect to its x value. Its x value is near the center of the other x values, but its y value is not consistent with the linear relationship. Observation 2 is an outlier with respect to its x value but not with respect to its y value. Its x value is outside the range of the majority of the x values, and its y value is consistent with the linear relationship. Observation 3 is probably an influential point. It is an outlier with respect to its x value, and its y value is not consistent with the linear relationship.

Technology

Technology Corner

All the concepts discussed in this chapter can be computed and illustrated through most statistical software packages. Most scientific calculators will not compute the correlation coefficient directly, slope and intercept for the line of best fit, and will not display scatter plots. However, some of the newer calculators with extensive statistical and graphical capabilities will compute the correlation coefficient directly, as well as the slope and the intercept for the regression line, and display scatter plots. If you own a calculator, you should consult the manual to determine what statistical features are included.

Illustration: **Figure 5-16** shows the regression analysis output computed by the MINITAB software. **Figure 5-17** shows the LinReg output computed by the TI-83/84 calculator. The data used in both cases were from **Example 5-2**. Observe that MINITAB has given the least-squares equation and the coefficient of determination R-Sq. (R^2). Also, MINITAB

```
Regression Analysis: y versus x

The regression equation is
y = 5.04 - 0.891 x


Predictor     Coef  SE Coef       T      P
Constant    5.0396   0.2737   18.41  0.000
x          -0.89109  0.05974  -14.92  0.000


S = 0.453807   R-Sq = 97.8%   R-Sq(adj) = 97.4%


Analysis of Variance

Source          DF      SS      MS       F      P
Regression       1  45.827  45.827  222.53  0.000
Residual Error   5   1.030   0.206
Total            6  46.857
```

Figure 5-16: MINITAB regression output for Example 5-2

Figure 5-17: TI-83/84 LinReg output for Example 5-2

computes other statistics that will not be discussed in this text. The TI-83/84 calculator output gives the values for the slope, the intercept, the correlation coefficient, and the coefficient of determination. *Note:* Care always should be taken when using the formulas to compute the values for *a* and *b*. One can use other features of the technologies to illustrate other concepts discussed in this chapter.

Note: MINITAB also uses the form $\hat{y} = ax + b$ for the line of best fit. Other texts and technology may use the form $\hat{y} = a + bx$.

Figure 5-18 shows the MINITAB fitted-line plot for **Example 5-2** with the line of best fit superimposed onto the scatter plot.

Figure 5-18: MINITAB output with regression line superimposed on the scatter plot for Example 5-2

 Linear relationships can be investigated through

✓ Scatter plots
✓ Correlation coefficient
✓ Line of best fit
✓ Coefficient of determination
✓ Appropriate technology

Care always should be taken when using the line of best fit to model data. One should be aware of outliers and influential points. One should make use of scatter plots and residual plots to determine whether the model is appropriate. One should be clear as to whether there is an association between two variables and be sure that causation is not being misinterpreted for association.

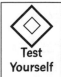

True/False Questions

1. In simple regression analysis, if the slope of the line is positive, then there is a positive correlation between the dependent variable *y* and the independent variable *x*.
2. In simple regression analysis, if the *y* intercept is negative, then there is a negative correlation between the dependent variable *y* and the independent variable *x*.

3. The variable that is being predicted in regression analysis is the independent variable.
4. The method of least squares provides the best approximation for the straight-line model that relates the dependent variable y and the independent variable x.
5. The value of the correlation coefficient r is always between -2 and $+2$.
6. A correlation coefficient of 0.95 indicates that the observations are widely scattered about the regression line.
7. A correlation of almost zero indicates that the strength of the relationship between the dependent and independent variables is very weak.
8. The coefficient of determination can assume negative values.
9. If the least-squares equation relating the dependent variable y and the independent variable x for a given problem is $y = 2x + 5$, then an increase of 1 unit in x is associated with an increase of 2 units in y.
10. In regression analysis, the units for the dependent and independent variables always will be the same.
11. A negative correlation between the dependent variable y and the independent variable x indicates that large values of x are associated with small values of y.
12. A scatter plot is a graphical display of the dependent and independent variables under study.
13. If the correlation between the dependent and independent variables is $+1$, then the slope of the regression line also will be $+1$.
14. If there is no correlation between the independent and dependent variables, then the value of the correlation coefficient must be -1.
15. Causation and correlation explain the same concept in that they both measure the strength of the linear relationship between two variables.
16. The sample correlation coefficient has possible values ranging from -1 to $+1$.
17. When data are measured on two variables to determine a possible linear association between those variables, this set of data is called bivariate data.
18. If the least-squares equation between the dependent variable y and the independent variable x for a given set of bivariate data is $y = 2x + 5$, then an increase in 2 units in x is associated with a 1 unit increase in y.
19. The coefficient of determination measures the variation in the dependent variable that is explained by the regression model.
20. The least-squares regression equation minimizes the error sum of squares.
21. If the slope of the regression equation is positive, then the correlation between the dependent variable y and the independent variable x must be 1.
22. If your computed correlation coefficient $r = +1.2$, then you have better than a perfect positive correlation.
23. The variable that is being predicted in regression analysis is the dependent variable.
24. A student might expect that there is a positive correlation between the age of his or her computer and its resale value.
25. Simple regression analysis is used when several independent variables contribute to the variation of the dependent variable.

Completion Questions

1. The value of the correlation coefficient equal to $(0, +1, -1)$ _____ indicates that there is a perfect negative relationship between the dependent variable y and the independent variable x.

2. A negative correlation coefficient between the dependent variable y and the independent variable x indicates that large values of x are associated with (large, small) _____ values of y.

3. The sample correlation coefficient has values ranging from _____ to _____.

4. In simple linear regression analysis, if the y intercept is positive, then the slope of the line of best fit must be (positive, negative, zero, any of the previous three responses) _____.

5. In regression analysis, the variable that is being predicted is called the (independent, dependent) _____ variable.

6. Correlation analysis is used to determine the _____ and _____of the relationship between the dependent and independent variables.

7. When there is not a significant relationship between the dependent variable y and the independent variable x, the value of the correlation coefficient will be approximately $(-2, -1, 0, +1, +2)$ _____.

8. You should expect a (positive, negative, zero) _____ correlation between the age of your computer and the resale value of your computer.

9. Which of the following values $(-1, 0.66, 0, 1, -1.01, -0.78)$ will not be a value of the correlation coefficient? _____

10. If the computed value of the correlation coefficient is 0.71, then the slope of the least-squares line will be (positive, negative, zero) _____.

11. A correlation coefficient of 0.97 indicates that the observations are (closely, widely) _____ scattered about the regression line.

12. When data are measured on two variables to determine whether there is any association between them, these kinds of data are called _____ data.

13. For the least-squares equation $\hat{y} = -x + 1$, the correlation between x and y is $(1, -1,$ positive, negative) _____.

14. The least-squares equation (minimizes, maximizes) _____ the error sum of squares.

15. Generally speaking, the larger the correlation (either positive or negative) between the independent variable x and the dependent variable y for the simple linear regression model, the (better, worse) _____ will be the predictions y for given values of x.

16. The value of the coefficient of determination lies between $(-1$ and $+1, -1$ and $0, 0$ and $+1, -0.5$ and $+0.5)$ _____.

17. The coefficient of determination can be obtained by squaring the value of the _____.

18. Regression analysis is used to find the (strength, direction, model) _____ of the linear relationship between the independent and dependent variables in simple regression analysis.

19. If the slope of the line of best fit is $+2$, this implies that for a 1-unit increase in the x value, there will be a 2-unit (increase, decrease) _____ in the y value.

20. Without a scatter plot and with a correlation close to zero, can one say for certain that there is no relationship between the variables? (yes, no) _____.

Multiple-Choice Questions

1. In simple linear regression analysis with x representing the independent variable and y representing the dependent variable, if the y intercept is negative, then
   (a) the correlation between x and y is negative.
   (b) the correlation between x and y is positive.
   (c) the correlation between x and y could be either negative, positive, or zero.
   (d) the predicted y value is always negative.

2. In regression analysis, the input variable that is used to get a predicted value is the same as
   (a) the dependent variable.
   (b) the independent variable.
   (c) the least-squares variable.
   (d) the random variable.

3. In a simple linear regression model with x representing the independent variable and y representing the dependent variable, correlation analysis is used to
   (a) find the least-squares regression line.
   (b) find the slope of the regression line.
   (c) measure the strength and direction of the linear relationship between x and y.
   (d) draw a scatter plot.

4. If the correlation coefficient is zero, the slope of a linear regression line will be
   (a) positive.
   (b) negative.
   (c) positive or negative.
   (d) none of the above.

5. In the simple linear regression model, if there is a very strong correlation between the independent and dependent variables, then the correlation coefficient should be
   (a) close to -1.
   (b) close to $+1$.
   (c) close to either -1 or $+1$.
   (d) close to zero.

6. For the simple linear regression model, if all the points on a scatter plot lie on a straight line with correlation coefficient $r = -1$, then the slope of the regression line is
   (a) -1.
   (b) $+1$.
   (c) positive.
   (d) negative.

7. The least-squares equation for the line of best fit
   (a) minimizes the error sum of squares.
   (b) maximizes the error sum of squares.
   (c) does not change the error sum of squares.
   (d) does none of the above.

8. If through some analysis one can conclude that the slope of the line of best fit is not equal to zero, then the simple linear regression model indicates that there is
    (a) a positive relationship between the independent and dependent variables.
    (b) a negative relationship between the independent and dependent variables.
    (c) a positive or negative relationship between the independent and dependent variables.
    (d) no relationship between the independent and dependent variables.

9. Which of the following is not a possible value of the correlation coefficient?
    (a) +1
    (b) −1
    (c) 0.011
    (d) 1.11

10. A negative correlation coefficient between the dependent variable y and the independent variable x indicates that
    (a) large values of x are associated with small values of y.
    (b) large values of x are associated with large values of y.
    (c) small values of x are associated with small values of y.
    (d) none of the answers is correct.

11. For the simple linear regression model, if the unit for the dependent variable is square feet, then the unit of the independent variable
    (a) must be square feet.
    (b) can be some unit of square measurement.
    (c) can be any unit.
    (d) cannot be a unit of square measurement.

12. In simple linear regression analysis, there
    (a) is only one independent variable in the model.
    (b) could be several linear independent variables in the model.
    (c) is only one nonlinear term in the model.
    (d) is at least one nonlinear term in the model.

13. For the regression equation $\hat{y} = 2(1 - x)$, the correlation coefficient
    (a) is +2.
    (b) is −2.
    (c) is −1.
    (d) cannot be determined from the information given.

14. In the least-squares regression line, the desired sum of the errors (residuals) should be
    (a) positive.
    (b) negative.
    (c) maximized.
    (d) equal to zero.

15. Which of the following is associated with correlation and regression analyses?
    (a) Least squares
    (b) Correlation coefficient
    (c) Coefficient of determination
    (d) All the above

16. You are given the following set of observations for the independent variable x and the dependent variable y:

x	-3	-1	1	3
y	8	4	5	-1

The correlation coefficient is

(a) -1.0.
(b) -0.8971.
(c) $+1$.
(d) 0.8971.

17. You are given the following set of observations for the independent variable x and the dependent variable y:

x	-3	-1	1	3
y	8	4	5	-1

The coefficient of determination is

(a) -1.0.
(b) -0.8048.
(c) $+1$.
(d) 0.8048.

18. You are given the following set of observations for the independent variable x and the dependent variable y:

x	-3	-1	1	3
y	8	4	5	-1

The least-squares estimate of slope of the regression line is

(a) $+4.0$.
(b) -1.3.
(c) -0.9.
(d) -4.0.

19. You are given the following set of observations for the independent variable x and the dependent variable y:

x	-3	-1	1	3
y	8	4	5	-1

The least-squares estimate for the y intercept of the regression line is

(a) -1.3.
(b) $+4$.
(c) -0.9.
(d) $+1.3$.

20. You are given the following set of observations for the independent variable x and the dependent variable y:

x	-3	-1	1	3
y	8	4	5	-1

The least-squares linear regression equation is
(a) $\hat{y} = -1.3 + 4x$.
(b) $\hat{y} = 4.0 - 1.3x$.
(c) $\hat{y} = -1.3 - 0.8971x$.
(d) $\hat{y} = -0.897 - 1.3x$.

21. You are given the following set of observations for the independent variable x and the dependent variable y:

x	-3	-1	1	3
y	8	4	5	-1

The predicted value $\hat{y}$ of the dependent variable y when $x = 2$ is
(a) 6.7.
(b) 1.4.
(c) -3.094.
(d) -3.497.

22. You are given the following information:

$$\Sigma x = 24 \quad \Sigma y = 16 \quad \Sigma x^2 = 180 \quad \Sigma y^2 = 90 \quad \Sigma xy = 75 \quad n = 10$$

The correlation coefficient will be
(a) 0.4122.
(b) 0.1700.
(c) 0.2990.
(d) 0.5683.

23. You are given the following information:

$$\Sigma x = 24 \quad \Sigma y = 16 \quad \Sigma x^2 = 180 \quad \Sigma y^2 = 90 \quad \Sigma xy = 75 \quad n = 10$$

The coefficient of determination will be
(a) 0.3230.
(b) 0.0894.
(c) 0.0289.
(d) 0.1699.

24. You are given the following information:

$$\Sigma x = 24 \quad \Sigma y = 16 \quad \Sigma x^2 = 180 \quad \Sigma y^2 = 90 \quad \Sigma xy = 75 \quad n = 10$$

The least-squares estimate of *a* is

(a) 0.4773.
(b) 0.2990.
(c) 0.2061.
(d) 0.9265.

25. You are given the following information:

$$\Sigma x = 24 \quad \Sigma y = 16 \quad \Sigma x^2 = 180 \quad \Sigma y^2 = 90 \quad \Sigma xy = 75 \quad n = 10$$

The least-squares estimate of *b* is

(a) 2.3176.
(b) 0.7176.
(c) 0.8824.
(d) 1.8990.

26. You are given the following information:

$$\Sigma x = 24 \quad \Sigma y = 16 \quad \Sigma x^2 = 180 \quad \Sigma y^2 = 90 \quad \Sigma xy = 75 \quad n = 10$$

The least-squares regression equation is

(a) $\hat{y} = 0.299 + 0.8824x$.
(b) $\hat{y} = 1.899 + 0.9265x$.
(c) $\hat{y} = 0.7176 + 0.2061x$.
(d) $\hat{y} = 0.8824 + 0.299x$.

27. You are given the following information:

$$\Sigma x = 24 \quad \Sigma y = 16 \quad \Sigma x^2 = 180 \quad \Sigma y^2 = 90 \quad \Sigma xy = 75 \quad n = 10$$

The predicted value $\hat{y}$ of the dependent variable *y* when *x* = 2 is

(a) 1.4804.
(b) 1.1296.
(c) 3.752.
(d) 3.2722.

28. The following table shows the age *x* and the systolic blood pressure *y* for a sample of six patients who were admitted to a hospital:

x	43	48	56	61	67	70
y	123	125	135	143	145	152

Note: In this problem we assume that the systolic blood pressure depends on age. That is, we are assuming that age is the independent variable, and systolic blood pressure is the dependent variable.

Which of the following scatter plots represents the data given in the preceding table?

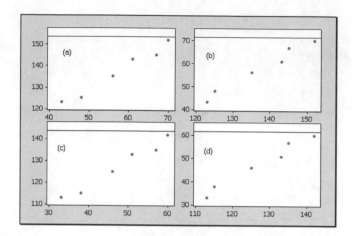

29. The following table shows the age x and the systolic blood pressure y for a sample of six patients who were admitted to a hospital:

x	43	48	56	61	67	70
y	123	125	135	143	145	152

Note: In this problem we assume that the systolic blood pressure depends on age. That is, we are assuming that age is the independent variable, and systolic blood pressure is the dependent variable.

What is the value of the correlation coefficient?

(a) 0.977
(b) 0.967
(c) 0.997
(d) 0.986

30. The following table shows the age x and the systolic blood pressure y for a sample of six patients who were admitted to a hospital:

x	43	48	56	61	67	70
y	123	125	135	143	145	152

Note: In this problem we assume that the systolic blood pressure depends on age. That is, we are assuming that age is the independent variable, and systolic blood pressure is the dependent variable.

What is the value of the coefficient of determination?

(a) 0.9545
(b) 0.9351
(c) 0.9722
(d) 0.9940

31. The following table shows the age x and the systolic blood pressure y for a sample of six patients who were admitted to a hospital:

x	43	48	56	61	67	70
y	123	125	135	143	145	152

Note: In this problem we assume that the systolic blood pressure depends on age. That is, we are assuming that age is the independent variable, and systolic blood pressure is the dependent variable.

If we use regression analysis to fit a linear model to the data, what will be the value of the y intercept for the line of best fit?

   (a) 1.077
   (b) 75.26
   (c) −66.47
   (d) 0.9038

32. The following table shows the age x and the systolic blood pressure y for a sample of six patients who were admitted to a hospital:

x	43	48	56	61	67	70
y	123	125	135	143	145	152

Note: In this problem we assume that the systolic blood pressure depends on age. That is, we are assuming that age is the independent variable, and systolic blood pressure is the dependent variable.

If we use regression analysis to fit a linear model to the data, what will be the value of the slope for the line of best fit?

   (a) 0.9038
   (b) 75.26
   (c) −66.47
   (d) 1.077

33. The following table shows the age x and the systolic blood pressure y for a sample of six patients who were admitted to a hospital:

x	43	48	56	61	67	70
y	123	125	135	143	145	152

Note: In this problem we assume that the systolic blood pressure depends on age. That is, we are assuming that age is the independent variable, and systolic blood pressure is the dependent variable.

If we use regression analysis to fit a linear model to the data, what will be the equation for the line of best fit?

   (a) $\hat{y} = 75.26 + 1.077\,x$
   (b) $\hat{y} = 1.077 + 75.26x$

(c) $\hat{y} = -66.47 + 0.9038x$

(d) $\hat{y} = 0.9038 - 66.47x$

34. The following table shows the age x and the systolic blood pressure y for a sample of six patients who were admitted to a hospital:

x	43	48	56	61	67	70
y	123	125	135	143	145	152

Note: In this problem we assume that the systolic blood pressure depends on age. That is, we are assuming that age is the independent variable, and systolic blood pressure is the dependent variable.

If we use regression analysis to fit a linear model to the data, what will be the predicted systolic blood pressure for a patient who is 65 years old?

(a) 145.265

(b) 144

(c) 143

(d) 141

Further Exercises

If possible, you could use any technology help to solve the following questions.

1. The scores x on a pretest for a college algebra course and the course grade y were recorded for 10 students. The results are given in **Table 5-3**.

Table 5-3

x	75	81	57	79	68	93	96	84	41	89
y	2	3	1	2	1	4	4	3	1	3

(a) Present a scatter plot for the data.

(b) Determine the correlation coefficient for the data, and interpret the value.

(c) Determine the coefficient of determination, and interpret the value.

(d) Compute the least-squares estimate for a.

(e) Compute the least-squares estimate for b.

(f) State the least-squares regression line.

(g) Find $\hat{y}$ for $x = 60$.

2. Engineers for a car manufacturer wanted to analyze the relationship between the speed x of their new model (The Bullet) and its gas mileage y (in mpg) for regular unleaded gasoline. The car was test driven at different speeds in the laboratory, and the data in **Table 5-4** were obtained.

Table 5-4

Speed x	30	40	50	60	70	80	90
Mpg y	39	38	36	32	27	24	22

(a) Present a scatter plot for the data.
(b) Determine the correlation coefficient for the data, and interpret the value.
(c) Determine the coefficient of determination, and interpret the value.
(d) Compute the least-squares estimate for a.
(e) Compute the least-squares estimate for b.
(f) State the least-squares regression line.
(g) Find $\hat{y}$ for $x = 65$.

3. Twelve people who were advised by their physicians to lose weight for health reasons enrolled in a special weight-loss program. **Table 5-5** gives the time in the program x (in days) and the weight lost in the program y (in pounds).

Table 5-5

x	30	41	16	32	54	43	68	91	15	13	59	90
y	2.9	4.5	1.8	3.6	6.8	4.7	11	13.6	1.6	1.5	7.8	14.2

(a) Present a scatter plot for the data.
(b) Determine the correlation coefficient for the data, and interpret the value.
(c) Determine the coefficient of determination, and interpret the value.
(d) Compute the least-squares estimate for a.
(e) Compute the least-squares estimate for b.
(f) State the least-squares regression line.
(g) Find $\hat{y}$ for $x = 50$.

4. In a given community, a survey was conducted to determine whether there is any relationship between the size of one's income x (in thousands of dollars) and the size of one's home y (in square feet). The data in **Table 5-6** were collected for 10 sample points.

Table 5-6

x	41.2	68.3	22.4	56.7	42.2	86.1	50.3	35.7	44.4	47.5
y	2.9	3.5	2.5	3.1	3.3	4	3.7	2.9	3	3.1

(a) Present a scatter plot for the data
(b) Determine the correlation coefficient for the data, and interpret the value.
(c) Determine the coefficient of determination, and interpret the value.
(d) Compute the least-squares estimate for a.
(e) Compute the least-squares estimate for b.
(f) State the least-squares regression line.
(g) Find $\hat{y}$ for $x = 40$.

ANSWER KEY
True/False Questions

1. T 2. F   3. F   4. T   5. F   6. F   7. T   8. F   9. T 10. F   11. T 12. T
13. F 14. F 15. F 16. T 17. T 18. F 19. T 20. T 21. F 22. F 23. T 24. F
25. F

Completion Questions

1. -1 2. small 3. $-1; +1$ 4. any of the previous three responses 5. dependent
6. strength; direction 7. 0 8. negative 9. -1.01 10. positive 11. closely
12. bivariate 13. negative 14. minimizes 15. better 16. 0 and $+1$ 17. correlation
coefficient 18. model 19. increase 20. no

Multiple-Choice Questions

1. (c) 2. (b) 3. (c) 4. (d) 5. (c) 6. (d) 7. (a) 8. (c) 9. (d) 10. (a)
11. (c) 12. (a) 13. (d) 14. (d) 15. (d) 16. (b) 17. (d) 18. (b) 19. (b)
20. (b) 21. (b) 22. (a) 23. (d) 24. (b) 25. (c) 26. (d) 27. (a) 28. (a)
29. (d) 30. (c) 31. (b) 32. (d) 33. (a) 34. (a)

Further Exercises

1. Solutions to (a), (c), (d), (e), and (f) can be obtained from the output below;
   (b) $r = 0.894$; (g) 1.394

2. Solutions to (a), (c), (d), (e), and (f) can be obtained from the output below; (b) $r = -0.985$; (g) 29.5705

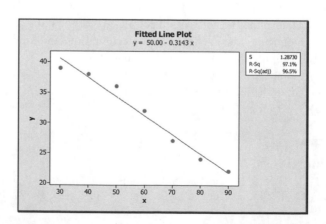

3. Solutions to (a), (c), (d), (e), and (f) can be obtained from the output below; (b) r = 0.987; (g) 6.829

4. Solutions to (a), (c), (d), (e), and (f) can be obtained from the output below; (b) r = 0.871; (g) 2.996

CHAPTER 6

Exploring Categorical Data

Do I Need to Read This Chapter?

Y ou should read this chapter if you need to review or to learn about

→ Two-way tables for a pair of categorical variables

→ Marginal and conditional distributions of categorical variables

→ Graphical displays for categorical variables

→ Independence between categorical variables

→ Simpson's paradox

In **Chapter 5** we dealt with bivariate data for which the variables were quantitative. In this chapter we will explore the relationship between categorical and qualitative variables.

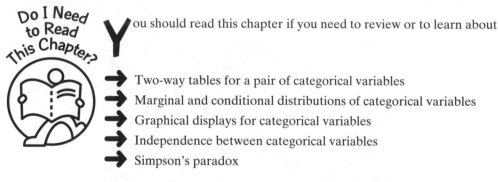

Get Started

When we are looking for associations between two qualitative variables, scatter plots will not work to help display any pattern. We use contingency tables to present the association between two or more qualitative or categorical variables. When there are just two qualitative variables, the table is usually called a *two-way contingency table* or a *bivariate frequency table.* Examples of categorical variables would be gender, ethnicity, and religious affiliation. These variables can assume values that are qualitative. Examples of values for these variables would be male, Asian, Methodist, etc. A quantitative variable such as age also could be a categorical variable when data are classified into age groups. For example, ages 20 to 25 would be an example of an appropriate category in which to classify a 24-year-old. Bar graphs will be used to display the relationship between the qualitative variables.

6-1 Marginal Distributions

In this section you will be introduced to the concepts of marginal and conditional distributions as they apply to contingency tables. You will learn how to compute the values for both marginal and conditional distributions.

Example 6-1: **Table 6-1** summarizes the information concerning the number of AIDS patients by age (in years) and race/ethnicity for females in San Francisco for cases reported for the first quarter through March 31, 2004. Information is presented only for whites, blacks, and Hispanics and for three broad age groups.

Table 6-1: Summary of the Number of AIDS Patients by Age and Ethnicity

AGE/ETHNICITY	WHITE	BLACK	HISPANIC	TOTAL
24 and younger	26	29	15	70
25–49	324	422	115	861
50 and older	65	60	19	144
Total	415	511	149	Grand Total 1,075

Source: www.dph.sf.ca.us/PHP/AIDSSurvUnit.htm.

Table 6-1 represents a two-way contingency table or a bivariate frequency table because there are only two qualitative variables. This table is sometimes called a **three-by-three (3 × 3) table** because we have three classifications for each of the two variables. The table shows how many observations are allocated to each category. Each row and column combination is called a **cell** in the table. The value of 65 in the first column for ethnicity and the third row for the age classifications indicate that 65 of the 1075 females are white and are 50 years of age or older. That is, about 6.05 percent of the total observed values were classified as white females who were age 50 and older. Also, there were only 19 female Hispanics in the age group of 50 and older. This would represent 1.77 percent of the total observed values. However, the 65 were out of a total of 415 white females, or 15.66 percent, whereas the 19 were out of a total of 149 Hispanic females, or 12.75 percent. Thus the relationship between these two qualitative variables may be better analyzed and understood by using the appropriate percentages. We will explore the relationship between two qualitative variables by using marginal distributions and conditional distributions.

Marginal Distributions

From the contingency table of frequencies (**Table 6-1**), one can obtain the **marginal distributions** by computing the appropriate percentages.

Explanation of the term—marginal distribution: A **marginal distribution** for a variable is the percentage of that variable expressed as the row or column totals relative to the grand total for the table.

To obtain the marginal distributions, divide the column or row totals by the grand total. This is usually expressed as a percentage.

Example 6-2: Compute the marginal distributions for the ethnicity variable.

Solution: We need to divide the values of 415, 511, and 149 by the grand total of 1,075. The marginal distributions, in percentages, for the classification variable of ethnicity are given in **Table 6-2**.

Table 6-2: Marginal Distributions for Ethnicity

WHITE	BLACK	HISPANIC	TOTAL
38.61%	47.53%	13.86%	100%

Observe that the sum of the marginal percentages equals 100 percent. From the marginal distribution, one can observe that 38.61 percent of the females with AIDS were white, 47.53 percent were black, and 13.86 percent were Hispanic. Also, one can observe that blacks outnumbered whites and Hispanics. In particular, blacks outnumbered Hispanics more than three to one for the displayed data.

Example 6-3: Compute the marginal distributions for the age group variable.

Solution: We need to divide the values of 70, 861, and 144 by the grand total of 1,075. The marginal distributions, in percentages, for the classification variable of age are given in **Table 6-3**.

Observe that the sum of the marginal percentages equals 100 percent. From the marginal distributions, one can observe that 6.51 percent of the females were 24 years of age or younger, 80.09 percent of the females were between 25 and 49 years of age, and 13.4 percent were 50 years of age or older. Also, one can observe that a very large proportion of the data was from the age classification of 25–49. One may want to further subdivide the age groupings to obtain and analyze other properties for the marginal distributions.

Table 6-3: Marginal Distributions for Age

24 and younger	6.51%
25–49	80.09%
50 and older	13.4%
Total	100%

6-2   Conditional Distributions

From the contingency table, one can obtain the distribution of one variable given the other variable. For example, one may be interested in finding the proportion of female AIDS patients who are 50 years of age or older, given that the female is white. In this case we are looking for a row classification given a column classification. One also can consider a column classification given a row classification. The proportions computed from such analysis are called **conditional distributions**.

Conditional Distributions

From the contingency table of frequencies, one can obtain the conditional distributions by computing the appropriate percentages.

Explanation of the term—conditional distribution: A **conditional distribution** for a (first) variable given another (second) variable is the percentage of items for the first variable that is contained in the second variable.

To obtain the conditional distributions for the row classifications, given the column classifications, divide the frequency values in the original table by the column totals. This is usually expressed as a percentage. The conditional distribution of the column variable, given the row variable, is obtained by dividing the frequency values in the original table by the row totals and expressing the results as percentages.

Example 6-4: Compute the conditional distributions for the age classifications (row) given the ethnic classifications (column). Use two decimal places.

Solution: From the original two-way distribution, we need to compute each frequency entry as a percentage of the respective column totals. For the class of 24 years of age and younger, the conditional distribution for the entry 26, given the white ethnic classification, will be $\frac{26}{415} \times 100$ percent = 6.27 percent. For the class of 50 years of age and older, the conditional distribution for the entry 19, given the Hispanic ethnic classification, will be $\frac{19}{149} \times 100$ percent = 12.75 percent. One can continue in this manner to compute the remaining conditional distributions for the rows given the columns. The conditional distributions are given in **Table 6-4**.

Table 6-4: Conditional Distributions for Age Given Ethnicity

AGE/ETHNICITY	WHITE	BLACK	HISPANIC
24 and younger	6.27	5.68	10.07
25–49	78.07	82.58	77.18
50 and older	15.66	11.74	12.75
Total	100%	100%	100%

Example 6-5: Interpret the 82.58 percent cell value in **Table 6-4** for **Example 6-4**.

Solution: The value indicates that 82.58 percent (approximately 83 percent) of females with AIDS who are black are between 25 and 49 years of age for the reported time period in San Francisco.

Example 6-6: Compute the conditional distributions for the ethnic classifications (columns) given the age classifications (rows). Use two decimal places.

Solution: From the original two-way distribution, **Table 6-1**, we need to compute each frequency cell entry as a percentage of the respective row total. For the ethnic class of whites, the conditional distribution for the entry 26, given the age group of 24 years of age and younger, will be $\frac{26}{70} \times 100$ percent = 37.14 percent. For the ethnic class of Hispanics, the conditional distribution for the entry 19, given the age group of 50 years of age and older, will be $\frac{19}{144} \times 100$ percent = 13.19 percent. One can continue in this manner to compute the remaining conditional distributions for the columns given the rows. The conditional distributions are given in **Table 6-5**.

Table 6-5: Conditional Distributions for Ethnicity Given Age

AGE/ETHNICITY	WHITE	BLACK	HISPANIC	TOTAL
24 and younger	37.14	41.43	21.43	100%
25–49	37.63	49.01	13.36	100%
50 and older	45.14	41.67	13.19	100%

Example 6-7: Interpret the 37.14 percent cell value in **Table 6-5** for **Example 6-6**.

Solution: The value indicates that 37.14 percent of females with AIDS who are 24 years of age and younger are white.

6-3   Using Bar Charts to Display Contingency Tables

The following bar charts display the different information given and derived for **Examples 6-1, 6-2, 6-3, 6-4**, and **6-6**. If you need to review the concept of bar charts, see **Chapter 1**.

The bar chart in **Figure 6-1** displays the information for the original contingency table. It uses the raw frequencies to construct the chart. We can observe from **Figure 6-1**, that for this sample of females with AIDS for the first quarter in 2004, the classification of 25- to 49-year-old black females has the highest frequency count. For white and Hispanic females, whites outnumber Hispanics for the 25- to 49-year age group more than two to one. For the age 50 and over classification, both black and white females with AIDS are observed approximately three times as often as the Hispanic females for this age group. For the age group 24 years and younger, both black and white females with AIDS are observed approximately twice as often as the Hispanic females for this age group.

Figure 6-1: Bar charts for the AIDS data

The next chart, **Figure 6-2**, shows the marginal distributions for the ethnicity classifications. Observe that approximately half the data are related to black females.

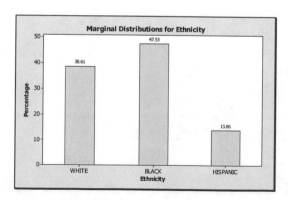

Figure 6-2: Bar chart of the marginal distributions for ethnicity

The next chart, **Figure 6-3**, shows the marginal distributions for the age group classifications for the females. Observe that a significant majority of the females are between the ages of 25 and 49 years. A further breakdown of the age classifications should be investigated; this may reveal other properties of the distributions.

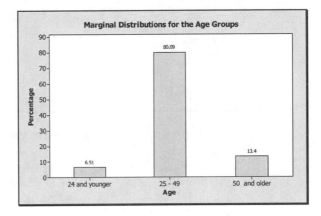

Figure 6-3: Bar chart of the marginal distributions for age

The next chart, **Figure 6-4**, presents the conditional distributions for the age classifications given the ethnic classifications. From the display, one can observe that there are small deviations within each age classification. Again, one can observe that the majority of the observations are in the 25- to 49-year age range for all three ethnic groups

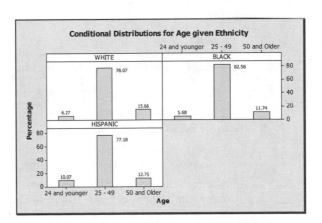

Figure 6-4: Bar chart of the conditional distributions for age given ethnicity

The next chart, **Figure 6-5**, presents the conditional distributions for the ethnic classifications given the age classifications. From the display, one can observe that within the age group of 24 years of age and younger and 25 to 49 years of age, black females have the highest incidence of AIDS. Observe that the highest incidence of AIDS for white females occurs in the 50 years of age and older classification. The highest incidence of AIDS for Hispanic females occurred in the 24 years of age and younger category.

Figure 6-5: Bar chart of the conditional distributions for ethnicity given age

6-4　Independence in Categorical Variables

Sometimes it is important to determine whether there is an association among the variables in a contingency table, that is, whether the variables are independent or dependent. This concept will be discussed further in **Chapter 14**. In this chapter we will use the concept of conditional distributions for contingency tables to determine whether there is an association among the variables.

Explanation of the term—independence: Two categorical variables are said to be **independent** of each other (have no association) if the conditional distributions of one variable are the same for every category of the other variable.

Example 6-8: A faculty member conducted a survey on a college campus to determine the favorability rating of the college president. One hundred randomly selected students were asked to indicate whether they view the president favorably or unfavorably. **Table 6-6** shows a 2 × 2 contingency table summarizing the results for both male and female students in the sample.

Table 6-6: Favorability Rating of the College President by Gender

GENDER/RATING	FAVORABLE	UNFAVORABLE	TOTAL
Male	54	21	75
Female	18	7	25
Total	72	28	100

(a) Construct a table of the conditional distributions for the gender classification given the favorable/unfavorable ratings.

Solution: Since we are conditioning on the favorable/unfavorable ratings, we need to divide each cell entry by the column totals in the original 2 × 2 table. These are expressed as percentages. The conditional distributions are given in **Table 6-7**.

Table 6-7: Conditional Distributions of Gender Given Ratings

GENDER/RATING	FAVORABLE	UNFAVORABLE
Male	75	75
Female	25	25
Total	100%	100%

(b) Construct a table of the conditional distributions for the favorable/unfavorable ratings given the gender classification.

Solution: Since we are conditioning on the gender classification, we need to divide each cell entry by the row totals in the original 2 × 2 table. These are expressed as percentages. The conditional distributions are given in **Table 6-8**.

Table 6-8: Conditional Distributions of Ratings Given Gender

GENDER/RATING	FAVORABLE	UNFAVORABLE	TOTAL
Male	72	28	100%
Female	72	28	100%

(c) Based on the results in parts (a) and (b), can one conclude that the gender variable and the favorable/unfavorable ratings variable are independent? That is, is there no association between the male and female responses of favorable or unfavorable?

Solution: From part (a), the distributions of gender of the students were conditioned on the ratings. From the computed conditional distributions for gender, we see that the values are the same for the male classification for both the favorable and unfavorable classifications. Also, for the female classification, the conditional distributions are the same. Based on the definition of independence for contingency tables, one can conclude that there is no association between the gender of the students and their responses of favorable or unfavorable. That is, these variables are independent of each other.

From part (b), the distributions of ratings were conditioned on the gender of the student. From the computed conditional distributions for ratings, we see that the values are the same for the favorable classification for both male and female genders. Also, for the unfavorable classification, the conditional distributions are the same for both genders. Based on the definition of independence for contingency tables, one again can conclude that there is no association between the gender of the students and their responses of favorable or unfavorable. That is, these variables are independent of each other.

In conclusion, if the faculty member knew the gender of the student, he or she would not be at an advantage over one who did not know the gender of the student in predicting the response.

Quick Tip

Contingency tables are not only restricted to 2 × 2 classifications. Other areas of statistics deal with much more complex tables.

6-5 Simpson's Paradox

For a 1973 study on sex bias in admissions to the graduate school at the University of California, Berkeley, **Table 6-9** shows the information obtained for the five largest majors on that campus.

Table 6-9: Admissions by Gender and Major

	MALES		FEMALES	
MAJOR/GENDER	NUMBER OF APPLICANTS	NUMBER ADMITTED	NUMBER OF APPLICANTS	NUMBER ADMITTED
Major 1	800	520	120	102
Major 2	550	341	32	23
Major 3	400	160	410	148
Major 4	350	126	347	129
Major 5	200	48	387	105
Total	2,300	1,195	1,296	507

There were actually a total of 8,442 males and 4,321 females who had applied for admission. Of the males that applied, 3,714 were accepted, and of the females, 1,512 were accepted. That is, $\frac{3,714}{8,442} \times 100$ percent $= 43.99 \approx 44$ percent of the males were accepted, and $\frac{1,512}{4,321} \times 100$ percent $= 34.99 \approx 35$ percent of the females were accepted. These percentages would suggest that there may be discrimination against females in admission to the graduate school. However, if this was so, then the discrimination also should be apparent in the admission rates for the different majors because admission was by department.

Let us consider the percentages that were admitted for both males and females. **Table 6-10** displays these data.

Table 6-10: Percentages of Males and Females Admitted

MAJOR/% ADMITTED	% OF MALES ADMITTED	% OF FEMALES ADMITTED
Major 1	65	85
Major 2	62	72
Major 3	40	36
Major 4	36	37
Major 5	24	27

For all majors except major 3, the admission rate is higher for the female applicants! This reveals that the female applicants were not discriminated against. If anything, it reveals the opposite. How can this reversal be true? By examining **Table 6-9**, one can see that the majors with the largest acceptance rates had a large number of male applicants and fewer females. The majors that had the lowest acceptance rates had fewer males applying and more females applying. That is, the variable of **major** was **confounding** the **gender** variable in the computation of the 44 percent and the 35 percent. The apparent bias in these percentages is due to the fact that, in general, the female applicants were applying to the most difficult majors for acceptance and not to gender bias. By considering the variable of **major**, the **gender** variable was removed from the bias. That is, we say we are controlling for this confounding variable.

To give a different perspective, we will analyze the sample information for the five majors using marginal and conditional distributions for the number of students admitted. The marginal distributions for gender are given in **Table 6-11**.

Table 6-11: Marginal Distributions for Gender

% OF MALES ADMITTED	% OF FEMALES ADMITTED
70	30

From this information, one should be alarmed. Here, 70 percent of the persons admitted to these five majors are males, and only 30 percent are females. **Table 6-12** shows the marginal distributions for major.

Table 6-12: Marginal Distributions for Majors

MAJOR	1	2	3	4	5
%	37	21	18	15	9

We can observe that **major 1** had the highest acceptance rate for all five majors.

Next we display the conditional distributions for the **gender** of the applicant given the **major** chosen. These distributions are given in **Table 6-13**.

Table 6-13: Conditional Distributions for Gender Given Major

MAJOR/GENDER	MALE (%)	FEMALE (%)	TOTAL (%)
Major 1	84	16	100
Major 2	94	6	100
Major 3	52	48	100
Major 4	49	51	100
Major 5	31	69	100

From these conditional distributions for **gender** given **major**, one can observe again that for the different majors, the percentages for the males and females generally are going in opposite directions. That is, for majors 1, 2, and 3, there are more males than females, and for majors 4 and 5, there are more females than males. One can make the argument that based on majors 1, 2, and 3, there is gender bias against females. However, one could also argue that there is not a male bias based on the conditional distributions for majors 4 and 5. Again, the variable of **major** is **confounding** the **gender** variable.

The next table, **Table 6-14**, shows the conditional distributions for the majors given the gender of the applicant.

Table 6-14: Conditional Distributions for Major Given Gender

MAJOR/GENDER	MALE (%)	FEMALE (%)
Major 1	44	20
Major 2	29	5
Major 3	13	29
Major 4	11	25
Major 5	3	21
Total	100	100

From these conditional distributions for **major** given the **gender** of the applicants, one can observe that for the males, the percentage decreases from major to major, whereas it stays relatively the same for the female applicants except for major 2. For the male applicants, more are accepted in majors 1 and 2, whereas more females than males are accepted in the other majors. Again, one can make counterarguments for bias. Here again, the variable of **major** is **confounding** the **gender** variable in the computation of the 70 percent of males being accepted compared with the 30 percent of females.

The apparent inconsistency in the example falls into a category of problems known as **Simpson's paradox**. One can claim that there is gender bias in either direction that is not apparent just by looking at the marginal distributions for gender. The moral is to make sure that you analyze the data thoroughly in order to see what information is hidden within the data.

Technology Corner

All the concepts discussed in this chapter can be computed and illustrated through all statistical software packages. However, using such software for the computations encountered in this chapter would be technology overkill. All that is required is simple calculations. All scientific and graphical calculators will aid directly in the computations.

Association between two categorical variables can be investigated through
- ✓ Contingency tables.
- ✓ Marginal distributions.
- ✓ Conditional distributions.
- ✓ Bar charts.

Care always should be taken when interpreting the marginal and conditional distributions that are associated with contingency tables. Care also should be taken when interpreting bar charts for contingency tables. One should be clear whether there is an association between variables in a contingency table by interpreting the conditional distributions appropriately.

True/False Questions

1. In finding the marginal distributions for the row variable in a contingency table, one must divide the column totals by the grand total.
2. In finding the marginal distributions for the column variable in a contingency table, one must divide the column totals by the grand total.

3. In finding the marginal distributions for the row variable in a contingency table, one must divide the row totals by the column totals.
4. In finding the conditional distributions for the row variable given the column variable in a contingency table, one must divide the cell frequencies by the grand total.
5. In finding the conditional distributions for the row variable given the column variable in a contingency table, one must divide the cell frequencies by their respective column totals.
6. In finding the conditional distributions for the column variable given the row variable in a contingency table, one must divide the cell frequencies by their respective column totals.
7. Scatter plots can be used to display the association between two qualitative variables.
8. Two categorical variables are said to be independent of each other if the conditional distributions of one variable are the same for every category of the other variable.
9. Bar charts are appropriate graphical displays for marginal and conditional distributions computed for contingency tables.
10. In a contingency table, if the two variables A and B, say, are independent of each other, then knowing the classifications of A will not give you an advantage over someone who does not know the classifications of A in predicting the responses for variable B.

Completion Questions

1. A two-way contingency table with four classifications for the row variable and three classifications for the column variable will have (how many?) _____ cells in the table.
2. Marginal distributions for the row variable in a contingency table are the percentages of that variable expressed as the row totals relative to the (row, column, grand) _____ total(s) for the table.
3. In computing the conditional distributions for the row variable given the column variable in a contingency table, the cell entries are divided by the (row, column) _____ totals.
4. Scatter plots are (appropriate, not appropriate) _____ graphical displays for investigating the association between qualitative variables.
5. Marginal distributions for the column variable in a contingency table are the percentages of that variable expressed as the (row, column) _____ totals relative to the grand total for the table.
6. In computing the conditional distributions for the column variable given the row variable in a contingency table, the cell entries are divided by the (row, column) _____ totals.
7. In a contingency table with variables X and Y, if knowing the classifications of X does not give you the advantage over someone who does not know the classifications of X in predicting the responses for variable Y, then X and Y are said to be _____.
8. (Bar, Pie, Pareto) _____ charts can be used to display the marginal and conditional distributions for the variables in a contingency table.
9. Two categorical variables are said to be independent of each other if the conditional distributions of one variable are the _____ for every category of the other variable.
10. Frequency tables that are used to describe the association between qualitative variables are called _____ tables.

Multiple-Choice Questions

1. The number of cells for a 5×7 contingency table is
    (a) 35.
    (b) 24.
    (c) 48.
    (d) 28.

2. A cross-classification of two categorical variables in tabular form is called a
    (a) frequency distribution table.
    (b) probability distribution table.
    (c) twofold table.
    (d) contingency table.

Consider **Table 6-15**, formed by cross-classifying age group and brand of cola consumed. **Use this information to answer Questions 3 to 8:**

Table 6-15

COLA/AGE	UNDER AGE 15	AGES 15–25	AGES 25–35	TOTAL
Cola 1	150	100	200	450
Cola 2	300	125	200	625
Cola 3	300	200	300	800
Total	750	425	700	1,875

3. The marginal distribution for the **under age 15** classification is
    (a) 40 percent.
    (b) 24 percent.
    (c) 20 percent.
    (d) 33.33 percent.

4. The observed cell frequency for **ages 15–25** and **cola 3** consumers is
    (a) 300.
    (b) 200.
    (c) 125.
    (d) 100.

5. The marginal distribution for the **cola 3** classification is
    (a) 40 percent.
    (b) 37.5 percent.
    (c) 42.67 percent.
    (d) 93.75 percent.

6. The conditional distribution of **cola 2**, given that the person is classified as having **ages 25–35** is
    (a) 42.67 percent.
    (b) 28.57 percent.
    (c) 32 percent.
    (d) 42.86 percent.

7. The conditional distribution of a person's being classified in the **under age 15** group given **cola 1** is
   (a) 20 percent.
   (b) 24 percent.
   (c) 50 percent.
   (d) 33.33 percent.

8. The conditional distributions for the three colas given the age group of **ages 15–25** are
   (a) 5.33, 6.67, and 10.67 percent.
   (b) 22.22, 20, and 25 percent.
   (c) 23.25, 29.41, and 47.06 percent.
   (d) 13.33, 29.41, and 28.57 percent.

A survey was done by a car manufacturer concerning a particular make and model. A group of 500 individuals was asked whether they purchased their cars because of appearance, performance ratings, or fixed price (no negotiating). The results are given in the contingency table, **Table 6-16**, for both male and female owners. **Use this information for Questions 9 to 17:**

Table 6-16

OWNER/REASON	APPEARANCE	PERFORMANCE	PRICE	TOTAL
Male	100	50	35	185
Female	80	170	65	315
Total	180	220	100	500

9. The marginal distribution for the **performance** classification is
   (a) 22.73 percent.
   (b) 77.27 percent.
   (c) 44 percent.
   (d) 78.57 percent.

10. The marginal distribution for the **female** classification is
    (a) 63 percent.
    (b) 25.4 percent.
    (c) 53.96 percent.
    (d) 20.63 percent.

11. The contingency table can be classified as
    (a) 4×5.
    (b) 3×4.
    (c) 3×3.
    (d) 2×3.

12. The observed cell frequency for the number of females who purchased the car because of **appearance** is
    (a) 315.
    (b) 180.
    (c) 80.
    (d) 100.

13. The marginal distribution for the **male** classification is
   (a) 37 percent.
   (b) 54.1 percent.
   (c) 27.03 percent.
   (d) 18.92 percent.

14. The conditional distribution of a **female** given that the reason was **price** is
   (a) 31.75 percent.
   (b) 13 percent.
   (c) 53.85 percent.
   (d) 65 percent.

15. The conditional distribution that the reason is **performance** given that the gender is **male** is
   (a) 27.03 percent.
   (b) 84.09 percent.
   (c) 22.73 percent.
   (d) 29.41 percent.

16. The conditional distributions for the three reasons given the **female** gender are
   (a) 16, 34, and 13 percent.
   (b) 25.4, 53.97, and 20.63 percent.
   (c) 44.44, 77.27, and 65 percent.
   (d) 54.05, 27.027, and 18.92 percent.

17. The conditional distributions for the gender given the **appearance** are
   (a) 20 and 16 percent.
   (b) 55.56 and 44.45 percent.
   (c) 54.05 and 25.4 percent.
   (d) 45.45 and 80 percent.

Further Exercises

If possible, you could use any technology help to solve the following questions.

1. A sample of four one-pound bags of Skittles was examined, and the different flavors of Skittles in each bag are summarized in **Table 6-17**. Observe that this can be considered as a 4 × 5 contingency table.

Table 6-17

BAG/FLAVOR	WILDBERRY	FRUIT PUNCH	RASPBERRY	WILD CHERRY	STRAWBERRY	TOTAL
Bag 1	85	87	84	92	89	437
Bag 2	108	85	88	71	86	438
Bag 3	95	99	61	84	80	419
Bag 4	103	80	82	71	98	434
Total	391	351	315	318	353	1728

  (a) Find the marginal distributions for the flavors.
  (b) Find the marginal distributions for the bags.
  (c) Use bar graphs to display the marginal distributions in parts (a) and (b). Discuss any observations.
  (d) Find the conditional distributions for the bags given the flavors. Display the percentages in tabular form.
  (e) Use bar charts to display the conditional distributions in part (d). Discuss any observations.
  (f) Find the conditional distributions for the flavors given the bags. Display the percentages in tabular form.
  (g) Use bar charts to display the conditional distributions in part (f). Discuss any observations.
  (h) Determine whether the variables are independent of each other. Discuss your results.

ANSWER KEY
True/False Questions

  1. F 2. T 3. F 4. F 5. T 6. F 7. F 8. T 9. T 10. T

Completion Questions

  1. 12 2. grand 3. column 4. not appropriate 5. column 6. row 7. independent 8. bar 9. same 10. contingency

Multiple-Choice Questions

  1. (a) 2. (d) 3. (a) 4. (b) 5. (c) 6. (b) 7. (d) 8. (c) 9. (c) 10. (a)
  11. (d) 12. (c) 13. (a) 14. (d) 15. (a) 16. (b) 17. (b)

Further Exercises

  1. (a) Marginal distributions for flavors.

WILDBERRY	FRUIT PUNCH	RASPBERRY	WILD CHERRY	STRAWBERRY	TOTAL
22.63%	20.31%	18.23%	18.40%	20.43%	100%

  (b) Marginal distributions for bags.

Bag 1	25.29%
Bag 2	25.35%
Bag 3	24.25%
Bag 4	25.12%
Total	100%

(c) Marginal distributions for flavors.

Marginal distribution for bags.

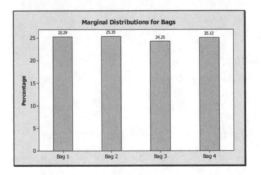

(d) Conditional distributions for bags given flavor.

BAG/FLAVOR	WILDBERRY	FRUIT PUNCH	RASPBERRY	WILD CHERRY	STRAWBERRY
Bag 1	21.74	24.79	26.67	28.93	25.21
Bag 2	27.62	24.22	27.94	22.33	24.36
Bag 3	24.30	28.21	19.37	26.42	22.66
Bag 4	26.34	22.79	26.03	22.33	27.76
Total	100%	≈100%	≈100%	≈100%	≈100%

Note: Totals in the table are approximated to 100 percent because of rounding.

(e) Bar chart for the conditional distributions for bags given flavors.

(f) Conditional distributions for flavors given bags.

BAG/FLAVOR	WILDBERRY	FRUIT PUNCH	RASPBERRY	WILD CHERRY	STRAWBERRY	TOTAL
Bag 1	19.45	19.91	19.22	21.05	20.37	100%
Bag 2	24.66	19.41	20.09	16.21	19.63	100%
Bag 3	22.67	23.63	14.56	20.05	19.09	100%
Bag 4	23.73	18.43	18.89	16.36	22.58	≈100%

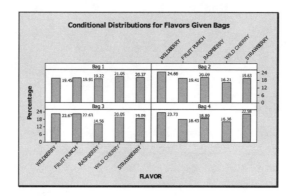

Note: Totals in the table are approximated to 100 percent because of rounding.

(g) Bar chart for the conditional distributions for flavors given bags.

(h) From the original data, the likelihood of selecting a wildberry-flavored Skittle (for example) is 391/1,728 = 0.2263 (22.63 percent). Also, the conditional distribution of selecting a wildberry-flavored Skittle given bag 1 (say) is 19.45 percent from part (f). Now, if these percentages were the same, then we would conclude that the event of selecting a wildberry-flavored Skittle is independent of bag 1. Since they are not the same, we generally can conclude that flavor of the Skittle is **not independent** of the bags from which the Skittles were selected.

PART II

Probability

CHAPTER 7

Randomness, Uncertainty, and Probability

Do I Need to Read This Chapter?

You should read this chapter if you need to review or to learn about

→ Relative frequency probability
→ The law of large numbers
→ The addition rule in probability
→ Conditional probability
→ The multiplication rule in probability
→ Independence in probability

Get Started

Probability statements are everywhere around us. Examples of probability statements include

- There is a 60 percent chance of its raining today.
- The chance of me winning the lottery is one in 80 million.
- There is a 50-50 chance of observing a head when a fair coin is tossed.

Just what is meant by *chance* in these statements? Chance is a measure of uncertainty, and we call this measure *probability*. In this chapter we will study this concept of probability.

7-1   Randomness and Uncertainty

Randomness

The term **randomness** suggests unpredictability. A simple example of randomness is the tossing of a coin. Unless someone consults a psychic for a "perfect reading" on the outcome when a coin is tossed, the outcome is uncertain. The outcome could be either an observed head (H) or an observed tail (T). Because the outcome of the toss cannot be predicted for sure, we say that it displays randomness. This is an example of an easily describable random process. However, other random processes can be quite intricate; for example, the fluctuating prices of stocks are difficult to explain because there are so many variables and combinations of variables that are influencing the prices.

Uncertainty

At some time or another, everyone will experience **uncertainty**. For example, if you are playing a game of softball and the pitch is on its way, you may be uncertain as to whether to take a swing at the ball or not. Or consider the case when you are approaching some traffic signals, and the light changes from green to amber. You have to decide whether you can make it through the intersection or not. You may be uncertain as to what the correct decision should be.

Probability

When you ask yourself the question as to whether you believe that you can make it through the amber light, the answer may be "Probably." That is, you believe that you can make it across the intersection, but you still may have some doubt. The concept of **probability** is used to quantify this measure of doubt. If you believe that you have a 0.99 probability of getting across the intersection before the light turns red, you have made a clear statement about your doubt. The probability statement provides a great deal of information, much more than such statements as, "Maybe I can make it across," "I should make it across," etc.

7-2   Random Experiments, Sample Space, and Events

Before we discuss the concept of probability, we need to introduce some terms that we will encounter later in this chapter.

Random Experiment

When we toss a coin, as mentioned earlier, we do not know the outcome. Let us refer to this process of tossing the coin as an **experiment**. We will define such an experiment as a **random** or **probability experiment** because we do not know the outcome in advance.

Explanation of the term—random experiment: A **random experiment** is an experiment in which the outcome on each trial is uncertain and distinct.

Examples of random experiments are rolling a die, selecting items at random from a manufacturing process to examine for defects, selection of numbers by a lottery machine, etc.

Sample Space

When we toss a coin, we have two possible outcomes, summarized by $\{H, T\}$. When a child is born, the gender of the child is either a boy (B) or a girl (G), summarized by $\{B, G\}$. If we consider a two-child family, the possibilities can be summarized by $\{BB, BG, GB, GG\}$. In each case, the outcomes enclosed in braces list all the possible outcomes. Such a list is called a **sample space**.

Explanation of the term—sample space: The **sample space** for an experiment is the list or set of all possible outcomes for the experiment.

Example 7-1: A fair regular six-sided die is rolled. List the sample space for this random experiment.

Solution: Let S represent the sample space. Then $S = \{1, 2, 3, 4, 5, 6\}$.

Example 7-2: List the sample space for a two-child family.

Solution: Let B represent the outcome of a boy and G for a girl. The diagram in **Figure 7-1**, called a **tree diagram**, depicts the possibilities.

From **Figure 7-1**, if you follow along the "branches" of the tree, you will trace out all the possible outcomes as listed on the right-hand side. Thus the sample space is $S = \{BB, BG, GB, GG\}$.

Figure 7-1: Tree diagram for a two-child family

Events

We may only be interested in part of the sample space. For example, we may only be concerned with one girl in a two-child family, that is, the outcomes of BG and GB. These two outcomes constitute a subset of the sample space. Such subsets are called **events**.

Explanation of the term—event: An **event** is a subset of the sample space.

Note: Each outcome in a sample space is an event. These events are called **simple events**.

7-3   Classical Probability

If we can assume that all the simple events in a sample space have the same chance of occurring, then we can measure the probability of an event as a proportion relative to the number of points in the sample space. Such a probability measure is referred to as **classical probability**.

Explanation of the term—classical probability of an event: If the outcomes in a sample space are equally likely to occur, then the **classical probability of an event A** is defined to be

$$P(A) = \frac{\text{number of simple events in } A}{\text{total number of simple events in the sample space}}$$

Example 7-3: If a two-child family is selected at random, what is the probability of there being two boys in the family?

Solution: Recall that the sample space is $S = \{BB, BG, GB, GG\}$. From this sample space, the event of two boys occurs once, and there are four simple events in the sample space. Thus $P(BB) = \dfrac{1}{4} = 0.25$.

Example 7-4: In a manufacturing process, a quality control inspector selects three items at random. Let D represent the event of a defective item, and let N represent the event of a nondefective item. List the possible outcomes for the sample space.

Solution: The possible points in the sample space are given in the set S.

   $S = \{DDD, DDN, DND, DNN, NDD, NDN, NND, NNN\}$

The sample space can be obtained from the tree diagram given in **Figure 7-2**. There are two possible outcomes when the first item is selected: a defective (D) or a nondefective (N). If a defective is selected, then on the second selection there are again two possibilities, D or N. If a nondefective was selected on the first selection, then on the second selection a defective or a nondefective can be selected. Continuing in this manner, you can display the outcomes by the tree diagram given in **Figure 7-2**.

Figure 7-2: Tree diagram for the selection of three items

Example 7-5: For **Example 7-4**, what is the probability of the quality control inspector's observing at least two defective items?

Solution: Let A be the event of at least two defectives. Then $A = \{DDD, DDN, DND, NDD\}$. Event A is made up of four simple events, and there are eight simple events in the sample space. Thus $P(A) = \dfrac{4}{8} = 0.5$.

7-4   Relative Frequency or Empirical Probability

If we flip a fair coin once, we say that the probability of getting a head is $\dfrac{1}{2} = 0.5$. This is so because we have two possible outcomes: a head or a tail. This probability of 0.5 is the theoretical (classical) probability of observing a head on a single toss of a coin. In an experiment, however, if we flip the coin 10 times, say, and observe 4 heads, then, based on this information, we say that the chance of observing a head will be $\dfrac{4}{10} = 0.4$, which is not the same as 0.5. If, however, we flip the coin a large number of times, we would expect about 50 percent of the flips to result in a head.

Observe that

$$\frac{4}{10} = \frac{\text{frequency of occurrence}}{\text{number of trials}}$$

That is, chance or probability can be measured by relative frequency in which the trials are exactly repeatable, as in the case of tossing a coin a repeated number of times. Thus the probability of an event occurring can be measured by the proportion of times the event occurs if the process is repeated a large number of times. This is called the **long-term relative frequency** of the event.

Explanation of the term—relative frequency or empirical probability of an event: The **relative frequency probability** of an event's occurring is the proportion of times the event occurs over a given number of trials.

If A is the event in which we are interested, then the relative frequency probability of A's occurring, denoted by $P(A)$, is computed from

$$P(A) = \frac{\text{frequency of occurrence}}{\text{number of trials}}$$

Example 7-6: For the first 43 presidents of the United States, 26 were lawyers. What is the probability of randomly selecting from those 43 presidents a president who was a lawyer?

Solution: Let A represent the event of a president being a lawyer. Thus, since there are 43 presidents and 26 were lawyers, then $P(A) = \dfrac{26}{43} = 0.605$ (correct to three decimal places).

Example 7-7: During a flu season, a campus health clinic observed that on one day 12 of 60 students examined had strep throats, whereas a week later on the same day 18 of 75 students examined had strep throats. Compute the relative frequencies for the given information.

Solution: The relative frequencies are $\dfrac{12}{60} = 0.2$ and $\dfrac{18}{75} = 0.24$. Observe that these relative frequencies are different. However, if data are collected over a long period of time, the clinic may be able to conclude that during the flu season, a student who is examined will have strep throat with a probability of 0.22.

7-5   The Law of Large Numbers

In any experiment, the relative frequency for an event will change from trial to trial. However, if the experiment is conducted for a large number of times, the relative frequency of the event will tend to converge toward a number that is called the **probability** of the event. This concept is called the **law of large numbers**.

Law of Large Numbers

When an experiment is conducted a large number of times, the relative frequency (empirical) probability of an event can be expected to be close to the theoretical probability of the event. This approximation will improve as the number of replications is increased. The following example will demonstrate this concept.

Example 7-8: A fair coin is tossed 200 times. Display the graph of the cumulative (running) relative frequency for the number of observed heads.

Note: Refer to **Chapter 1** for a review of cumulative relative frequency.

Solution: Since we are using a fair coin, the probability of observing a head on a single toss is $P(H) = 0.5$, where H represents the outcome of a head, which is the (theoretical) probability of observing a head. We should expect as the number of trials increases that the proportion of observed heads will approach 0.5. The experiment is simulated using the MINITAB statistical software package, and the graph of the relative frequency is displayed in **Figure 7-3**.

Observe that the relative frequency varies a great deal at first but then starts to level off at around 0.5. Recall that $P(H) = 0.5$, and thus one can observe that as the number of trials increases, the relative frequency probability tends toward the probability of observing a head. The display in **Figure 7-4** shows the simulation for 1,000 tosses of the coin. Observe a distinct convergence of the relative frequencies to a value of 0.5. This can be expected because the number of trials is increased to 1,000.

Figure 7-3: Relative frequency graph for 200 trials

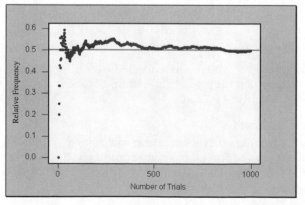

Figure 7-4: Relative frequency graph for 1,000 trials

Figure 7-5 shows what is happening as the number of trials gets very large. The proportion flattens out around the 0.5 mark, which is the theoretical probability of observing a head when a coin is tossed.

Figure 7-5: Relative frequency graph for 10,000 trials

7-6 Subjective Probability

Subjective probability is a measure of belief. This measure depends on your life experiences. Thus, based on life experiences, two reasonable persons may have different measures of belief for a particular event's occurring. An example of a subjective probability is a probability value that you assign to the chance of passing an exam. This will be based on your experiences—number of hours you studied, number of classes missed, etc. Subjective probability cannot be used uniformly to define the chance of an event's occurring because the value may be different for different people.

7-7 Some Basic Laws of Probability

Following are four basic laws of probability:

Law 1: If the probability of an event is 1, then the event must occur.

For example, the probability of each of us dying is 1. We know that dying is certain to occur.

Law 2: If the probability of an event is 0, then the event will never occur.

For example, the probability of a person who was born outside the United States becoming its president is zero. This is the decree of the United States Constitution.

Law 3: The probability of any event must assume a value between 0 and 1, inclusively.

For example, the probability of it raining today is $0.7 = 70$ percent. We cannot be more than 100 percent certain that it will rain, nor we cannot be less than 0 percent certain that it will rain.

Law 4: The sum of the probabilities of all the simple events in a sample space must equal 1. Another way of saying this is to say that the probability of the sample space in any experiment is always 1.

For example, if we consider the sample space for **Example 7-4**, there are eight simple events. By the classical approach, each simple event has an equal chance of occurring. That is, each simple event has a $\frac{1}{8}$ chance of occurring. When we sum these probabilities we have $8 \times \frac{1}{8} = 1$.

7-8   Other Probability Rules

Here we will consider other rules that will enable us to find probabilities between events.

Compound Events

Sometimes we may have to combine events in order to define another event. Such events are called **compound events**.

Explanation of the term—compound event: A **compound event** is an event that is defined by combining two or more events.

To illustrate, consider the following example.

Example 7-9: Let A be the event of a student owning an iPod. Let B be the event of a student owning a laptop computer. Let C be the event of a student owning both an iPod and a laptop computer. Discuss the event C that is common to both A and B.

Solution: From the given information, C is the event that is common to both A and B. Since the event C is obtained by combining A and B, C is a compound event.

Union of Events

Consider two events A and B. We may be interested in the event that is obtained by considering the elements that are in A, in B, or in both A and B. Such a compound event is called the **union** of events A and B.

Explanation of the term—union of two events: The **union of two events** A and B is the set of outcomes that are included in A or B or both A and B.

Notation: The union of A and B will be denoted by $A \cup B$.

The diagram in **Figure 7-6**, called a **Venn diagram**, depicts the union of events A and B. The shaded area represents the event of $A \cup B$.

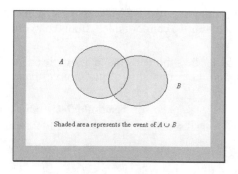

Shaded area represents the event of $A \cup B$

Figure 7-6: Venn diagram for $A \cup B$

Example 7-10: Let *A* be the event of rolling a fair six-sided die. Let *B* be the event of an even number between 0 and 9. What are the elements of $A \cup B$?

Solution: Recall that $A = \{1, 2, 3, 4, 5, 6\}$ and $B = \{2, 4, 6, 8\}$. Thus $A \cup B = \{1, 2, 3, 4, 5, 6, 8\}$. Note that elements that are common to both *A* and *B* are not repeated when listing the elements in $A \cup B$. This is shown in **Figure 7-7**.

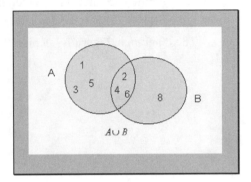

Figure 7-7: Elements in $A \cup B$

Quick Tip

In the union of events, elements common to different events are not repeated.

Example 7-11: Given that the probability that **only** event *A* will occur is 0.3, the probability of **only** event *B* occurring is 0.4, and the probability that **both** events *A* and *B* occurring is 0.1. Depict this information on a Venn diagram.

Solution: The information is displayed in **Figure 7-8**. Note that the sum of the probabilities in the Venn diagram equals 1.

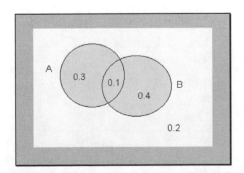

Figure 7-8: Venn diagram displaying information for Example 7-11

Intersection of Events

Consider two events A and B. We may be interested in the event that is obtained by considering the elements that are in **both** A and B. Such a compound event is called the **intersection** of events A and B.

Explanation of the term—intersection of two events: The **intersection of two events** A and B is the set of outcomes that are included in both A and B.

Notation: The intersection of A and B will be denoted by $A \cap B$.

The diagram in **Figure 7-9** depicts the intersection of the events A and B.

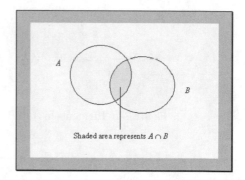

Shaded area represents $A \cap B$

Figure 7-9: Venn diagram for $A \cap B$

Example 7-12: Let A be the event of rolling a fair six-sided die. Let B be the event of an even number between 0 and 9. What is $A \cap B$?

Solution: Recall that $A = \{1, 2, 3, 4, 5, 6\}$ and $B = \{2, 4, 6, 8\}$. Thus $A \cap B = \{2, 4, 6\}$. The event of $A \cap B$ is shown in **Figure 7-7** for **Example 7-10**.

Example 7-13: In a sample of 100 college students, 60 said that they own a car, 30 said that they own a stereo, and 10 said that they own both a car and a stereo. Compute probabilities for these events, and depict this information on a Venn diagram.

Solution: Let C be the event that a student owns a car, and let D be the event that a student owns a stereo.

Thus $P(C) = \dfrac{60}{100} = 0.6$, $P(D) = \dfrac{30}{100} = 0.3$, and $P(C \cap D) = \dfrac{10}{100} = 0.1$.

Thus the probability of **only** C occurring is $0.6 - 0.1 = 0.5$, and the probability of **only** D occurring is $0.3 - 0.1 = 0.2$. Note that we have to subtract the portion that is common to both C and D in order to get **only** C and **only** D. This information is depicted in **Figure 7-10**.

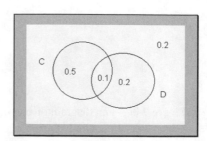

Figure 7-10: Venn diagram for
Example 7-13

Mutually Exclusive Events

Sometimes events may have nothing in common. In such cases, we may deal with the concept known as **mutually exclusive events**.

Explanation of the term—mutually exclusive events: Two events A and B are said to be **mutually exclusive** if they have no elements in common—in other words, if the intersection is empty.

Figure 7-11 shows two mutually exclusive events. Observe that they do not have any common portion.

A and B are mutually exclusive

Figure 7-11: Venn diagram depicting two mutually exclusive events A and B

Law 5: If two events A and B are mutually exclusive, then $P(A \cup B) = P(A) + P(B)$.

Quick Tips

- If two events are mutually exclusive, then if one of them occurs, the other cannot occur.
- Another term used for mutually exclusive is *disjoint*.

Example 7-14: Persons are being selected for a survey. Let M be the event that a male is selected. Let F be the event that a female is selected. Are these mutually exclusive events?

Solution: These events are mutually exclusive because when a person is selected, that person will be either a male or female. There is no commonality to these two events.

Complement of an Event

Sometimes it is more convenient to consider what is outside of a given event than to consider what is inside the given event itself. This deals with the **complement** of the event.

Explanation of the term—complement of an event: The **complement of an event** A is the set of all outcomes that are not in A.

Notation: We will let A^c represent the complement of event A.

The diagram in **Figure 7-12** depicts the complement of event A.

Example 7-15: If a fair six-sided die with faces numbered 1 to 6 is rolled and A is the event of rolling a 2, compute $P(A^c)$.

Solution: Now $P(A) = \dfrac{1}{6}$. Thus $P(A^c) = P\{1, 3, 4, 5, 6\} = \dfrac{5}{6}$.

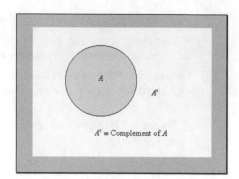

Figure 7-12: Venn diagram depicting the complement of an event

The Complement Rule

Observe that the complement of an event and the event itself are mutually exclusive. If we are dealing with only a single event in a sample space, then the union of the event and its complement will be the same as the event of the sample space. If A is the event, then $A \cup A^c = S$, where S is the sample space. Thus $P(A \cup A^c) = P(S)$. Now, the probability of the sample space for any experiment is 1. That is, $P(S) = 1$. Thus $P(A \cup A^c) = 1$. Since A and A^c are mutually exclusive, $P(A \cup A^c) = P(A) + P(A^c)$. This gives us that $P(A) + P(A^c) = 1$. We usually state this as a law.

Law 6: The sum of the probability of an event and the probability of its complement equals 1.

$$P(A) + P(A^c) = 1$$
$$or$$
$$P(A^c) = 1 - P(A)$$

Example 7-16: The probability of your favorite college basketball team's winning a game is 0.6. What is the probability of the team not winning the next game?

Solution: Let A be the event that your team wins the next game, so $P(A) = 0.6$. Thus A^c is the event that your team will not win the next game. Thus

$$P(\text{not winning the next game}) = P(A^c) = 1 - P(A)$$
$$= 1 - 0.6$$
$$= 0.4$$

The Addition Rule

A more generalized rule for the union of two events is given next.

Law 7: For any two events A and B, the probability of their union is given by

$$P(A \cup B) = P(A) + P(B) - P(A \cap B)$$

This is usually called the **addition rule** of probability. The Venn diagram in **Figure 7-13** depicts this law. The striped area represents $P(A \cup B)$.

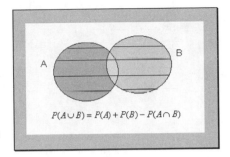

$$P(A \cup B) = P(A) + P(B) - P(A \cap B)$$

Figure 7-13: Venn diagram depicting the addition rule

Example 7-17: In **Example 7-13**, what is the probability of a student's having a car, a stereo, or both a car and a stereo?

Solution: We need to find $P(C \cup D)$. From the Venn diagram in **Figure 7-10** for **Example 7-13**, $P(C) = 0.6$, $P(D) = 0.3$, and $P(C \cap D) = 0.1$. Thus $P(C \cup D) = 0.6 + 0.3 - 0.1 = 0.8$.

7-9   Conditional Probability

Sometimes it is important to find the probability of an event **given** that another event has occurred. Such a probability is called a **conditional probability**.

Explanation of the term—conditional probability: This is the probability of a particular event occurring, given that another event has occurred.

Notation: We will let $P(A \mid B)$ represent the conditional probability of the event A given that event B has occurred. It is read as "the probability of A given B."

Law 8. The conditional probability of an event A, given that event B has occurred, is computed from the following formula:

$$P(A \mid B) = \frac{P(A \cap B)}{P(B)}, \text{ where } P(B) \neq 0$$

Example 7-18: In **Example 7-13**, what is the probability of a student's having a stereo given the student has a car?

Solution: We need to compute $P(D \mid C)$. From the Venn diagram in **Figure 7-10** for **Example 7-13**, $P(C) = 0.6$, $P(D) = 0.3$, and $P(C \cap D) = 0.1$. Thus

$$P(D \mid C) = \frac{P(D \cap C)}{P(C)} = \frac{P(C \cap D)}{P(C)} = \frac{0.1}{0.6} = 0.167 \quad \text{(correct to three decimal places)}$$

Quick Tip

In finding a conditional probability, we restrict the sample space to the event on which we condition.

In **Example 7-18**, we are restricting the sample space to the event C. This is shown in **Figure 7-14**.

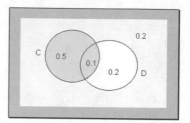

Figure 7-14: Venn diagram for Example 7-18

Law 9 (multiplication rule for two dependent events): If events A and B are dependent, then $P(A \cap B) = P(A) \times P(B \mid A)$ or $P(A \cap B) = P(B) \times P(A \mid B)$.

7-10 Independence

Independence illustrates a special relationship between events. If having knowledge of one event does not affect the probability of occurrence of another event, then these two events are said to be **independent**. For example, if $P(A \mid B) = 0.5$ and $P(A) = 0.5$, then having information about event B does not affect the probability of A occurring.

Explanation of the term—independence in probability: Two events are **independent** if the occurrence of one does not alter the probability of the other. Thus, if two events A and B are independent, then symbolically we can express them as

$$P(A \mid B) = P(A)$$
or
$$P(B \mid A) = P(B)$$

If events A and B are not independent, then the events are said to be **dependent**.

Example 7-19: A part-time student is enrolled in a course in geometry (G) and a course in music (M). The probabilities that the student will pass geometry, music, or both subjects are, respectively, $P(G) = 0.8$, $P(M) = 0.7$, and $P(G \cap M) = 0.56$.

(a) What is the probability that the student will pass geometry given that the student passes music?

Solution: We need to find $P(G \mid M)$. Thus

$$P(G \mid M) = \frac{P(G \cap M)}{P(M)} = \frac{0.56}{0.7} = 0.8$$

(b) Are the events G and M independent?

Solution: From part (a), $P(G \mid M) = 0.8$, and also $P(G) = 0.8$. That is, $P(G|M) = P(G)$. Thus G and M are independent.

Law 10 (multiplication rule for two independent events): If events A and B are independent, then $P(A \cap B) = P(A) \times P(B)$.

Example 7-20: For the information given in **Example 7-19**, use this law to verify that the events G and M are independent.

Solution: We need to show that $P(G \cap M) = P(G) \times P(M)$. We are given that $P(G \cap M) = 0.56$ and $P(G) \times P(M) = 0.8 \times 0.7 = 0.56$. Thus $P(G \cap M) = P(G) \times P(M)$ so one can conclude that events G and M are independent. This was also established in **Example 7-19(b)**.

Example 7-21: A consumer group studied the service provided by fast-food restaurants in a given community. One of the things they looked at was the relationship between service and whether the server had a high school diploma or not. The information is summarized in **Table 7-1**.

Table 7-1: Table for Example 7-21

QUALIFICATION/SERVICE	GOOD SERVICE	POOR SERVICE	TOTAL
HS diploma	61	28	89
No HS diploma	30	81	111
Total	91	109	Grand total = 200

Let

G = the event of good service

B = the event of poor service

H = the event of having a high school diploma

N = the event of not having a high school diploma.

(a) Find $P(G)$.

Solution: $P(G) = \dfrac{91}{200} = 0.455$. Recall from **Chapter 6** that this is equivalent to the marginal distribution of the variable **good service**.

(b) Find $P(N)$.

Solution: $P(N) = \dfrac{111}{200} = 0.555$. Again, recall from **Chapter 6** that this is equivalent to the marginal distribution of the variable **no high school diploma**.

(c) Find $P(B \cap N)$.

Solution: The number of observations in $B \cap N$ is 81. Thus $P(B \cap N) = \dfrac{81}{200} = 0.405$.

(d) Find $P(B \mid N)$.

Solution: Now $P(B \mid N) = \dfrac{P(B \cap N)}{P(N)} = \dfrac{0.405}{0.555} = 0.73$. Again, recall from **Chapter 6** that this equivalent to the conditional distribution of the variable **poor service** given **no high school diploma**.

Technology Corner

All the concepts discussed in this chapter can be computed and illustrated using any statistical software package. However, using such software for the computations encountered in this chapter again would be technology overkill. All that is required is simple calculations. All scientific and graphical calculators will aid directly in the computations.

It's a Wrap

Probability concepts can be investigated through

✓ Relative frequency

✓ The law of large numbers

✓ Sample spaces

✓ Tree diagrams

✓ Union and intersection of events

Care always should be taken when computing the probability of an event. In certain branches of work in the real world, such as the insurance field, a great deal of emphasis is placed on probabilities.

Test Yourself

True/False Questions

1. The sample space for an experiment is the set of all possible outcomes in that experiment.
2. An event is a subset of the sample space.
3. The probability of an event is a measure of the likelihood of that event not occurring.
4. If we toss a coin 100 times and 50 heads are observed, we can estimate the probability of a head occurring to be 50 percent. This estimate is known as the law of large numbers.
5. In the classical interpretation of probability, it is not necessary to assume that the outcomes in the sample space are equally likely.
6. If two events A and B are independent, the $P(A \mid B) \neq P(A)$.
7. Two events are mutually exclusive if the occurrence of one depends on the occurrence of the other.
8. If events A and B are independent, then the probability of both of them occurring, $P(A \cap B)$, is the sum of their respective probabilities.
9. Two events A and B are dependent if $P(A \mid B) \neq P(A)$.
10. In a Venn diagram, the intersection of two events indicates that the two events are not mutually exclusive.
11. If two events are mutually exclusive, then they are independent.
12. The complement of an event and the event itself are mutually exclusive.
13. The probability of an event is always a number between 0 and 1 inclusive.
14. In selecting a card from a regular deck of cards, the event of "drawing a queen" and the event of "drawing a king" are mutually exclusive.
15. The outcome of an event and the complement of that event together make up the sample space.
16. If a regular six-sided die is rolled, then the complement of "rolling an even number" is the set {2, 4, 6}.
17. A sample space is a list of all the possible outcomes of the experiment.
18. Two events are mutually exclusive if they both cannot occur at the same time.
19. If two events A and B are independent, then $P(A \cap B) = P(A) \times P(B)$.
20. If $P(A \cap B) = 0$, then the two events must be independent.

Completion Questions

1. If A and B are mutually exclusive, then $P(A \cap B)$ must equal (0, 0.5, 1) _____.
2. The probability of an event occurring will assume values between (0, 0.5, 1) _____ and (0, 0.5, 1) _____.
3. An event is an (outcome, subset) _____ of a sample space.
4. If the probability of an event is zero, then it will (always, never) _____ occur.
5. The sum of the probabilities of all simple events in a sample space must be equal to (0, 0.5, 1) _____.
6. If events A and B are mutually exclusive, then $P(A \cup B) = \{P(A) + P(B); P(A) \times P(B)\}$ _____.

7. If events A and B are independent, then $P(A \cap B) = \{P(A) + P(B); P(A) \times P(B)\}$ _____.

8. If the probability of an event's occurring is equal to $(1, 0)$ _____, then the event must occur.

9. A sample space is the collection of all possible (outcomes, compound events, heads) _____ for an experiment.

10. In classical probability, it is assumed that all outcomes in the sample space are (equally, likely, never) _____ to occur.

11. The complement of an event A is the event that A (will, will not) _____ occur.

12. When any one of the outcomes in an experiment has the same likelihood of occurring as any other, we say the outcomes are (independent, mutually inclusive, equally likely) _____.

13. Suppose that we toss a fair coin (with the likelihood of the coin's staying on its edge being zero) a large number of times and we use the observed number of tails to help compute the probability of a tail occurring for this coin. This approach to probability is known as the (relative frequency, classical, subjective) _____ concept of probability.

14. The addition rule for probability is helpful when we are computing the probability for (independent, mutually exclusive) _____ events.

15. If $P(A|B) = P(A)$, then A and B must be (independent, dependent) _____ events.

16. If two events A and B have nonzero probabilities and are mutually exclusive, then $P(A \cup B)$ must be $(0, 1, \text{neither})$ _____.

17. Rolling a regular six-sided die and observing a 6 and then rolling the die again and observing another 6 would be an example of (independent, mutually exclusive) _____ events.

18. If a regular six-sided die is rolled and the outcomes are equally likely, then this is an example of (relative frequency, classical, subjective) _____ probability.

19. The intersection of two events A and B is the set of outcomes included in (both A and B, only A, only B, A or B) _____.

20. If A and B are independent, then if $P(A) = 0.7$, $P(B) = 0.8$, and $P(A \cap B) = 0.4$; these assigned probabilities are (valid or invalid) _____.

Multiple-Choice Questions

1. If $P(A) = 0.5$, $P(B) = 0.6$, and $P(A \cap B) = 0.3$, then $P(A \cup B)$ is
   (a) 0.8000.
   (b) 0.5000.
   (c) 0.6000.
   (d) 0.0000.

2. If $P(A) = 0.6$, $P(B) = 0.5$, and $P(A \cup B) = 0.9$, then $P(A \cap B)$ is
   (a) impossible.
   (b) 0.2000.
   (c) 0.3000.
   (d) 0.6000.

3. If $P(A) = 0.3$, $P(B) = 0.5$, and $P(A \cup B) = 0.6$, then $P(A \mid B)$ is
   (a) 0.5000.
   (b) 0.8333.
   (c) 0.4000.
   (d) 0.4500.

4. If $P(A) = 0.5$, $P(B) = 0.4$, and $P(B \mid A) = 0.3$, then $P(A \cap B)$ is
   (a) 0.7500.
   (b) 0.6000.
   (c) 0.1200.
   (d) 0.1500.

5. If $P(A) = 0.6$, $P(B) = 0.3$, and $P(A \mid B) = 0.4$, then $P(A \cup B)$ is
   (a) 0.7800.
   (b) 0.1200.
   (c) 0.6667.
   (d) 0.2200.

6. If A and B are mutually exclusive events and $P(A) = 0.5$ and $P(B) = 0.4$, then $P(A \cup B)$ is
   (a) 0.0000.
   (b) 0.9000.
   (c) 0.2000.
   (d) 0.8000.

7. If A and B are independent events and $P(A) = 0.3$ and $P(B) = 0.6$, then $P(A \cap B)$ is
   (a) 0.7200.
   (b) 0.9000.
   (c) 0.1800.
   (d) 0.5000.

8. If A and B are independent events and $P(A) = 0.3$ and $P(B) = 0.6$, then $P(A \cup B)$ is
   (a) 0.9000.
   (b) 0.1800.
   (c) 0.5000.
   (d) 0.7200.

9. If $P(A) = 0.6$, $P(B) = 0.3$, and $P(A \mid B) = 0.4$, then $P(A^c)$ is
   (a) 0.4000.
   (b) 0.1000.
   (c) 0.6000.
   (d) 0.1200.

10. If A and B are mutually exclusive events and $P(A) = 0.2$ and $P(B) = 0.7$, then $P(A \cap B)$ is
    (a) 0.1400.
    (b) 0.0000.
    (c) 0.9000.
    (d) 0.7600.

Problems 11 to 18 are based on the following information:

In a survey of 120 college students living in the dorms, 60 said that they had **only** a stereo set in their rooms, 40 said they had **only** a microcomputer in their rooms, and 15 said they had **both** a stereo and a microcomputer in their rooms. The remaining 5 students had neither.

11. If a student is randomly chosen from this group, the probability that the student has both a stereo and a microcomputer is
    (a) 0.1250.
    (b) 0.2174.
    (c) 0.2143.
    (d) 0.8333.

12. If a student is randomly chosen from this group, the probability that the student has either a stereo or a microcomputer or both is
    (a) 0.9583.
    (b) 0.8333.
    (c) 0.8000.
    (d) 0.7273.

13. If a student is randomly chosen from this group, the probability that the student does not have a stereo is
    (a) 0.4783.
    (b) 0.4583.
    (c) 0.5000.
    (d) 0.3750.

14. If a student is randomly chosen from this group, the probability that the student does not have a microcomputer is
    (a) 0.6522.
    (b) 0.2727.
    (c) 0.5417.
    (d) 0.6667.

15. If a student is randomly selected from this group, the probability that the student has a stereo given that the student does not have a microcomputer is
    (a) 0.9286.
    (b) 0.9231.
    (c) 0.8889.
    (d) 0.8000.

16. If a student is randomly chosen from this group, the probability that the student does have a microcomputer given that the student has a stereo is
    (a) 0.2000.
    (b) 0.6667.
    (c) 0.1500.
    (d) 0.3750.

17. If a student is randomly chosen from this group, the probability that the student does not have either a stereo or a microcomputer is
    (a) 0.0435.

    (b) 0.0417.

    (c) 0.8696.

    (d) 0.8750.

18. If a student is randomly chosen from this group, the probability that the student does have a stereo given that the student has a microcomputer is

    (a) 0.5333.

    (b) 0.6667.

    (c) 0.3750.

    (d) 0.2727.

19. The probability that any one of two engines on an aircraft will fail is 0.001. Assuming that the engines operate independently of each other, then the probability that both engines will not fail is

    (a) $(0.001)^2$.

    (b) 0.002.

    (c) $(0.001)(0.999)$.

    (d) $(0.999)^2$.

20. If two nontrivial events (probability not equal to zero) A and B are mutually exclusive, which of the following must be true?

    (a) $P(A \cap B) = P(A) + P(B)$

    (b) $P(A \cup B) = P(A) + P(B)$

    (c) $P(A \cup B) = P(A) \times P(B)$

    (d) $P(A \cap B) = P(A) \times P(B)$

Problems 21 to 27 are based on the following information:

A clothing store that targets young customers (ages 18 through 22) wishes to determine whether the size of the purchase is related to the method of payment. A sample of 300 customers was analyzed, and the information is given in **Table 7-2**.

Table 7-2

SIZE OF PURCHASE/ METHOD OF PAYMENT	CASH	CREDIT CARD	LAYAWAY PLAN	TOTAL
Under $40	60	30	10	100
$40 or more	40	100	60	200
Total	100	130	70	Grand total = 300

21. If a customer is selected at random from this group of customers, the probability that the customer paid cash is

    (a) 1/3.

    (b) 3/5.

    (c) 2/5.

    (d) 2/3.

22. If a customer is selected at random from this group of customers, the probability that the customer paid with a credit card is

    (a) 17/30.

    (b) 13/30.

(c) 3/13.

(d) 10/13.

23. If a customer is selected at random from this group of customers, the probability that the customer paid with the layaway plan is

(a) 6/7.

(b) 1/10.

(c) 7/30.

(d) 1/7.

24. If a customer is selected at random from this group of customers, the probability that the customer purchased under $40 is

(a) 3/5.

(b) 2/5.

(c) 2/3.

(d) 1/3.

25. If a customer is selected at random from this group of customers, the probability that the customer purchased $40 or more is

(a) 2/3.

(b) 2/5.

(c) 6/7.

(d) 10/13.

26. If a customer is selected at random from this group of customers, the probability that the customer paid with a credit card given that the purchase was under $40 is

(a) 3/10.

(b) 13/30.

(c) 1/3.

(d) 2/3.

27. If a customer is selected at random from this group of customers, the probability that the customer paid with a layaway plan given that the purchase was $40 or more is

(a) 3/10.

(b) 2/3.

(c) 7/30.

(d) 7/20.

28. Manufactured bolts are collected in a large bin. Suppose that one bolt is selected at random and examined to determine whether it is defective or nondefective. The bolt is returned to the bin, and another is selected and examined. If the probability of a defective bolt is 0.01, the probability of selecting two nondefective bolts is

(a) 2(0.01).

(b) 2(0.99).

(c) $(0.01)^2$.

(d) $(0.99)^2$.

29. In a particular rural region, 65 percent of the residents are smokers, and research indicates that 15 percent of the smokers have some form of lung cancer. The probability of a resident's having lung cancer given that the resident is a smoker is

(a) 0.0975.

(b) 0.2308.

(c) 0.1500.

(d) 0.6500.

30. From past experience, an instructor estimates that the probability that a student will cheat on an exam is 0.05. The probability that a student cheats and will be caught is 0.01. The probability that a student will be caught, given the student is cheating, is

(a) 0.0005.

(b) 0.0600.

(c) 0.0400.

(d) 0.2000.

31. For a certain brand of tire, the probability that it will last beyond 40,000 miles is 0.8, and the probability that it will last beyond 50,000 miles is 0.25. Given that a tire lasts beyond 40,000 miles, the probability that it will last beyond 50,000 miles is

(a) 0.2500.

(b) 0.0000.

(c) 0.3125.

(d) 0.2000.

32. Given $P(A) = 0.5$, $P(B) = 0.6$, and $P(A \cup B) = 0.8$, then $P(A \mid B)$ is

(a) 0.5000.

(b) 0.7500.

(c) 0.6250.

(d) 0.0480.

33. If $P(\text{only } A) = 0.4$, $P(\text{only } B) = 0.2$, and $P(A \cup B) = 0.8$, then $P(A \cap B)$ is

(a) 0.5000.

(b) 0.2000.

(c) 0.0800.

(d) 0.2500.

34. If $P(A) = 0.6$, $P(B) = 0.3$, and $P(A \mid B) = 0.4$, then $P(A \cup B)$ is

(a) 0.1200.

(b) 0.9000.

(c) 0.7800.

(d) 0.2400.

35. If $P(A) = 0.5$, $P(B) = 0.4$, and $P(A \mid B) = 0.9$, then $P(B \mid A)$ is

(a) 0.4500.

(b) 0.3600.

(c) 0.5556.

(d) 0.7200.

36. If A and B are two mutually exclusive events with $P(A) = 0.15$ and $P(B) = 0.7$, then $P(A \cup B)$ is

(a) 0.2143.

(b) 0.8500.

    (c) 0.0980.

    (d) 0.5500.

37. If A and B are two independent events with $P(A) = 0.15$ and $P(B) = 0.7$, then $P(A \cap B)$ is

    (a) 0.5500.

    (b) 0.2143.

    (c) 0.1050.

    (d) 0.8500.

38. If A and B are two independent events with $P(A) = 0.35$ and $P(B) = 0.6$, then $P(A \mid B)$ is

    (a) 0.6000.

    (b) 0.3500.

    (c) 0.2100.

    (d) 0.5833.

39. If A and B are two independent events with $P(A) = 0.15$ and $P(B) = 0.4$, then $P(A \cup B)$ is

    (a) 0.5500.

    (b) 0.3750.

    (c) 0.0600.

    (d) 0.4900.

40. In a three-child family, the probability that there are at least two girls is

    (a) 3/7.

    (b) 1/2.

    (c) 4/7.

    (d) 3/8.

41. If A and B are two mutually exclusive events with $P(A) = 0.15$ and $P(B) = 0.4$, then $P(A \cap B^c)$ is

    (a) 0.8500.

    (b) 0.1500.

    (c) 0.4000.

    (d) 0.6000.

Problems 42 to 51 are based on the following information:

Six hundred registered voters were surveyed and asked their political affiliation and whether they support the idea of the federal government investing a portion of their Social Security contributions. A summary of the survey is given in **Table 7-3**.

Table 7-3

POLITICAL AFFILIATION/ SUPPORT OR NOT	DEMOCRAT	REPUBLICAN	INDEPENDENT	TOTAL
Yes	35	90	10	135
No	165	100	200	465
Total	200	190	210	Grand total = 600

42. If a voter is selected at random from the results of this survey, the probability that the voter is a Democrat is
   (a) 0.3500.
   (b) 0.3167.
   (c) 0.3333.
   (d) 0.1750.

43. If a voter is selected at random from the results of this survey, the probability that the voter is a Republican is
   (a) 0.3500.
   (b) 0.3167.
   (c) 0.3333.
   (d) 0.4737.

44. If a voter is selected at random from the results of this survey, the probability that the voter is an independent is
   (a) 0.3500.
   (b) 0.3167.
   (c) 0.3333.
   (d) 0.0476.

45. If a voter is selected at random from the results of this survey, the probability that the voter supports the plan is
   (a) 0.1750.
   (b) 0.4737.
   (c) 0.0476.
   (d) 0.2250.

46. If a voter is selected at random from the results of this survey, the probability that the voter does not support the plan is
   (a) 0.7750.
   (b) 0.4737.
   (c) 0.0476.
   (d) 0.2250.

47. If a voter is selected at random from the results of this survey, the probability that the voter is an independent and does not support the plan is
   (a) 0.3333.
   (b) 0.7750.
   (c) 0.9524.
   (d) 0.3500.

48. If a voter is selected at random from the results of this survey, the probability that the voter is an independent given that the voter does not support the plan is
   (a) 0.9523.
   (b) 0.3333.
   (c) 0.4301.
   (d) 0.7547.

49. If a voter is selected at random from the results of this survey, the probability that the voter is a Republican and supports the plan is
   (a) 0.4737.
   (b) 0.9000.
   (c) 0.1500.
   (d) 0.6667.

50. If a voter is selected at random from the results of this survey, the probability that the voter is a Democrat given that the voter supports the plan is
   (a) 0.1750.
   (b) 0.2122.
   (c) 0.2250.
   (d) 0.2593.

51. If a voter is selected at random from the results of this survey, the probability that the voter is a Republican given that the voter does not support the plan is
   (a) 0.2151.
   (b) 0.5263.
   (c) 0.1667.
   (d) 0.4086.

52. If a voter is selected at random from the results of this survey, the probability that the voter supports the plan given that the voter is a Democrat is
   (a) 0.2593.
   (b) 0.0583.
   (c) 0.1750.
   (d) 0.2121.

53. If a voter is selected at random from the results of this survey, the probability that the voter does not support the plan given that the voter is a Republican is
   (a) 0.2151.
   (b) 0.1667.
   (c) 0.2740.
   (d) 0.5263.

54. If a voter is selected at random from the results of this survey, the probability that the voter supports the plan given that the voter is an independent is
   (a) 0.0476.
   (b) 0.0500.
   (c) 0.0741.
   (d) 0.0167.

ANSWER KEY

True/False Questions

1. T 2. T 3. F 4. F 5. F 6. F 7. F 8. F 9. T 10. T
11. F 12. T 13. T 14. T 15. T 16. F 17. T 18. T 19. T 20. F

Completion Questions

1. 0 2. 0, 1 3. subset 4. never 5. 1 6. $P(A) + P(B)$
7. $P(A) \times P(B)$ 8. 1 9. outcomes 10. equally likely 11. will not
12. equally likely 13. relative frequency 14. mutually exclusive 15. independent
16. neither 17. independent 18. classical 19. both A and B 20. invalid

Multiple-Choice Questions

1. (a) 2. (b) 3. (c) 4. (d) 5. (a) 6. (b) 7. (c) 8. (d) 9. (a)
10. (b) 11. (a) 12. (a) 13. (d) 14. (c) 15. (b) 16. (a) 17. (b) 18. (d)
19. (d) 20. (b) 21. (a) 22. (b) 23. (c) 24. (d) 25. (a) 26. (a) 27. (a)
28. (d) 29. (c) 30. (d) 31. (c) 32. (a) 33. (b) 34. (c) 35. (d) 36. (b)
37. (c) 38. (b) 39. (d) 40. (b) 41. (b) 42. (c) 43. (b) 44. (a) 45. (d)
46. (a) 47. (a) 48. (c) 49. (c) 50. (d) 51. (a) 52. (c) 53. (d) 54. (a)

CHAPTER 8

Discrete Probability Distributions

Do I Need to Read This Chapter?

You should read this chapter if you need to review or to learn about

→ Probability distributions

→ Expectation or expected values

→ Variance

→ Bernoulli trials

→ The binomial distribution

Get Started

Here we will discuss ideas relating to randomness for the sample space produced by a random experiment. For example, if a fair coin is tossed, then the resulting sample space is $S = \{H, T\}$. Using the classical definition of probability, we can summarize the outcomes with the associated probabilities as

OUTCOME	PROBABILITY
H	0.5
T	0.5

To analyze more complex random experiments, we will introduce and use the ideas of random variables and probability distributions.

8-1   Random Variables

Let us consider the experiment of tossing a single coin. Recall the sample space $S = \{H, T\}$. Let X represent the number of heads. Thus X can assume the values 0 and 1. We will let x be these values. That is, $x = 0, 1$. What is the relationship between the sample space and the values of X? The relationship is shown in **Figure 8-1**.

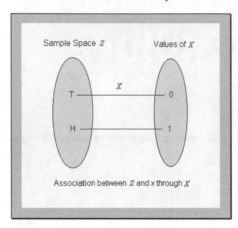

Figure 8-1: Outcomes on tossing a single coin and values of X

Next, consider the example of a two-child family. Recall that the sample space is $S = \{BB, BG, GB, GG\}$. Let X represent the number of girls. Possible numbers of girls in S are 0, 1, 2. Thus $x = 0, 1, 2$. **Figure 8-2** shows the relationship between the sample space S and the values of X.

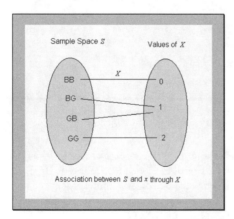

Figure 8-2: Outcomes for a two-child family and values of X

By observing **Figures 8-1** and **8-2**, you will see that the points in the sample space are associated with values on the number line through X. Also observe that these numbers are based on the random outcome of the experiment. Because of this, we refer to the variable X as a **random variable**.

Explanation of the term—random variable: A **random variable** assigns one and only one numerical value to each point in the sample space for a random experiment.

Note: Random variables usually are denoted by **uppercase** letters near the end of the alphabet, such as X, Y and Z. We will use **lowercase** letters to represent the values of the random variables, such as x, y, and z.

Types of Random Variables

We will encounter two types of random variables, **discrete** and **continuous**.

Explanation of the term—discrete random variable: A **discrete random variable** is one that can assume a countable number of possible values.

For example, the number of days it rained in your community during the month of March is an example of a discrete random variable. If X is the number of days it rained during the month of March, then the possible values for X are $x = 0, 1, 2, 3, \ldots, 31$.

Explanation of the term—continuous random variable: A **continuous random variable** is one that can assume any value in an interval on the real number line.

For example, the amount (in inches) of rainfall in your community during the month of March is an example of a continuous random variable. If X is the amount it rained during the month of March, then the possible values for X will be in the interval $(0, \infty)$. That is, the amount can vary from zero inches to an infinite number of inches. Theoretically, the number of inches of rainfall can go to infinity (∞), but from a practical standpoint, this may never happen. A practical continuous interval may be [0, 12] inches, as shown in **Figure 8-3**.

Figure 8-3: Continuous interval of rainfall

Note: We will deal only with discrete random variables in this chapter.

8-2   Probability Distributions for Discrete Random Variables

Recall the two-child family example from **Chapter 7**. The sample space was given as $S = \{BB, BG, GB, GG\}$, and the tree diagram is repeated in **Figure 8-4** for convenience.

Figure 8-4: Tree diagram for a two-child family

Let X represent the number of girls in the family; then the values for X are $x = 0, 1, 2$. Using the classical definition of probability,

$$P(X = 0) = P(BB) = \frac{1}{4} = 0.25$$

$$\begin{aligned}
P(X = 1) &= P(BG \text{ or } GB) \\
&= P(BG \cup GB) \\
&= P(BG) + P(GB) \quad \text{since } BG \text{ and } GB \text{ are mutually exclusive events} \\
&= \frac{1}{4} + \frac{1}{4} = \frac{1}{2} = 0.5
\end{aligned}$$

$$\begin{aligned}
P(X = 2) &= P(GG) \\
&= \frac{1}{4} = 0.25
\end{aligned}$$

We can arrange the values of the random variable and the associated probabilities in tabular form, as shown in **Table 8-1**.

Table 8-1: Probability Distribution for a Two-Child Family

x	$P(X = x)$
0	0.25
1	0.50
2	0.25
	$\Sigma P(x) = 1$

Such a table is called a **probability distribution**. In particular, it is a **discrete probability distribution** because the random variable is discrete.

Explanation of the term—discrete probability distribution: A **discrete probability distribution** consists of all possible values of a discrete random variable with their corresponding probabilities.

The diagram in **Figure 8-5** shows a bar graph representation of the probability distribution for the number of girls in a two-child family.

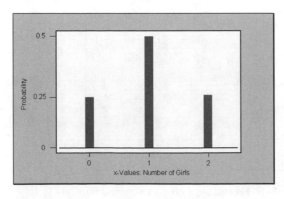

Figure 8-5: Bar graph for the probability distribution for the number of girls in a two-child family

8-3   Expected Value for a Discrete Random Variable

A very important concept in probability is the idea of expected values. The **expected value** for a random variable is the long-term mean or average value of the random variable. If the random variable is observed over a long period of time, the expected value should be close to the average value of the observations generated by the random process. The larger the number of observations, the closer the expected value will be to the average value of the observations.

Expected Value

Explanation of the term—expected value for a discrete random variable: The **expected value for a discrete random variable** X is the mean value of the random variable. It is denoted by $E(X)$ and is obtained by computing

$$\mu = E(X) = \Sigma\, x \times P(x)$$

Example 8-1: Find the expected number of girls in a two-child family.

Solution: Let X represent the number of girls in a two-child family. Using the formula and the information from the probability distribution in **Table 8-1**, we have

$$E(X) = 0 \times 0.25 + 1 \times 0.5 + 2 \times 0.25 = 1$$

That is, if we sample from a large number of two-child families, on average, there will be one girl in each family.

Sometimes it is convenient to create a table to compute the expected value for a random variable. Using the information for **Example 8-1**, we can create the following, as shown in **Table 8-2**.

Table 8-2: Table Showing the Probability Distribution and Expected
Value Computations for Example 8-1

VALUES OF X (x)	$P(x)$	$X \cdot P(x)$
0	0.25	$0 \times 0.25 = 0.0$
1	0.50	$1 \times 0.50 = 0.5$
2	0.25	$2 \times 0.25 = 0.5$
		$\Sigma x \times P(x) = 1.0$

From **Table 8-2**, we see that if we sum the values in the third column, we get the value of the expected value.

Figure 8-6 shows the result of a simulation for the average values for the observations generated for the number of girls for a two-child family distribution. Observe that as the number of simulation is increasing, the average value for the observations is fluctuating about the value of 1. Recall that the expected value for the number of girls in a two-child family was 1, so this pattern in the simulation should be expected.

Figure 8-6: Simulation illustrating the expected number of girls in a two-child family

---

Quick Tip

For discrete random variables, the expected value is very seldom one of the possible outcomes of the random variable.

Example 8-2: If 1,000 raffle tickets were sold for a bicycle worth $400, and a ticket number is drawn at random to determine the winner, what is the expected value of the raffle?

Solution: The probability of winning the bicycle is $\dfrac{1}{1,000}$ because there were 1,000 raffle tickets and the ticket number is drawn at random. Thus the expected value of the raffle will be $\$400 \times \dfrac{1}{1000} = \$0.40$, or 40 cents. That is, if you purchase a large number of tickets, on average, the return on each ticket will be 40 cents. Thus it would be unwise to spend more than 40 cents for the ticket. Of course, if the money is going to a worthy cause, you may wish to take that into consideration.

Example 8-3: What is the expected value of a raffle with a first prize of $400, a second prize of $300, and a third prize of $200 if 1,000 tickets are sold?

Solution: If the raffle were repeated a large number of times, we would lose $\frac{997}{1,000} \times 100$ percent = 99.7 percent of the time. We would win the first prize $\frac{1}{1,000} \times 100$ percent = 0.1 percent of the time because we could choose from 1,000 tickets. We would win the second prize $\frac{1}{999} \times 100$ percent = 0.1 percent of the time because we would only have 999 remaining tickets to choose from for the second prize. We would win the third prize $\frac{1}{998} \times 100$ percent = 0.1 percent of the time because we would only have 998 remaining tickets from which to choose the third prize. Converting the percentages to probabilities, we would have the probability distribution given in **Table 8-3**.

Table 8-3: Probability Distribution for Example 8-3

PRIZE VALUE x (IN $)	P(x)
0	0.997
200	0.001
300	0.001
400	0.001

Thus the expected value of the raffle is $0 \times 0.997 + 200 \times 0.001 + 300 \times 0.001 + 400 \times 0.001 = \$0.90$, or 90 cents. It would be unwise to spend more than 90 cents for a ticket.

Once again, one also can use the tabular presentation to help find the expected value. This is shown in **Table 8-4**.

Table 8-4: Probability Distribution and Expected Value Computations for Example 8-3

VALUES OF X (x)	P(x)	x × P(x)
0	0.997	$0 \times 0.997 = 0.0$
200	0.001	$200 \times 0.001 = 0.2$
300	0.001	$300 \times 0.001 = 0.3$
400	0.001	$400 \times 0.001 = 0.4$
		$\Sigma x \times P(x) = 0.9$

Example 8-4: A game is set up such that you have a $\frac{1}{5}$ chance of winning $350 and a $\frac{4}{5}$ chance of losing $50. What is your expected gain?

Solution: Let X represent the amount of gain. Note that a loss will be considered as a negative gain. The probability distribution for X is given in **Table 8-5**.

Table 8-5: Probability Distribution for Example 8-4

x (IN $)	$P(x)$
350	1/5
−50	4/5

Thus the expected value of the game is $E(X) = 350 \times \frac{1}{5} + (-50) \times \frac{4}{5} = \$30$. That is, if you play the game a large number of times, on average, you will win $30 per game.

Sometimes we may be able to use expected values to help make a decision. The following example illustrates this.

Example 8-5: Suppose that you are given the option of two investment portfolios, A and B, with potential profits and the associated probabilities displayed in **Table 8-6.** Based on expected profits, which portfolio will you choose?

Table 8-6: Probability Distributions for Portfolios A and B

PORTFOLIO A		PORTFOLIO B	
PROFIT	PROBABILITY	PROFIT	PROBABILITY
−1,500	0.2	−2,500	0.2
−100	0.1	−500	0.1
500	0.4	1,500	0.3
1,500	0.2	2,500	0.3
3,500	0.1	3,500	0.1

Let X represent the profit for portfolio A, and let Y represent the profit for portfolio B. Then

$E(X) = (-1,500) \times 0.2 + (-100) \times 0.1 + 500 \times 0.4 + 1,500 \times 0.2 + 3,500 \times 0.1 = \$540$

$E(Y) = (-2,500) \times 0.2 + (-500) \times 0.1 + 1,500 \times 0.3 + 2,500 \times 0.3 + 3,500 \times 0.1 = \$1,000$

Since $E(Y) > E(X)$, you should invest in portfolio B based on the expected profit. That is, in the long run, portfolio B will outperform portfolio A. Thus, under repeated investments in portfolio B, you will, on average, gain $\$(1,000 - 540) = \$460$ over portfolio A.

8-4 Variance and Standard Deviation of a Discrete Random Variable

The following diagrams in **Figures 8-7** through **8-11** show the shapes of different distributions about a mean of zero for different random variables. Observe that some are more spread out about zero, whereas others are more clustered about zero. The spread gives us an idea about the **variability** of the random variable about the mean.

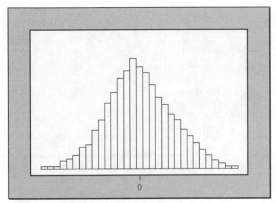

Figure 8-7: Distribution with a fair amount of spread about the mean of zero

Figure 8-8: Distribution with a large amount of spread about the mean of zero

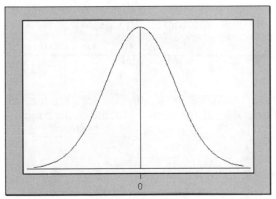

Figure 8-9: Distribution with a moderate amount of spread about the mean of zero

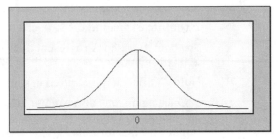

Figure 8-10: Distribution with a fair amount of spread about the mean of zero

Figure 8-11: Distribution with a large amount of spread about the mean of zero

Variance

Explanation of the term—variance for a discrete random variable: The **variance for a discrete random variable** X measures the spread of the random variable about the expected value (mean) and is computed from the following formula:

$$V(X) = \Sigma(x - \mu)^2 \times P(x)$$

where μ is the expected value for the random variable.

An equivalent computational formula for the variance is given as

$$V(X) = \Sigma \left[x^2 \times P(x) \right] - \mu^2$$

Note: In the preceding formula, the summation is only for $[x^2 \times P(x)]$ over all the x values.

Quick Tip

- Some texts may use the symbols σ^2 or σ_x^2 to represent the variance of the random variable X.
- The variance and standard deviation for a probability distribution are equal to its population variance and standard deviation, respectively.

Example 8-6: Find the variance for the winnings in the raffle for **Example 8-3**.

Solution: If we let X represent the winnings, then $V(X) = 0^2 \times 0.997 + 200^2 \times 0.001 + 300^2 \times 0.001 + 400^2 \times 0.001 - 0.90^2 = 289.19$. The units here will be (dollar)^2.

Note: Variance is measured in square units.

Once again, one also can use the tabular presentation to help find the variance for a discrete random variable. We can work out the values for the different terms in the computational variance formula $V(X) = \Sigma \left[x^2 \times P(x) \right] - \mu^2$. This is illustrated in **Table 8-7**.

Table 8-7: Probability Distribution, Expected Value, and Variance Computations for Example 8-3

VALUE (X)	$P(x)$	$X \times P(x)$	X^2	$X^2 \times P(x)$
0	0.997	$0 \times 0.997 = 0.0$	0	0
200	0.001	$200 \times 0.001 = 0.2$	40,000	40
300	0.001	$300 \times 0.001 = 0.3$	90,000	90
400	0.001	$400 \times 0.001 = 0.4$	160,000	160
		$\Sigma x \times P(x) = 0.9$		$\Sigma x^2 \times P(x) = 290$

Thus, from **Table 8-7**, we see that $V(X) = 290 - 0.9^2 = 289.19$.

Example 8-7: Find the variance for the gain in **Example 8-4**.

Solution: If we let X be the amount of gain, then $V(X) = 350^2 \times \frac{1}{5} + (-50)^2 \times \frac{4}{5} - 30^2 = 25,600$.

Example 8-8: Find the variance for the profits in the two portfolios in **Example 8-5**.

Solution: Let X represent the profit for portfolio A, and let Y represent the profit for portfolio B. Then

$$V(X) = (-1,500)^2 \times 0.2 + (-100)^2 \times 0.1 + 500^2 \times 0.4 + 1,500^2 \times 0.2 + 3,500^2 \times 0.1 - 540^2 = 1,934,400$$

$$V(Y) = (-2,500)^2 \times 0.2 + (-500)^2 \times 0.1 + 1,500^2 \times 0.3 + 2,500^2 \times 0.3 + 3,500^2 \times 0.1 - 1,000^2 = 4,050,000$$

Now, if you select a portfolio based on the variance, then you should select the one with the smaller variability because this would involve lesser risk. Thus, in this case, you should select portfolio *A* because it has the smaller variability.

Standard Deviation

It is easier to deal with a quantity that has the same units as the variable itself. If we take the square root of a square unit, we will get the unit itself. Thus, if we take the square root of the variance, called the **standard deviation**, we will get a quantity that has the same unit as the random variable.

Explanation of the term—standard deviation for a random variable: The **standard deviation for a random variable** X is defined to be the positive square root of the variance. It is computed from the following formula:

$$SD(X) = \sqrt{V(X)}$$

Quick Tip

The standard deviation is a rough estimate of the average distance of the values of the random variable from the expected value (mean).

Example 8-9: Find the standard deviation for the profits in the two portfolios in **Example 8-5**.

Solution: Let X represent the profit for portfolio *A*, and let *Y* represent the profit for portfolio *B*. Then

$$SD(X) = \sqrt{1,934,400} = 1,390.83$$

$$SD(Y) = \sqrt{4,050,000} = 2,012.46$$

A larger standard deviation indicates that there is greater variability in profits and hence an inherently larger risk for your investment, and vice versa. You would need to consider these issues and weigh the risks against the gains to make an informed decision as to the portfolio in which you should invest.

8-5 Bernoulli Trials and the Binomial Probability Distribution

When a coin is tossed once, the outcome can be classified in one of two possible mutually exclusive ways: a head (*H*) or a tail (*T*). Similarly, in selecting an item from a manufacturing process, we can have a defective (*D*) item or a nondefective (*N*) item. Such experiments are called **Bernoulli experiments**. In the case of tossing a coin, we may be interested in the outcome of a head. In such a case, we will classify a head as a successful outcome. In the case of selecting an item, a success may be the selection of a defective item.

Explanation of the term—Bernoulli experiment: A **Bernoulli experiment** is a random experiment, the outcome of which can be classified as one of two simple events.

Of course, we can repeat a Bernoulli experiment several times. When we do this under certain conditions, we say we have a sequence of **Bernoulli trials**.

Explanation of the term—Bernoulli trials: **Bernoulli trials** occur when a Bernoulli experiment is repeated several **independent** times so that the probability of success, say, p, remains the **same** from trial to trial.

In a sequence of Bernoulli trials, we often are interested in the total number of successes. For example, if we examine 18 items off a production line, we may be interested in the number of defectives we observe in the sample of size 18. If we let X be the random variable that represents the number of defective items in the sample, then X is called a **binomial random variable,** and the associated experiment is called a **binomial experiment**.

Explanation of the term—binomial experiment: A **binomial experiment** is a random experiment that satisfies the following conditions:

• There are two possible outcomes (success or failure) on each trial.
• There is a fixed number of trials, say, n.
• The probability of success, say, p, is fixed from trial to trial.
• The trials are independent.
• The binomial random variable is the number of successes in the n trials.

Binomial experiments occur quite frequently in the real world, and a model has been developed to help compute the probabilities associated with such experiments. Before we discuss the binomial distribution, however, we need to introduce the concept of factorials.

Factorials

Suppose that there are five job positions to be filled by five different applicants. There will be five choices for the first position. Once this is filled, there are only four applicants remaining; thus there will be four choices for the second position. We can continue in this manner until all the positions are filled. Note that there will only be one choice for the last position. By a counting principle, there will be $5 \times 4 \times 3 \times 2 \times 1 = 120$ ways of filling the five positions. We say that there are **5 factorial ways** of filling these positions.

Notation: We will use the symbol ! to represent factorial.

For example

$$5! = 5 \times 4 \times 3 \times 2 \times 1 = 120$$
$$10! = 10 \times 9 \times 8 \times \cdots \times 1 = 3,628,800$$
$$1! = 1$$

We define $0! = 1$.

Binomial Distribution

The function that generates binomial probabilities is given below. It represents the probability of exactly x successes in n trials in a binomial experiment.

$$P(x) = \frac{n!}{x!(n-x)!} p^x (1-p)^{n-x} \quad for \ x = 0,1,2,...,n$$

Example 8-10: Five items are selected at random from a production line. What is the probability of selecting **exactly** two defectives if it is known that the probability of a defective item from this production system is 0.05?

Solution: Let X represent the number of defectives. Then X is a binomial random variable with $n = 5$, $x = 2$, and $p = 0.05$. Substituting into the formula gives

$$P(2)=\frac{5!}{2!(5-2!)}0.05^2(1-0.5)^{5-2}=0.0214$$

That is, the probability of observing two defectives in this binomial experiment is 0.0214, correct to four decimal places.

Example 8-11: A student randomly guesses at 10 multiple-choice questions. Find the probability that the student guesses **exactly** three correctly. Each question has four possible answers with only one correct answer, and each question is independent of every other question.

Solution: Observe that this can be considered as a binomial experiment. We have a fixed number of trials (10 questions), with a probability of success (probability of guessing correctly) of 0.25. Also, the trials (questions) are independent of each other, and there are two possible outcomes on each question (correct guess or incorrect guess). Let X be the number of correct guesses. Then X is a binomial random variable with $n = 10$, $x = 3$, and $p = 0.25$. Substituting into the formula gives

$$P(3)=\frac{10!}{3!(10-3!)}0.25^3(1-0.25)^{10-3}=0.2503$$

That is, the probability of guessing exactly three of the questions correctly is 0.2503, correct to four decimal places.

Example 8-12: For the information given in **Example 8-11**, what is the probability of guessing fewer than three correctly?

Solution: The probability of guessing fewer than three correctly is equivalent to finding $P(X < 3)$. That is, we need to find $P(X < 3) = P(X \leq 2) = P(X = 0 \text{ or } X = 1 \text{ or } X = 2)$. Since $X = 0$ or $X = 1$ or $X = 2$ are mutually exclusive events, then $P(X = 0 \text{ or } X = 1 \text{ or } X = 2) = P(X = 0) + P(X = 1) + P(X = 2)$. Thus

$P(X < 3) = P(X \leq 2) = 0.0563 + 0.1877 + 0.2816 = 0.5256$

Example 8-13: For the information given in **Example 8-11**, what is the probability of guessing more than eight correctly?

Solution: The probability of guessing more than eight correctly is equivalent to finding $P(X > 8)$. That is, we need to find $P(X > 8) = P(X = 9) + P(X = 10)$. Thus

$P(X > 8) = P(X \geq 9) = 0.0000 + 0.0000 = 0.000$ correct to four decimal places.

Quick Tip

Extensive tables can be generated and used to find probabilities of binomial random variables. The drawback, however, is that there is an infinite number of values between 0 and 1 for the probability of success, and therefore, one would not have an exhaustive table for reference.

Example 8-14: From the information given in **Example 8-11**, a table of probabilities and cumulative probabilities was generated. This information is given in **Table 8-8**.

Table 8-8: Binomial Probabilities and Cumulative Probabilities for Example 8-11

x	$P(X = x)$	$P(X \leq x)$
0	0.0563	0.0563
1	0.1877	0.2440
2	0.2816	0.5256
3	0.2503	0.7759
4	0.1460	0.9219
5	0.0584	0.9803
6	0.0162	0.9965
7	0.0031	0.9996
8	0.0004	1.0000
9	0.0000	1.0000
10	0.0000	1.0000

(a) Find the probability that a student correctly guesses between four and six answers, inclusive. Use the **exact** probability values $P(X = x)$ to solve the problem.

Solution: The probability of guessing between four and six answers (inclusive) correctly is equivalent to finding $P(4 \leq X \leq 6)$. That is, we need to find $P(4 \leq X \leq 6) = P(X = 4) + P(X = 5) + P(X = 6) = 0.1460 + 0.0584 + 0.0162 = 0.2206$.

(b) Find the probability of the student correctly guessing between four and six answers, inclusive. Use the **cumulative** probability values $P(X \leq x)$ to solve the problem.

Solution: Note that $P(4 \leq X \leq 6) = P(X \leq 6) - P(X \leq 3)$, as shown in **Figure 8-12**.

Figure 8-12: Display to help find $P(4 \leq X \leq 6)$

Thus $P(4 \leq X \leq 6) = P(X = 4) + P(X = 5) + P(X = 6) = P(X \leq 6) - P(X \leq 3) = 0.9965 - 0.7759 = 0.2206$. Note that by subtracting out $P(X \leq 3)$, we are making sure that the probability of 4 is included in the required probability computations. If we had subtracted out $P(X \leq 4)$, then the probability of 4 would not have been included in the required probability computations, and the solution would have been incorrect.

Mean (Expected Value), Variance, and Standard Deviation for a Binomial Random Variable

The mean, variance, and standard deviation of a binomial random variable can be computed using the following formulas:

$$\boxed{\begin{aligned} \text{Mean } \mu &= np \\ \text{Variance } \sigma^2 &= np(1 - p) \\ \text{Standard deviation} &= \sqrt{np(1 - p)} \end{aligned}}$$

Example 8-15: What is the expected value of the number of correct guesses in **Example 8-11**?

Solution: Since $\mu = n \times p$, then $\mu = 10 \times 0.25 = 2.5$. That is, if the exam is taken a repeated number of times, on average, the student will guess 2.5 of the answers correctly. Observe that 2.5 is an average value, because the student cannot guess 0.5 of an answer correctly.

Technology Corner

All the concepts discussed in this chapter can be computed and illustrated using most statistical software packages. However, using such software for the simpler computations encountered in this chapter would be technology overkill. All scientific and graphical calculators will aid directly in the computations. In addition, the newer calculators, such as the TI-83/84, may have the binomial distribution, from which you can compute binomial probabilities. If you own such a calculator, you should consult the owner's manual to determine what statistical features are included.

Illustration: Figure 8-13 shows the solutions for **Examples 8-11** and **8-12** computed by the MINITAB software. **Figure 8-14** shows the same solutions computed by the TI-83/84 calculator. Other solutions can be obtained with a little mathematical manipulation by the software and the calculator.

```
Example 8-11

Probability Density Function

Binomial with n = 10 and p = 0.250000

      x        P( X = x)
   3.00         0.2503

Example 8-12

Cumulative Distribution Function

Binomial with n = 10 and p = 0.250000

      x        P( X <= x)
   2.00         0.5256
```

Figure 8-13: MINITAB output for Examples 8-11 and 8-12

Example 8-11

Example 8-12

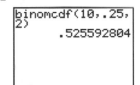

Figure 8-14: TI-83/84 output for Examples 8-11 and 8-12

It's a Wrap Discrete random variable concepts can be investigated through

✓ Discrete probability distributions

✓ Expectation, variance, and standard deviation

✓ Special probability distributions such as the binomial distribution

Again, care always should be taken when computing probabilities. Also, care should be taken when using the expected value and the standard deviation to aid in decision making.

Test Yourself

True/False Questions

1. A random variable can assume only one value with a given probability.
2. A discrete random variable can assume any set of values that can be counted or listed.
3. The values of a continuous random variable cannot be counted or listed.
4. The probability associated with a regular six-sided die falls between 0 and 6 inclusive.
5. The sum of all associated probabilities for an experiment is sometimes less than 1.
6. The expected value for any discrete random variable X is always, $\Sigma x \times P(x)$, where $P(x)$ is the probability of x.
7. The variance for any discrete random variable X is $\sqrt{\Sigma (x - \mu)^2 P(x)}$
8. In a binomial experiment, the number of trials is infinite.
9. In a binomial experiment, the trials can be dependent on each other.
10. In a binomial experiment, there are exactly two possible outcomes for each trial.
11. The amount of time you study for an exam is a discrete random variable.
12. The formula $\mu = np$ can be used to find the expected value for any discrete random variable.
13. Discrete random variables may assume only positive values.
14. The length of any page in any of your textbooks is a continuous random variable.
15. The height of a basketball player is a continuous random variable.
16. Sometimes a continuous random variable may be discrete.
17. The expected value of a binomial random variable consisting of nine trials and probability of failure of 0.3 is 2.7 if a failure is considered to be a successful outcome.
18. The mean of a discrete random variable is also called the expected value of the random variable.
19. The standard deviation for a binomial distribution is equal to $np(1 - p)$, where n is the number of trials, and p is the probability of success.
20. A random variable is a rule that assigns one and only one numerical value to each point in the sample space for a random experiment.

Completion Questions

1. A discrete random variable takes on different values, with each value with an associated (probability, mean) _____.
2. A random variable that can assume any of a set of possible values that can be counted or listed is a (discrete, continuous) _____ random variable.
3. A random variable that can assume any value in an interval on the real number line is a (discrete, continuous) _____ random variable.
4. For any discrete probability distribution, the sum of all associated probabilities must be equal to (0, 1) _____.
5. The mean μ of a discrete random variable X with probability $P(x)$ is given by ($x P(x)$, $\Sigma x P(x)$) _____.
6. In a binomial experiment, the individual trials are (independent, dependent) _____ of each other.
7. The variance for a binomial distribution with n trials and probability of success p is obtained by computing $\{np, np(1 - p), p(1 - p)\}$ _____.
8. The average value for a discrete random variable is called the _____ of the random variable.
9. Name a discrete probability distribution. _____

10. The number of pages in your statistics book is a (discrete, continuous) _____ random variable, and the length of any page in the text is a (discrete, continuous) _____ random variable.

11. Every probability value associated with a discrete random variable in a probability distribution must lie between (0, 0.5, 1) _____ and (0, 0.5, 1) _____, inclusive.

12. In a binomial experiment, if the probability of success is p, then the probability of failure is (1, p, 1 − p) _____.

13. A (discrete, continuous) _____ random variable is one that can assume any of an infinite number of different values in an interval that cannot be counted or listed.

14. A random variable is a rule that assigns one and only one numerical value to each point in the (sample space, number line) _____ for a random experiment.

15. The standard deviation is used instead of the variance because it has the same (value, units) _____ as the associated variable.

Multiple-Choice Questions

1. Given the following probability distribution for a random variable X:

x	1	2	3	4	5	6	7
P(x)	0.15	0.2	0.1	0.2	0.1	0.15	0.1

the probability that X is an odd number is

(a) 0.65.

(b) 0.35.

(c) 0.55.

(d) 0.45.

2. Given the following probability distribution for a random variable X:

x	1	2	3	4	5	6	7
P(x)	0.15	0.2	0.1	0.2	0.1	0.15	0.1

the mean of X is

(a) 3.75.

(b) 4.00.

(c) 1.65.

(d) 2.10.

3. Given the following probability distribution for a random variable X:

x	1	2	3	4	5	6	7
P(x)	0.15	0.2	0.1	0.2	0.1	0.15	0.1

the standard deviation of X is

(a) 1.9378.
(b) 1.9462.
(c) 3.7875.
(d) 3.7550.

4. Which of the following **does not** represent a probability distribution?

(a)		(b)		(c)		(d)	
X	P(X)	X	P(X)	X	P(X)	X	P(X)
3	0.4	−2	0.60	0	0.2	0.25	0.2
5	0.3	−1	0.30	1	0.6	0.50	0.3
7	0.3	0	0.10	2	0.3	0.75	0.5

5. In an experiment where the probability of a success is 0.4 and you are interested in the probability of two successes out of seven trials, the correct probability for this situation is
(a) 0.0774.
(b) 0.1600.
(c) 0.2613.
(d) 0.0016.

6. A statistics instructor (with at least 20 years of teaching experience with the same course) has established that 10 percent of all the students who take his course receive a failing grade. If 10 students have enrolled in his course for the next semester, the probability that **at most one** of these students will fail is
(a) 0.387.
(b) 0.100.
(c) 0.651.
(d) 0.736.

7. A statistics instructor (with at least 20 years of teaching experience with the same course) has established that 10 percent of all the students who take his course receive a failing grade. If 10 students have enrolled in his course for the next semester, the probability that **more than one** of these students will fail is
(a) 0.349.
(b) 0.264.
(c) 1.000.
(d) 0.613.

8. A statistics instructor (with at least 20 years of teaching experience with the same course) has established that 10 percent of all the students who take his course receive a failing grade. If 10 students have enrolled in his course for the next semester, the mean number of students who will fail is
(a) 1.0.
(b) 2.0.
(c) 0.5.
(d) 20.

9. A statistics instructor (with at least 20 years of teaching experience with the same course) has established that 10 percent of all the students who take his course receive a failing grade. If 10 students have enrolled in his course for the next semester, the variance for the number of students who fail is
    (a) 1.0000.
    (b) 9.0000.
    (c) 0.9000.
    (d) 0.9487.

10. A multiple-choice examination has 15 questions. Each question has four possible answers, of which only one is correct. The probability that by just guessing a student will get **exactly** 7 correct is
    (a) 0.039.
    (b) 0.727.
    (c) 0.273.
    (d) 0.561.

11. The probability distribution for a random variable X is given below:

x	-3	-2	0	2	3
$P(x)$	0.1	0.3	0.2	0.3	0.1

The mean of the distribution is
    (a) 0.00.
    (b) -2.5.
    (c) $+2.5$.
    (d) 2.00.

12. The probability distribution for a random variable X is given below:

x	-3	-2	0	2	3
$P(x)$	0.1	0.3	0.2	0.3	0.1

The variance of the distribution is
    (a) 0.0000.
    (b) 4.2000.
    (c) 2.0494.
    (d) $2\sqrt{13}$.

13. Which of the following is **not** a property of a binomial experiment?
    (a) The number of trials is fixed.
    (b) There are exactly two possible outcomes for each trial.
    (c) The individual trials are dependent on each other.
    (d) The probability of success is the same for each trial.

14. If n is the number of trials and p is the probability of success for a binomial experiment, the standard deviation for the resulting binomial distribution is

    (a) $\sqrt{n(1-p)}$.

    (b) $\sqrt{p(1-p)}$.

    (c) $\sqrt{np}$.

    (d) $\sqrt{np(1-p)}$.

15. $n!$ (n factorial) could be defined as

    (a) $n(n-1)(n-2)\cdots(3)(2)(1), n > 0$.

    (b) $n(n-1)(n-2)\cdots(3)(2)(1), n \geq 0$.

    (c) $n(n-1)(n-2)\cdots(3)(2)(1), n > 1$.

    (d) $n(n-1)(n-2)\cdots(3)(2)(1), n \geq 1$.

16. Given the following distribution function,

x	0	1	2	3	4
$P(x)$	0.3	0.05	0.1	0.35	0.2

the computed mean is

    (a) 2.0000.

    (b) 2.1000.

    (c) 0.2000.

    (d) 2.4000.

17. If a fair coin is tossed five times and the number of tails is observed, the probability that exactly two tails are observed is

    (a) 2/5.

    (b) 5/16.

    (c) 1/2.

    (d) 15/64.

18. A loan officer has indicated that 80 percent of all loan application forms have zero errors. If six forms are selected at random, the probability that **exactly** two of them will have at least one error is

    (a) 0.150.

    (b) 0.040.

    (c) 0.850.

    (d) 0.246.

19. A loan officer has indicated that 80 percent of all loan application forms have zero errors. If six forms are selected at random, the probability that **at most** one of them will have at least one error is

    (a) 0.655.

    (b) 0.002.

    (c) 0.393.

    (c) 0.607.

20. A loan officer has indicated that 80 percent of all loan application forms have zero errors. If six forms are selected at random, the mean number of forms that will have **at least** one error is

(a) 4.8.

(b) 1.2.

(c) 1/6.

(d) 0.0.

21. A loan officer has indicated that 80 percent of all loan application forms have zero errors. If six forms are selected at random, the standard deviation for the number of forms with **at least** one error is

(a) 4.8000.

(b) 1.2000.

(c) 0.9600.

(d) 0.9798.

22. Which of the following **does not** represent a probability distribution?

(a)			(b)			(c)			(d)	
X	$P(X)$		X	$P(X)$		X	$P(X)$		X	$P(X)$
3	0.5		−2	0.60		0	0.04		0.25	0.32
5	0.5		−1	−0.30		1	0.63		0.50	0.30
7	0.0		0	0.70		2	0.33		−0.75	0.38

23. The value of p that makes the following table a probability distribution is

X	−2	−1	0	1	2
$P(x)$	0.13	0.17	p	0.19	0.22

(a) 0.3000.

(b) 0.1800.

(c) 0.4100.

(d) 0.2900.

24. If X is a random variable with the following probability distribution

X	1	2	3	4
$P(x)$	p	0.4	0.25	0.3

then the mean for X

(a) cannot be determined.

(b) is 2.75.

(c) is $2.75 + p$.

(d) is 2.8.

25. The owner of a pawn shop knows that 80 percent of the customers who enter her store will pawn an item. If there are 13 customers in the shop, the probability that **at most** 6 will pawn an item is

(a) 0.006.

(b) 0.001.

(c) 0.930.

(d) 0.007.

26. If a fair six-sided die with face values numbered 1, 3, 5, 7, 9, and 11 is rolled a very large number of times, then the average face value will be

(a) 3.5.

(b) 6.0.

(c) 7.0.

(d) 5.0.

27. A statistics professor (with at least 20 years of teaching a particular statistics course) has established a probability distribution for grades a student can earn in that course. The following table gives the distribution, where x is the grade and $P(x)$ is the corresponding probability for the grade:

GRADE	F	D	C	B	A
x	0	1	2	3	4
$P(x)$	0.12	0.15	0.35	0.30	0.08

The mean grade will be

(a) 2.00.

(b) 2.19.

(c) 2.07.

(d) 2.17.

28. A statistics professor (with at least 20 years of teaching a particular statistics course) has established a probability distribution for grades a student can earn in that course. The following table gives the distribution, where x is the grade and $P(x)$ is the corresponding probability for the grade:

GRADE	F	D	C	B	A
x	0	1	2	3	4
$P(x)$	0.12	0.15	0.35	0.30	0.08

The variance for the grade distribution will be

(a) 3.4600.

(b) 1.2451.

(c) 3.5300.

(d) 1.5300.

29. A statistics professor (with at least 20 years of teaching a particular statistics course) has established a probability distribution for grades a student can earn in that course. The following table gives the distribution, where x is the grade and $P(x)$ is the corresponding probability for the grade:

GRADE	F	D	C	B	A
x	0	1	2	3	4
$P(x)$	0.12	0.15	0.35	0.30	0.08

The standard deviation for the grade distribution will be

(a) 1.8601.

(b) 1.2369.

(c) 1.8788.

(d) 1.1158.

30. A statistics professor (with at least 20 years of teaching a particular statistics course) has established a probability distribution for grades a student can earn in that course. The following table gives the distribution, where x is the grade and $P(x)$ is the corresponding probability for the grade:

GRADE	F	D	C	B	A
x	0	1	2	3	4
$P(x)$	0.12	0.15	0.35	0.30	0.08

What is the probability that a student will earn a grade of A for this course?

(a) 0.20

(b) 0.08

(c) 0.92

(d) 0.12

31. A statistics professor (with at least 20 years of teaching a particular statistics course) has established a probability distribution for grades a student can earn in that course. The following table gives the distribution, where x is the grade and $P(x)$ is the corresponding probability for the grade:

GRADE	F	D	C	B	A
x	0	1	2	3	4
$P(x)$	0.12	0.15	0.35	0.30	0.08

What is the probability that a student will earn a grade of C or better for this course?

(a) 0.38

(b) 0.62

(c) 0.73

(d) 0.35

32. A statistics professor (with at least 20 years of teaching a particular statistics course) has established a probability distribution for grades a student can earn in that course. The following table gives the distribution, where x is the grade and $P(x)$ is the corresponding probability for the grade:

GRADE	F	D	C	B	A
x	0	1	2	3	4
$P(x)$	0.12	0.15	0.35	0.30	0.08

What is the probability that a student will earn a grade of D or worse for this course?

(a) 0.15

(b) 0.27

(c) 0.88

(d) 0.73

33. A statistics professor (with at least 20 years of teaching a particular statistics course) has established a probability distribution for grades a student can earn in that course. The following table gives the distribution, where x is the grade and $P(x)$ is the corresponding probability for the grade:

GRADE	F	D	C	B	A
x	0	1	2	3	4
$P(x)$	0.12	0.15	0.35	0.30	0.08

What is the probability that a student will earn a grade of at least B for this course?

(a) 0.30

(b) 0.62

(c) 0.38

(d) 0.92

34. A telephone company claims that 90 percent of the time when customers call for directory assistance, the customer is given the correct number. If 10 customers call directory assistance for help with telephone numbers, what is the probability that **exactly** 6 of them will be given the correct number?

(a) 0.0111

(b) 0.0001

(c) 0.9999

(d) 0.0000

35. A telephone company claims that 90 percent of the time when customers call for directory assistance, the customer is given the correct number. If 10 customers call directory assistance for help with telephone numbers, what is the probability that **at least** 6 of them will be given the correct number?

(a) 0.0016

(b) 0.0128

(c) 0.9984

(d) 0.9872

36. A telephone company claims that 90 percent of the time when customers call for directory assistance, the customer is given the correct number. If 10 customers call directory assistance for help with telephone numbers, what is the probability that **more than** 6 of them will be given the correct number?

(a) 0.0128

(b) 0.0112

(c) 0.0015

(d) 0.9872

37. A telephone company claims that 90 percent of the time when customers call for directory assistance, the customer is given the correct number. If 10 customers call directory assistance for help with telephone numbers, what is the probability that **between** 6 **and** 8 (including both end points) of them will be given the wrong number?

(a) 0.2623
(b) Approximately zero
(c) 0.0574
(d) 0.2511

38. A telephone company claims that 90 percent of the time when customers call for directory assistance, the customer is given the correct number. If repeated numbers of 10 customers who call directory assistance for help with telephone numbers are sampled, what will be the average number of correct telephone numbers given out to the customers?
    (a) 5
    (b) 1
    (c) 90
    (d) 9

39. A telephone company claims that 90 percent of the time when customers call for directory assistance, the customer is given the correct number. If repeated numbers of 10 customers who call directory assistance for help with telephone numbers are sampled, what will be the average number of incorrect telephone numbers given out to the customers?
    (a) 5
    (b) 1
    (c) 90
    (d) 9

40. A telephone company claims that 90 percent of the time when customers call for directory assistance, the customer is given the correct number. If 10 customers call directory assistance for help with telephone numbers, what is the probability that **none** of them will be given the wrong number?
    (a) 0.0000
    (b) 0.6513
    (c) 0.3487
    (d) 1.0000

Further Exercises

If possible, you could use any technology help available to solve the following problems.

1. Suppose that on a very large campus 2.5 percent of the students are foreign students. If 30 students are selected at random from the student body,

    (a) find the probability that fewer than 7 from this group are foreign students.
    (b) find the probability that the number of foreign students in this group will be between 2 and 8 inclusive.
    (c) find the mean number of foreign students if repeated groups of 30 students are selected at random.

2. For a binomial distribution with $n = 20$ and $p = 0.4$, which of the following is(are) not true?

(a) The largest probability for this distribution occurs at a random variable value of 8.
(b) The distribution is symmetrical.
(c) The mean for this distribution is 8.
(d) The standard deviation for this distribution is 2.1909.

3. From past studies it is known that 60 percent of the students at a given campus read the weekly campus newspaper. Your statistics professor recently wrote an article on the odds of winning the state lottery in this paper and would like to refer to this article during his lecture. If the class size is 20,

(a) what is the probability that none of the students read the article?
(b) what is the probability that fewer than 5 students read the article?
(c) what is the probability that at least 5 of the students read the article?
(d) what is the probability that at least 75 percent of the students read the article?
(e) what is the mean number of students who did not read the article?
(f) what is the variance for the number of students who read the article?

4. Because of no-shows, airlines commonly overbook their flights. An airline sells 100 tickets for a flight that could carry at most 95 passengers. If the probability that a passenger is a no-show is 0.10 and that passengers arrive for the flight independent of each other, find

(a) the probability that every passenger that shows up will be able to get on the flight.
(b) the probability that not every passenger that shows up will be able to get on the flight.
(c) the probability that the plane departs with empty seats.

5. A college finds that 40 percent of all students take a course in statistics. If a group of 8 students is considered, find the probability that

(a) precisely 6 of them take statistics.
(b) at least 6 of them take statistics.

6. (a) Find the value of the unknown probability p that makes the following table into probability distribution.

x	0	1	2	3	4
$P(x)$	0.226	p	0.328	0.215	0.106

(b) If X represents the number of successes in an experiment, use the table to find the probability of at most three successes.
(c) Find the mean of X.
(d) Find the standard deviation of X.

7. A small town has 15 walk−do-not-walk traffic signals that operate independently of one another. The probability is 0.98 that at any given time these signals will be operating properly.

(a) If X is the random variable representing the number of signals that operate properly, what kind (give a name) of random variable is X?
(b) Find the mean of the random variable named in (a).

(c) Find the variance of the random variable named in (a).

(d) Find the probability that all 15 signals are operating properly.

(e) Find the probability that exactly 13 of the signals will be operating properly.

(f) Find the probability that more than 10 of the signals are operating properly.

8. In a recent study it was found that 1 of every 50 Pap smears sampled was misdiagnosed by a certain lab. In a sample of 100,

(a) find the probability that exactly 3 will be misdiagnosed.

(b) find the probability that between 2 and 4 (inclusive) will be misdiagnosed.

(c) find the probability that at most 4 will be misdiagnosed.

9. In a religious survey of southerners it was found that 82 percent believed in angels. In a sample of 20 southerners,

(a) find the probability that exactly 5 will believe in angels.

(b) find the probability that between 12 and 14 (inclusive) will believe in angels.

(c) find the probability that at most 4 will not believe in angels.

ANSWER KEY

True/False Questions

1. F   2. T   3. T   4. F   5. F   6. T   7. F   8. F   9. F   10. T
11. F   12. F   13. F   14. T   15. T   16. F   17. T   18. T   19. F   20. T

Completion Questions

1. probability   2. discrete   3. continuous   4. 1   5. $\Sigma xP(x)$ 6. independent
7. $np(1 - p)$ 8. mean (expected value)   9. Binomial   10. discrete, continuous
11. 0, 1   12. $(1 - p)$ 13. continuous   14. sample space   15. units

Multiple-Choice Questions

1. (d)   2. (a)   3. (b)   4. (c)   5. (c)   6. (d)   7. (b)   8. (a)   9. (c)
10. (a)   11. (a)   12. (b)   13. (c)   14. (d)   15. (d)   16. (b)   17. (b)   18. (d)
19. (a)   20. (b)   21. (d)   22. (b)   23. (d)   24. (d)   25. (d)   26. (b)   27. (c)
28. (b)   29. (d)   30. (b)   31. (c)   32. (b)   33. (c)   34. (a)   35. (c)   36. (d)
37. (b)   38. (d)   39. (b)   40. (c)

Further Exercises

1. (a) 0.9999; (b) 0.1721; (c) 0.75 (exact average) or approximately 1.

2. (a) True; probability = 0.1797; (b) Not true—slightly skewed to the right;

   (c) True; mean = $n \times p = 20 \times 0.4 = 8$;

   (d) True; standard deviation $\sqrt{n \times p \times (1 - p)} = \sqrt{20 \times 0.4 \times 0.6} = 2.1909$.

3. (a) 0; (b) 0.0003; (c) 0.9997; (d) 0.1256.

4. (a) $P(x \le 95) = 1$; (b) $P(x > 95) = 0$; (c) $P(x < 95) = 1$, where x is the number of passengers who show up for the flight.

5. (a) 0.0413; (b) 0.0498.

6. (a) 0.894; (b) 1.85; (c) 1.2828.

7. (a) binomial; (b) 14.7; (c) 0.294; (d) 0.7386; (e) 0.0323; (f) 0.9999 (approximately 1).

8. (a) 0.1823; (b) 0.5459; (c) 0.9492.

9. (a) 0; (b) 0.1307; (c) 0.7151.

CHAPTER 9

The Normal Probability Distribution

You should read this chapter if you need to review or to learn about

→ The normal probability distribution

→ The standard normal probability distribution

→ z scores

→ Probability associated with any normal probability distribution

---

Get Started

Here we will focus on a special continuous random variable that can assume any value in the interval $(-\infty, +\infty)$. That is, the random variable can assume any value on the real number line. The distribution for this random variable is called the *normal distribution* and originally was called the *Gaussian distribution* in honor of Karl Gauss, who in 1833 published a work describing it. This distribution is considered the most important probability distribution in all of statistics. A picture of a normal distribution is shown in Figure 9-1.

Figure 9-1: The normal probability distribution

9-1   The Normal Probability Distribution

The normal distribution can be viewed as the limiting distribution of a binomial random variable. That is, in a binomial experiment, if we use a fixed probability of success p, we can analyze what happens as the number of trials n increases. One way to visualize what happens is to construct histograms for a fixed p and increasingly large n. **Figures 9-2** through **9-7** show histograms for $n = 5, 10, 25$, and 50, with $p = 0.1$ when the simulation was done 1,000 times. Superimposed on the histograms are smooth curves that show the shapes of the distributions. Observe that as n increases for a fixed $p = 0.1$, the shape of the smooth curve becomes increasingly bell-shaped. This bell-shaped curve is associated with the normal distribution. Similar results can be observed for different p values.

Note: If you have access to statistical software, simulate values for a binomial random variable with different p and n values, and graph to observe other patterns.

Figure 9-2 shows the histogram for 1,000 simulations from a binomial distribution with the number of trials $n = 5$ and the probability of success $p = 0.1$. The number of simulations with 0, 1, 2, 3, 4, and 5 successes was recorded, and a frequency histogram with these values is shown in **Figure 9-2**. Observe that the smooth curve that is used to approximate the distrubution is skewed to the right.

Figure 9-2: Histogram with curve for $n = 5$ and $p = 0.1$

Figure 9-3 shows the histogram for 1,000 simulations of a binomial distribution with the number of trials $n = 10$ and the probability of success $p = 0.1$. The number of simulations with 0, 1, 2, 3, 4, ..., 10 successes was recorded, and a frequency histogram with these values is shown in **Figure 9-3**. Observe that the smooth curve that is used to approximate the distrubution is still skewed to the right but not as acute as in **Figure 9-2**.

Figure 9-3: Histogram with curve for $n = 10$ and $p = 0.1$

Figure 9-4 shows the histogram for 1,000 simulations of a binomial distribution with the number of trials $n = 25$ and the probability of success $p = 0.1$. The number of simulations with $0, 1, 2, 3, 4, \ldots, 25$ successes was recorded, and a frequency histogram with these values is shown in **Figure 9-4**. Observe that the smooth curve that is used to approximate the distrubution is still slightly skewed to the right but not as acute as in **Figure 9-3**.

Figure 9-4: Histogram with curve for $n = 25$ and $p = 0.1$

Figure 9-5 shows the histogram for 1,000 simulations of a binomial distribution with the number of trials $n = 50$ and the probability of success $p = 0.1$. The number of simulations with $0, 1, 2, 3, 4, \ldots, 50$ successes was recorded, and a frequency histogram with these values is shown in **Figure 9-5**. Observe that the smooth curve that is used to approximate the distrubution is almost symmetrical.

Figure 9-5: Histogram with curve for $n = 50$ and $p = 0.1$

Figures 9-2 through **9-5** show that as the number of trials is increased and the probability of success is held fixed, the approximation to the frequency distribution for the number of successes becomes more and more bell-shaped.

The following two diagrams, **Figures 9-6** and **9-7**, show distributions for $n = 10$ and $p = 0.5$ and $n = 100$ and $p = 0.6$, respectively.

Figures 9-6 and **9-7** show that as the probability of success remains around 0.5 and the number of trials increases, the approximation to the frequency distribution for the number of successes becomes more and more bell-shaped.

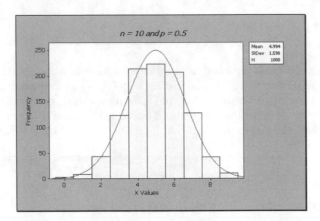

Figure 9-6: Histogram with curve for $n = 10$ and $p = 0.5$

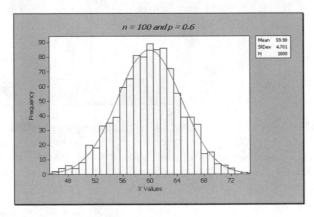

Figure 9-7: Histogram with curve for $n = 100$ and $p = 0.6$

As mentioned earlier, the normal distribution is considered to be the most important probability distribution in all of statistics. It is used to describe the distribution of many natural phenomena, such as the height of a person, IQ score, weight, blood pressure, etc.

9-2 Properties of the Normal Distribution

The mathematical equation for the normal distribution is

$$y = \frac{e^{-(x-\mu)^2/2\sigma^2}}{\sigma\sqrt{2\pi}}$$

where $e \approx 2.718$, $\pi \approx 3.14$, μ = population mean, and σ = population standard deviation. When this equation is graphed for a given μ and σ, a continuous, bell-shaped, symmetrical graph will result. Thus we can display an infinite number of graphs for this equation, depending on the values of μ and σ. In such a case we say that we have a **family** of normal curves. Some representations of normal distribution curves are shown in **Figures 9-8** through **9-10**.

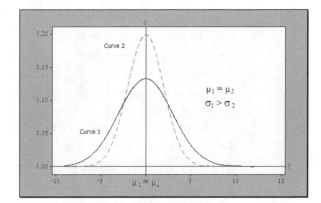

Figure 9-8: Normal distributions with the same mean but with different standard deviations

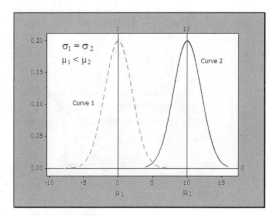

Figure 9-9: Normal distributions with different means but with the same standard deviations

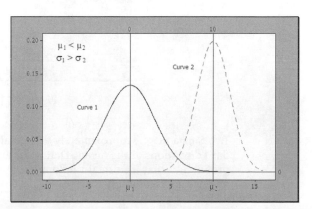

Figure 9-10: Normal distributions with different means and different standard deviations

Note that these normal curves have similar shapes but are located at different points along the x axis. Also, the larger the standard deviation, the more spread out is the distribution, and the curves are symmetrical about the mean value.

Explanation of the term—normal distribution: A **normal distribution** is a continuous, symmetrical, bell-shaped distribution of a normal random variable.

Summary of the Properties of the Normal Distribution

- The curve is continuous.
- The curve is bell-shaped.
- The curve is symmetrical about the mean.
- The mean, median, and mode are located at the center of the distribution and are equal to each other.
- The curve is unimodal (single mode).
- The curve never touches the x axis.
- The total area under the normal curve is equal to 1.

A very important property of any normal distribution is that within a fixed number of standard deviations from the mean, all normal distributions have the same fraction of their probabilities. **Figures 9-11** through **9-13** illustrate this for $\pm 1\sigma$, $\pm 2\sigma$, and $\pm 3\sigma$ from the mean. Recall that this was discussed in **Chapter 3** as the **empirical rule**.

Empirical Rule Revisited

One Sigma Rule: Approximately 68 percent of the data values should lie within one standard deviation of the mean. That is, regardless of the shape of the normal distribution, the probability that a normal random variable will be within one standard deviation of the mean is approximately equal to 0.68. This is illustrated in **Figure 9-11**.

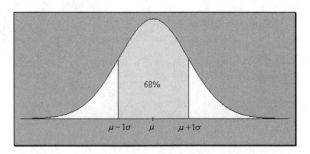

Figure 9-11: One sigma rule

Two Sigma Rule: Approximately 95 percent of the data values should lie within two standard deviations of the mean. That is, regardless of the shape of the normal distribution, the probability that a normal random variable will be within two standard deviations of the mean is approximately equal to 0.95. This is illustrated in **Figure 9-12**.

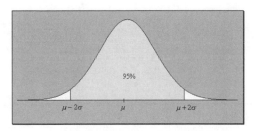

Figure 9-12: Two sigma rule

Three Sigma Rule: Approximately 99.7 percent of the data values should lie within three standard deviations of the mean. That is, regardless of the shape of the normal distribution, the probability that a normal random variable will be within three standard deviations of the mean is approximately equal to 0.997. This is illustrated in **Figure 9-13**.

Figure 9-13: Three sigma rule

Quick Tip

1. The total area under the normal curve is equal to 1.
2. The probability that the normal random variable is equal to a given discrete value is always zero because the normal random variable is continuous.
3. The probability that a normal random variable is between two values is given by the area under the normal curve between the two given values and the horizontal axis.

9-3 The Standard Normal Distribution

Since each normally distributed random variable has its own mean and standard deviation, the shape and central location of the normal curves will vary. Thus one would have to have information on the areas for all the normal distributions. This, of course, would be impractical. Therefore, we use information for a special normal distribution called the **standard normal distribution** to simplify this situation.

Explanation of the term—standard normal distribution: The **standard normal distribution** is a normal distribution with a mean of 0 and a standard deviation of 1.

Any normal random variable can be converted to a standard normal random variable by computing the corresponding *z* **score**. The *z* score is computed from the following formula:

$$z = \frac{\text{value} - \text{mean}}{\text{standard deviation}} = \frac{x - \mu}{\sigma}$$

In this equation, x is the value of a normal random variable X with mean μ and standard deviation σ.

Quick Tip

The z score is a random variable that is normally distributed with a mean of 0 and a standard deviation of 1.

Recall that a z score gives the number of standard deviations that a specific value is above or below the mean.

Extensive tables can be constructed for the standard normal random variable to aid in finding areas (probabilities) under the standard normal curve. Usually, standard normal tables give the area between the mean of 0 and a value z, as shown in **Figure 9-14**.

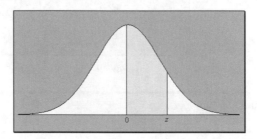

Figure 9-14: Area under standard normal curve between 0 and z

A sample portion of a table using four decimal places is shown in **Table 9-1**.

Table 9-1: Sample of the Standard Normal Table

z	0.00	0.01	0.02	0.03
0.0	0.0000	0.0040	0.0080	0.0120
0.1	0.0398	0.0438	0.0478	0.0517
0.2	0.0793	0.0832	0.0871	0.0910
0.3	0.1179	0.1217	0.1255	0.1293
0.4	0.1554	0.1591	0.1628	0.1664
0.5	0.1915	0.1950	0.1985	0.2019
0.6	0.2257	0.2291	0.2324	0.2357
0.7	0.2580	0.2611	0.2642	0.2673
0.8	0.2881	0.2910	0.2939	0.2967
0.9	0.3159	0.3186	0.3212	0.3238
1.0	0.3413	0.3438	0.3461	0.3485

The first column in **Table 9-1** gives the z values correct to one decimal place, and the first row gives the second decimal place for a z score. For example, if we wanted to find the area between $z = 0$ and $z = 0.92$, we will find $z = 0.9$ in the first column and then look for $z = 0.02$ along the first row. Where the corresponding row and column intersect gives the value of 0.3212. This is the area between $z = 0$ and $z = 0.92$. This is equivalent to finding $P(0 \leq z \leq 0.92)$, and the area is depicted in **Figure 9-15**.

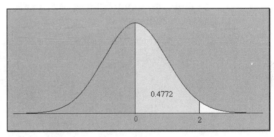

Figure 9-15: Area representing $P(0 \leq z \leq 0.92)$

More extensive tables are given in the **Appendix** of this text. Refer to them to solve problems in this chapter.

Example 9-1: Find the area under the standard normal curve between $z = 0$ and $z = 2.0$.

Solution: This is equivalent to finding $P(0 \leq z \leq 2.0)$. From the standard normal tables in the **Appendix**, for $z = 2.0$, the corresponding value is 0.4772. Thus $P(0 \leq z \leq 2) = 0.4772$. This is shown in **Figure 9-16**.

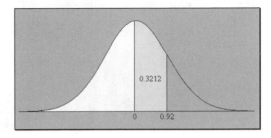

Figure 9-16: Area for $P(0 \leq z \leq 2)$

Example 9-2: Find the area under the standard normal curve between $z = 0$ and $z = -1.8$.

Solution: This is equivalent to finding $P(-1.8 \leq z \leq 0)$. Now, from the symmetry of the distribution, $P(-1.8 \leq z \leq 0) = P(0 \leq z \leq 1.8)$. From the standard normal tables in the **Appendix** the end of the text, for $z = 1.8$, the corresponding value is 0.4641. Thus $P(-1.8 \leq z \leq 0) = 0.4641$. This is shown in **Figure 9-17**.

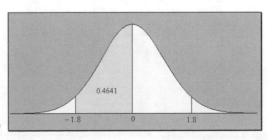

Figure 9-17: Area for $P(-1.8 \leq z \leq 0)$

Example 9-3: Find the area under the standard normal distribution curve to the right of z = 1.5.

Solution: This is equivalent to finding $P(z \geq 1.5)$. From the standard normal tables in the **Appendix** the end of the text, for $z = 1.5$, the corresponding value is 0.4332. But this is the area between 0 and 1.5. Since the total area under the curve is 1, and because of the symmetry of the distribution, the total area to the right of 0 will be equal to 0.5. Thus the required area for $P(z \geq 1.5) = 0.5 - 0.4332 = 0.0668$. This is shown in **Figure 9-18**.

Figure 9-18: Area for $P\ (z \geq 1.5)$

Example 9-4: Find the area under the standard normal distribution curve to the left of z = −1.75.

Solution: This is equivalent to finding $P(z \leq -1.75)$. Now, from the symmetry of the distribution, $P(z \leq -1.75) = P(z \geq 1.75)$. So now this is a similar problem to **Example 9-3**. From the standard normal tables in the **Appendix** for $z = 1.75$, the corresponding value is 0.4599. But this is the area between 0 and 1.75. Since the total area under the curve is 1, and because of the symmetry of the distribution, the total area to the right of 0 will be equal to 0.5. Thus the required area for $P(z \leq -1.75) = P(z \geq 1.75) = 0.5 - 0.4599 = 0.0401$. This is shown in **Figure 9-19**.

Figure 9-19: Area for $P(z \leq -1.75)$

Example 9-5: Find the area under the standard normal distribution curve between $z = 1.5$ and $z = 2.5$.

Solution: We need to find $P(1.5 \leq z \leq 2.5)$. This is equivalent to finding $P(0 \leq z \leq 2.5) - P(0 \leq z \leq 1.5)$. From the standard normal tables in the **Appendix**, for $z = 2.5$, the corresponding value is 0.4938, and for $z = 1.5$, the corresponding value is 0.4332. Thus the required area for $P(1.5 \leq z \leq 2.5) = P(0 \leq z \leq 2.5) - P(0 \leq z \leq 1.5) = 0.4938 - 0.4332 = 0.0606$. This is shown **Figure 9-20**.

Figure 9-20: Area for $P(1.5 \leq z \leq 2.5)$

Example 9-6: Find the area under the standard normal distribution curve between $z = -2.78$ and $z = -1.66$.

Solution: This is equivalent to finding $P(-2.78 \leq z \leq -1.66)$. Because of the symmetry of the distribution, this is equivalent to finding $P(1.66 \leq z \leq 2.78) = P(0 \leq z \leq 2.78) - P(0 \leq z \leq 1.66)$. From the standard normal tables in the **Appendix**, for $z = 2.78$, the corresponding value is 0.4973, and for $z = 1.66$, the corresponding value is 0.4515. Thus the required area for $P(1.66 \leq z \leq 2.78) = P(0 \leq z \leq 2.78) - P(0 \leq z \leq 1.66) = 0.4973 - 0.4515 = 0.0458$. This is shown in **Figure 9-21**.

Figure 9-21: Area for $P(-2.78 \leq z \leq -1.66)$

Example 9-7: Find the area under the standard normal distribution curve between $z = -2.79$ and $z = 1.71$.

Solution: We need to find $P(-2.79 \leq z \leq 1.71)$. This is equivalent to finding $P(-2.79 \leq z \leq 0) + P(0 \leq z \leq 1.71) = P(0 \leq z \leq 2.79) + P(0 \leq z \leq 1.71) = 0.4974 + 0.4564 = 0.9538$. This is shown in **Figure 9-22**.

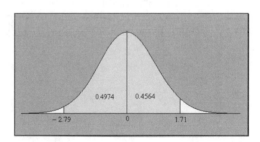

Figure 9-22: Area for $P(-2.79 \leq z < 1.71)$

Example 9-8: Find the area under the standard normal distribution curve to the right of $z = -2.79$.

Solution: We need to find $P(z \geq -2.79)$. Now, $P(z \geq -2.79) = 0.4974 + 0.5 = 0.99974$. This is shown in **Figure 9-23**.

Figure 9-23: Area for $P(z \geq -2.79)$

Note: Other problems can be illustrated that may involve any combination of the preceding situations.

Quick Tips

In solving problems relating to the standard normal distribution, it might be helpful if you use the following procedure:
• Write out the equivalent probability statement.
• Draw a normal curve.
• Shade in the desired area.
• Use the standard normal distribution table to find the shaded area.

9-4   Applications of the Normal Distribution

We can use the standard normal distribution curve to solve problems involving variables that are normally or approximately normally distributed. To solve problems involving normal random variables, we need to transform the original normal variable into a standard normal random variable by using

$$z = \frac{\text{value} - \text{mean}}{\text{standard deviation}} = \frac{x - \mu}{\sigma}$$

In this equation, x is the value of a normal random variable X with mean μ and standard deviation σ. Once the transformation is made, the problem may be reduced to one similar to those presented in the preceding section.

Figure 9-24: Area for $P(X > 110) = P$ $(z > 2)$

Example 9-9: If IQ scores are normally distributed with a mean of 100 and a standard deviation of 5, what is the probability that a person chosen at random will have an IQ score greater than 110?

Solution: Let X = IQ score. Then we need to find $P(X > 110)$. The equivalent z score is $z = (110 - 100)/5 = 2$. Thus $P(X > 110) = P(z > 2) = 0.5 - 0.4772 = 0.0228$. That is, only 2.28 percent of this population will have an IQ score greater than 110. This is shown in **Figure 9-24**.

Quick Tip

All application problems involving the normal distribution can be reduced to simple problems using z scores. These reduced problems can be solved in the same way as the preceding examples or combinations of them.

Example 9-10: Suppose that family incomes in a town are normally distributed with a mean of \$1,200 and a standard deviation of \$600 per month. What is the probability that a family has an income between \$1,400 and \$2,250?

Solution: Let X = family income. Thus we need to find $P(1,400 \leq X \leq 2,250)$. First, we need to transform the values of 1,400 and 2,250 to z scores. Let $z_1 = (1,400 - 1,200)/600 = 0.33$ and $z_2 = (2,250 - 1,200)/600 = 1.75$. Thus $P(1,400 \leq X \leq 2,250) = P(0.33 \leq z \leq 1.75)$. Now $P(0.33 \leq z \leq 1.75) = P(0 \leq z \leq 1.75) - P(0 \leq z \leq 0.33) = 0.4599 - 0.1293 = 0.3306$. This is shown in **Figure 9-25**.

Figure 9-25: Area for $P(1400 \leq X \leq 2250) = P(0.33 \leq z \leq 1.75)$

Quick Tip

In solving application problems relating to the normal distribution, it may be helpful if you use the following procedure:

* Define the appropriate normal variable with appropriate parameters (mean and standard deviation).
* Write out an appropriate probability statement.
* Write out an equivalent transformed probability statement using the z score.
* Draw a normal curve.
* Shade in the desired area.
* Use the normal distribution table to find the shaded area.

Example 9-11: A four-year college will accept any student ranked in the top 60 percent on a national examination. If the test score is normally distributed with a mean of 500 and a standard deviation of 100, what is the cutoff score for acceptance?

Solution: Let X = test score, and let x_0 be the cutoff score. We need to find x_0 such that $P(X > x_0) = 0.6$. What we need to do is to find the corresponding z score, say, z_0, such that an area of 0.6 is to the right of z_0. **Figure 9-26** illustrates the desired area.

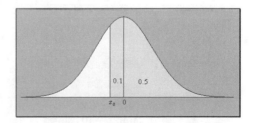

Figure 9-26: Area associated with z_0 such $P(z \geq z_0) = 0.6$

Using the area of 0.1, we have from the body of the standard normal table in the **Appendix**, a corresponding z score of 0.25. Since, from **Figure 9-26**, z_0 is to the left of 0, then $z_0 = -0.25$. We can use this information to solve for x_0 by using the equation $z_0 = \dfrac{x_0 - \mu}{\sigma}$, or

$-0.25 = (x_0 - 500)/100$. Solving gives $x_0 = 475$. That is, the minimum score the college will accept is 475.

Technology

Technology Corner

All the concepts discussed in this chapter can be computed and illustrated through some statistical software packages. All scientific and graphical calculators will aid directly in the computations. In addition, the newer calculators may have the normal distribution from which you can compute the normal probabilities, such as the TI-83/84 series. Some calculators will allow you to shade under the normal curve as well, such as the TI-83/84 series. If you own a calculator, you should consult the owner's manual to determine what statistical features are included.

Illustration: Figures 9-27a and **9-27b** show the solution for **Example 9-10** computed by the MINITAB/EXCEL software. **Figure 9-28** shows the same solution computed by the TI-83/84 calculator. Other alternative approaches to the solution can be obtained with a little mathematical manipulation by the software and the calculator.

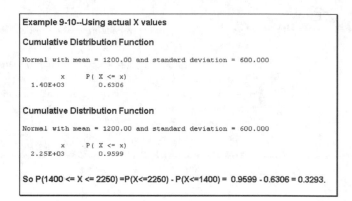

Figure 9-27a: MINITAB output for Example 9-10 using exact X values

Figure 9-27b: EXCEL output for Example 9-10 using z values

Figure 9-28: TI-83/84 output for Example 9-10 using both the X values and the z values

Note: When the actual values for the random variable are used, the computed probability is slightly different from when the standard normal distribution is used. Using the actual values of the random variable, we get 0.3293, and using the z values, we get 0.3306.

The normal random variable can be investigated through
  ✓ Simulation
  ✓ z scores
  ✓ Tables
  ✓ Technology

Again, care always should be taken when computing probabilities. Also, care should be taken when using the normal probability tables.

True/False Questions

1. Continuous random variables typically arise from counting some type of quantity.
2. The probability that a continuous random variable assumes any single value always will be nonzero.
3. The normal distribution is centered at its mean.
4. The area under the normal curve left of its mean is -0.5.
5. Approximately 68 percent of a normal population will lie within one standard deviation of its mean.
6. The total area under the normal curve is approximately 1.
7. The probability that a normal random variable X is **at least** some number a can be denoted as $P(X > a)$.
8. The z value or z score is computed from the equation $z = \dfrac{\mu - x}{\sigma}$, where x is the value of a normal random variable X with mean μ and standard deviation σ.
9. A positive z score gives the number of standard deviations a specified value of a normal random variable is above its mean.
10. A random variable that can assume any value in the set of real numbers must be normally distributed.
11. For any continuous random variable X, $P(X > 2) = P(X \geq 2)$.
12. The standard normal distribution is symmetrical about 0.
13. The area under any normal curve between a and b gives the probability that the normal random variable lies between a and b.

14. The standard normal distribution has a mean of zero and a variance of 1.
15. The mean, the median, and the mode for a normal distribution are all equal.
16. If X is a normal random variable, then $P(X > 0) = 0.5$ is always true.
17. Because of the right and left tails of the normal curve, we can say that the normal distribution is skewed to both the left and right.
18. Not all normal distributions can be transformed to a standard normal distribution.
19. If the computed z value is negative, you definitely have made a computational error.
20. A z value of 1 indicates that 1 percent of the area under the standard normal curve is to the right of the z value of 0.

Completion Questions

1. Any normal distribution is (symmetrical, asymmetrical) _____ about its mean.
2. The total area under any normal curve is always (0.5, 1) _____.
3. The standard normal distribution is specified by a mean of (0, 1) _____ and a standard deviation of (0, 1) _____.
4. If a computed z value is zero, then the value of the normal random variable must be (greater than, equal to, less than) _____ the mean of this normal random variable.
5. If z is the standard normal random variable, then $P(z < 0) = P(z > 0) = (0, 0.5, 1)$ _____.
6. If z is the standard normal random variable, then $P(-1 < z < 1) \approx (0.68, 0.95, 0.997)$ _____.
7. The second quartile of the standard normal random variable corresponds to a z score of $(-3, -2, -1, 0, 1, 2, 3)$ _____.
8. The percentage of the standard normal distribution that lies within three standard deviations of the mean is approximately (68, 95, 99.7) _____.
9. A z score of $z = (-2, 2)$ _____ corresponds to a value of the standard normal random variable that is above the mean by two standard deviations.
10. Transforming a normal distribution to a standard normal distribution will not change the (shape, mean, standard deviation) _____ of the distribution.
11. If two values of a normal random variable from the same distribution correspond to the same z score, then these values must be (negative, positive, equal) _____.
12. When a normal random variable is transformed to a z score, the resulting distribution of z scores will have a standard deviation value of (0, 1) _____.
13. A (negative, positive) _____ z score always corresponds to a value of the normal random variable that is less than the mean of the random variable.
14. The z scores for a standard normal random variable is the set of all (whole, real) _____ numbers.
15. The normal probability distribution is a (continuous, discrete) _____ probability distribution.
16. The mean, the median, and the mode for a normal random variable are all (equal, not equal) _____ to one another.
17. The probability that a continuous random variable assumes a discrete value is always (0, 1) _____.
18. The total area under any standard normal curve is always (0.5, 1) _____.

19. When normal scores are transformed into z scores, the resulting z scores will have a mean of (0, 1) _____.

20. For a normal random variable, the probability of observing a value less than or equal to its mean is (0, 0.5, 1) _____.

21. The z value associated with a given value of a normal random variable measures how far (above, below, above or below) _____, in terms of standard deviations, the value is from the mean of the distribution.

22. When the value of the standard deviation increases, the value of the z score generally will tend to (increase, decrease) _____.

23. Very large positive or negative z scores will correspond to raw scores that generally are (more, less) _____ likely to occur.

Multiple-Choice Questions

1. The area under the standard normal curve between -2.0 and -1 is
   (a) 0.0228.
   (b) 0.1359.
   (c) 0.4772.
   (d) 0.3413.

2. The probability that an observation taken from a standard normal population will be between -1.96 and 1.28 is
   (a) 0.0753.
   (b) -0.0753.
   (c) 0.1253.
   (d) 0.8747.

3. The value of z_0 such that $P(z \le z_0) = 0.8997$ is
   (a) 1.28.
   (b) 0.00.
   (c) 0.1003.
   (d) none of the above.

4. The two z values such that the area bounded by them is equal to the middle 68.26 percent of the standard normal distribution is
   (a) ± 3.
   (b) ± 1.
   (c) ± 2.
   (d) ± 1.96.

5. The area under the standard normal curve between $z = -1.68$ and $z = 0$ is
   (a) 0.4535.
   (b) 0.0465.
   (c) 0.9535.
   (d) -0.4535.

6. If X is a normal random variable with a mean of 15 and a variance of 9, then $P(X < 18)$ is

(a) 0.7486.
(b) 0.8413.
(c) 0.3413.
(d) 0.1587.

7. If X is a normal random variable with a mean of 15 and a variance of 9, then $P(X = 18)$ is
(a) 0.8413.
(b) 0.0000.
(c) 0.3413.
(d) 0.1587.

8. The two z values such that the area bounded by them is equal to the middle 90 percent of the standard normal distribution is
(a) ± 1.640.
(b) ± 1.650.
(c) ± 2.000.
(d) ± 1.645.

9. The time it takes for a dose of a certain drug to be effective as a sedative on laboratory animals is normally distributed with a mean of 1 hour and a standard deviation of 0.1 hour. If X represents this time, then $P(X > 1.1)$ is
(a) 0.0000.
(b) 0.5000.
(c) 0.3643.
(d) 0.1587.

10. The area under any normal curve that is within two standard deviations of the mean is approximately
(a) 0.950.
(b) 0.680.
(c) 0.997.
(d) 0.500.

11. Which of the following does not apply to the normal distribution?
(a) The normal curve is unimodal
(b) The total probability under the curve is 1
(c) The normal curve is symmetrical about its standard deviation
(d) The mean, the median, and the mode are all equal to each other

12. If z is a standard normal random variable, then the probability that $z > 1$ or $z < -2$ is
(a) 0.1587.
(b) 0.0228.
(c) 0.8185.
(d) 0.1815.

13. A standard normal distribution is a normal distribution with
(a) $\mu = 1$ and $\sigma = 0$.
(b) $\mu = 0$ and $\sigma = 1$.

(c) any mean and $\sigma = 0$.

(d) any mean and any standard deviation.

14. If IQ scores are normally distributed with a mean of 100 and a standard deviation of 20, then the probability of a person's having an IQ score of at least 130 is

(a) 0.4332.

(b) 0.3000.

(c) 0.9332.

(d) 0.0668.

15. A bank finds that the balances for its customers in their savings accounts are normally distributed with a mean of $500 and a standard deviation of $50. The probability that a randomly selected account has a balance more than $600 is

(a) 0.4772.

(b) 0.0228.

(c) 0.9772.

(d) 0.0000.

16. The lifetime of a certain brand of tires is normally distributed. The average lifetime of a tire is 50,000 miles with a lifetime standard deviation of 8,400 miles. The probability that a randomly selected tire will last beyond 55,000 miles is

(a) 0.2257.

(b) 0.7257.

(c) 0.0000.

(d) 0.2743.

17. The waiters in a restaurant receive an average tip of $20 per table with a standard deviation of $5. The amounts of tips are normally distributed, and management of the restaurant has established that a waiter has provided excellent service if the tip is more than $25. The probability that a waiter has provided excellent service to a table is

(a) 0.1587.

(b) 0.8413.

(c) 0.8000.

(d) 0.6587.

18. The waiters in a bar receive an average tip of $20 per table with a standard deviation of $5. The amounts of tips are normally distributed, and a waiter feels that he has provided excellent service if the tip is more than $25. The probability that a waiter has not provided excellent service (according to the waiters' theory) to a table is

(a) 0.1587.

(b) 0.8413.

(c) 0.8000.

(d) 0.6587.

19. Suppose that family incomes in a town are normally distributed with a mean of $1,200 and a standard deviation of $600 per month. The probability that a given family has an income over $2,000 per month is

(a) 0.0918.

(b) 0.9082.

    (c) 0.4082.

    (d) 0.5918.

20. Suppose that family incomes in a town are normally distributed with a mean of $1,200 and a standard deviation of $600 per month. The probability that a given family has an income between $1,000 and $2,050 per month is

    (a) 0.4585.

    (b) 0.7001.

    (c) 0.4222.

    (d) 0.5515.

21. The life of a brand of battery is normally distributed with a mean of 62 hours and a standard deviation of 6 hours. The probability that a single randomly selected battery will last more than 70 hours is

    (a) 0.0000.

    (b) 0.0918.

    (c) 0.4082.

    (d) 0.9082.

22. The life of a brand of battery is normally distributed with a mean of 62 hours and a standard deviation of 6 hours. The probability that a single randomly chosen battery will last from 55 to 65 hours is

    (a) 0.4295.

    (b) 0.6875.

    (c) 0.5705.

    (d) 0.3125.

23. For any z distribution, the sum of all the associated z scores always will be

    (a) equal to 1.

    (b) less than 1.

    (c) greater than 1.

    (d) equal to 0.

24. The average score on one of your statistics examination was 75 with a standard deviation of 10. If your corresponding z score was 2, then your corresponding raw score and percentile rank (approximate) would be

    (a) 55; 48 percent.

    (b) 65; 12 percent.

    (c) 85; 75 percent.

    (d) 95; 98 percent.

25. If the z score associated with a given raw score is equal to 0, this implies that

    (a) the raw score equals 0.

    (b) the raw score does not exist.

    (c) the raw score is extremely large.

    (d) the raw score is the same as the mean.

26. Which of the following is not needed in computing the z score for a normal random variable?

(a) The value of the raw score

(b) The percentile rank of the raw score

(c) The standard deviation for the random variable

(d) The mean score for the random variable

27. The U.S. Bureau of Census reports that the average annual alimony income received by women is $3,000 with a standard deviation of $7,500. If the annual alimony income is assumed to be normally distributed, then the proportion of women who receive less than $2,000 in annual alimony income is

(a) −0.0517.

(b) 0.5517.

(c) 0.8966.

(d) 0.4483.

28. The weights of male basketball players on a certain campus are normally distributed with a mean of 180 pounds and a standard deviation of 26 pounds. If a player is selected at random, the probability that the player will weigh more than 225 pounds is

(a) 0.0418.

(b) 0.4582.

(c) 0.9582.

(d) 0.5418.

29. The weights of male basketball players on a certain campus are normally distributed with a mean of 180 pounds and a standard deviation of 26 pounds. If a player is selected at random, the probability that the player will weigh less than 225 pounds is

(a) 0.5418.

(b) 0.9582.

(c) 0.4582.

(d) 0.0418.

30. The weights of male basketball players on a certain campus are normally distributed with a mean of 180 pounds and a standard deviation of 26 pounds. If a player is selected at random, the probability that the player will weigh between 180 and 225 pounds is

(a) 0.5000.

(b) 0.5418.

(c) 0.4582.

(d) 0.9582.

31. If X is a normally distributed random variable with a mean of 6 and a variance of 4, then the probability that X is less than 10 is

(a) 0.8413.

(b) 0.9772.

(c) 0.3413.

(d) 0.4772.

32. If X is a normally distributed random variable with a mean of 6 and a variance of 4, then the probability that X is greater than 10 is

(a) 0.1587.

(b) 0.0228.

    (c) 0.6587.

    (d) 0.5228.

33. In a normal distribution, the distribution will be less spread out when

    (a) the mean of the raw scores is small.

    (b) the median of the raw scores is small.

    (c) the mode of the raw scores is small.

    (d) the standard deviation of the raw scores is small.

34. For the standard normal random variable z, $P(z = 0)$ is

    (a) 0.5.

    (b) less than 0.5.

    (c) same as $P(-0.5 \leq z \leq 0.5)$.

    (d) 0.

35. A statistics professor has established that the final overall percentage per student in her elementary statistics course is normally distributed with a mean and standard deviation of 79 and 7 respectively. If the professor decides to assign her grades, for this current semester, based on a curve such that only the bottom 10 percent of her students receive a failing grade, then the cutoff percentage to earn a failing grade is

    (a) less than or equal to 70.03.

    (b) less than or equal to 65.00.

    (c) less than or equal to 71.10.

    (d) less than or equal to 63.20.

36. The lifetime of a certain brand of tire is normally distributed with an average of 50,000 miles and a standard deviation of 8,400 miles. The probability that a randomly selected tire will last beyond 52,000 miles is

    (a) 0.6406.

    (b) 0.1406.

    (c) 0.2812.

    (d) 0.4059.

37. The manager of a local cell phone store believes that the annual revenue of the store can be approximated by a normal distribution with a mean of $250,000 and a standard deviation of $30,000. If this is the model the manager is using to predict next year's total revenue, then the probability that the total sales will be greater than the mean by at least $10,000 is

    (a) 0.3694.

    (b) 0.6293.

    (c) 0.1293.

    (d) 0.8307.

38. The manager of a local cell phone store believes that the yearly revenue of the store can be approximated by a normal distribution with a mean of $250,000 and a standard deviation of $30,000. If this is the model the manager is using to predict next year's revenue, then the probability that the total sales will be more than the mean by at least $10,000 is

    (a) 0.1293.

    (b) 0.8707

(c) 0.6306.

(d) 0.3694.

39. The manager of a local crafts store believes that the yearly revenue of the store can be approximated by the normal distribution with a mean of $250,000 and a standard deviation of $40,000. If this is the model the manager is using to predict next year's revenue and the break-even revenue is $180,000 (this is the total cost to run the business for one year), then the probability that the store will make a profit is

(a) 0.4599.

(b) 0.9198.

(c) 0.9599.

(d) 0.0401.

40. Which of the following situations may not require a z score to be computed?

(a) A college basketball player wants to know the probability that he will get more than 72 percent of his 3-point shots based on his performance during the last two seasons.

(b) A college baseball player wants to know the median batting average for his team during the last season.

(c) A college softball player wants to know the minimum batting average that she would have to achieve to be in the top 10 percent of her team.

(d) A statistics professor wants to "curve" the overall average for his course such that the bottom 5 percent of the students in his class will receive a failing grade.

41. The systolic blood pressure of adults is approximately normally distributed with a mean of 128 and a standard deviation of 20. Give an interval in which the blood pressures of approximately 95 percent of the population will fall.

(a) 88 to 168

(b) 68 to 188

(c) 108 to 148

(d) 88 to 188

42. The scores on a standardized test are normally distributed with a mean of 400 and a standard deviation of 100. If a certain university will only consider applicants with scores in the upper 10 percent, what is the minimum score required for consideration at this university?

(a) 450

(b) 500

(c) 529

(d) 600

43. If Z is a standard normal random variable, which of the following statements is correct?

(a) $P(Z > -2.5) = P(Z > 2.5)$

(b) $P(Z > -2.5) = P(Z < -2.5)$

(c) $P(Z > -2.5) = P(-2 < Z < 2.5)$

(d) $P(Z > -2.5) = P(Z < 2.5)$

44. The length of time it takes to find a parking spot during the summer terms on campus follows a normal distribution with a mean of 3.5 minutes and a standard deviation of 1

minute. The probability that a student attending classes during the summer terms will take more than 3 minutes to find a parking spot is
(a) 0.8085.
(b) 0.6915.
(c) 0.3085.
(d) 0.1915.

45. A company that bottles apple juice has a machine that automatically fills 12-ounce bottles. From quality control data it was found that the average amount of apple juice dispensed into the bottles was 12 ounces with a standard deviation of 0.5 ounce. If a bottle is chosen at random from the production line, what is the probability that the machine will overfill the bottle if the amount dispensed is assumed to be normally distributed?
(a) 0.5000
(b) 0.1587
(c) 0.0000
(d) 0.8413

46. The time it takes a driver to react to the brake lights on a decelerating vehicle is normally distributed with a mean of 1.30 seconds and standard deviation of 0.3 second. What is the probability that the reaction time of a driver is between 1.00 and 1.50 seconds?
(a) 0.3893
(b) 0.2743
(c) 0.5889
(d) 0.8849

47. The time it takes a driver to react to the brake lights on a decelerating vehicle is normally distributed with a mean of 1.30 seconds and standard deviation of 0.3 second. What is the probability that the reaction time of a driver is less than 1.00 second?
(a) 0.1587
(b) 0.4514
(c) 0.7257
(d) 0.5486

48. The time it takes a driver to react to the brake lights on a decelerating vehicle is normally distributed with a mean of 1.30 seconds and standard deviation of 0.3 second. If the reaction time is more than 2 seconds, a rear-end collision is likely to occur in heavy traffic. What is the probability of a rear-end collision in heavy traffic?
(a) 0.9192
(b) 0.4192
(c) 0.0096
(d) 0.8385

49. The specification for the diameter of a steel washer is set by the buyer to be 2 ± 0.01 cm. Any washer with a diameter outside this specification will be scrapped. What percentage of the washers will be accepted if the diameter is normally distributed with a mean of 2 cm and standard deviation of 0.005 cm?
(a) 95.45 percent
(b) 2.275 percent

(c) 97.725 percent

(d) 4.55 percent

50. The speeds of cars traveling on Kentucky's highways are normally distributed with a mean 60 mph and a standard deviation 5 mph. If Kentucky's police follow a policy of not ticketing the slowest 90 percent, at what speed will the police start to issue tickets? (Round up all answers to the next whole number.)

(a) 54 mph

(b) 52 mph

(c) 66 mph

(d) 68 mph

Further Exercises

If possible, you could use any technology to help solve the following questions.

1. The Test of English as a Foreign Language (TOEFL) is required by most universities to help in their admission of international students. From past records at a certain university, these scores are approximately normally distributed with a mean of 490 and a variance of 6400. If an international student's application is selected at random,

   (a) what is the probability that the student's TOEFL score is at most 450?

   (b) what is the probability that the student's TOEFL score is at least 520?

   (c) what is the probability that the student's TOEFL score is equal to the mean score?

   (d) what is the probability that the student's TOEFL score is between 475 and 525?

   (e) what is the student's percentile rank if her score is 500?

2. The amount of hot chocolate dispensed by a hot chocolate machine is normally distributed with a mean of 16 ounces and a standard deviation of 2 ounces.

   (a) If the cups can hold a maximum of 18 ounces each, what is the probability that a selected cup will be overfilled?

   (b) If the cups can hold a maximum of 18 ounces each, what is the probability that a selected cup will be underfilled?

   (c) If the cups can hold a maximum of 18 ounces each, what is the probability that a selected cup will be less than half-filled?

3. The annual rainfall in a particular region of the country has a mean of 75 inches and a standard deviation of 10 inches. If the rainfall is assumed to be normally distributed, find in any given year

   (a) the probability that it rained more than 100 inches.

   (b) the probability that it rained at most 65 inches.

   (c) the probability that it rained between 60 and 95 inches.

   (d) the percentile corresponding to 75 inches of rainfall.

4. The diameters of ball bearings manufactured by a particular machine are normally distributed with a mean of 2 cm and a standard deviation of 0.02 cm. If a ball bearing is selected at random,

   (a) find the probability that the diameter is greater than 1.77 cm.

   (b) find the 70th percentile for the distribution ball bearing diameters.

   (c) find the probability that the diameter is between 1.79 to 2.11 cm.

5. A company manufactures a certain brand of lightbulb. The lifetime for these bulbs is normally distributed with a mean of 4,000 hours and a standard deviation of 200 hours.

(a) What proportion of these bulbs will last beyond 4,200 hours?

(b) What lifetime should the company claim for these bulbs in order that only 2 percent of the bulbs will burn out before the claimed lifetime.

ANSWER KEY
True/False Questions

1. F   2. F   3. T   4. F   5. T   6. F   7. T   8. F   9. T   10. F   11. T
12. T   13. T   14. T   15. T   16. F   17. F   18. F   19. F   20. F

Completion Questions

1. symmetrical   2. 1   3. 0, 1   4. equal to   5. 0.5   6. 0.68   7. 0   8. 99.7   9. 2
10. shape   11. equal   12. 1   13. negative   14. real   15. continuous   16. equal
17. 0   18. 1   19. 0   20. 0.5   21. above or below   22. decrease   23. less

Multiple-Choice Questions

1. (b)   2. (d)   3. (a)   4. (b)   5. (a)   6. (b)   7. (b)   8. (d)   9. (d)
10. (a)   11. (c)   12. (d)   13. (b)   14. (d)   15. (b)   16. (d)   17. (a)   18. (b)
19. (a)   20. (d)   21. (b)   22. (c)   23. (d)   24. (d)   25. (d)   26. (b)   27. (d)
28. (a)   29. (b)   30. (c)   31. (b)   32. (b)   33. (d)   34. (d)   35. (a)   36. (d)
37. (a)   38. (d)   39. (c)   40. (b)   41. (a)   42. (c)   43. (d)   44. (b)   45. (a)
46. (c)   47. (a)   48. (c)   49. (a)   50. (c)

Further Exercises

1. (a) 0.3085; (b) 0.3538; (c) 0; (d) 0.5744; (e) 55th percentile

2. (a) 0.1587; (b) 0.8413; (c) 0.0002

3. (a) 0.0062; (b) 0.1587; (c) 0.9104; (d) 50th percentile

4. (a) 0.8749; (b) 70th percentile ≈ 2.1049; (c) 0.5620

5. (a) 0.1587; (b) approximately 4,411 hours

CHAPTER 10

Sampling Distributions and the Central Limit Theorem

Do I Need to Read This Chapter?

You should read this chapter if you need to review or to learn about

→ Sampling distribution of a sample mean

→ Sampling distribution of a sample proportion

→ The central limit theorem

→ Sampling distribution of the difference between two independent sample means

→ Sampling distribution of the difference between two independent sample proportions

---

Get Started

Here we will focus on sampling distributions and the central limit theorem. Sampling distributions for the sample mean, the sample proportion, differences of sample proportions from two independent populations, and differences of sample means from two independent populations will be investigated, along with the central limit theorem for these situations. We will only consider sampling populations that are infinite. The central limit theorem will lay the foundation for the broad area of statistical inference.

10-1 Sampling Distribution of a Sample Proportion

Suppose that we are interested in the true proportion of Americans who favor doctor-assisted suicide. If we let the population proportion be denoted by p, then p can be defined by

$$p = \frac{\text{number of Americans who favor doctor-assisted suicide}}{\text{total number of Americans}}$$

Since the population of interest is too large for us to observe in its entirety, we can estimate the true proportion by observing a random sample of the population. If we let the sample proportion be denoted by $\hat{p}$ (read as "p hat"), then the point estimate $\hat{p}$ can be defined by

$$\hat{p} = \frac{\text{number of Americans who favor doctor-assisted suicide in the sample}}{\text{sample size}}$$

Explanation of the term—point estimate: A **point estimate** is a single number that is used to estimate a population parameter.

Suppose that we assume that the true proportion of Americans who favor doctor-assisted suicide is 68 percent (*Source*: *USA TODAY* Snapshot). (In general, we will not know the true population proportion.) If we select a random sample of, say, 50 Americans, we may observe that 35 of them favor doctor-assisted suicide. Thus our sample proportion of Americans who favor doctor-assisted suicide will be $\hat{p} = \dfrac{35}{50} = 0.7$, or 70 percent. If we were to select another random sample of size 50, we most likely would obtain a different value for $\hat{p}$. If we selected 50 different samples of the same size and computed the proportion of Americans who favor doctor-assisted suicide for all 50 samples, we should not expect these values to all be the same. That is, there will be some variability in these computed proportions. Pictorially, the situation is demonstrated in **Figure 10-1**.

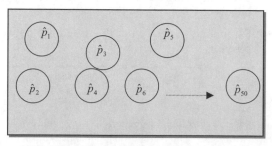

Figure 10-1: Sample proportions for 50 samples of size 50

These 50 sample proportions constitute a **sampling distribution of a sample proportion.**

Explanation of the term—sampling distribution of a sample proportion: A **sampling distribution of a sample proportion** is a distribution obtained by using the proportions computed from random samples of a specific size obtained from a population.

In order to investigate properties of the sampling distribution of a sample proportion, simulations of the situation can be done. For example, the MINITAB statistical software can be used for the simulation. In the example, 50 samples of size 50 were generated. The distribution used in the simulation was the binomial distribution with parameters $n = 50$ and $p = 0.68$. This assumed distribution is reasonable because we are interested in the proportion (number) of persons in the sample of size 50 who support doctor-assisted suicide. You may try your own simulation if you have access to such statistical software. The descriptive statistics for a simulation are shown in **Figure 10-2**.

```
Descriptive Statistics

Variable                 N        Mean      Median    TrMean    StDev     SE Mean
Sample Proportion        50       0.67600   0.68000   0.67682   0.06337   0.00896

Variable             Minimum     Maximum    Q1        Q3
Sample Proportion    0.54000     0.82000    0.64000   0.72500
```

Figure 10-2: MINITAB descriptive statistics of simulation for sample proportion

Let $\mu_{\hat{p}}$ represent the mean of the sample proportions, and $\sigma_{\hat{p}}$ represent the standard deviation of the sample proportions. **Table 10-1** shows some summary information, obtained from **Figure 10-2**, for the 50 simulated sample proportions.

Table 10-1: Some Summary Information for the Simulation on Sample Proportions

True proportion $p = 0.68$	Mean of sample proportions $\mu_{\hat{p}} = 0.6760$
$\sqrt{p(1-p)/n} = 0.0660$	Standard deviation of the sample proportions $\sigma_{\hat{p}} = 0.0634$

Observe that $p \approx \mu_{\hat{p}}$ and $\sqrt{p(1-p)/n} \approx \sigma_{\hat{p}}$, where again the symbol $\approx$ represents "approximately equal to." Of course, if we do a large number of these simulations and take averages, we should expect that these values would be closer, if not equal, to each other. The main purpose of this illustration was to help in understanding the stated properties given in **Table 10-2**.

Table 10-2: Properties of the Sampling Distribution for the Sample Proportion

SAMPLING DISTRIBUTION OF THE SAMPLE PROPORTION $\hat{p}$

Suppose that random samples of size n are selected from a population (distribution) in which the true proportion of the attribute of interest is p. Then the sampling distribution of the sample proportions $\hat{p}$ has the following properties.

- The mean of the sample proportions is equal to the true population proportion. That is, symbolically, $\mu_{\hat{p}} = p$.
- The standard deviation of the sample proportions is given by $\sigma_{\hat{p}} = \sqrt{p(1-p)/n}$.

Next, we can investigate the shape of the distribution for these sample proportions. **Figure 10-3** shows a histogram for the simulation.

Figure 10-3: Histogram for simulated sample proportions

Observe that the distribution of the simulated sample proportions is approximately bell-shaped. That is, the distribution of the sample proportions is approximately normally distributed.

We can investigate with other sample sizes and probability p. However, we will generally observe the same properties when the sample size is "large enough" ($n \geq 30$) or $np > 5$.

We can generalize the observations in a very important theorem called the **central limit theorem for sample proportions**. This theorem is given in **Table 10-3**.

Table 10-3: Central Limit Theorem for Sample Proportions

THE CENTRAL LIMIT THEOREM FOR SAMPLE PROPORTIONS
Suppose that random samples of size n are selected from a population (distribution) in which the true proportion of the attribute of interest is p. Then, provided that $np > 5$ and $n(1 - p) > 5$, the sampling distribution of the sample proportion $\hat{p}$ will be approximately normally distributed with mean $\mu_{\hat{p}} = p$, and the standard deviation of the sample proportions is given by $\sigma_{\hat{p}} = \sqrt{p(1 - p)/n}$.
Note: The normality assumption will improve with large sample size.

Quick Tip

Since the sampling distribution of the sample proportion $\hat{p}$ is approximately normally distributed for large enough sample sizes, with mean $\mu_{\hat{p}} = p$ and standard deviation $\sigma_{\hat{p}} = \sqrt{p(1 - p)/n}$, we can compute z scores for observed $\hat{p}$ values. Also, we will be able to compute probabilities associated with these $\hat{p}$ values. The equation that we use to compute the associated z score is

$$z = \frac{\hat{p} - \mu_{\hat{p}}}{\sigma_{\hat{p}}} = \frac{\hat{p} - p}{\sqrt{p(1-p)/n}}$$

Example 10-1: In a survey it was reported that 33 percent of women believe in the existence of aliens. If 100 women are selected at random, what is the probability that more than 45 percent of them will say that they believe in aliens?

Solution: We need to find $P(\hat{p} > 0.45)$. Now $n = 100$, $np = 33 > 5$, $n(1 - p) > 5$, $\hat{p} = 0.45$, $\mu_{\hat{p}} = p = 0.33$, and $\sigma_{\hat{p}} = \sqrt{p(1 - p)/n} = \sqrt{0.33(1-0.33)/100} = 0.0470$. The corresponding z score is $z = (0.45 - 0.33)/0.0470 = 2.55$. Thus $P(\hat{p} > 0.45) = P(z > 2.55) = 0.5 - 0.4946 = 0.0054$, or 0.54 percent. That is, the probability is rather small (less than 1 percent) that more than 45 percent of the women in the sample will believe in aliens. This is depicted in **Figure 10-4**.

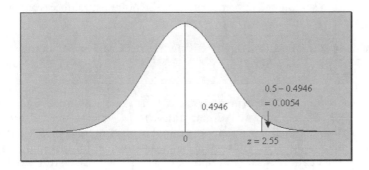

Figure 10-4: Area for $P(\hat{p} > 0.45) = P(z > 2.55)$ in Example 10-1

Example 10-2: It is estimated that approximately 53 percent of college students graduate in 5 years or less. This figure is affected by the fact that more students are attending college on a part-time basis. If 500 students on a large campus are selected at random, what is the probability that between 50 and 60 percent of them will graduate in 5 years or less?

Solution: We need to find $P(0.5 \leq \hat{p} \leq 0.6)$. Now $n = 500$, $np = 265 > 5$, $n(1 - p) = 235 > 5$, $\hat{p} = 0.5$ and 0.6, $\mu_{\hat{p}} = p = 0.53$, and $\sigma_{\hat{p}} = \sqrt{p(1-p)/n} = \sqrt{0.53(1-0.53)/500} = 0.0223$. The corresponding z scores are $z = (0.5 - 0.53)/0.0223 = -1.35$ and $z = (0.6 - 0.53)/0.0223 = 3.14$. Thus $P(0.5 \leq \hat{p} \leq 0.6) = P(-1.35 \leq z \leq 3.14) = 0.4115 + 0.4990 = 0.9105$. This is depicted in **Figure 10-5**.

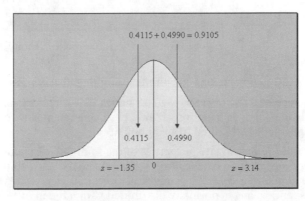

Figure 10-5: Area for $P(0.5 \leq \hat{p} \leq 0.6) = P(-1.35 \leq z \leq 3.14)$ in Example 10-2

10-2 Sampling Distribution of a Sample Mean

Suppose that we are interested in the true daily mean time men spend driving their motor vehicles in the United States. If we let the population mean be denoted by μ, then μ can be defined by

$$\mu = \frac{\text{total daily amount of time spent driving by American males}}{\text{total number of American males who drive}}$$

Since the population of interest is too large for us to observe in its entirety, we can estimate the true mean by observing a random sample of the population of American males who drive. If we let the sample mean be denoted by the point estimate $\bar{x}$ (read as "x bar"), then $\bar{x}$ can be defined by

$$\bar{x} = \frac{\text{total daily amount of time spent driving by Americans males in the sample}}{\text{sample size}}$$

Suppose that we assume that the true daily mean time American males spend driving is 81 minutes (*Source:* Federal Highway Administration). (In general, we will not know the mean of the population.) If we select a random sample of 50 American males who drive, we may observe that the average daily time spent behind the wheel for this sample is 85 minutes. If we were to select another random sample of size 50, we most likely would obtain a different value for $\bar{x}$. If we selected 100 different samples, say, of the same sample size and compute the average time spent behind the wheel by American males, we should not expect these 100 sample means to all be the same. That is, there will be some variability in these computed sample means. Pictorially, the situation is demonstrated in **Figure 10-6.**

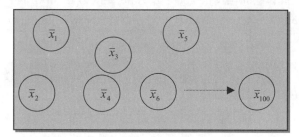

Figure 10-6: One hundred random samples of size 50

This 100 sample means constitute a **sampling distribution of sample means.**

Explanation of the term—sampling distribution of a sample mean: A **sampling distribution of a sample mean** is a distribution obtained by using the means computed from random samples of a specific size obtained from a population.

In order to investigate properties of the sampling distribution of a sample mean, simulations of the situation can be done. Again, the MINITAB statistical software was used to aid in the simulation, and 100 samples of size of 50 were used. Here we will assume that the time spent driving is normally distributed with a mean of 81 and a standard deviation of 1 for the sake of the simulation. You may try your own simulation if you have access to such statistical software. The descriptive statistics for a simulation are shown in **Figure 10-7.**

```
Descriptive Statistics

Variable               N      Mean    Median    TrMean    StDev   SE Mean
Sample Means          100    81.001   81.018    81.003    0.140    0.014

Variable           Minimum  Maximum      Q1        Q3
Sample Means        80.667   81.342    80.890    81.090
```

Figure 10-7: MINITAB descriptive statistics of simulation for sample means

Let $\mu_{\bar{x}}$ represent the mean of the sample means and $\sigma_{\bar{x}}$ represent the standard deviation of the sample means. **Table 10-4** shows some summary statistics for the 100 simulated sample means.

Table 10-4: Some Summary Information for the Simulation on Sample Means

True mean $\mu = 81$	Mean of sample means $\mu_{\bar{x}} = 81.007$
$\dfrac{\sigma}{\sqrt{n}} = \dfrac{1}{\sqrt{50}} = 0.141$	Standard deviation of the sample means $\sigma_{\bar{x}} = 0.140$

Observe that $\mu \approx \mu_{\bar{x}}$ and $\dfrac{\sigma}{\sqrt{n}}, \approx \sigma_{\bar{x}}$, where again the symbol $\approx$ represents "approximately equal to." Of course, if we do a large number of these simulations and compute averages, we should expect that these values would be closer, if not equal, to each other. Also, if we assume different standard deviations for the drive time distribution, we would observe similar results. The main purpose of this illustration was to help in understanding the stated properties given in **Table 10-5**.

Table 10-5: Properties of the Sampling Distribution for the Sample Mean

SAMPLING DISTRIBUTION OF THE SAMPLE MEAN $\bar{X}$

If all possible random samples of size n are selected from a population with mean μ and standard deviation σ, then the sampling distribution of $\bar{x}$ has the following properties:
- The mean of the sample means is equal to the population mean. That is, symbolically $\mu_{\bar{x}} = \mu$.
- The standard deviation of the sample means is equal to the standard deviation of the sampling population divided by the square root of the sample size. That is, symbolically $\sigma_{\bar{x}} = \dfrac{\sigma}{\sqrt{n}}$.

Next, we can investigate the shape of the distribution for these sample means. **Figure 10-8** shows a histogram of the simulation for this situation.

Figure 10-8: Histogram for simulated sample means

Observe that the distribution of the simulated sample means is approximately bell-shaped. That is, the distribution of the sample means is approximately normally distributed.

We can investigate with other sample sizes, other population means, and other distributions. However, we generally will observe the same properties when the sample size is "large enough" ($n \geq 30$).

We can generalize the observations in a very important theorem called the **central limit theorem for sample means.** This is given in **Table 10-6**.

Table 10-6: Central Limit Theorem for Sample Means

THE CENTRAL LIMIT THEOREM FOR SAMPLE MEANS

As the sample size n increases, the shape of the distribution of the sample means obtained from **any** population (distribution) with mean μ and standard deviation σ will approach a normal distribution. This distribution (the distribution of the sample means) will have a

mean $\mu_{\bar{x}} = \mu$ and a standard deviation of $\sigma_{\bar{x}} = \dfrac{\sigma}{\sqrt{n}}$.

Note: If the sampling distribution is an exact normal distribution, the distribution of the sample means also will be an exact normal distribution for **any** sample size.

Note: In applying the central limit theorem for sample means, the sampling population can be **any** distribution.

Quick Tip

Since the sampling distribution of the sample mean $\bar{x}$ is approximately normally distributed, with mean $\mu_{\bar{x}} = \mu$ and standard deviation $\sigma_{\bar{x}} = \sigma/\sqrt{n}$, we can compute z scores for observed $\bar{x}$ values. Also, we will be able to compute probabilities that are associated with these $\bar{x}$ values. The equation that is used to compute the z score is

$$z = \frac{\bar{x} - \mu_{\bar{x}}}{\sigma_{\bar{x}}} = \frac{\bar{x} - \mu}{\sigma/\sqrt{n}}$$

Example 10-3: A tire manufacturer claims that its tires will last an average of 60,000 miles with a standard deviation of 3,000 miles. Sixty-four tires were placed on test, and the average failure miles for these tires was recorded. What is the probability that the average failure miles will be more than 59,500 miles?

Solution: Observe here that we do not know the distribution of failure miles, but the sample size is large, so we can apply the central limit theorem for the sample means. We need to find $P(\bar{x} > 59,500)$. Now, $\bar{x} = 59,500$, $\mu = 60,000$, $\sigma = 3,000$, and $n = 64$. From this information, $z = \dfrac{\bar{x} - \mu}{\sigma/\sqrt{n}} = \dfrac{59,500 - 60,000}{(3,000/\sqrt{64})} = -1.33$ Thus, $P(\bar{x} > 59,500) = P(z > -1.33) = 0.4082$

$+\, 0.5 = 0.9082$. This area is displayed in **Figure 10-9**.

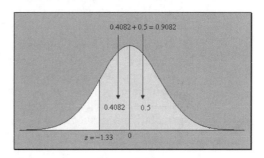

Figure 10-9: Area for $P(\bar{x} > 59,500) = P(z > -1.33)$ in Example 10-3

Example 10-4: A supervisor has determined that the average salary of the employees in his department is $40,000 with a standard deviation of $15,000. A sample of 25 of the employees' salaries was selected at random. Assuming that the distribution of the salaries is normal, what is the probability that the average for this sample is between $36,000 and $42,000?

Solution: Here we know the salaries are normally distributed, so the size of the sample does not matter. Thus we can proceed to apply the central limit theorem for the sample means. We need to find $P(36,000 \le \bar{x} \le 42,000)$. Now $n = 25$, $\bar{x} = 36,000$ and $42,000$, $\mu = 40,000$, and $\sigma = 15,000$. The corresponding z scores are

$$z = \frac{(36,000 - 40,000)}{15,000/\sqrt{25}} = -1.33 \quad \text{and} \quad z = \frac{(42,000 - 40,000)}{15,000/\sqrt{25}} = 0.67$$

Thus $P(36,000 \le \bar{x} \le 42,000) = P(-1.33 \le z \le 0.67) = 0.4082 + 0.2486 = 0.6568$. The probability is depicted in **Figure 10-10**.

Figure 10-10: Area for $P(36,000 \le \bar{x} \le 42,000) = P(-1.33 \le z \le 0.67)$ in Example 10-4

10-3 Sampling Distribution of a Difference between Two Independent Sample Proportions

We may be interested in comparing the proportions of two populations. For example, we may have to compare the effectiveness of two different drugs, drug 1 and drug 2, say, on a certain medical condition. One way of doing this is to select a homogeneous group of people with the given medical condition and randomly divide them into two groups. These groups then can be treated with the different medications over a period of time, and then the effectiveness of the medication for these two groups can be determined.

In the preceding illustration, we may consider the two homogeneous groups as samples from two different populations who were treated with the two drugs. Information obtained about the number of patients who were helped in the two samples then can be used to make comparisons concerning the proportion of patients who were helped by the two different medications.

To be specific, we will let the subscript 1 be associated with population 1 and the subscript 2 be associated with population 2. We will let n_1 and n_2 denote the sample sizes for the two independent samples from the two populations, and we will let x_1 and x_2 be the respective number of successes. We will let p_1 and p_2 denote the population proportions of interest. Also, we will let $\hat{p}_1$ and $\hat{p}_2$ represent the sample proportions from population 1 and population 2, respectively. This sampling situation, showing the case where one sample is taken from each population, is presented in **Figure 10-11**.

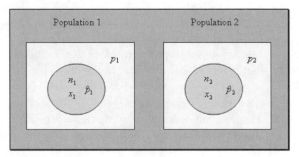

Figure 10-11: Sampling representation to investigate the sampling distribution for two sample proportions

We then can investigate the sampling distribution of $\hat{p}_1 - \hat{p}_2$ by taking repeated samples from the two populations and computing the differences for the sample proportions for these repeated samples. Through simulations and theory, we can state some properties of the sampling distribution of $\hat{p}_1 - \hat{p}_2$.

Explanation of the term—sampling distribution of the difference between two independent sample proportions: A **sampling distribution of the difference between two independent sample proportions** is a distribution obtained by using the difference of the proportions computed from random samples obtained from the two populations.

In order to investigate properties of the sampling distribution of the difference between two sample proportions, simulations of the situation can be done. Again, the MINITAB statistical software was used to aid in the simulation, and 100 samples of size of 100 were simulated from binomial distributions with $p_1 = 0.8$ and $p_2 = 0.5$. The descriptive statistics for a simulation are shown in **Figure 10-12**.

```
Descriptive Statistics

Variable                N       Mean    Median    TrMean    StDev    SE Mean
Differences            100    0.30920   0.30000   0.30867   0.06100   0.00610
of Proportions

Variable            Minimum   Maximum      Q1        Q3
Differences         0.18000   0.45000   0.27000   0.35000
of Proportions
```

Figure 10-12: MINITAB descriptive statistics of simulation for difference between two sample proportions

Let $\mu_{\hat{p}_1-\hat{p}_2}$ represent the mean of the differences of the sample proportions, and let $\sigma_{\hat{p}_1-\hat{p}_2}$ represent the standard deviation of the differences of the sample proportions. **Table 10-7** shows some summary statistics for the 100 simulated sample proportion differences.

Table 10-7: Some Summary Information for the Simulation on the Difference between Two Sample Proportions

True mean $p_1 - p_2 = 0.8 - 0.5$ $= 0.3$	Mean of the differences of the sample proportions $\mu_{\hat{p}_1-\hat{p}_2} = 0.3092$.
$\sqrt{\dfrac{p_1(1-p_1)}{n_1}+\dfrac{p_2(1-p_2)}{n_2}}=0.0640$	Standard deviation of the differences sample proportions $\sigma_{\hat{p}_1-\hat{p}_2} = 0.0610$.

Observe that

$$p_1-p_2\approx\mu_{\hat{p}_1-\hat{p}_2} \quad \text{and} \quad \sqrt{\frac{p_1(1-p_1)}{n_1}+\frac{p_2(1-p_2)}{n_2}} \approx\sigma_{\hat{p}_1-\hat{p}_2}$$

Again, if we perform a large number of these simulations and take averages, we should expect that these values will be close, if not equal, to each other in the long run. Also, if we assume different sample sizes and different population proportions, we will observe similar results. The main purpose of this illustration was to help in understanding the stated properties given in **Table 10-8**.

Table 10-8: Properties of the Sampling Distribution for the Difference between Two Independent Sample Proportions

SAMPLING DISTRIBUTION OF $\hat{p}_1-\hat{p}_2$

If all possible random samples of sizes n_1 and n_2 are selected from two populations with given proportions p_1 and, p_2, then the sampling distribution of $\hat{p}_1 - \hat{p}_2$ has the following properties:

- The mean of the differences of the sample proportions, denoted by, $\mu_{\hat{p}_1-\hat{p}_2}$, is equal to $p_1 - p_2$, the difference of the population proportions.
- The standard deviation of the differences of sample proportions, denoted by $\sigma_{\hat{p}_1-\hat{p}_2}$, is approximately equal to

$$\sqrt{\frac{p_1(1-p_1)}{n_1}+\frac{p_2(1-p_2)}{n_2}}$$

Next, we can investigate the shape of the distribution for these differences of the sample proportions. **Figure 10-13** shows a histogram for the simulation for this situation.

Figure 10-13: Histogram for simulated differences of sample proportions

Observe that the distribution of the simulated differences of sample proportions is approximately bell-shaped or normal.

We can investigate with other sample sizes, population proportions, and other distributions. However, we generally will observe the same properties when $n_1 p_1 > 5$, $n_1 (1 - p_1) > 5$, $n_2 p_2 > 5$, and $n_2 (1 - p_2) > 5$.

We can generalize the observations in a very important theorem called the **central limit theorem for the difference between two sample proportions**. This theorem is given in **Table 10-9**.

Table 10-9: Central Limit Theorem for the Difference between Two Sample Proportions

THE CENTRAL LIMIT THEOREM FOR THE DIFFERENCE BETWEEN TWO SAMPLE PROPORTIONS
As the sample sizes n_1 and n_2 increase, the shape of the distribution of the differences of the sample proportions obtained from **any** population (distribution) will approach a normal distribution. This distribution (the distribution of the differences of the sample proportions) will have a mean of $\mu_{\hat{p}_1 - \hat{p}_2} = p_1 - p_2$ and a standard deviation of $$\sigma_{\hat{p}_1 - \hat{p}_2} = \sqrt{\frac{p_1(1-p_1)}{n_1} + \frac{p_2(1-p_2)}{n_2}}$$ where p_1 and p_2 are the respective population proportions of interest.

Quick Tip

Since the sampling distribution of the differences of the sample proportions $\hat{p}_1 - \hat{p}_2$ is approximately normally distributed, with mean $\mu_{\hat{p}_1 - \hat{p}_2} = p_1 - p_2$ and standard deviation

$$\sigma_{\hat{p}_1 - \hat{p}_2} = \sqrt{\frac{p_1(1-p_1)}{n_1} + \frac{p_2(1-p_2)}{n_2}}$$

we can compute z scores for observed $\hat{p}_1 - \hat{p}_2$ values. Also, we will be able to compute probabilities that are associated with these $\hat{p}_1 - \hat{p}_2$ values. The equation that is used to compute the z score is

$$z = \frac{(\hat{p}_1 - \hat{p}_2) - \mu_{\hat{p}_1 - \hat{p}_2}}{\sigma_{\hat{p}_1 - \hat{p}_2}} = \frac{(\hat{p}_1 - \hat{p}_2) - (p_1 - p_2)}{\sqrt{\dfrac{p_1(1-p_1)}{n_1} + \dfrac{p_2(1-p_2)}{n_2}}}$$

Example 10-5: A study was conducted to determine whether remediation in developmental mathematics enabled students to be more successful in an elementary statistics course. Success here means that a student received a grade of C or better, and remediation was for one year. **Table 10-10** shows the summary results of the study.

Table 10-10: Information Related to Example 10-5

	REMEDIAL	NONREMEDIAL
Sample size	100	40
Number of successes	70	16

Based on past history, it is known that 75 percent of students who enroll in remedial mathematics are successful, whereas only 50 percent of nonremedial students are successful. What is the probability that the difference in proportion of success for the remedial and nonremedial students is at least 10 percent?

Solution: From the information given, we have $n_1 = 100$, $n_2 = 40$, $p_1 = 0.75$, $p_2 = 0.5$, $\hat{p}_1 = \frac{70}{100} = 0.7$, and $\hat{p}_2 = \frac{16}{40} = 0.4$. We need to determine $P(\hat{p}_1 - \hat{p}_2 \geq 0.1)$. Substituting in the preceding equation to find the z score, we have that the z score value is 0.56. Thus $P(\hat{p}_1 - \hat{p}_2 \geq 0.1) = P(z \geq 0.56)$. Using the standard normal distribution table in the **Appendix** $P(z \geq 0.56) = 0.5 - 0.2123 = 0.2877$. That is, the probability that the difference in the proportion of success for the remedial and nonremedial students is at least 10 percent is 0.2877. **Figure 10-14** shows the distribution.

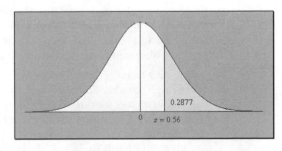

Figure 10-14: Area for $P(\hat{p}_1 - \hat{p}_2 \geq 0.1)$ = $P(z \geq 0.56)$ in Example 10-5

10-4 Sampling Distribution of a Difference between Two Independent Sample Means

We may be interested in comparing the means of two populations. For example, we may have to compare the effectiveness of two different diets, diet 1 and diet 2, say, for weight loss. One way of doing this is to select a homogeneous group of people who are classified as overweight and randomly divide them into two groups. These groups then can be treated with the different diets over a period of time, and the effectiveness of the diets for these two groups can be determined.

Again, in the preceding illustration we may consider the two homogeneous groups as samples from two different independent populations who were treated with the two diets. Information obtained about the weight loss in the two samples then can be used to make comparisons concerning the average weight loss with the two diets.

To be specific, we will let subscript 1 be associated with population 1 and subscript 2 be associated with population 2. We will let n_1 and n_2 denote the sample sizes for the two independent samples from the two populations. We will let μ_1 and μ_2 denote the respective population means. We will let σ^2_1 and σ^2_2 denote the respective population variances and the corresponding sample variances as s^2_1 and s^2_2. Also, we will let $\bar{x}_1$ and $\bar{x}_2$ represent the sample means for the samples from population 1 and population 2, respectively. We can then investigate the sampling distribution of $\bar{x}_1 - \bar{x}_2$. Through simulations and theory, we can state some properties of the sampling distribution for $\bar{x}_1 - \bar{x}_2$. This sampling situation, showing the case where one sample is taken from each population, is shown in **Figure 10-15**.

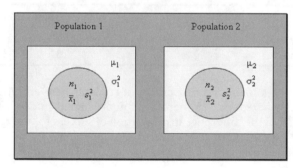

Figure 10-15: Sampling representation to investigate the sampling distribution for two sample means

We then can investigate the sampling distribution of $\bar{x}_1 - \bar{x}_2$ by taking repeated samples from the two populations and computing the differences for the sample means for these repeated samples. Through simulations and theory, we can state some properties of the sampling distribution $\bar{x}_1 - \bar{x}_2$.

Explanation of the term—sampling distribution of the difference between two independent sample means A **sampling distribution of the difference between two independent sample means** is a distribution obtained by using the difference of the sample means computed from random samples obtained from the two populations.

In order to investigate properties of the sampling distribution of the difference between two sample means, simulations of the situation can be done. Again, the MINITAB statistical software was used to aid in the simulation, and 100 samples of size 25 were simulated from normal distributions with means $\mu_1 = 2$ and $\mu_2 = 5$ and standard deviations $\sigma_1 = 1$ and $\sigma_2 = 4$. The descriptive statistics for the differences of the sample means for a simulation are given in **Figure 10-16**.

```
Descriptive Statistics

Variable              N      Mean    Median    TrMean    StDev    SE Mean
Differences         100    3.0096    2.9089    2.9856    0.7302    0.0730
of Means

Variable        Minimum    Maximum       Q1        Q3
Differences      1.1910     5.1450    2.4402    3.4479
of Means
```

Figure 10-16: MINITAB descriptive statistics of simulation for the difference between two sample means

Let $\mu_{\bar{x}_1-\bar{x}_2}$ represent the mean of the differences of the sample means and $\sigma_{\bar{x}_1-\bar{x}_2}$ represent the standard deviation of the differences of the sample means. **Table 10-11** shows some summary statistics for the differences of the 100 simulated sample means.

Table 10-11: Some Summary Information for the Simulation on the Difference between Two Sample Means

True mean difference $\mu_1 - \mu_2 = 3$	Mean of the differences of the sample means $\mu_{\bar{x}_1-\bar{x}_2} = 3.0067$
$\sqrt{\dfrac{\sigma_1^2}{n_1} + \dfrac{\sigma_2^2}{n_2}} = 0.8246$	Standard deviation of the differences of the sample means $\sigma_{\bar{x}_1-\bar{x}_2} = 0.7302$

Observe that $\mu_1 - \mu_2 \approx \mu_{\bar{x}_1-\bar{x}_2}$ and $\sqrt{\dfrac{\sigma_1^2}{n_1} + \dfrac{\sigma_2^2}{n_2}} \approx \sigma_{\bar{x}_1-\bar{x}_2}$. Again, if we perform a large number of these simulations and take averages, we should expect that these values will be close, if not equal, to each other in the long run. Also, if we assume different sample sizes and different population means and variances, we will observe similar results. The main purpose of this illustration was to help in understanding the stated properties given in **Table 10-12.**

Table 10-12: Properties of the Sampling Distribution for the Difference between Two Independent Sample Means

SAMPLING DISTRIBUTION OF $\overline{X}_1 - \overline{X}_2$

If all possible random samples of size n_1 and n_2 are selected from two populations with given means μ_1 and μ_2, then the sampling distribution of $\bar{x}_1 - \bar{x}_2$ has the following properties:

- The mean of the differences of the sample means, denoted by $\mu_{\bar{x}_1-\bar{x}_2}$, is equal to $\mu_1 - \mu_2$, the difference of the population means.
- The standard deviation of the differences of sample means, denoted by $\sigma_{\bar{x}_1-\bar{x}_2}$, is approximately equal to

$$\sqrt{\frac{\sigma_1^2}{n_1} + \frac{\sigma_2^2}{n_2}}$$

Next, we can investigate the shape of the distribution for these differences of the sample means. **Figure 10-17** shows a histogram of the simulation for this situation.

Figure 10-17: Histogram for simulated differences of sample means

Observe that the distribution of the simulated differences of sample means is approximately bell-shaped, or normal. We can investigate with other sample sizes, population means, and variances. However, we generally will observe the same properties.

We can generalize the observations in a very important theorem called the **central limit theorem for the difference between two sample means.** This theorem is stated in **Table 10-13.**

Table 10-13: Central Limit Theorem for the Difference between Two Sample Means

CENTRAL LIMIT THEOREM FOR THE DIFFERENCE BETWEEN TWO SAMPLE MEANS
As the sample sizes n_1 and n_2 increase, the shape of the distribution of the differences of the sample means obtained from **any** population (distribution) will approach a normal distribution. This distribution (the distribution of the differences of the sample means) will have a mean $\mu_{\bar{x}_1 - \bar{x}_2} = \mu_1 - \mu_2$, and a standard deviation $$\sigma_{\bar{x}_1 - \bar{x}_2} = \sqrt{\frac{\sigma_1^2}{n_1} + \frac{\sigma_2^2}{n_2}}$$ where μ_1 and μ_2 are the respective population means of interest.

Note: If the population standard deviations are unknown but the sample sizes are large (n_1 and $n_2 \geq 30$), then we can approximate the population variances by the corresponding sample variances.

Since the sampling distribution of the differences of the sample means $\bar{x}_1 - \bar{x}_2$ is approximately normally distributed, with mean $\mu_{\bar{x}_1 - \bar{x}_2} = \mu_1 - \mu_2$, and standard deviation

$$\sigma_{\bar{x}_1 - \bar{x}_2} = \sqrt{\frac{\sigma_1^2}{n_1} + \frac{\sigma_2^2}{n_2}}$$

we can compute z scores for observed $\bar{x}_1 - \bar{x}_2$ values. Also, we will be able to compute probabilities that are associated with these $\bar{x}_1 - \bar{x}_2$ values. The equation that is used to compute the z score is

$$z = \frac{(\bar{x}_1 - \bar{x}_2) - \mu_{\bar{x}_1 - \bar{x}_2}}{\sigma_{\bar{x}_1 - \bar{x}_2}} = \frac{(\bar{x}_1 - \bar{x}_2) - (\mu_1 - \mu_2)}{\sqrt{\frac{\sigma_1^2}{n_1} + \frac{\sigma_2^2}{n_2}}}$$

Example 10-6: Based on extensive use of two methods (method 1 and method 2) of teaching a high school advance placement (AP) statistics course, the following summary information, given in **Table 10-14,** for a random sample of final scores for each teaching method was obtained.

Table 10-14: Information Related to Example 10- 6

	METHOD 1	METHOD 2
Sample size	45	55
Mean	85	76
Standard deviation	16	19

Find the probability that method 1, on average, was more successful than method 2? That is, we need to find $P(\bar{x}_1 \geq \bar{x}_2) \equiv P(\bar{x}_1 - \bar{x}_2 \geq 0)$.

Solution: From the information given, we need to determine $P(\bar{x}_1 \geq \bar{x}_2)$. We have $n_1 = 45$, n_2 = 55, $\mu_1 = 85$, $\mu_2 = 76$, $\sigma_1 = 16$, $\sigma_2 = 19$, $\sqrt{\frac{\sigma_1^2}{n_1} + \frac{\sigma_2^2}{n_2}} = 3.5$, and $z = [0 - (85 - 76)]/3.5 = $

-2.57. Substituting, $P(\bar{x}_1 - \bar{x}_2 \geq 0) = P(z \geq -2.57)$. Using the standard normal distribution table in the **Appendix**, $P(z \geq -2.57) = 0.4949 + 0.5 = 0.9949$. This is a rather large probability, so if one is given the choice of the two methods to teach or to receive instruction by, one should choose method 1. It seems, based on this probability value, that method 1 is more effective. **Figure 10-18** shows the distribution.

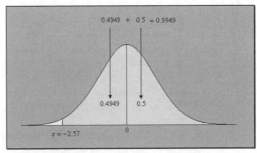

Figure 10-18: Area for $P(\bar{x}_1 - \bar{x}_2 \geq 0) = P(z \geq -2.57)$ in Example 10-6

Quick Tip

If the sample sizes are large enough to apply the central limit theorem ($n_1 \geq 30$ and $n_2 \geq 30$), then the assumption of normal populations is less crucial because the distribution of $\bar{x}_1 - \bar{x}_2$ will be approximately normal.

Technology

Technology Corner

All the concepts discussed in this chapter can be computed and illustrated through some statistical software packages. All scientific and graphical calculators can be used for the computations. In addition, some of the newer calculators (such as the TI- 83/84 series) will allow you to simulate data from different distributions to aid in understanding of the concepts presented in this chapter. If you own a calculator, you should consult the owner's manual to determine what statistical features are included. In addition, the MINITAB software (and other statistical packages) can be used to compute the probabilities presented in the examples.

The sampling distributions of both single and two proportions and means can be investigated through

✓ Simulation

✓ Histograms

✓ Descriptive statistics

✓ Technology

Here we consider only sampling populations that are infinitely large. Other formulas can be presented that would accommodate a finite population. However, finite population analysis will not be presented in this text. Again, care always should be taken when computing probabilities. Also, care should be taken when using the normal probability tables.

Test Yourself

True/False Questions

1. A single-value prediction for a parameter is called a point estimate.
2. The distribution of the difference of sample means is obtained by observing a fixed number of sample means from two populations.
3. The expected value (the average of all possible samples of a given size) of the sample mean is equal to the mean of the population from which the random samples are taken.
4. If we take every possible random sample of a fixed size from a normal population with a given variance, then the variance of the distribution of the sample means will be larger than the variance of the given normal distribution.
5. The sampling distribution of the sample mean is approximately normal for all sample sizes.
6. One of the properties of the central limit theorem (for all situations) is that if the sampling population is *not* normally distributed, then the sampling distribution will be approximately normally distributed, provided that the sample size(s) is(are) large enough [sample size(s) ≥ 30].

7. One property of the distribution of sample means is that if the original population is normally distributed, then the distribution of the sample means is also normally distributed, regardless of the sample size.

8. If σ is the standard deviation of the sampling population, then the variance of the sample means is $\frac{\sigma}{\sqrt{n}}$, where n is the sample size of the random samples selected from the sampling population.

9. The standard deviation of a set of differences of sample proportion is approximately equal to

$$\sqrt{\frac{p_1(1-p_1)}{n_1}+\frac{p_2(1-p_2)}{n_2}}$$

where p_1 and p_2 are the population proportions of interest, and n_1 and n_2 are the respective sample sizes.

10. If we sample from a normal population with mean μ and standard deviation σ, then the z score associated with $\bar{x}$ is $z = \frac{\bar{x}-\mu}{\sigma/\sqrt{n}}$, where n is the sample size.

11. If the sample sizes are large enough to apply the central limit theorem ($n_1 \geq 30$ and $n_2 \geq 30$), then the assumption of normal populations is less crucial in considering the sampling distribution of the difference of two sample means $\bar{x}_1 - \bar{x}_2$ because the distribution of $\bar{x}_1 - \bar{x}_2$ will be approximately normal.

12. The central limit theorem applies only to normal distributions from which samples are obtained.

13. If all possible samples of the same size have the same chance of being selected, these samples are said to be random samples.

14. The distribution of the sample mean is obtained by considering a single sample.

15. The central limit theorem cannot be applied to sampling distributions when the samples are obtained from discrete distributions.

16. The smaller the variance for the distribution of the sample mean, the closer the sample mean is to the population mean.

17. The probability distribution of the sample means is referred to as the sampling distribution of the mean.

18. The central limit theorem applies only to continuous distributions.

19. The sampling distribution of the sample proportion is approximately normal for large enough sample sizes.

20. When considering the sampling distribution for the sample proportions from a single population, the mean of the sample proportions, for large enough sample sizes, will equal the population proportion of interest.

Completion Questions

1. A single-value estimate for μ is known as a(n) (point, interval) _____ estimate.

2. The population of sample means of every possible sample size n is known as the (sampling, normal) _____ distribution of the mean.

3. In the central limit theorem for the sample mean, if the original population is not normally distributed, then the sampling distribution will be (exactly, approximately) _____ normally distributed, provided that the sample size is large enough.

4. The distribution of sample proportions will be approximately normal if the sample size is (greater, smaller) _____ than 30.

5. If the sampling population is normal, then for any sample size, the distribution of the sample mean will be (approximately, exactly) _____ normally distributed.

6. The mean of the distribution of sample means is always equal to the (mean, standard deviation) _____ of the population from which the samples are obtained.

7. As the sample size increases, the standard deviation for the sampling distribution of sample mean, when samples are taken from a single population, will (increase, decrease) _____.

8. If we sample from a normal population with mean μ and standard deviation σ, then the z score associated with $\bar{x}$ for sample size n is $\left[z=\dfrac{\bar{x}-\mu}{\sigma/\sqrt{n}} \; ; \; z=\dfrac{\bar{x}-\mu}{\sigma/\sqrt{n}} \; ; \; z=\dfrac{\bar{x}-\mu}{\sigma/\sqrt{n}} \right]$ _____.

9. The central limit theorem for the sample mean applies to (some, only discrete, only continuous, all) _____ distributions from which samples are obtained.

10. For a sample size of 36 and a standard deviation for the distribution of sample mean of 5, the standard deviation for the population will be (5/36, 5/6, 36/5, 6/5) _____.

11. List two statistics that we can find the sampling distributions of: _____ and _____.

12. If σ is the standard deviation of the sampling population, then for fixed sample size n, the standard deviation of the sample mean can be computed from (give a formula) (σ, σ/n, $\sigma\sqrt{n}$, σ^2/n^2)_____.

13. When we consider the sampling distribution of the difference between two sample proportions, the mean for the sampling distribution will be the difference between the two (sample, population) _____ proportions.

14. When we consider the sampling distribution of the difference between two sample proportions, as the sample sizes n_1 and n_2 increase, the shape of the sampling distribution obtained from (any, some, discrete, continuous) _____ populations will approach a normal distribution.

15. When we consider the sampling distribution of the difference between two sample means, if the sample sizes are large enough to apply the central limit theorem ($n_1 \geq 30$ and $n_2 \geq 30$), then the assumption of normal populations is (less, very) _____ crucial because the distribution of $\bar{x}_1 - \bar{x}_2$ will be approximately normal.

16. If we sample from any population with proportion of interest p, then the z score associated with $\hat{p}$ for sample size n is $\left[z=\dfrac{\hat{p}-p}{p(1-p)} ; z=\dfrac{\hat{p}-p}{\sqrt{p(1-p)}} ; z=\dfrac{\hat{p}-p}{\sqrt{p(1-p)/n}} \right]$ _____.

Multiple-Choice Questions

1. As the sample size increases,
   (a) the population mean decreases.
   (b) the population standard deviation decreases.
   (c) the standard deviation for the distribution of the sample means increases.
   (d) the standard deviation for the distribution of the sample means decreases.

2. The concept of sampling distribution applies to
   (a) only discrete probability distributions from which random samples are obtained.
   (b) only continuous probability distributions from which random samples are obtained.
   (c) only the normal probability distribution.
   (d) any probability distribution from which random samples are obtained.

3. When considering sampling distributions, if the sampling population is normally distributed, then the distribution of the sample means
   (a) will be exactly normally distributed.
   (b) will be approximately normally distributed.
   (c) will have a discrete distribution.
   (d) none of the above.

4. The expected value of the sampling distribution of the sample mean is equal to
   (a) the standard deviation of the sampling population.
   (b) the mean of the sampling population.
   (c) the mean of the sample.
   (d) the population size.

5. The sample statistic $\bar{x}$ is the point estimate of
   (a) the population standard deviation σ.
   (b) the population median.
   (c) the population mean μ.
   (d) the population mode.

6. If repeated random samples of size 40 are taken from an infinite population, the distribution of sample means
   (a) always will be normal because we do not know the distribution of the population.
   (b) always will be normal because the sample mean is always normal.
   (c) always will be normal because the population is infinite.
   (d) will be approximately normal because of the central limit theorem.

7. The mean TOEFL score of international students at a certain university is normally distributed with a mean of 490 and a standard deviation of 80. Suppose that groups of 30 students are studied. The mean and the standard deviation for the distribution of sample means, respectively, will be
   (a) 490 and 8/3.
   (b) 16.33 and 80.
   (c) 490 and 14.61.
   (d) 490 and 213.33.

8. A certain brand of lightbulb has a mean lifetime of 1,500 hours with a standard deviation of 100 hours. If the bulbs are sold in boxes of 25, the parameters of the distribution of sample means are
   (a) 1,500 and 100.
   (b) 1,500 and 4.
   (c) 1,500 and 2.
   (d) 1,500 and 20.

9. Samples of size 49 are drawn from a population with a mean of 36 and a standard deviation of 15. Then $P(\bar{x} < 33)$ is
   (a) 0.5808.
   (b) 0.4192.
   (c) 0.1608.
   (d) 0.0808.

10. A tire manufacturer claims that its tires will last an average of 40,000 miles with a standard deviation of 3,000 miles. Forty-nine tires were placed on test, and the average failure miles was recorded. The probability that the average value of failure miles is less than 39,500 is
   (a) 0.3790.
   (b) 0.8790.
   (c) 0.1210.
   (d) 0.6210.

11. A tire manufacturer claims that its tires will last an average of 40,000 miles with a standard deviation of 3,000 miles. Forty-nine tires were placed on test, and the average failure miles was recorded. The probability that the average value of failure miles is equal to 39,500 is
   (a) 0.4525.
   (b) 0.9525.
   (c) 0.0475.
   (d) 0.0000.

12. A tire manufacturer claims that its tires will last an average of 40,000 miles with a standard deviation of 3,000 miles. Forty-nine tires were placed on test, and the average failure miles was recorded. The probability that the average value of failure miles is more than 39,500 is
   (a) 0.3790.
   (b) 0.8790.
   (c) 0.1210.
   (d) 0.6210.

13. A tire manufacturer claims that its tires will last an average of 40,000 miles with a standard deviation of 3000 miles. Forty-nine tires were placed on test, and the average failure miles was recorded. The probability that the average value of failure miles is between 39,500 and 40,000 is
   (a) 0.3790.
   (b) 0.8790.
   (c) 0.1210.
   (d) 0.6210.

14. Lloyd's Cereal Company packages cereal in 1-pound boxes (1 pound = 16 ounces). It is assumed that the amount of cereal per box varies according to a normal distribution with a standard deviation of 0.05 pound. One box is selected at random from the production line every hour, and if the weight is less than 15 ounces, the machine is adjusted to increase the amount of cereal dispensed. The probability that the amount dispensed per box will have to be increased during a 1-hour period is

(a) 0.3944.

(b) 0.8944.

(c) 0.1056.

(d) 0.6056.

15. Lloyd's Cereal Company packages cereal in 1-pound boxes (1 pound = 16 ounces). It is assumed that the amount of cereal per box varies according to a normal distribution. A sample of 16 boxes is selected at random from the production line every hour, and if the average weight is less than 15 ounces, the machine is adjusted to increase the amount of cereal dispensed. If the mean for an hour is 1 pound and the standard deviation is 0.1 pound, the probability that the amount dispensed per box will have to be increased is

(a) 0.5062.

(b) 0.0062.

(c) 0.4938.

(d) 0.9938.

16. Lloyd's Cereal Company packages cereal in 1-pound boxes (1 pound = 16 ounces). It is assumed that the amount of cereal per box varies according to a normal distribution. A sample of 16 boxes is selected at random from the production line every hour, and if the average weight is less than 15 ounces, the machine is adjusted to increase the amount of cereal dispensed. If the mean for an hour is 1 pound and the standard deviation is 0.1 pound, the probability that the amount dispensed per box will not have to be increased is

(a) 0.5062.

(b) 0.0062.

(c) 0.4938.

(d) 0.9938.

17. Suppose that a very large number of random samples of size 25 are selected from a population with mean μ and standard deviation σ. If the mean of all the $\bar{x}$'s found is 300 and the standard deviation of these $\bar{x}$'s is 20, the estimates of the true mean μ and the true standard deviation σ of the distribution from which the samples were drawn are, respectively,

(a) 300 and 100.

(b) 300 and 4.

(c) 300 and 16.

(d) 300 and 80.

18. Suppose that a very large number of random samples of size 25 are selected from a population with mean μ and standard deviation σ. If the mean of all the $\bar{x}$'s found is 300 and the standard deviation of these $\bar{x}$'s is 20, the estimates of the true mean and the true standard deviation of the distribution of sample means are, respectively,

(a) 300 and 100.

(b) 300 and 4.

(c) 300 and 20.

(d) 300 and 16.

19. A waiter estimates that his average tip per table is $20, with a standard deviation of $4. If his tables seat nine customers, the probability that the average tip for one table will be less than $21 when the tip per table is normally distributed is

(a) 0.2734.

(b) 0.2266.

(c) 0.7734.

(d) 0.7266.

20. A waiter estimates that his average tip per table is $20, with a standard deviation of $4. If his tables seat nine customers, the probability that the average tip for one table will be more than $21 when the tip per table is normally distributed is

(a) 0.2734.

(b) 0.2266.

(c) 0.7734.

(d) 0.7266.

21. A waiter estimates that his average tip per table is $20, with a standard deviation of $4. If his tables seat nine customers, the probability that the average tip for one table will be equal to $21 when the tip per table is normally distributed is

(a) 0.2734.

(b) 0.2266.

(c) 0.7734.

(d) 0.0000.

22. A waiter estimates that his average tip per table is $20, with a standard deviation of $4. If his tables seat nine customers, the probability that the average tip for one table will be between $19 and $21 when the tip per table is normally distributed is

(a) 0.2734.

(b) 0.2266.

(c) 0.7734.

(d) 0.5468.

23. Samples of size 49 are selected at random from an infinite population whose mean and variance are both 25. It is assumed that the distribution of the population is unknown. The mean and the standard deviation of the distribution of sample means are, respectively,

(a) 49 and 3.5714.

(b) 25 and 5.

(c) 25 and 0.7143.

(d) 25 and 0.5102.

Use the following information for Questions 24 to 26:

Two machines are used to fill 50-pound bags of dog food. Sample information for these two machines is given below:

	MACHINE 1	MACHINE 2
Sample size	81	64
Sample mean (pounds)	51	48
Sample variance	16	12

24. The point estimate for the difference between the two population means $(\mu_1 - \mu_2)$ is
    (a) 17.
    (b) 3.
    (c) 4.
    (d) -4.

25. The standard deviation for the distribution of differences of sample means $(\mu_1 - \mu_2)$ is
    (a) 0.6205.
    (b) 0.1931.
    (c) 0.3850.
    (d) 0.3217.

26. Find $P(\bar{x}_1 - \bar{x}_2 \geq 2)$.
    (a) 0.4463
    (b) 0.0537
    (c) 0.9463
    (d) 0.5537

Use the following information for Questions 27 to 29:

A study was conducted to determine whether remediation in mathematics enabled students to be more successful in college algebra. Success here means that a student received a grade of C or better, and remediation was for one year (students took an equivalent of one year of high school algebra). The following table shows the results of this study:

	REMEDIAL (1)	NONREMEDIAL (2)
Sample size	$n_1 = 34$	$n_2 = 150$
Number of successes	$x_1 = 28$	$x_2 = 104$

27. The point estimate for $p_1 - p_2$ is
    (a) -0.1302.
    (b) 0.1302.
    (c) 0.2280.
    (d) -0.2280.

28. If it is known from past history that the success rates for students in the remedial and nonremedial groups are 90 and 75 percent, respectively, then the standard deviation for the sampling distribution of $\hat{p}_1 - \hat{p}_2$ is
    (a) 0.0057.
    (b) 0.0624.
    (c) 0.0755.
    (d) 0.0039.

29. If it is known from past history that the success rates for students in the remedial and nonremedial groups are 90 and 75 percent, respectively, find $P(\hat{p}_1 - \hat{p}_2 \geq 0.2)$.
    (a) 0.2881
    (b) 0.2119
    (c) 0.7881
    (d) 0.7119

30. A single number computed from sample data used to estimate a population parameter is called
    (a) the sample mean.
    (b) a parameter.
    (c) a point estimate.
    (d) a population statistic.

31. A sampling distribution of a sample proportion, when samples are taken from a single population, has a
    (a) mean that is equal to the sample proportion for a single sample.
    (b) standard deviation that is equal to the population proportion.
    (c) variance that is equal to the sample variance for a single sample.
    (d) mean that is equal to the population proportion.

32. The sample statistic $\bar{x}$ is the point estimate of the
    (a) population standard deviation.
    (b) sample mean.
    (c) population mode.
    (d) population mean.

33. If a simulation produces 400 random samples of size 35 from the same population, then
    (a) the mean of these 400 random sample means likely will be approximately equal to the population mean.
    (b) the sample variances will all be the same.
    (c) the mean of these 400 random sample means will be exactly equal to the population mean.
    (d) the sample means will all be the same.

34. The test scores of an exit exam on a certain campus are normally distributed with a mean of 490 and a standard deviation of 80. Suppose samples of 25 students are selected. The mean and the variance for the distribution of sample means will be, respectively,
    (a) 490 and 3.2.
    (b) 490 and 1.7889.
    (c) 490 and 256.
    (d) 490 and 16.

35. A teachers' union is gathering information for teachers in a particular state in order to lobby to represent them in the future. The union has determined that the average salary of all its members across the country is $40,000, with a standard deviation of $15,000. If the union selected a random sample of 25 salaries from the given state, and assuming that the distribution of the salaries is normally distributed, then the probability that the average for this sample is less than $35,000 is
    (a) 0.9522.
    (b) 0.4522.
    (c) 0.5478.
    (d) 0.0478.

36. The Burger Joint believes that 80 percent of all students on a particular campus prefer their hamburgers over the hamburgers served at the campus grill. The owner of the

Burger Joint decides to give a taste test to a sample of 225 students. What is the probability that at least 183 of the students in the sample prefer the hamburger from the Burger Joint?

(a) 0.1615
(b) 0.3085
(c) 0.8385
(d) 0.6915

37. The sampling distribution of the sample proportions can be approximated generally by a normal distribution when

(a) $np > 5$.
(b) $n \geq 30$.
(c) both $np > 5$ and $n(1 - p) > 5$.
(d) all the above are true.

38. The IQ scores of students at a college are normally distributed with a mean of 100 and a standard deviation of 15. If a sample of 16 students is selected from this college, what is the probability the sample average IQ will be greater than 115?

(a) Approximately 1.0
(b) Approximately 0.0
(c) 0.8413
(d) 0.1587

39. Suppose that during a national election a survey indicates that 48 percent of the population favors a particular candidate. If a random sample of size 200 is chosen, what is the probability that at most 99 people favor this candidate?

(a) 0.5563
(b) 0.4160
(c) 0.5840
(d) 0.4437

40. Equal dosages of two drugs were used to treat the same pain level for headaches. Sample information for the time (minutes) to complete pain relief for these two medications, along with the sample means, is given below, along with the standard deviation from previous studies. We will assume that these standard deviations correspond to the respective populations.

	DRUG 1	DRUG 2
Sample size	81	75
Sample mean (minutes)	32	28
Population standard deviation	4	3

Find the probability that the average time to complete relief of the headache from drug 1 exceeds the average time for drug 2 by 3 minutes. That is, find $P(\bar{x}_1 - \bar{x}_2 \geq 3)$.

(a) 0.0384
(b) 0.9616
(c) 0.4616
(d) 0.9232

41. A study was conducted to determine whether two teaching methods of the same course materials would produce equal success for the course. Success here is measured by the proportion of students gaining a C or better in the course. The following table shows the results of this study for this semester:

	METHOD 1	METHOD 2
Sample size	$n_1 = 102$	$n_2 = 150$
Number of successes	$x_1 = 84$	$x_2 = 104$

If it is known from past history that the success rates for students in courses using these two methods are 90 and 75 percent, respectively, find the probability, for this semester, that the proportion of success using method 1 will exceed the proportion of success using method 2 by 20 percent. That is, find $P(\hat{p}_1 - \hat{p}_2 \geq 0.2)$.

(a) 0.9345
(b) 0.0655
(c) 0.5655
(d) 0.4345

Further Exercises

If possible, you could use any technology help to solve the following questions.

1. Consider a population that consists of the elements {1, 3, 5}. Write down all possible samples of size 2 (chosen with replacement) from this population, and give the sample mean $\bar{x}$ in each case. Show that the mean of all possible samples of size 2 equals the mean of the population.

2. A population has a distribution with $\mu = 50$ and $\sigma = 12$. A random sample of size 100 is selected.

   (a) Calculate the standard deviation of the sample mean.
   (b) Find $P(51 < \bar{x} < 53)$

3. Suppose that the high daily temperatures in a small town in the eastern United States are normally distributed with a mean of 58.6°F and a standard deviation of 9.8°F.

   (a) Find the probability that the average high daily temperature is between 45 and 55°F.
   (b) Find the probability that the average high daily temperature is less than 60°F.
   (c) If a random sample of size four of average high daily temperatures is selected, find the probability that the mean of this sample of average high daily temperatures is less than 57°F.
   (d) If a random sample of size four of average high daily temperatures is selected, find the probability that the mean of this sample of average high daily temperatures is between 57 and 61°F.
   (e) Suppose that a random sample of 16 high temperatures was chosen and that the sample mean was recorded. Give the values of the mean and standard deviation of the sample mean.

4. Suppose that the heights of female adults in the United States are normally distributed with a mean of 65.4 inches and a standard deviation of 2.8 inches. Let X denote the height of a randomly chosen adult female.

   (a) Find the probability that X is between 66 and 70 inches.
   (b) Suppose that a random sample of 10 adult females was chosen and that the sample mean was recorded. Give the values of the mean and standard deviation of the sample mean, and describe the shape of the distribution.
   (c) Using the information in part (b), find the probability that the sample mean is greater than 68 inches.

5. A manufacturing company produces steel bolts to be used on a certain truck. The lengths of the bolts are normally distributed with a mean length of 6 inches and a standard deviation of 0.1 inch. Samples of size 20 are examined at random, and if the average length is outside the interval from 5.98 to 6.02 inches, the entire production for the day is examined. Find the probability that a daily production will have to be examined.

6. Two instructors offer extra help designed to improve the scores on the MCAT exam for students. Suppose that 85 percent of the students under tutelage from instructor 1 improve their scores, whereas 76 percent of the students under tutelage from instructor 2 improve their scores. In a random sample of 55 students taking instructor 1 and 60 students taking instructor 2, compute the probability that the difference between the percentages of students improving their scores is more than 25 percent.

7. In a highly publicized murder trial it was estimated that 25 percent of the TV viewers watched (at least three hours of) the trial on TV. A statistics student felt that the estimate was too small for his community and selected a random sample of 100 residents from the community and found that 35 of them actually watched the trial on TV. Find the probability that more than 33 percent watched the proceedings on TV.

ANSWER KEY
True/False Questions

1. T   2. F   3. T   4. F   5. F   6. T   7. T   8. F   9. T   10. T
11. T   12. F   13. T   14. F   15. F   16. T   17. T   18. F   19. T   20. T

Completion Questions

1. point   2. sampling   3. approximately   4. greater   5. exactly   6. mean

7. decrease   8. $\dfrac{\bar{x}-\mu}{\sigma/\sqrt{n}}$ 9. all   10. 5/6   11. sample mean, sample proportion

12. $\sigma/\sqrt{n}$ 13. population   14. any   15. less   16. $\dfrac{\hat{p}-p}{\sqrt{p(1-p)/n}}$

Multiple-Choice Questions

1. (d)   2. (d)   3. (a)   4. (b)   5. (c)   6. (d)   7. (c)   8. (d)   9. (d)
10. (c)   11. (d)   12. (b)   13. (a)   14. (c)   15. (b)   16. (d)   17. (a)   18. (c)

19. (c) 20. (b) 21. (d) 22. (d) 23. (c) 24. (b) 25. (a) 26. (b) 27. (b)
28. (b) 29. (b) 30. (c) 31. (d) 32. (d) 33. (a) 34. (d) 35. (d) 36. (b)
37. (c) 38. (b) 39. (c) 40. (b) 41. (a)

Further Exercises

1. Mean of population $\mu = (1 + 3 + 5)/3 = 3$. Table with samples and sample means:

SAMPLES	SAMPLE MEANS, $\bar{X}$
(1, 1)	1
(1, 3)	2
(1, 5)	3
(3, 3)	3
(3, 1)	2
(3, 5)	4
(5, 5)	5
(5, 3)	4
(5, 1)	3

Mean of the sample means $= (1 + 2 + 3 + 3 + 2 + 4 + 5 + 4 + 3)/9 = 3 = \mu$.

2. (a) $\sigma_{\bar{x}} = 1.2$ (b) 0.1961

3. (a) 0.2741   (b) 0.5568   (c) 0.3720   (d) 0.3158
   (e) $\mu_{\bar{x}} = 58.6°F$, $\sigma_{\bar{x}} = 2.45°F$.

4. (a) 0.3650   (b) $\mu_{\bar{x}} = 65.4$ inches; $\sigma_{\bar{x}} = 0.8854$ inches; exactly normal   (c) 0.0017

5. 0.3711   6. 0.0143

7. 0.3353 [*Hint*: Find $P(p > 0.33) = P(-p < -0.33) = P(\hat{p} - p < 35/100 - 0.33$. Next, divide on both sides of the "less than" symbol within the parentheses by the appropriate radical to convert to a z score, and then find the probability.]

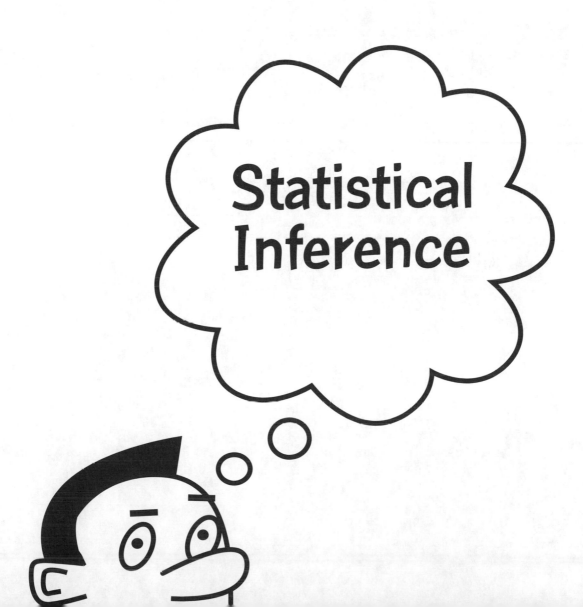

PART III

Statistical Inference

CHAPTER 11

Confidence Intervals: Large Samples

Do I Need to Read This Chapter?

You should read this chapter if you need to review or to learn about

→ Large-sample confidence intervals for a single population proportion

→ Large-sample confidence intervals for a single population mean

→ Large-sample confidence intervals for the difference between two population proportions

→ Large-sample confidence intervals for the difference between two population means

Get Started

Here we will focus on confidence intervals. When a point estimate is used to estimate the parameter of interest, it is unlikely that the value of the point estimate will be equal to the value of the parameter. Therefore, we will use the value of the point estimate to help construct an interval estimate for the parameter. We will be able to state, with some confidence, that the parameter lies within the interval, and because of this, we refer to these intervals as *confidence intervals*. Typically, we consider 90, 95, and 99 percent confidence interval estimates for parameters, but any other percentage can be considered. Here we will consider large-sample confidence intervals for a single population proportion and mean and for the difference between two population proportions and means.

11-1 Large-Sample Confidence Interval for a Single Population Proportion

From **Chapter 10** we can summarize the properties of the central limit theorem for sample proportions with the following statements:

- Random samples of size n are selected from a population in which the true proportion of the attribute of interest is p.

- Provided that $np > 5$ and $n(1 - p) > 5$, the sampling distribution of the sample proportion $\hat{p}$ will be approximately normally distributed with a mean of $\mu_{\hat{p}} = p$ and a standard deviation of $\sigma_{\hat{p}} = \sqrt{p(1 - p)/n}$.

Now, in finding confidence interval estimates for the unknown parameter p, we would need to compute $\sigma_{\hat{p}} = \sqrt{p(1 - p)/n}$, the standard deviation for the sampling distribution of the sample proportion $\hat{p}$. The question then is: How do we compute $\sigma_{\hat{p}}$ because we are estimating p, and p is unknown? A reasonable approach would be to replace p with $\hat{p}$, the point estimate for p, in the formulas. Thus we will use $\sigma_{\hat{p}} \approx \sqrt{\hat{p}(1 - \hat{p})/n}$.

Before we state the formula relating to confidence intervals for a population proportion, let us consider the following example.

Example 11-1: In a random sample of 100 men in the United States, 55 of them were married. Determine an approximate 95 percent confidence interval estimate for the true proportion of men in the United States who are married.

Solution: Since $n = 100$, x(number of successes) $= 55$; then $\hat{p} = 0.55$. Also, $\sigma_{\hat{p}} \approx \sqrt{\hat{p}(1 - \hat{p})/n} = 0.0497$. The sampling distribution for $\hat{p}$ is approximately normally distributed, so from the empirical rule, approximately 95 percent of the observed $\hat{p}$ values will lie within two standard deviations of the mean, $p \approx \hat{p}$. This situation can be described by **Figure 11-1**.

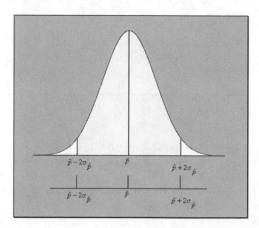

Figure 11-1: Display of two standard deviations from the mean of $\hat{p}$

Thus the approximate 95 percent confidence interval estimate for the proportion of men in the United States who are married is $0.55 \pm 2 \times 0.0497 = 0.55 \pm 0.0994$. That is, we are (approximately) 95 percent confident that the proportion of males in the United States who are married will lie between 0.4506 and 0.6494, or between 45.06 and 64.94 percent.

Note: We say the margin of error is ± 0.0994, or ± 9.94 percent.

In order to state a general formula that can be used to compute the confidence interval for any population proportion, we need to be familiar with the notation z_α, read as "z sub alpha." This will enable us to use any number of standard deviations from the mean in constructing the confidence interval.

Explanation of the notation—z_α: z_α is a z score such that the α area is to the right of the z-score value, where $0 \le \alpha \le 1$.

Figure 11-2 shows a diagram that explains the notation.

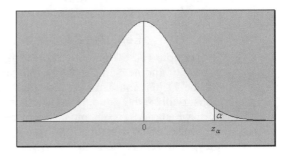

Figure 11-2: Area associated with z_α

Table 11-1 lists values for z_α and $z_{\alpha/2}$ when $\alpha = 0.1, 0.05, 0.02$, and 0.01. These values can be obtained from the standard normal tables in the **Appendix** of this text.

Table 11-1: Selected z Values for Selected α Values

α	z_α	$z_{\alpha/2}$
0.10	1.28	1.645
0.05	1.645	1.96
0.02	2.05	2.33
0.01	2.33	2.575

Note: The notation $z_{\alpha/2} \ne \dfrac{z_\alpha}{2}$. First, you have to divide α by 2 and then find the corresponding z-score value. For example, if we are given that $\alpha = 0.1$ and we need to find $z_{\alpha/2}$, first we find $\alpha/2$. This is equivalent to $0.1/2 = 0.05$. Thus we then would find the value of $z_{0.05}$. From **Table 11-1**, this value will be 1.645.

The relationship between α and the confidence level is that the stated confidence level is the percentage equivalent to the decimal value $1 - \alpha$. For example, if we are constructing a 98 percent confidence interval, then $0.98 = 1 - \alpha$, from which $\alpha = 0.02$.

The general equation used in constructing a $(1 - \alpha) \times 100$ percent confidence interval for the population proportion for large samples is given next:

$$\hat{p} \pm z_{\alpha/2} \sqrt{\frac{\hat{p}(1-\hat{p})}{n}}$$

Note: The margin of error is given by $E = z_{\alpha/2} \sqrt{\dfrac{\hat{p}(1-\hat{p})}{n}}$

Example 11-2: In a random sample of 100 persons, 77 percent of them said that when they pray, they pray for world peace. Determine a 90 percent confidence interval estimate for the true proportion of people who pray for world peace when they pray.

Solution: Since $\hat{p} = 0.77$, then $\sigma_{\hat{p}} \approx \sqrt{\hat{p}(1-\hat{p})/n} = 0.0421$. Since we need to find the 90 percent confidence interval, then $\alpha = 10$ percent $= 0.1$. From **Table 11-1**, $z_{\alpha/2} = 1.645$. Thus the 90 percent confidence interval estimate for the proportion of people who pray for world peace when they pray, using the formula, is $0.77 \pm 1.645 \times 0.0421 = 0.77 \pm 0.0692$. That is, we are 90 confident that the true proportion of people who pray for world peace when they pray will lie between 0.7008 and 0.8392, or between 70.08 and 83.92 percent.

Repeated-Sample Interpretation of a Confidence Interval

In **Example 11-2**, 77 percent of the sample said that they prayed for world peace when they prayed. If another sample of size 100 is taken, it is unlikely that the sample proportion again will be 77 percent. Thus, in repeated sampling, we should not expect the sample proportions to all be the same. If we use these sample proportions to construct confidence intervals, we should expect most, if not all, to be different. However, we should expect 90 percent of them to contain the true proportion of people who pray for world peace when they pray. This is the reason why we say that we are 90 percent confident that the population proportion will lie between 0.7008 and 0.8392 in the example.

Note: We **do not** say that the probability is 0.90 that the population proportion of people who pray for world peace when they pray is between 0.7008 and 0.8392. Once the sample is obtained and the confidence interval is constructed, the population proportion of people who pray for world peace when they pray will lie in the interval or it will not lie in the interval.

Quick Tip

The repeated-sampling interpretation of a confidence interval generally can be applied to any confidence interval for any population parameter.

Sample Size: Sample size determination is closely related to estimation. You may need to know how large a sample is necessary to make an accurate estimate for the population proportion p. The answer depends on

- The margin of error
- The point estimate for the population proportion
- The degree of confidence

For example, you may need to know how far away from the population proportion you would like the estimate to be and how confident you are of this. Since

$E = z_{\alpha/2}\sqrt{\dfrac{\hat{p}(1-\hat{p})}{n}}$, we can solve to find n, the sample size. Solving, we have

$$n = \hat{p}(1-\hat{p})\left(\frac{z_{\alpha/2}}{E}\right)^2$$

Note: This will be the minimum sample size that is required.

Example 11-3: A statistician wishes to estimate, with 99 percent confidence, the proportion of people who trust DNA testing. A previous study shows that 91 percent of those who were surveyed trusted DNA testing. The statistician wishes to be accurate within 3 percent of the true proportion. What is the minimum sample size necessary for the statistician to carry out this analysis?

Solution: We are given that $\alpha = 0.01$, $z_{\alpha/2} = 2.575$, $\hat{p} = 0.91$, and $E = 0.03$. Substituting into the formula, we get that the sample size:

$$n = \hat{p}(1-\hat{p})\left(\frac{z_{\alpha/2}}{E}\right)^2 = (0.91)(1-0.91)\left(\frac{2.575}{0.03}\right)^2 = 603.38 \approx 604$$

That is, in order for the statistician to be 99 percent certain that the estimate is within 3 percent of the true proportion of people who trust DNA testing, a sample of at least 604 is needed.

Quick Tips

- When computing the sample size to make an accurate estimate for the population proportion p, if $\hat{p}$ is unknown, use a value of 0.5 in the formula for $\hat{p}$.
- By using $\hat{p} = 0.5$, the maximum sample size will be computed.

- The formula will be reduced to $n = 0.25 \times \left(\frac{z_{\alpha/2}}{E}\right)^2$

Example 11-4: A confidence interval for a population proportion is to be constructed and must be accurate to within 0.01 (1 percent) unit of measurement. What is the largest sample size n needed to provide the desired accuracy with 95 percent confidence?

Solution: We are given that $\alpha = 0.05$, $z_{\alpha/2} = 1.96$, $\hat{p} = 0.5$ (because no estimate for $\hat{p}$ is given), and $E = 0.01$. Substituting into the formula, we get that the sample size:

$$n = \hat{p}(1-\hat{p})\left(\frac{z_{\alpha/2}}{E}\right)^2 = (0.5)(1-0.5)\left(\frac{1.96}{0.01}\right)^2 = 9,604$$

That is, in order to be 95 percent certain that the estimate is within 1 percent of the true population proportion, the largest sample size needed is 9,604.

11-2 Large-Sample Confidence Interval for a Single Population Mean

From **Chapter 10** we can summarize the properties of the central limit theorem for sample means with the following statements:

- Sampling is from any distribution with mean μ and standard deviation σ.

- Provided that n is large ($n \geq 30$ as a rule of thumb), the sampling distribution of the sample mean $\bar{x}$ will be approximately normally distributed with a mean of $\mu_{\bar{x}} = \mu$ and a standard deviation of $\sigma_{\bar{x}} = \frac{\sigma}{\sqrt{n}}$.

- If the sampling distribution is normal, the sampling distribution of the sample means will be an exact normal distribution for any sample size.

Now, in finding confidence interval estimates for the unknown parameter μ, we would need to compute $\sigma_{\bar{x}} = \frac{\sigma}{\sqrt{n}}$. The general equation used in constructing a $(1 - \alpha) \times 100$ percent confidence interval for the population mean is given below:

$$\overline{x} \pm z_{\alpha/2} \frac{\sigma}{\sqrt{n}}$$

Note: The margin of error is given by $E = z_{\alpha/2} \times \frac{\sigma}{\sqrt{n}}$.

Example 11-5: A random sample of 100 public school teachers in a particular state has a mean salary of \$31,578. It is known from past history that the standard deviation of the salaries for the teachers in the state is \$4,415. Construct a 99 percent confidence interval estimate for the true mean salary for public school teachers for the given state.

Solution: We are given that $\alpha = 0.01$, $z_{\alpha/2} = 2.575$, $\overline{x} = 31,578$, $n = 100$, $\sigma = 4,415$, and $\sigma_{\overline{x}} = \frac{\sigma}{\sqrt{n}} = 441.5$. Thus the 99 percent confidence interval estimate for the mean salary, using the formula, is $31,578 \pm 2.575 \times 441.5 = 31,578 \pm 1,136.86$. That is, we are 99 percent confident that the average salary for public school teachers for the given state will lie between \$30,441.14 and \$32,714.86.

Quick Tip

In computing a confidence interval for a single population mean, when the population standard deviation σ is unknown, it can be replaced with the sample standard deviation s if the sample size is large ($n \geq 30$).

Example 11-6: The president of a large community college wishes to estimate the average distance commuting students travel to the campus. A sample of 64 students who commute to the campus was randomly selected and yielded a mean of 35 miles and a standard deviation of 5 miles. Construct a 95 percent confidence interval estimate for the true mean distance commuting students travel to the campus.

Solution: We are given that $\alpha = 0.05$, $z_{\alpha/2} = 1.96$, $\overline{x} = 35$, $s = 5$, $n = 64$, and $\sigma_{\overline{x}} \approx \frac{s}{\sqrt{n}} = 0.625$. The 95 percent confidence interval estimate for the mean distance, using the formula, is $35 \pm 1.96 \times 0.625 = 35 \pm 1.225$. That is, we are 95 percent confident that the average distance commuting students travel to the campus will lie between 33.775 and 36.225 miles.

Sample Size: In considering large-sample confidence intervals for the mean, since the error of estimate is given by $E = z_{\alpha/2} \frac{\sigma}{\sqrt{n}}$, we can solve to find n, the sample size. Solving, we have

$$n = \left(\frac{z_{\alpha/2} \times \sigma}{E} \right)^2$$

Quick Tip

When computing sample sizes, you always should round up the next whole-number value.

Example 11-7: What sample size should be selected to estimate the mean age of workers in a large factory within ± 1 year at a 95 percent confidence level if the standard deviation for the ages is 3.5 years?

Solution: We are given that $\alpha = 0.05$, $z_{\alpha/2} = 1.96$, $\sigma = 3.5$, and $E = 1$. Substituting into the formula, we get that the sample size:

$$n = \left(\frac{z_{\alpha/2} \times \sigma}{E} \right)^2 = \left(\frac{1.96 \times 3.5}{1} \right)^2 = 47.0596 \approx 48$$

That is, in order to be 95 percent certain that the estimate is within 1 year of the true mean age, a sample of at least 48 is needed.

Note: For large enough sample size ($n \geq 30$), when the population standard deviation σ is unknown, we can replace σ with the sample standard deviation s in the preceding equation.

11-3 Large-Sample Confidence Interval for the Difference between Two Population Proportions

From **Chapter 10** we can summarize the properties of the sampling distribution for the difference between two independent sample proportions with the following statements:

- As the sample sizes n_1 and n_2 increase, the shape of the distribution of the differences of the sample proportions obtained from any population (distribution) will approach a normal distribution.
- The distribution of the differences of the sample proportions will have a mean given by $\mu_{\hat{p}_1 - \hat{p}_2} = p_1 - p_2$.
- The distribution of the differences of the sample proportions will have a standard deviation given by

$$\sigma_{\hat{p}_1 - \hat{p}_2} = \sqrt{ \frac{p_1(1-p_1)}{n_1} + \frac{p_2(1-p_2)}{n_2} }$$

where p_1 and p_2 are the respective population proportion of interest.

These properties can aid us in the construction of a $(1 - \alpha) \times 100$ percent confidence interval for the difference of two population proportions. Again, since we do not know the values of the true proportions, we will use the corresponding point estimates for these true proportions. The general equation used in constructing a $(1 - \alpha) \times 100$ percent confidence interval for the difference between two population proportions for large samples, that is, when $n_1 p_1 \geq 5$, $n_1(1 - p_1) \geq 5$, $n_2 p_2 \geq 5$, and $n_2 (1 - p_2) \geq 5$, is given next:

$$\boxed{(\hat{p}_1 - \hat{p}_2) \pm z_{\alpha/2} = \sqrt{ \frac{\hat{p}_1(1-\hat{p}_1)}{n_1} + \frac{\hat{p}_2(1-\hat{p}_2)}{n_2} }}$$

Example 11-8: A study was conducted to determine whether remediation in basic mathematics enabled students to be more successful in an elementary statistics course. Success here means that a student received a grade of C or better, and remediation was for one year. **Table 11-2** shows the results of the study.

Table 11-2: Information Related to Example 11-8

	REMEDIAL	NONREMEDIAL
Sample size	100	40
Number of successes	70	16

Construct a 95 percent confidence interval for the difference between the proportions of success for the remedial and nonremedial (remedial − nonremedial) groups.

Solution: From the information given, we have $n_1 = 100$, $n_2 = 40$, $\hat{p}_1 = \dfrac{70}{100} = 0.7$,

$$\hat{p}_2 = \frac{16}{40} = 0.4, \sqrt{\frac{\hat{p}_1(1-\hat{p}_1)}{n_1}+\frac{\hat{p}_2(1-\hat{p}_2)}{n_2}} = \sqrt{\frac{0.7(1-0.7)}{100}+\frac{0.4(1-0.4)}{40}} = 0.09$$

$\alpha = 0.05$, and $z_{\alpha/2} = 1.96$. Thus the 95 percent confidence interval estimate for the difference of the proportions is $(0.7 - 0.4) \pm 1.96 \times 0.09 = 0.3 \pm 0.1764$. That is, we are 95 percent confident that the difference between the proportions for the remedial and nonremedial groups will lie between 0.1236 and 0.4764, or between 12.36 and 47.64 percent. Since both limits for the interval are positive, one may conclude that the proportion of success for the remedial group is larger than the proportion of success for the nonremedial group. That is, for the elementary statistics course, we can conclude that remediation seems to help the students do better than those students who do not obtain remediation.

Sample Sizes: In considering large-sample confidence intervals for the difference between two population proportions, that is, when $n_1 p_1 \geq 5$, $n_1(1 - p_1) \geq 5$, $n_2 p_2 \geq 5$, and $n_2(1 - p_2) \geq 5$, we may need to estimate the sample sizes needed in order to collect data. The formula given here is for when the sample sizes are the same. Also, this will be the equation for the minimum sample size. The formula is given next:

$$n=0.5\times\left(\frac{z_{\alpha/2}}{E}\right)^2$$

Note: The formula given is for when we use equal sample sizes to obtain the estimates. When the sample sizes are not the same, the formula(s) is(are) much more complex and will not be presented in this text.

Example 11-9: A researcher wants to determine the difference between the proportions of males and females who believe in aliens. If a margin of error of ± 0.02 is acceptable at the 95 percent confidence level, what is the minimum sample size that should be taken from each population? Assume that equal sample sizes are selected for the two sample proportions.

Solution: We are given $\alpha = 0.05$ and $E = 0.02$. Since $\alpha = 0.05$, then $z_{\alpha/2} = 1.96$. Thus

$$n=0.5\times\left(\frac{z_{\alpha/2}}{E}\right)^2 =0.5\times\left(\frac{1.96}{0.02}\right)^2 =4,802$$

That is, the researcher should sample at least 4,802 males and 4,802 females in the research study.

11-4 Large-Sample Confidence Interval for the Difference between Two Population Means

From **Chapter 10** we can summarize the properties of the sampling distribution for the difference between two independent sample means with the following statements:

- As the sample sizes n_1 and n_2 increase, the shape of the distribution of the differences of the sample means obtained from any population (distribution) will approach a normal distribution.

- The distribution of the differences of the sample means will have a mean of $\mu_{\bar{x}_1 - \bar{x}_2} = \mu_1 - \mu_2$, where μ_1 and μ_2 are the respective population means of interest.
- The distribution of the differences of the sample means will have a standard deviation of

$$\sigma_{\bar{x}1 - \bar{x}1} = \sqrt{\frac{\sigma_1^2}{n_1} + \frac{\sigma_2^2}{n_2}} \quad \text{where } \sigma_1 \text{ and } \sigma_2 \text{ are the respective population standard deviations}$$

of interest.

These properties can aid us in the construction of a $(1 - \alpha) \times 100$ percent confidence interval for the difference of two population means. The general equation used in constructing a $(1 - \alpha) \times 100$ percent confidence interval for the difference between two population means for large samples is given next:

$$(\bar{x}_1 - \bar{x}_2) \pm z_{\alpha/2} \sqrt{\frac{\sigma_1^2}{n_1} + \frac{\sigma_2^2}{n_2}}$$

Quick Tip

For large samples ($n_1 \geq 30$ and $n_2 \geq 30$), the population variances can be replaced by the sample variances if the population variances are unknown.

Example 11-10: A random sample of size $n_1 = 36$ selected from a normal distribution with standard deviation $\sigma_1 = 4$ has a mean $\bar{x}_1 = 75$. A second random sample of size $n_2 = 25$ selected from a different normal distribution with a standard deviation $\sigma_2 = 6$ has a mean $\bar{x}_2 = 85$. Find a 95 percent confidence interval for $\mu_1 - \mu_2$.

Solution: From the information given, we have $n_1 = 36$, $n_2 = 25$, $\bar{x}_1 = 75$, $\bar{x}_2 = 85$, $\sigma_1 = 4$,

$\sigma_2 = 6$, $\sqrt{\frac{\sigma_1^2}{n_1} + \frac{\sigma_2^2}{n_2}} = 1.3728$, $\alpha = 0.05$, and $z_{\alpha/2} = 1.96$. Thus the 95 percent confidence inter-

val estimate for $\mu_1 - \mu_2$ is $(75 - 85) \pm 1.96 \times 1.3728 = -10 \pm 2.6907$. That is, we are 95 percent confident that the difference between the means will lie between -12.6907 and -7.3093. Since both limits are negative, one may conclude that the mean from population 2 is larger than the mean from population 1.

Example 11-11: Two methods were used to teach a high school algebra course. A sample of 75 scores was selected for method 1, and a sample of 60 scores was selected for method 2, with the summary results given in **Table 11-3.**

Table 11-3: Information Related to Example 11-11

	METHOD 1	METHOD 2
Sample size	75	60
Sample mean	85	76
Sample standard deviation	3	2

Construct a 99 percent confidence interval for the difference (method 1 − method 2) in the mean scores for the two methods. Assume that the scores are normally distributed.

Solution: From the information given, we have $n_1 = 75$, $n_2 = 60$, $\bar{x}_1 = 85$, $\bar{x}_2 = 76$, $s_1 = 3, s_2 = 2, \sqrt{\dfrac{s_1^2}{n_1} + \dfrac{s_2^2}{n_2}} = 0.4320$, $\alpha = 0.01$, and $z_{\alpha/2} = 2.576$. Thus the 99 percent confidence interval estimate for the difference of the means for the two methods (method 1 − method 2) is $(85 - 76) \pm 2.576 \times 0.4320 = 9 \pm 1.1128$. That is, we are 99 percent confident that the difference between the mean scores for the two teaching methods will lie between 7.8872 and 10.1128. Since both limits are positive, one may conclude that method 1 seems to be the better of the two methods.

Sample Sizes: In considering large-sample confidence intervals for the difference between two population means, we may need to estimate the sample sizes needed in order to collect data. The formula given here is for the minimum sample sizes when the sample sizes are the same. The formula is given next:

$$n = \left(\frac{z_{\alpha/2}}{E}\right)^2 \times \left(\sigma_1^2 + \sigma_2^2\right)$$

Example 11-12: A researcher wishes to study the difference between the average score on a standardized test for students who major in marketing and art. The standard deviation for the scores is 5 for both groups of students. How large a sample (equal in this case) must the researcher use if she wishes to be 99 percent certain of knowing the difference of the average of the scores for the two populations to be within ±3 points.

Solution: We are given $\alpha = 0.01$, $E = 3$, and $\sigma_1 = \sigma_2 = 5$. Since $\alpha = 0.01$, then $z_{\alpha/2} = 2.576$. Thus

$$n = \left(\frac{z_{\alpha/2}}{E}\right)^2 \times \left(\sigma_1^2 + \sigma_2^2\right) = \left(\frac{2.576}{3}\right)^2 \times \left(5^2 + 5^2\right) = 36.8654 \approx 37$$

That is, the researcher should sample at least 37 students from each group.

Note: The formulas for nonequal sample sizes are much more complex when considering confidence intervals (inferences) for the differences of parameters.

Technology Corner

All the concepts discussed in this chapter can be computed and illustrated through most statistical software packages. All scientific and graphical calculators will aid directly in the computations. In addition, some of the newer calculators, such as the TI-83/84 (all versions), will allow you to compute the confidence intervals directly. If you own a calculator, you should consult the owner's manual to determine what statistical features are included.

Illustration: **Figure 11-3** shows the outputs computed by the MINITAB software for **Examples 11-2** and **11- 8**. The MINITAB software also allows you to construct confidence intervals for a population mean directly if you have summary data as in **Examples 11- 5**. However, MINITAB (version 14 and earlier) will not allow you to construct a large-sample confidence interval for the difference of two means. The MINITAB output for **Example**

11-5 is shown in **Figure 11-4**. **Figure 11-5** shows the outputs computed by the TI-83/84 calculator for **Examples 11-2, 11-5, 11-8,** and **11-10**. The TI-83/84 calculator allows you to use both summary data and raw data to compute confidence intervals for both means and proportions. Care always should be taken when using the formulas in computing confidence intervals. One can use other features of the technologies to illustrate other concepts discussed in this chapter.

Test and Confidence Interval for One Proportion - Example 11-2

Test of p = 0.5 vs p not = 0.5

Sample	X	N	Sample p	90% CI	Z-Value	P-Value
1	77	100	0.770000	(0.700779, 0.839221)	5.40	0.000

Test and Confidence Interval for Two Proportions - Example 11 - 8

Sample	X	N	Sample p
1	70	100	0.700000
2	16	40	0.400000

Difference = p (1) - p (2)
Estimate for difference: 0.3

95% CI for difference: (0.123603, 0.476397)

Test for difference = 0 (vs not = 0):   Z = 3.29   P-Value = 0.001

Figure 11-3: MINITAB output for Examples 11-2 and 11-8

One-Sample Z Test and Confidence Interval - Example 11 - 5

Test of mu = 0 vs not = 0
The assumed standard deviation = 4415

N	Mean	SE Mean	99% CI	Z	P
100	31578.0	441.5	(30440.8, 32715.2)	71.52	0.000

Figure 11-4: MINITAB output for Example 11-5

Example 11-2

```
1-PropZInt
 (.70078,.83922)
 p=.77
 n=100
```

Example 11-5

```
ZInterval
 (30441,32715)
 x̄=31578
 n=100
```

Example 11-8

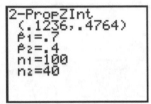

```
2-PropZInt
 (.1236,.4764)
 p₁=.7
 p₂=.4
 n₁=100
 n₂=40
```

Example 11-10

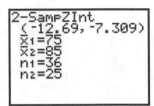

```
2-SampZInt
 (-12.69, -7.309)
 x̄₁=75
 x̄₂=85
 n₁=36
 n₂=25
```

Figure 11-4: TI-83/84 outputs for Examples 11-2, 11-5, 11-8, and 11-10

Here the focus was on confidence intervals and sample sizes. We considered large-sample confidence intervals for a population proportion and mean and for the difference between two population proportions and means. We also considered formulas for finding sample sizes under different conditions. We computed 90, 95, and 99 percent confidence interval estimates for these parameters, but any other percentage also can be considered. These concepts were presented through

✓ Formulas

✓ Examples

✓ Technology

Test Yourself

True/False Questions

1. The best point estimate for the population mean μ is the sample mean $\bar{x}$.
2. As the length of a confidence interval increases, the degree of confidence in its actually containing the population parameter being estimated also increases.
3. If the length of a confidence interval is very large, then the corresponding prediction is very meaningful.
4. The z score corresponding to a 98 percent confidence level is 1.96.
5. The confidence interval for the population mean μ can be computed from $\bar{x} \pm z_{\alpha/2} \dfrac{\sigma}{n}$, where σ is the population standard deviation and n is the sample size.
6. For a fixed confidence level, when the sample size increases, the length of the confidence interval for a population mean decreases.
7. For a fixed confidence level, when the sample size decreases, the length of the confidence interval for a population mean decreases.
8. The distribution of sample proportions is approximately normal provided that the sample size $n \geq 30$.

9. The confidence interval for the population proportion p can be computed from $\hat{p} \pm z_{\alpha/2}\,\hat{p}(1 - \hat{p})/n$, where $\hat{p}$ is the point estimate for p.

10. A 90 percent confidence interval for a population mean implies that there is a 0.90 probability that the population mean will be contained in the confidence interval.

11. A 90 percent confidence interval for a population parameter means that if a large number of confidence intervals were constructed from repeated samples, then, on average, 90 percent of these intervals would contain the true parameter.

12. The point estimate of a population parameter is always at the center of the confidence interval for the parameter.

13. When repeated samples are selected from a population, the point estimate for a given parameter always will be the same value.

14. The larger the level of confidence, the shorter is the confidence interval.

15. The best point estimate for a population parameter is its corresponding sample statistic.

16. In order to determine the sample size when considering confidence intervals for the population mean μ, it is necessary to know the level of confidence, the margin of error, and either an estimate of the population standard deviation or the standard deviation itself.

17. In order to determine the sample size when determining the population proportion, it is necessary to know the level of confidence, the margin of error, and an estimate of the population mean.

18. The maximum error of estimate gives a measure of accuracy when computing the sample size required to make inferences.

19. Based on the central limit theorem for the difference of two population proportions, we can assume, for large enough sample sizes, that the sampling distribution for the difference between two sample proportions is exactly normally distributed.

20. In computing equal sample sizes when considering confidence intervals for the difference between two population proportions, the sample size will increase when the margin of error is decreased and the significance level is held fixed.

21. When computing large sample confidence intervals for the difference between two population means, it is necessary to know the variances for the two populations.

Completion Questions

1. As the length of the confidence interval for the population mean increases, the degree of confidence in the interval's actually containing the population mean (increases, decreases) _____.

2. The z score associated with the 99 percent confidence level is (1.28, 1.645, 2.33, 2.576) _____.

3. The confidence interval for the population mean μ, when the population standard deviation σ is known, will be given by the relation ($\mu \pm z_x \times \sigma/5\sqrt{n}$, $\mu \pm z_{\alpha/2} \times \sigma/5\sqrt{n}$, $\bar{x} \pm z_{\alpha/2} \times \sigma/5\sqrt{n}$) _____ $\pm$ _____.

4. For a fixed level of confidence, when the sample size increases, the length of the confidence interval for a population mean will (increase, decrease) _____.

5. For a fixed level of confidence, when the sample size decreases, the length of the confidence interval for a population proportion will (increase, decrease) _____.

6. When constructing confidence intervals for the population mean, if the population standard deviation is unknown but the sample size is large enough and the sampling population is normally distributed, then the distribution that is used to help compute the maximum error of estimate is the (normal, standard normal) _____distribution.

7. Provided that the sample size is large enough, the distribution of the sample proportions is approximately normal with standard deviation $\sigma_{\hat{p}} = \left[\hat{p}(1 - \hat{p})/n, \sqrt{\hat{p}(1 - \hat{p})/n}, p(1 - p)/n, \sqrt{p(1 - p)/n} \right]$ _____.

8. Provided that the sample size is large enough from a population with proportion p, the distribution of the sample proportions $\hat{p}$ is approximately normal with mean $\mu_{\hat{p}} = $ _____.

9. When constructing confidence intervals for the population mean μ based on large samples ($n \geq 30$) when the population standard deviation is unknown, the maximum error of estimate is given by $E = (z_{\alpha/2} \times \sigma/5\sqrt{n}, z_{\alpha/2} \times \sigma/5\sqrt{n}, z_{\alpha} \times \sigma/5\sqrt{n})$ _____.

10. The (point, interval) _____ estimate of a population parameter is always at the center of the confidence interval for that parameter.

11. A point estimate for a population parameter is the value of the corresponding sample (parameter, statistic) _____.

12. The z value for a 97.8 percent confidence interval estimation is (2.29, 1.96, 2.33) _____.

13. If we change a 90 percent confidence interval estimate to a 95 percent confidence interval estimate, the width of the confidence interval will (increase, decrease) _____.

14. A confidence interval is a range of values used to estimate a population (parameter, statistic) _____.

15. The maximum error of estimate E will (decrease, increase) _____ when larger sample sizes are used in constructing confidence intervals for the difference between two population means.

16. The maximum error of estimate E will (decrease, increase) _____ when a larger confidence level is used.

17. When constructing confidence intervals for the population proportion, for a given confidence level and maximum error of estimate, the maximum sample size is obtained when $p = (0.25, 0.50, 0.75)$ _____.

18. The best point estimate for the population standard deviation is the _____ standard deviation.

19. The best point estimate for the population mean is the _____ mean.

20. As the sample sizes increase, the shape of the distribution of the differences of the sample means obtained from any population will approach a(n) _____ distribution.

21. In estimating equal sample sizes when inference is made on the difference between two population proportions, the sample size will (increase, decrease) _____ when the error of estimate decreases and the level of confidence remains fixed.

22. When confidence intervals for the difference between two population means are constructed, if the population variances are unknown, they can be estimated by their respective _____ variances for large enough sample sizes.

Multiple-Choice Questions

1. If we are constructing a 98 percent confidence interval for the population mean, the confidence level will be
   (a) 2 percent.
   (b) 2.29.
   (c) 98 percent.
   (d) 2.39.

2. The z value corresponding to a 97 percent confidence interval is
   (a) 1.88.
   (b) 2.17.
   (c) 1.96.
   (d) 3 percent.

3. As the sample size increases, the confidence interval for the population mean will
   (a) decrease.
   (b) increase.
   (c) stay the same.
   (d) decrease and then increase.

4. If we change the confidence level from 98 to 95 percent when constructing a confidence interval for the population mean, we can expect the size of the interval to
   (a) increase.
   (b) decrease.
   (c) stay the same.
   (d) None of the above

5. Generally, lower confidence levels will yield
   (a) smaller standard deviations for the sampling distribution.
   (b) a larger margin of error.
   (c) broader confidence intervals.
   (d) narrower confidence intervals.

6. If the 98 percent confidence limits for the population mean μ are 73 and 80, which of the following could be the 95 percent confidence limits?
   (a) 73 and 81
   (b) 72 and 79
   (c) 72 and 81
   (d) 74 and 79

7. A 90 percent confidence interval for a population mean indicates that
   (a) we are 90 percent confident that the interval will contain all possible sample means with the same sample size taken from the given population.
   (b) we are 90 percent confident that the population mean will be the same as the sample mean used in constructing the interval.
   (c) we are 90 percent confident that the population mean will fall within the interval.
   (d) none of the above is true.

8. Interval estimates of a parameter provide information on
  (a) how close an estimate of the parameter is to the parameter.
  (b) what proportion of the estimates of the parameter are contained in the interval.
  (c) exactly what values the parameter can assume.
  (d) the z score.

9. Which of the following confidence intervals will be the widest?
  (a) 90 percent
  (b) 95 percent
  (c) 80 percent
  (d) 98 percent

10. The best point estimate for the population variance is
  (a) a statistic.
  (b) the sample standard deviation.
  (c) the sample mean.
  (d) the sample variance.

11. When determining the sample size in constructing confidence intervals for the population mean μ, for a fixed maximum error of estimate and level of confidence, the sample size will
  (a) increase when the population standard deviation is decreased.
  (b) increase when the population standard deviation is increased.
  (c) decrease when the population standard deviation is increased.
  (d) decrease and then increase when the population standard deviation is increased.

12. When computing the sample size to help construct confidence intervals for the population proportion, for a fixed margin of error of estimate and level of confidence, the sample size will be maximum when
  (a) $p = 0.25$.
  (b) $(1 - p) = 0.25$.
  (c) $p(1 - p) = 0.5$.
  (d) $p = 0.5$.

13. What value of the population proportion p will maximize $p(1 - p)$?
  (a) 0.50
  (b) 0.25
  (c) 0.75
  (c) 0.05

14. Suppose that a sample of size 100 is selected from a population with unknown variance. If this information is used in constructing a confidence interval for the population mean, which of the following statements is true?
  (a) The sample must have a normal distribution.
  (b) The population is assumed to have a normal distribution.
  (c) Only 95 percent confidence intervals may be computed.
  (d) The sample standard deviation cannot be used to estimate the population standard deviation because the sample size is large.

15. A 95 percent confidence interval for the mean of a population is to be constructed and must be accurate to within 0.3 unit. A preliminary sample standard deviation is 2.9. The smallest sample size n that provides the desired accuracy with 95 percent confidence is
    (a) 253.
    (b) 359.
    (c) 400.
    (d) 380.

16. A 95 percent confidence interval for the population proportion is to be constructed and must be accurate to within 0.1 unit. The largest sample size n that provides the desired accuracy with 95 percent confidence
    (a) cannot be determined.
    (b) is 73.
    (c) is 97.
    (d) is 100.

17. In a survey about a murder case that was widely reported by the TV networks, 201 of 300 persons surveyed said that they believed that the accused was guilty. The 95 percent confidence interval for the proportion of people who did *not* believe that the accused was guilty is
    (a) 0.617 to 0.723.
    (b) 0.277 to 0.383.
    (c) 0.285 to 0.375.
    (d) 0.625 to 0.715.

18. In constructing a confidence interval for the population mean μ, if the level of confidence is changed from 98 to 90 percent, the standard deviation of the mean will
    (a) be equal to 90 percent of the original standard deviation of the mean.
    (b) increase.
    (c) decrease.
    (d) remain the same.

19. Suppose that the heights of the population of basketball players at a certain college are normally distributed with a standard deviation of 2 feet. If a sample of heights of size 16 is randomly selected from this population with a mean of 6.2 feet, the 90 percent confidence interval for the mean height of these basketball players is
    (a) 4.555 to 7.845 feet.
    (b) 5.378 to 7.022 feet.
    (c) 4.447 to 7.953 feet.
    (d) 5.324 to 7.077 feet.

20. A 99 percent confidence interval is to be constructed for the population mean from a random sample of size 22. If the population standard deviation is known, the table value to be used in the computation is
    (a) 2.518.
    (b) 2.330.
    (c) 2.831.
    (d) 2.580.

21. The most common confidence levels and corresponding z values are listed below. Which corresponding z value is incorrect?
  (a) 99 percent, z value = 1.280
  (b) 95 percent, z value = 1.960
  (c) 98 percent, z value = 2.330
  (d) 90 percent, z value = 1.645

22. The heights (inches) of the students on a campus are assumed to have a normal distribution with a standard deviation of 4 inches. A random sample of 49 students was taken with a mean of 68 inches. The 95 percent confidence interval for the population mean μ is
  (a) 67.06 to 68.94 inches.
  (b) 66.88 to 69.12 inches.
  (c) 63.42 to 72.48 inches.
  (d) 64.24 to 71.76 inches.

23. The length of time it takes a car salesperson to close a deal on a car sale is assumed to be normally distributed. A random sample of 100 such times was selected and yielded a mean of 3 hours and variance of 0.5 hour. The 98 percent confidence interval for the mean length of time it takes a car salesperson to sell a car is
  (a) 2.8835 to 3.1165 hours.
  (b) 2.8176 to 3.1824 hours.
  (c) 2.8352 to 3.1648 hours.
  (d) 2.8710 to 3.1290 hours.

24. In a recent study it was found that 11 of every 100 Pap smears sampled were misdiagnosed by a certain lab. If a sample of 100 is taken, the 99 percent confidence interval for the proportion of misdiagnosed Pap smears is
  (a) 0.1075 to 0.1125.
  (b) 0.0371 to 0.1829.
  (c) 0.1077 to 0.1123.
  (d) 0.0293 to 0.1908.

25. In a religious survey of southerners it was found that 164 of 200 believed in angels. The 90 percent confidence interval for the true proportion of southerners who believe in angels
  (a) is 0.7753 to 0.8647.
  (b) is 0.7499 to 0.8901.
  (c) is 0.8188 to 0.8212.
  (d) cannot be computed because the assumptions that are required to compute this confidence interval are violated.

26. In a random sample of 150 drunk drivers, 90 percent were males. The 99 percent confidence interval for the proportion of male drunk drivers is
  (a) 0.8716 to 0.9484.
  (b) 0.8369 to 0.9631.
  (c) 0.8641 to 0.9559.
  (d) 0.8555 to 0.9645.

27. The heights (inches) of the students on a campus are assumed to have a normal distribution with a variance of 25 inches. Suppose that we want to construct a 95 percent confidence interval for the population mean μ and have it accurate to within 0.5 inch. The minimum sample size required is

    (a) 9,604.
    (b) 269.
    (c) 98.
    (d) 385.

28. The 95 percent confidence interval for the proportion of female drunk drivers is to be constructed and must be accurate to within 0.08. A preliminary sample provides an initial estimate of $\hat{p} = 0.09$. The smallest sample size that will provide the desired accuracy with 95 percent confidence is

    (a) 26.
    (b) 77.
    (c) 50.
    (d) 151.

29. If the population proportion is being estimated, the sample size needed to be 90 percent confident that the estimate is within 0.05 of the true proportion is

    (a) 20.
    (b) 271.
    (c) 196.
    (d) 400.

30. In a random sample of 100 observations, the sample population $\hat{p} = 0.1$. The 84 percent confidence interval for the population proportion p is

    (a) 0.1 ± 0.578.
    (b) 0.1 ± 0.282.
    (c) 0.1 ± 0.0423.
    (d) 0.1 ± 0.001.

31. When computing the sample size needed to estimate the population proportion p, which of the following is not necessary?

    (a) The required confidence level
    (b) The margin of error
    (c) An estimate of p
    (d) An estimate of the population variance

32. In a religious survey of southerners it was found that 82 of 100 believed in angels. If we wanted to construct a 99 percent confidence interval for the true proportion of southerners who believe in angels, what would be the margin of error?

    (a) 0.0991
    (b) 0.9191
    (c) 0.0381
    (d) 0.7209

33. A statistician wishes to investigate the difference between the proportions of males and the proportion of females who believe in aliens. How large a sample should be taken

(equal sample size for each group) to be 95 percent certain of knowing the difference to within ± 0.02?

(a) 3,383

(b) 4,802

(c) 2,048

(d) 6,787

34. A researcher wishes to investigate the difference between the mean scores on a standardized test for students who were exposed to two different methods of teaching. How large a sample should the researcher take (equal sample size for each method) to be 99 percent certain of knowing the difference of the average scores to within ±3 points if the standard deviations for the populations are 5 and 8?

(a) 66

(b) 38

(c) 27

(d) 54

35. In 1973, the Graduate Division at the University of California, Berkeley, did an observational study on sex bias in admissions to the graduate school. It was found that in a particular major, of 800 male applicants, 65 percent were admitted, and of 120 female applicants, 85 percent were admitted. Establish a 95 percent confidence interval estimate of the difference in proportions of females and males for this particular major.

(a) 0.2 ± 0.09

(b) 0.2 ± 0.07

(c) 0.2 ± 0.11

(d) 0.2 ± 0.12

36. Two brands of similar tires were tested, and their lifetimes, in miles, were compared. The data are given below. Find the 95 percent confidence interval for the true difference in the means (brand A − brand B). Assume that the lifetimes are normally distributed.

BRAND A	BRAND B
$\bar{x}_1 = 41,000$	$\bar{x}_2 = 39,600$
$s_1 = 3,000$	$s_2 = 2,600$
$n_1 = 100$	$n_2 = 100$

(a) $1,400 \pm 1,022.5$

(b) $1,400 \pm 653$

(c) $1,400 \pm 508.1$

(d) $1,400 \pm 778.1$

37. When will it be reasonable to construct a confidence interval for a parameter if the values for the entire population are known?

(a) Never

(b) When the population size is greater than 30

(c) When the population size is less than 30

(d) When only lower confidence levels are used

38. A researcher wants to determine the difference between the proportions of males and females who do volunteer work. If a margin of error of ±0.02 is acceptable at the 90 percent confidence level, what is the maximum sample size that should be taken? Assume that equal sample sizes are selected for the two sample proportions.
   (a) 3,383
   (b) 2,048
   (c) 6,787
   (d) 8,295

39. In a random sample of 100 observations, the sample proportion $\hat{p} = 0.1$. The 95 percent confidence interval for the population proportion p is
   (a) 0.1 ± 0.0384.
   (b) 0.1 ± 0.0699.
   (c) 0.1 ± 0.0588.
   (d) 0.1 ± 0.0494.

40. A study was conducted on a college campus to determine the type (foreign or domestic) of car owned by female students. A random sample of 150 female students revealed that 50 of them owned a foreign car. A 90 percent confidence interval for the proportion of female students on this campus who own a foreign car is
   (a) 0.3333 ± 0.0385.
   (b) 0.3333 ± 0.0024.
   (c) 0.3333 ± 0.1097.
   (d) 0.3333 ± 0.0633.

41. A study is to be conducted to investigate the proportion of college professors who are left handed. Two hundred colleges are selected, and random samples of the faculty are interviewed. The collected information is used to construct 99 percent confidence intervals for a proportion of professors who are left handed for those 200 different samples. How many of the intervals would you expect to contain the true proportion of professors who are left handed?
   (a) 99
   (b) 199
   (c) 198
   (d) 200

42. Which of the following statements is true?
   (a) An estimate is a statistic whose value depends on the particular sample that is selected.
   (b) An estimate is a parameter whose value depends on the particular sample that is selected.
   (c) An estimate is a statistic whose value depends on the particular population that was selected.
   (d) An estimate is a parameter whose value depends on the particular population that was selected.

43. Which of the following statements is true?
   (a) An interval estimate of a population parameter is an interval that definitely contains any parameter of the population.

(b) Once an interval estimate of a population parameter is computed, we will be able to state with certainty that the interval will contain the parameter.

(c) An interval estimate of a population parameter is no better than a point estimate because both may not estimate the parameter.

(d) An interval estimate of a population parameter is an interval that is predicted to contain the parameter with some confidence.

44. Suppose that a quality control manager wishes to measure the average amount of hot chocolate mix dispensed in a 12-ounce package. From preliminary samples, the standard deviation was estimated to be 0.3 ounce. How large a sample must be taken to be 95 percent confident that the margin of error will be within 0.05 ounce?

(a) 98

(b) 12

(c) 10

(d) 139

45. A study is to be conducted to investigate the proportion of college professors who wear eyeglasses. In a random sample of 123 female professors, 34 of them wear eyeglasses. In a corresponding random sample of 95 male professors, 27 of them wear eyeglasses. Construct a 95 percent confidence interval for the difference in proportions of female to male professors (female − male) who wear eyeglasses.

(a) $(-0.1281, 0.1125)$

(b) $(-0.1125, 0.1281)$

(c) $(-0.1503, 0.1659)$

(d) $(-0.1659, 0.1503)$

46. An elementary school teacher is studying the reading speeds of boys and girls in a sixth grade class. They all have the same assignment for the reading test, with the following summary information with regard to the time (minutes) taken to complete the test for two separate random samples of boys and girls. Construct a 90 percent confidence interval for the difference in the average time to complete the test between the boys and the girls. *Note:* Approximate the population standard deviations with the sample standard deviations.

BOYS	GIRLS
$\bar{x}_1 = 12$	$\bar{x}_2 = 11$
$s_1 = 4$	$s_2 = 3$
$n_1 = 36$	$n_2 = 39$

(a) $(-0.9116, 2.9116)$

(b) $(-0.3516, 2.3516)$

(c) $(-0.6105, 2.6105)$

(d) $(-1.117, 3.1166)$

47. A cancer researcher is investigating the life expectancy of men diagnosed with terminal prostate cancer. In particular, he is interested in determining whether the life expectancy of the patients is increased from the time of diagnosis to the time of death by using a new drug with minimal side effects. He randomly selects a homogeneous

group of terminal prostate cancer patients and then randomly divides them into two groups. One group is treated with the drug, and the other group is used as the control group. That is, the control group is not given any treatment. The summary information is given in the following table. Construct a 99 percent confidence interval for the difference in the average time (in years) to death between the treated group and the control group. *Note:* Approximate the population standard deviations with the sample standard deviations.

TREATED GROUP	CONTROL GROUP
$\bar{x}_1 = 6.3$	$\bar{x}_2 = 5$
$s_1 = 0.8$	$s_2 = 0.7$
$n_1 = 50$	$n_2 = 50$

(a) (1.0527, 1.5473)
(b) (1.0054, 1.5946)
(c) (0.9503, 1.6497)
(d) (0.9128, 1.6872)

48. Two different brands of batteries were tested to establish the manufacturers' claims of their lasting beyond 2,500 hours. A random sample of 1,200 of the brand A battery was selected and placed on test. A corresponding random sample of 1,000 of the brand B battery also was put on test. The number of batteries lasting beyond 2,500 hours (successes) and sample sizes are given in the following table. Construct a 95 percent confidence interval for the difference in the proportions of batteries that lasted beyond 2,500 hours for brand B relative to brand A.

BRAND A	BRAND B
$x_1 = 900$	$x_2 = 800$
$n_1 = 1,200$	$n_2 = 1,000$

(a) (0.0208, 0.0793)
(b) (0.0086, 0.0914)
(c) (0.0152, 0.0849)
(d) (0.0042, 0.0958)

49. A quality control manager is comparing shipments of cell phones from two suppliers. She randomly selects samples of cell phones from two shipments, one from each supplier, and tests them for defects. The sample information is shown in the following table. Construct a 99 percent confidence interval for the proportion of defectives from supplier A − supplier B.

	SUPPLIER A	SUPPLIER B
Sample sizes	$n_1 = 400$	$n_2 = 300$
Number of defectives	$x_1 = 25$	$x_2 = 5$

(a) (0.0128, 0.0788)

(b) (0.0225, 0.0692)

(c) (0.0180, 0.0736)

(d) (0.0093, 0.0824)

50. A company makes two models of lawn mowers. These two models are placed on test to determine how long (in hours) they would run on a full tank of gasoline. The summary information for the two models is given in the following table. Construct a 95 percent confidence interval for the difference of the mean running time for a full tank of gasoline for the two models. Consider model 1 − model 2.

MODEL 1	MODEL 2
$\bar{x}_1 = 10.5$	$\bar{x}_2 = 9.8$
$s_1 = 0.5$	$s_2 = 0.8$
$n_1 = 45$	$n_2 = 51$

(a) (0.4787, 0.9213)

(b) (0.3534, 1.0466)

(c) (0.4363, 0.9637)

(d) (0.3870, 1.013)

Further Exercises

If possible, you could use any technology to help solve the following exercises.

1. State in your own words what the phrase "90 percent confidence for μ" tells you about the relationship between the population mean μ and the confidence interval.

2. A study is to be conducted to investigate the proportion of college professors who wear eyeglasses.

   (a) A random sample of 250 professors results in 139 of them wearing eyeglasses. From this information, generate a 90 percent confidence interval for the proportion of professors who wear eyeglasses.

   (b) Suppose that a 90 percent confidence interval for this proportion of professors who wear eyeglasses is to have a margin of error of ±2 percent. A preliminary random sample of 100 professors results in 52 of them wearing eyeglasses. How many additional adults must be surveyed?

3. The average annual salary of public school teachers who graduated from a certain college is to be studied.

   (a) A random sample of 100 teachers has a mean salary of $31,578, with a standard deviation of $4,415. Construct a 99 percent confidence interval for the average salary of the population of public school teachers who graduated from this specific college.

   (b) Interpret in your own words what the confidence interval in (a) means.

   (c) If 100 different 99 percent confidence intervals were generated, how many of them would you expect to contain the average salary of the teachers of this population?

4. A study was conducted to determine the type of car owned by female students. A sample of 150 female students revealed that 50 of them owned a foreign car.

   (a) Construct a 90 percent confidence interval for the proportion of female students who own foreign cars.

   (b) Interpret in your own words what the confidence interval in (a) means.

   (c) If the information given in this exercise can be considered as a preliminary study, compute the sample size necessary to construct a 95 percent confidence interval for the true proportion of female students who own a foreign car with a maximum error of ±2 percentage points.

5. (a) In a survey of 800 adults, it was found that 72 ate the recommended amount of fruits and vegetables each day. Construct a 99 percent confidence interval for the proportion of this population who follows these recommendations.

   (b) Express in your own words what the interval in (a) means.

   (c) Suppose that no preliminary study was done. Compute the sample size necessary to construct a 95 percent confidence interval for the population proportion with a margin of error of ±3 percent point.

6. The TOEFL (Test of English as a Foreign Language) scores for international students from two different countries were studied. The information is given below. Construct a 90 percent confidence interval for the difference in the average scores for the two countries.

COUNTRY 1	COUNTRY 2
$\bar{x}_1 = 490$	$\bar{x}_2 = 462$
$s_1 = 80$	$s_2 = 85$
$n_1 = 110$	$n_2 = 120$

7. Two different brands of lightbulbs were tested to establish the manufacturers' claims of their lasting beyond 2,000 hours. The number of successes and sample sizes are given below. Construct a 99 percent confidence interval for the difference in the average scores for the two countries.

BRAND A	BRAND B
$x_1 = 500$	$x_2 = 462$
$n_1 = 1200$	$n_2 = 1000$

ANSWER KEY
True/False Questions

1. T 2. T 3. F 4. F 5. F 6. T 7. F 8. T 9. F 10. F 11. T
12. T 13. F 14. F 15. T 16. T 17. F 18. T 19. F 20. T 21. F

Completion Questions

1. increases   2. 2.576   3. $\bar{x} \pm z_{\alpha/2}(\sigma/\sqrt{n})$ 4. decrease   5. increase

6. standard normal or z   7. $\sqrt{p(1-p)/n}$ 8. p 9. $z_{\alpha/2} \times (s/\sqrt{n})$

10. point   11. statistic   12. 2.29   13. increase   14. parameter   15. decrease
16. increase   17. 0.5   18. sample   19. sample   20. normal   21. increase
22. sample

Multiple-Choice Questions

1. (c)   2. (b)   3. (a)   4. (b)   5. (d)   6. (d)   7. (c)   8. (a)   9. (d)
10. (d)   11. (b)   12. (d)   13. (a)   14. (b)   15. (b)   16. (c)   17. (b)   18. (d)
19. (b)   20. (d)   21. (a)   22. (b)   23. (c)   24. (d)   25. (a)   26. (b)   27. (d)
28. (c)   29. (b)   30. (c)   31. (d)   32. (a)   33. (b)   34. (a)   35. (b)   36. (d)
37. (a)   38. (a)   39. (c)   40. (d)   41. (c)   42. (a)   43. (d)   44. (d)   45. (a)
46. (b)   47. (d)   48. (c)   49. (d)   50. (c)

Further Exercises

1. One would be 90 percent confident that the mean μ will lie within the interval.

2. (a) (0.5043, 0.6077); (b) $n = 1689 - 100 = 1589$

3. (a) ($30,441,$32,715)

   (b) We are 99 percent confident that the interval in part (a) will contain the true mean salary.

   (c) 99

4. (a) 0.2700, 0.3966)

   (b) We are 90 percent confident that the interval in part (a) will contain the true proportion of females who own a foreign car.

   (c) $1504 - 150 = 1354$.

5. (a) (0.0639, 0.1161)

   (b) We are 99 percent confident that the interval in part (a) will contain the true proportion of people who follow the recommendations.

   (c) 1068

6. (10.103, 45.897)

7. (-0.1, 0.0094)

CHAPTER 12

Hypothesis Tests: Large Samples

You should read this chapter if you need to review or to learn about

→ Large-sample hypothesis tests for a population proportion

→ Large-sample hypothesis tests for a population mean

→ Large-sample hypothesis tests for the difference between two population proportions

→ Large-sample hypothesis tests for the difference between two population means

Get Started

Here we will focus on large-sample hypothesis tests for population proportions and population means. We will, through these tests, make inferences on these parameters.

12-1 Some Terms Associated with Hypothesis Testing

Every situation that requires a hypothesis test starts with a statement of a hypothesis.

Explanation of the term—statistical hypothesis: A **statistical hypothesis** is an opinion about a population parameter. The opinion may or may not be true.

Example 12-1: A researcher feels that the proportion of a particular rare fish that is in the Great Lakes is 4 percent. What statistical hypothesis is the researcher proposing?

Solution: The opinion expressed by the researcher is that 4 percent of the entire population of fishes in the Great Lakes will constitute this particular rare fish. The parameter of interest here would be the proportion of this rare fish in the Great Lakes.

There are two types of statistical hypotheses: (1) the **null hypothesis** and (2) the **alternative hypothesis**.

Explanation of the term—null hypothesis: The **null hypothesis** is a claim about the value of a population parameter.

Notation: The null hypothesis is denoted by H_0.

Quick Tips

· H_0 must contain the condition of equality and must be written with the symbol $=$, $\leq$, or $\geq$.
· When a statistical test is actually performed, we will assume that the parameter equals a specific value.

Explanation of the term—alternative hypothesis: The **alternative hypothesis** states that there is a precise difference between a parameter (or parameters) and a specific value.

Notation: The alternative hypothesis is denoted by H_1.

Quick Tips

· H_1 is the negation of H_0.
· H_1 is the statement that must be true if H_0 is false.
· H_1 must be written with the symbol $\neq$, $>$, or $<$.

After the hypotheses are stated, the next step is to design the study. An appropriate statistical test will be selected, the level of significance will be chosen, and a plan to conduct the study will be formulated. To make an inference for the study, the **statistical test** and **level of significance** are used.

Explanation of the term—statistical test: A **statistical test** uses the data collected from a study to make a decision about the null hypothesis. This decision will be to reject or not to reject the null hypothesis.

We will need to compute a **test value** or a **test statistic** in order to make the decision. The formula that is used to compute this value will vary depending on the statistical test.

Possible Outcomes for a Hypothesis Test

When a test is done, there are four possible outcomes. These outcomes are summarized in **Table 12-1** along with the types of errors one can commit when performing hypothesis tests.

Table 12-1: Possible Outcomes and Types of Errors Committed When Performing a Hypothesis Test

	H_0 IS TRUE	H_0 IS FALSE
Reject H_0	Error, type I	Correct decision
Do not reject H_0	Correct decision	Error, type II

Observe that there are two possibilities for a correct decision and two possibilities for an incorrect decision.

Types of Error for a Hypothesis Test

From **Table 12-1** we can observe that there are two ways of making a mistake when doing a hypothesis test. These two errors are called a **type I error** and a **type II error**.

Explanation of the term—type I error: A **type I error** occurs if the null hypothesis is rejected when it is true.

Explanation of the term—type II error: A **type II error** occurs if the null hypothesis is not rejected when it is false.

When we reject or do not reject the null hypothesis, how confident are we that we are making the correct decision? This question can be answered by the specified **level of significance**.

Explanation of the term—level of significance: The **level of significance**, denoted by α, is the probability of a type I error.

Typical values for α are 0.1, 0.05, 0.02, and 0.01. For example, if $\alpha = 0.1$ for a test, and the null hypothesis is rejected, then one will be 90 percent certain that this is the correct decision.

Note: We will not address the probability of a type II error in this text because of its complexity.

Once the level of significance is selected, a **critical value** for the appropriate test is selected from a table. If a z test is used, the z table will be used to obtain the appropriate critical value.

Explanation of the term—critical value: A **critical value** separates the critical or rejection region from the noncritical or do-not-reject region.

Next, a **test statistic** or **test value** will be computed. This value will depend on the test being performed and the formula used in the computation.

Explanation of the term—test statistic or test value: A **test statistic** is a value computed from sample data that is used in making a decision about rejection of the null hypothesis.

Explanation of the term—critical or rejection region: A **critical** or **rejection region** is a range of test statistic values for which the null hypothesis should be rejected. This range of values will indicate that there is a significant or large enough difference between the postulated parameter value and the corresponding point estimate for the parameter.

Explanation of the term—noncritical or do-not-reject region: A **noncritical** or **do-not-reject region** is a range of test statistic values that indicates that the difference between the postulated value for the parameter and the corresponding point estimate value is probably due to chance and that the null hypothesis should not be rejected.

Figure 12-1 illustrates the idea of a critical or rejection and noncritical or do-not-reject region. Here we assume that a z test is used.

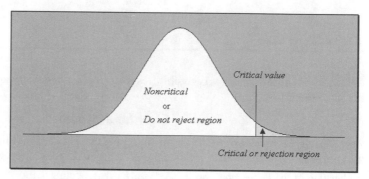

Figure 12-1: Diagram depicting the critical (rejection) and non-critical (do-not-reject) regions

There are two broad classifications of hypothesis tests: (1) one-tailed tests and (2) two-tailed tests.

A **one-tailed test** points out that the null hypothesis should be rejected when the test statistic value is in the critical region on one side of the parameter value being tested. A **two-tailed test** points out that the null hypothesis should be rejected when the test statistic value is in either side of the two critical regions.

12-2 Five-Step Process of Hypothesis Testing

Tests presented in this and subsequent chapters will follow a five-step procedure.

Step 1: State the null hypothesis H_0.

Step 2: State the alternative hypothesis H_1.

Step 3: State the formula for the test statistic and compute its value, T.S.

Step 4: State the decision rule for rejecting the null hypothesis for a given level of significance, D.R.

Step 5: State a conclusion in the context of the information given in the problem.

12-3 Large-Sample Test for a Population Proportion

Here we will present tests of hypotheses that will enable us to determine, based on sample data, whether the true value of a proportion equals a given constant. Samples of size n will be obtained and the number or proportion of successes observed. It will be assumed that the trials in the experiment are independent and that the probability of success is the same for each trial. That is, we are assuming that we have a binomial experiment, and we are testing hypotheses about the parameter p of a binomial population.

Summary of Hypothesis Tests

1. One-tailed (right-tailed)

H_0: $p \le p_0$ (where p_0 is a specified proportion value)

H_1: $p > p_0$

T.S.: $z = \dfrac{x - np_0}{\sqrt{np_0(1 - p_0)}}$

D.R.: For a specified significance level α, reject the null hypothesis if the computed test statistic value z is greater than $+z_\alpha$.

Conclusion:

Note: This is a right-tailed test because the direction of the inequality sign in the alternative hypothesis is to the right.

2. One-tailed (left-tailed)

H_0: $p \ge p_0$ (where p_0 is a specified proportion value)

H_1: $p < p_0$

T.S.: $z = \dfrac{x - np_0}{\sqrt{np_0(1 - p_0)}}$

D.R.: For a specified significance level α, reject the null hypothesis if the computed test statistic value z is less than $-z_\alpha$.

Conclusion:

Note: This is a left-tailed test because the direction of the inequality sign in the alternative hypothesis is to the left.

3. Two-tailed

H_0: $p = p_0$ (where p_0 is a specified proportion value)

H_1: $p \ne p_0$

T.S.: $z = \dfrac{x - np_0}{\sqrt{np_0(1 - p_0)}}$

D.R.: For a specified significance level α, reject the null hypothesis if the computed test statistic value z is less than $-z_{\alpha/2}$ or if it is greater than $+z_{\alpha/2}$.

Conclusion:

Note: This is a two-tailed test because of the not-equal-to symbol in the alternative hypothesis. Also note that the level of significance is shared equally when finding the critical z value ($z_{\alpha/2}$).

Note: The test statistics in the preceding tests, $z = \dfrac{x - np_0}{\sqrt{np_0(1 - p_0)}}$ is equivalent to

$$z = \dfrac{\dfrac{x}{n} - p_0}{\sqrt{\dfrac{p_0(1 - p_0)}{n}}} = \dfrac{\hat{p} - p_0}{\sqrt{\dfrac{p_0(1 - p_0)}{n}}}$$

Observe that this is similar to the z score discussed in **Chapter 10** when dealing with the sampling distribution for a population proportion.

Accept/Fail to Reject/Do Not Reject H_0

In hypothesis testing, some authors may use the phrase "accept the null hypothesis" instead of "fail to reject the null hypothesis" or "do not reject the null hypothesis." It does not matter which of the phrases is used when making a decision about H_0; one always should keep in mind that we are not proving the null hypothesis. All that is being inferred is that the sample evidence is not strong enough to warrant rejection of H_0. In this book, the phrase **do not reject the null hypothesis** will be used instead of "accept the null hypothesis" or "fail to reject the null hypothesis." In addition, when we do not reject the null hypothesis, we may infer that there is not enough or insufficient sample evidence to conclude that the alternative hypothesis is true because whatever we are trying to conclude about the population is stipulated in the alternative hypothesis. **Figure 12-2** gives an idea of the wording of the conclusion in hypothesis testing.

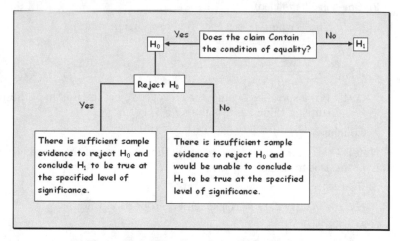

Figure 12-2: Wording of the final conclusion

Quick Tip

In writing up the final conclusion for a hypothesis test, you must express your conclusion to the problem at hand regardless of whether you rejected H_0 or not. For example, if you wanted to establish that the proportion of teachers who prefer to use a color of ink other than red to grade their tests, then in the write-up of the conclusion you would need to refer to this attribute.

Example 12-2: Your teacher claims that 60 percent of American males are married. You feel that the proportion is higher. In a random sample of 100 American males, 65 of them were married. Test your teacher's claim at the 5 percent level of significance.

Solution: We are given $n = 100$, x (number of successes) $= 65$, $\alpha = 0.05$, $z_\alpha = 1.645$, and $p_0 = 0.6$. Also, $\sqrt{np_0 (1 - p_0)} = 4.8990$. Since you would like to establish that the proportion is higher, then the alternative hypothesis should reflect this counterbelief. Thus

H_0: $p \le 0.6$

H_1: $p > 0.6$

T.S.: $z = \dfrac{x - np_0}{\sqrt{np_0(1 - p_0)}} = \dfrac{65 - 100 \times 0.6}{4.8990} = 1.0206$

D.R.: For a significance level of $\alpha = 0.05$, reject the null hypothesis if the computed test statistic value $z = 1.0206 > z_\alpha = 1.645$.

Conclusion: Since $1.0206 < 1.645$, do not reject H_0. There is insufficient sample evidence to refute your teacher's claim. That is, there is insufficient sample evidence to claim that more than 60 percent of American males are married at the 5 percent level of significance. Any difference between the sample proportion and the postulated proportion of 0.6 may be due to chance.

Figure 12-3 depicts the rejection region.

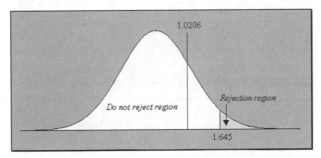

Figure 12-3: Diagram depicting the rejection region for Example 12-2

Example 12-3: A preacher would like to establish that of people who pray, less than 80 percent pray for world peace. In a random sample of 110 persons, 77 of them said that when they pray, they pray for world peace. Test at the 10 percent level of significance.

Solution: We are given $n = 110$, x (number of successes) $= 77$, $\alpha = 0.1$, $z_\alpha = 1.28$, and $p_0 = 0.8$. Also, $\sqrt{np_0(1 - p_0)} = 4.1952$. Since the preacher would like to establish that less than 80 percent of people pray for world peace when they pray, then the alternative hypothesis should reflect this. Thus

H_0: $p \ge 0.8$

H_1: $p < 0.8$

T.S.: $z = \dfrac{x - np_0}{\sqrt{np_0(1 - p_0)}} = \dfrac{77 - 110 \times 0.8}{4.1952} = -2.6220$

D.R.: For a significance level of $\alpha = 0.01$, reject the null hypothesis if the computed test statistic value $z = -2.6220 < -z_\alpha = -1.28$.

Conclusion: Since $-2.6220 < -1.28$, reject H_0. There is sufficient sample evidence to support the notion that less than 80 percent of people pray for world peace when they pray at the 10 percent level of significance. That is, there is a significant difference between the sample proportion and the postulated proportion of 0.8.

Figure 12-4 depicts the rejection region.

Figure 12-4: Diagram depicting the rejection region for Example 12-3

Example 12-4: A researcher claims that 90 percent of people trust DNA testing. In a survey of 100 people, 91 of them said that they trusted DNA testing. Test the researcher's claim at the 1 percent level of significance.

Solution: We are given $n = 100$, x (number of successes) = 91, $\alpha = 0.01$, $z_{\alpha/2} = 2.576$, and p_0 = 0.9. Also, $\sqrt{np_0 (1 - p_0)} = 3$. Since we are asked to test the researcher's claim, then the alternative hypothesis should contradict this claim. Thus

H_0: $p = 0.9$

H_1: $p \neq 0.9$

T.S.: $z = \dfrac{x - np_0}{\sqrt{np_0(1 - P_0)}} = \dfrac{91 - 100 \times 0.9}{3} = -0.3333$

D.R.: For a significance level of $\alpha = 0.01$, reject the null hypothesis if the computed test statistic value $z = 0.3333 < -z_{\alpha/2} = -2.576$ or if $z = 0.3333 > z_{\alpha/2} = 2.576$.

Conclusion: Since neither of the conditions are satisfied in the decision rule, do not reject H_0. There is insufficient sample evidence to refute the researcher's claim that the proportion of people who believe in DNA testing is equal to 90 percent at the 1 percent level of significance. That is, there is not a significant difference between the sample proportion and the postulated proportion of 0.9.

Figure 12-5 depicts the rejection region.

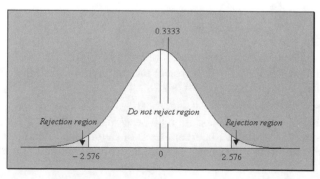

Figure 12-5: Diagram depicting the rejection region for Example 12-4

12-4 Large-Sample Test for a Population Mean

We refer to tests based on the statistic $z = \dfrac{\bar{x} - \mu_0}{\sigma/\sqrt{n}}$ or $z = \dfrac{\bar{x} - \mu_0}{s/\sqrt{n}}$ as **large-sample tests** for the population mean because we are assuming that the sampling distribution for the sample means is approximately normally distributed. The test requires that the sample size $n \geq 30$ when σ is unknown, unless the sampling population is exactly normally distributed. If the sampling distribution is normal, the test is appropriate for any sample size.

Following is a summary of the tests for a population mean.

Summary of Hypothesis Tests

1. One-tailed (right-tailed)

H_0: $\mu \leq \mu_0$ (where μ_0 is a specified value of the population mean)

H_1: $\mu > \mu_0$

T.S.: $z = \dfrac{\bar{x} - \mu_0}{\sigma/\sqrt{n}}$ or $z = \dfrac{\bar{x} - \mu_0}{s/\sqrt{n}}$, for σ unknown and $n \geq 30$

D.R.: For a specified significance level α, reject the null hypothesis if the computed test statistic value z is greater than $+z_\alpha$.

Conclusion:

Note: This is a right-tailed test because the direction of the inequality sign in the alternative hypothesis is to the right.

2. One-tailed (left-tailed)

H_0: $\mu \geq \mu_0$ (where μ_0 is a specified value of the population mean)

H_1: $\mu < \mu_0$

T.S.: $z = \dfrac{\bar{x} - \mu_0}{\sigma/\sqrt{n}}$ or $z = \dfrac{\bar{x} - \mu_0}{s/\sqrt{n}}$, for σ unknown and $n \geq 30$

D.R.: For a specified significance level α, reject the null hypothesis if the computed test statistic value z is less than $-z_\alpha$.

Conclusion:

Note: This is a left-tailed test because the direction of the inequality sign in the alternative hypothesis is to the left.

3. Two-tailed

H_0: $\mu = \mu_0$ (where μ_0 is a specified value of the population mean)

H_1: $\mu \neq \mu_0$

T.S.: $z = \dfrac{\bar{x} - \mu_0}{\sigma/\sqrt{n}}$ or $z = \dfrac{\bar{x} - \mu_0}{s/\sqrt{n}}$, for σ unknown and $n \geq 30$

D.R.: For a specified significance level α, reject the null hypothesis if the computed test statistic value z is less than $-z_{\alpha/2}$ or if it is greater than $+z_{\alpha/2}$.

Conclusion:

Note: This is a two-tailed test because of the not-equal-to symbol in the alternative hypothesis. Also, note that the level of significance is shared equally when finding the critical z value ($z_{\alpha/2}$).

Example 12-5: A teachers' union would like to establish that the average salary for high school teachers in a particular state is less than $32,500. A random sample of 100 public high school teachers in the particular state has a mean salary of $31,578. It is known from past history that the standard deviation of the salaries for the teachers in the state is $4,415. Test the union's claim at the 5 percent level of significance.

Solution: We are given $\alpha = 0.05$, $z_\alpha = 1.645$, $\bar{x} = 31,578$, $n = 100$, $\sigma = 4,415$, $\mu_0 = 32,500$, and $\dfrac{\sigma}{\sqrt{n}} = \dfrac{4,415}{\sqrt{100}} = 441.5$. Since the union would like to establish that the average salary is less than $32,500, this will be a left-tail test. Thus

H_0: $\mu \geq 32,500$

H_1: $\mu < 32,500$

T.S.: $z = \dfrac{\bar{x} - \mu_0}{\sigma/\sqrt{n}} = \dfrac{31578 - 32500}{441.5} = -2.0883$

D.R.: For a significance level of $\alpha = 0.05$, reject the null hypothesis if the computed test statistic value $z = -2.0883 < -z_\alpha = -1.645$.

Conclusion: Since $-2.0883 < -1.645$, reject H_0. There is sufficient sample evidence to support the claim that the average salary for high school teachers in the state is less than $32,500 at the 5 percent level of significance. That is, there is a significant difference between the sample mean and the postulated value of the population mean of $32,500.

Figure 12-6 depicts the rejection region.

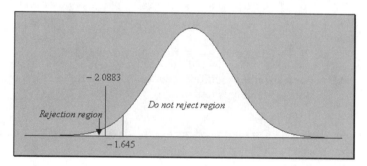

Figure 12-6: Diagram depicting the rejection region for Example 12-5

Example 12-6: The dean of students of a large community college claims that the average distance commuting students travel to the campus is 32 miles. The commuting students feel otherwise. A sample of 64 students was randomly selected and yielded a mean of 35 miles and a standard deviation of 5 miles. Test the dean's claim at the 5 percent level of significance.

Solution: We are given $\alpha = 0.05$, $z_{\alpha/2} = 1.96$, $\bar{x} = 35$, $s = 5$, $n = 64$, $\mu_0 = 32$, and $\dfrac{s}{\sqrt{n}} = 0.625$. This will be a two-tailed test because the students feel that the dean's claim is not correct, but whether they feel that the average distance is less than 32 miles or more than 32 miles is not specified. Thus

H_0: $\mu = 32$

H_1: $\mu \neq 32$

T.S.: $z = \dfrac{\bar{x}-\mu_0}{\sigma/\sqrt{n}} = \dfrac{35-32}{0.625} = 4.8$

D.R.: For a significance level $\alpha = 0.05$, reject the null hypothesis if the computed test statistic value $z = 4.8 < -z_\alpha = -1.96$ or if $z = 4.8 > z_\alpha = 1.96$.

Conclusion: Since $4.8 > 1.96$, reject H_0. There is sufficient sample evidence to refute the dean's claim. The sample evidence supports the students' claim that the average distance commuting students travel to the campus is not equal to 32 miles at the 5 percent level of significance. That is, there is a significant difference between the sample mean and the postulated value of the population mean of 32 miles.

Figure 12-7 depicts the rejection region.

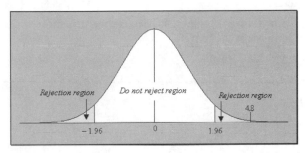

Figure 12-7: Diagram depicting the rejection region for Example 12-6

12-5 Large-Sample Test for the Difference between Two Population Proportions

There may be problems in which one must decide whether the observed difference between two sample proportions is due to chance or to the fact that the corresponding population proportions are not the same or that proportions are from different populations. Here we will discuss such problems.

Recall from **Chapter 11** that the differences of the sample proportions will have a mean of $\mu_{\hat{p}_1-\hat{p}_2} = p_1-p_2$ and a standard deviation (or standard error) of

$$\sigma_{\hat{p}_1-\hat{p}_2} = \sqrt{\dfrac{p_1(1-p_1)}{n_1} + \dfrac{p_2(1-p_2)}{n_2}}$$

where p_1 and p_2 are the respective population proportions of interest. When we test the null hypothesis $p_1 = p_2 (=p)$ against an appropriate alternative hypothesis, the mean $\mu_{\hat{p}_1-\hat{p}_2} = p_1 - p_2$ will be zero, and the standard error can be written as

$$\sqrt{p(1-p)\left(\dfrac{1}{n_1} + \dfrac{1}{n_2}\right)}$$

Since the value of p is unknown, we can estimate the value by

$$\hat{p} = \dfrac{x_1+x_2}{n_1+n_2}$$

$\hat{p}$ is sometimes called the pooled estimate for p.

Below is a summary of the tests for the difference between two population proportions using the preceding information.

Summary of Hypothesis Tests

1. One-tailed (right-tailed)

H_0: $p_1 \leq p_2$

H_1: $p_1 > p_2$

T.S.: $z = \dfrac{\hat{p}_1 - \hat{p}_2}{\sqrt{\hat{p}(1-\hat{p})\left(\dfrac{1}{n_1} + \dfrac{1}{n_2}\right)}}$

D.R.: For a specified significance level α, reject the null hypothesis if the computed test statistic value z is greater than $+z_\alpha$.

Conclusion:

Note: This is a right-tailed test because the direction of the inequality sign in the alternative hypothesis is to the right.

2. One-tailed (left-tailed)

H_0: $p_1 \geq p_2$

H_1: $p_1 < p_2$

T.S.: $z = \dfrac{\hat{p}_1 - \hat{p}_2}{\sqrt{\hat{p}(1-\hat{p})\left(\dfrac{1}{n_1} + \dfrac{1}{n_2}\right)}}$

D.R.: For a specified significance level α, reject the null hypothesis if the computed test statistic value z is less than $-z_\alpha$.

Conclusion:

Note: This is a left-tailed test because the direction of the inequality sign in the alternative hypothesis is to the left.

3. Two-tailed

H_0: $p_1 = p_2$

H_1: $p_1 \neq p_2$

T.S.: $z = \dfrac{\hat{p}_1 - \hat{p}_2}{\sqrt{\hat{p}(1-\hat{p})\left(\dfrac{1}{n_1} + \dfrac{1}{n_2}\right)}}$

D.R.: For a specified significance level α, reject the null hypothesis if the computed test statistic value z is less than $-z_{\alpha/2}$ or if it is greater than $+z_{\alpha/2}$.

Conclusion:

Note: This is a two-tailed test because of the not-equal-to symbol in the alternative hypothesis. Also note that the level of significance is shared equally when finding the critical z value ($z_{\alpha/2}$).

Example 12-7: A study was conducted to determine whether remediation in basic mathematics enabled students to be more successful in an elementary statistics course. Success in the course means that a student received a grade of C or better and remediation was for one year. **Table 12-2** shows the results of the study.

Table 12-2: Sample data for Example 12-7

	REMEDIAL	NONREMEDIAL
Sample size	100	40
Number of successes	70	16

Test, at the 5 percent level of significance, whether remediation helped the students to be more successful.

Solution: From the information given, we have $n_1 = 100$, $n_2 = 40$, $\hat{p}_1 = \dfrac{70}{100} = 0.7$, $\hat{p}_2 = \dfrac{16}{40}$

$= 0.4$, $\hat{p} = \dfrac{x_1 + x_2}{n_1 + n_2} = \dfrac{70 + 16}{100 + 40} = 0.6143$, $\alpha = 0.05$, and $z_\alpha = 1.645$. Since we would like to

establish whether remediation helped the students to be more successful, this is equivalent to establishing whether the proportion of students under remediation who were successful is greater than the proportion of those who were not under remediation. Thus we have a right-tail test in favor of remediation.

H_0: $p_1 \leq p_2$

H_1: $p_1 > p_2$

T.S.: $z = \dfrac{\hat{p}_1 - \hat{p}_2}{\sqrt{\hat{p}(1-\hat{p})\left(\dfrac{1}{n_1} + \dfrac{1}{n_2}\right)}} = \dfrac{0.7 - 0.4}{\sqrt{0.6143 \times (1 - 0.6143)\left(\dfrac{1}{100} + \dfrac{1}{40}\right)}} = 3.2944$

D.R.: For a significance level $\alpha = 0.05$, reject the null hypothesis if the computed test statistic value $z = 3.2944 > z_\alpha = 1.645$.

Conclusion: Since $3.2944 > 1.645$, reject the null hypothesis. Thus we can conclude that the proportion of success in the elementary statistics course for the remediation group is larger than that for the nonremedial group. That is, at the 5 percent level of significance, we can conclude that remediation is helping the students to do better in elementary statistics.

Figure 12-8 depicts the rejection region.

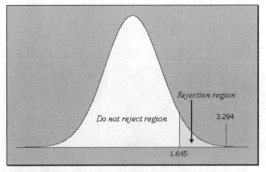

Figure 12-8: Diagram depicting the rejection region for Example 12-7

Example 12-8: A researcher wants to determine whether there is a difference between the proportions of male and female students who believe that an individual has the right to smoke in his or her dorm room on a particular campus because some students regard their dorm rooms as their homes when attending the college. The sample information is given in **Table 12-3**.

Table 12-3: Sample data for Example 12-8

	MALES	FEMALES
Sample size	75	100
Number who said "yes"	50	45

Test at the 1 percent level of significance.

Solution: From the information given, we have $n_1 = 75$, $n_2 = 100$, $\hat{p}_1 = \dfrac{50}{75} = 0.6667$,

$\hat{p}_2 = \dfrac{45}{100} = 0.45$, $\hat{p} = \dfrac{x_1 + x_2}{n_1 + n_2} = \dfrac{50 + 45}{75 + 100} = 0.5459$, $\alpha = 0.01$, and $z_{\alpha/2} = 2.576$. This is a two-

tail test because we are just testing whether there is a difference or not. Thus

H_0: $p_1 = p_2$

H_1: $p_1 \neq p_2$

T.S.: $z = \dfrac{\hat{p}_1 - \hat{p}_2}{\sqrt{\hat{p}(1-\hat{p})\left(\dfrac{1}{n_1} + \dfrac{1}{n_2}\right)}} = \dfrac{0.6667 - 0.45}{\sqrt{0.5429 \times (1 - 0.5429) \times \left(\dfrac{1}{75} + \dfrac{1}{100}\right)}} = 2.8478$

D.R.: For a significance level $\alpha = 0.01$, reject the null hypothesis if the computed test statistic value $z = 2.8478 < -z_{\alpha/2} = -2.576$ or if $z = 2.8478 > z_{\alpha/2} = 2.576$.

Conclusion: Since $2.8478 > 2.576$, reject the null hypothesis. That is, we can conclude, at the 1 percent level of significance, that the proportions of male and female students who believe that students should be allowed to smoke in their dorm rooms on this particular campus are significantly different from each other.

Figure 12-9 depicts the rejection region.

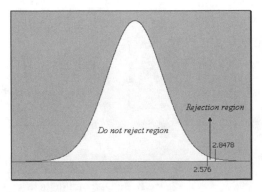

Figure 12-9: Diagram depicting the rejection region for Example 12-8

12-6 Large-Sample Test for the Difference between Two Population Means

There may be problems in which one must decide whether the observed difference between two sample means is due to chance or to the fact that the population means are not the same or that the samples are not from the same population. Here we will discuss such problems.

Recall from **Chapter 11** that the differences of the sample means will have a mean of $\mu_{\bar{x}_1 - \bar{x}_2} = \mu_1 - \mu_2$ an a standard deviation (or standard error) of

$$\sigma_{\bar{x}_1 - \bar{x}_2} = \sqrt{\frac{\sigma_1^2}{n_1} + \frac{\sigma_2^2}{n_2}}$$

where σ_1 and σ_2 are the respective population standard deviations of interest. Recall that the samples are assumed to have been obtained from normal populations. Also, when σ_1 and σ_2 are unknown, if the sample sizes are large enough ($n_1 \geq 30$ *and* $n_2 \geq 30$), we can estimate the population variances σ_1^2 and σ_2^2 with the sample variances s_1^2 and s_2^2.

Below is a summary of the tests for the difference between two population means using the preceding information.

Summary of Hypothesis Tests

1. One-tailed (right-tailed)

H_0: $\mu_1 \leq \mu_2$

H_1: $\mu_1 > \mu_2$

T.S.: $z = \dfrac{\bar{x}_1 - \bar{x}_2}{\sqrt{\dfrac{\sigma_1^2}{n_1} + \dfrac{\sigma_2^2}{n_2}}}$ or $\dfrac{\bar{x}_1 - \bar{x}_2}{\sqrt{\dfrac{s_1^2}{n_1} + \dfrac{s_2^2}{n_2}}}$, for $n_1 \geq 30$ and $n_2 \geq 30$

D.R.: For a specified significance level α, reject the null hypothesis if the computed test statistic value z is greater than $+z_\alpha$.

Conclusion:

Note: This is a right-tailed test because the direction of the inequality sign in the alternative hypothesis is to the right.

2. One-tailed (left-tailed)

H_0: $\mu_1 \geq \mu_2$

H_1: $\mu_1 < \mu_2$

T.S.: $z = \dfrac{\bar{x}_1 - \bar{x}_2}{\sqrt{\dfrac{\sigma_1^2}{n_1} + \dfrac{\sigma_2^2}{n_2}}}$ or $\dfrac{\bar{x}_1 - \bar{x}_2}{\sqrt{\dfrac{s_1^2}{n_1} + \dfrac{s_2^2}{n_2}}}$, for $n_1 \geq 30$ and $n_2 \geq 30$

D.R.: For a specified significance level α, reject the null hypothesis if the computed test statistic value z is less than $-z_\alpha$.

Conclusion:

Note: This is a left-tailed test because the direction of the inequality sign in the alternative hypothesis is to the left.

3. Two-tailed

H_0: $\mu_1 = \mu_2$

H_1: $\mu_1 \neq \mu_2$

T.S.: $z = \dfrac{\bar{x}_1 - \bar{x}_2}{\sqrt{\dfrac{\sigma_1^2}{n_1} + \dfrac{\sigma_2^2}{n_2}}}$ or $\dfrac{\bar{x}_1 - \bar{x}_2}{\sqrt{\dfrac{s_1^2}{n_1} + \dfrac{s_2^2}{n_2}}}$, for $n_1 \geq 30$ and $n_2 \geq 30$

D.R.: For a specified significance level α, reject the null hypothesis if the computed test statistic value z is less than $-z_{\alpha/2}$ or if it is greater than $+z_{\alpha/2}$.

Conclusion:

Note: This is a two-tailed test because of the not-equal-to symbol in the alternative hypothesis. Also note that the level of significance is shared equally when finding the critical z value ($z_{\alpha/2}$).

Example 12-9: A random sample of size $n_1 = 36$ selected from a normal distribution with standard deviation $\sigma_1 = 4$ has a mean $\bar{x}_1 = 75$. A second random sample of size $n_2 = 25$ selected from a different normal distribution with a standard deviation $\sigma_2 = 6$ has a mean $\bar{x}_2 = 85$. Is there a significant difference between the population means at the 5 percent level of significance?

Solution: From the information given, we have $n_1 = 36$, $n_2 = 25$, $\bar{x}_1 = 75$, $\bar{x}_2 = 85$, $\sigma_1 = 4$,

$\sigma_2 = 6$, $\sqrt{\dfrac{\sigma_1^2}{n_1} + \dfrac{\sigma_2^2}{n_2}} = 1.3728$, $\alpha = 0.05$, and $z_{\alpha/2} = 1.96$. Since we are just determining

whether there is a difference between the population means, this will be a two-tail test. Hence

H_0: $\mu_1 = \mu_2$

H_1: $\mu_1 \neq \mu_2$

T.S.: $z = \dfrac{\bar{x}_1 - \bar{x}_2}{\sqrt{\dfrac{\sigma_1^2}{n_1} + \dfrac{\sigma_2^2}{n_2}}} = \dfrac{75 - 85}{1.3728} = -7.2844$

D.R.: For a significance level $\alpha = 0.05$, reject the null hypothesis if the computed test statistic value $z = -7.2844 < -z_{\alpha/2} = -1.96$ or if $z = -7.2844 > +z_{\alpha/2} = 1.96$.

Conclusion: Since $-7.2844 < -1.96$, reject the null hypothesis. That is, at the 5 percent significance level, we can conclude that the means are significantly different from each other.

Example 12-10: Two methods, method 1 and method 2, were used to teach a high school algebra course. At the end of the semester, random samples of the final averages for the two methods were obtained. The sample information is given in summary form in **Table 12-4**.

Table 12-4: Sample data for Example 12-10

	METHOD 1	METHOD 2
Sample size	75	60
Sample mean	85	83
Sample standard deviation	3	2

Test whether method 1 was more successful than method 2 at the 1 percent significance level.

Solution: From the information given, we have $n_1 = 75$, $n_2 = 60$, $\bar{x}_1 = 85$, $\bar{x}_2 = 83$, $s_1 = 3$, $s_2 = 2$, $\sqrt{\dfrac{s_1^2}{n_1}+\dfrac{s_2^2}{n_2}} = 0.4321$, $\alpha = 0.01$, and $z_\alpha = 2.33$. Since we are testing whether method 1 was more successful than method 2, this is equivalent to establishing whether the mean score for method 1 is greater than that for method 2. Thus

H_0: $\mu_1 \le \mu_2$

H_1: $\mu_1 > \mu_2$

T.S.: $z = \dfrac{\bar{x}_1-\bar{x}_2}{\sqrt{\dfrac{s_1^2}{n_1}+\dfrac{s_2^2}{n_2}}} = \dfrac{85-83}{0.4321} = 4.6291$

D.R.: For a significance level $\alpha = 0.01$, reject the null hypothesis if the computed test statistic value $z = 4.6291 > z_\alpha = 2.33$.

Conclusion: Since $4.6291 > 2.33$, reject the null hypothesis. At the 1 percent significance level, we can conclude that method 1 was more successful than method 2. That is, we can conclude that the average score for the algebra course using method 1 is significantly greater than the average score using method 2.

12-7 *P*-Value Approach to Hypothesis Testing

With the advent of the computer and other technologies, certain probabilities can be computed readily and used to help make decisions in hypothesis testing. One such probability value is called the **P-value**.

Explanation of the term—P-value: A **P-value** is the smallest significance level at which a null hypothesis may be rejected.

Determining P-Values

For each of the preceding tests, we can determine a *P*-value.

1. **Right-tailed test:** *P*-value $= P(z > z^*) =$ area to the right of the test statistic value, where z^* is the computed value for the test statistic. The *P*-value for the right-tailed test is depicted in **Figure 12-10**.

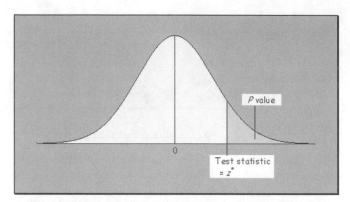

Figure 12-10: Depiction of the *P*-value for a right-tailed test

2. **Left-tailed test:** *P*-value $= P(z < z^*)$ = area to the left of the test statistic value, where z^* is the computed value for the test statistic. The *P*-value for the left-tailed test is depicted in **Figure 12-11**.

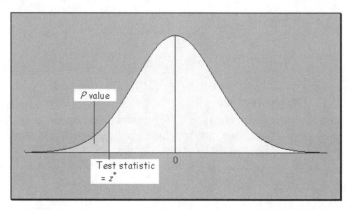

Figure 12-11: Depiction of the *P*-value for a left-tailed test

3. **Two-tailed test:** *P*-value $= 2 \times P(z > |z^*|)$, where z^* is the computed value for the test statistic. In this case, the test statistic could be to the right or to the left of the center of the distribution. This is why we use the absolute value of the test statistic in the computation of the *P*-value. Thus, for the two-tailed test, we could have a depiction as in **Figure 12-10** or **12-11**. We then multiply that area by 2 to get the *P*-value for the two-tailed test.

Example 12-11: Compute the *P*-value for the test in **Example 12.2.**

Solution: The test was a right-tailed test with $z^* = 1.0206$. Thus the *P*-value will be *P*-value $= P(z > 1.0206) = 0.5 - 0.3461 = 0.1539$. Note we have to subtract 0.3461 from 0.5 because the standard tables are set up such that we find the area from $z = 0$ to $z = 1.02$.

Example 12-12: Compute the *P*-value for the test in **Example 12-3**.

Solution: The test was a left-tailed test with $z^* = -2.622$. Thus the *P*-value will be *P*-value $= P(z < -2.622) = 0.5 - 0.4956 = 0.0044$.

Example 12-13: Compute the *P*-value for the test in **Example 12-4**.

Solution: The test was a two-tailed test with $z^* = 0.3333$. Thus the *P*-value will be *P*-value $= 2 \times P(z > |0.3333|) = 2 \times (0.5 - 0.1293) = 0.3707 = 0.7414$.

Note: The *P*-values for any of the presented tests can be computed using the preceding procedures.

Interpreting *P*-Values

We can use the *P*-value for a statistical test to measure the strength of the evidence against the null hypothesis for that test. The smaller the *P*-value, the stronger will be the evidence against the null hypothesis. That is, the smaller the *P*-value, the stronger is the evidence that we should reject the null hypothesis in favor of the alternative hypothesis. Several cut-off points can be used for *P*-values. Typical or a rule-of-thumb cutoff points are given next:

- *P*-value $> 0.1 \Rightarrow$ little evidence against H_0
- $0.05 <$ *P*-value $\leq 0.1 \Rightarrow$ some evidence against H_0
- $0.01 <$ *P*-value $\leq 0.05 \Rightarrow$ moderate evidence against H_0
- $0.001 <$ *P*-value $\leq 0.01 \Rightarrow$ strong evidence against H_0
- *P*-value $< 0.001 \Rightarrow$ very strong evidence against H_0

Using this guide to make a decision, for **Examples 12-11** and **12-13** we will not reject the null hypothesis because both *P*-values are greater then 0.1. However, the *P*-value for **Example 12-12** is 0.0044, which indicates strong evidence against the null hypothesis. In this case we would reject the null hypothesis and conclude that the alternative hypothesis is true at the 0.0044 level of significance.

Quick Tip

Note that there is a clear distinction between the α value (level of significance) and the *P*-value. The α value is chosen before the statistical test is carried out, and the *P*-value is computed after an experiment is run and a sample statistic is computed.

General Approach to Interpreting *P*-Values

A more general approach in using the *P*-value to help in making a decision for a test is to compare it with a specified significance level α. The following can be used:

- *P*-value $< \alpha \Rightarrow$ reject the null hypothesis
- *P*-value $\geq \alpha \Rightarrow$ do not reject the null hypothesis

Hypothesis Tests with *P*-Values

When using the *P*-value to help with a decision in hypothesis testing, the five-step procedure in **Section 12-2** again is employed. However, the test statistic will now be the *P*-value, and the decision rule will compare the *P*-value with the level of significance α to determine whether to reject the null hypothesis.

Example 12-14: Using the information in **Example 12-2** and the *P*-value from **Example 12-11**, write up the hypothesis test using the *P*-value approach.

Solution: Recall in **Example 12-2** that your teacher claimed that 60 percent of American males were married. You felt that the proportion was higher. In a random sample of 100

American males, 65 of them were married, and you wanted to test your teacher's claim at the 5 percent level of significance.

Here, $\alpha = 0.05$, and the P-value $= 0.1539$. Since you would like to establish that the proportion was higher, the alternative hypothesis should reflect this counterbelief. Thus

H_0: $p \leq 0.6$

H_1: $p > 0.6$

T.S.: P-value $= 0.1539$

D.R.: For a significance level of $\alpha = 0.05$, reject the null hypothesis if the computed P-value $= 0.1539 <$ level of significance $\alpha = 0.05$.

Conclusion: Since $0.1539 > 0.05$, do not reject H_0. There is insufficient sample evidence to refute your teacher's claim. That is, there is insufficient sample evidence to claim that more than 60 percent of American males are married at the 5 percent level of significance. Any difference between the sample proportion and the postulated proportion of 0.6 may be due to chance.

Note: The decision is the same as in **Example 12-2.**

Example 12-15: Using the information in **Example 12-6** write up the hypothesis test using the P-value approach.

Solution: Recall in **Example 12-6** that the dean of students of a large community college wanted to claim that the average distance commuting students travel to the campus was 32 miles. The commuting students felt otherwise and took a random sample of 64 students that yielded a mean of 35 miles and a standard deviation of 5 miles. The dean's claim was tested at the 5 percent level of significance.

Solution: We are given that $\alpha = 0.05$, and from **Example 12-6**, the test statistic z value is 4.8. We first need to use this test statistic value to help find the P-value. Observe that this will be a two-tailed test because the students feel that the dean's claim is not correct, but whether they feel that the average distance is less than 32 miles or more than 32 miles is not specified. Thus the P-value $= 2 \times P(z > |4.8|) \approx 0$. Hence, using the P-value approach, the test can be written up as follows:

H_0: $\mu = 32$

H_1: $\mu \neq 32$

T.S.: P-value $= 0$ (for all practical purposes)

D.R.: For a significance level $\alpha = 0.05$, reject the null hypothesis if the computed P-value $= 0.0 <$ level of significance $\alpha = 0.05$.

Conclusion: Since $0 < 0.05$, reject H_0. There is sufficient sample evidence to refute the dean's claim. The sample evidence supports the students' claim that the average distance commuting students travel to the campus is not equal to 32 miles at the 5 percent level of significance. That is, there is a significant difference between the sample mean and the postulated value of the population mean of 32 miles.

Technology Corner

Technology

All the computations and concepts discussed in this chapter can be computed and illustrated through most statistical software packages. All scientific and graphical calculators can be used for the computations. In addition, some of the newer calculators, such as the

TI-83/84 (all versions), will allow you to do the test directly on the calculator. If you own a calculator, you should consult the owner's manual to determine what statistical features are included.

Illustration: Figure 12-12 shows the outputs computed by the MINITAB software for **Examples 12-14** and **12-15**. Note that the outputs also give the *P*-values for the tests. **Figure 12-13** shows the outputs computed by the TI-83/84 calculator for **Examples 12-2, 12-6, 12-7**, and **12-10**. Both the MINITAB software and the TI-83/84 calculator allow you to use both summary data and raw data to do hypothesis tests for both means and proportions. The *P*-values provided by both the MINITAB and TI-83/84 outputs can be used to perform the tests. Care always should be taken when using the formulas for computations in hypothesis testing. One can use other features of the technologies to illustrate other concepts discussed in this chapter.

Figure 12-12: MINITAB output for Examples 12-14 and 12-15

Below are TI-83/84 outputs for various examples.

Figure 12-13: TI-83/84 output for Examples 12-2, 12-6, 12-7 and 12-10

Figure 12-14 shows the EXCEL output for **Example 12-10**. It gives the z test statistic value, and the critical (table) and P-values for both the one-tail and two-tail tests.

	A	B	C
1	z-Test: Two Sample for Means		
2			
3		Variable 1	Variable 2
4	Mean	85	83
5	Known Variance	9	4
6	Observations	75	60
7	Hypothesized Mean Difference	0	
8	z	4.629100499	
9	P(Z<=z) one-tail	1.83629E-06	
10	z Critical one-tail	1.644853627	
11	P(Z<=z) two-tail	3.67258E-06	
12	z Critical two-tail	1.959963985	
13			

Figure 12-14: EXCEL output for Example 12-10

Here the focus was on hypothesis testing for a single mean and a single proportion. Also, tests for the difference between two population proportions and the difference between two population means were addressed. In all tests, we assumed large samples. These concepts were presented through

✓ Formulas

✓ Examples

✓ Use of technology

True/False Questions

1. A claim or statement about a population parameter is classified as the null hypothesis.
2. A statement contradicting the claim in the null hypothesis about a population parameter is classified as the alternative hypothesis.
3. If we want to claim that a population parameter is different from a specified value, such a situation can be considered as a one-tailed test.
4. The null hypothesis is considered correct until proven otherwise.
5. A type I error is the error we make in failing to reject an incorrect null hypothesis.
6. The probability of making a type I error and the level of significance are equal or the same.
7. The range of z values that indicates that there is a significant difference between the value of the sample statistic and the proposed parameter value is called the rejection region or the critical region.
8. If the sample size n is less than 30, then a z score always will be associated with any hypothesis that deals with the mean.
9. In the P-value approach to hypothesis testing, if the P-value is less than a specified significance level, we fail to reject the null hypothesis.
10. In the P-value approach to hypothesis testing, if $0.01 < P$-value < 0.05, then there is insufficient sample evidence to reject the null hypothesis.
11. In the P-value approach to hypothesis testing, if the P-value is less than 0.001, then there is very strong sample evidence to reject the null hypothesis.

12. When large samples ($n \geq 30$) are associated with hypothesis tests for population proportions, the associated test statistic is a z score.
13. The distribution of sample proportions from a single population is approximately normal provided that the sample size is large enough ($n \geq 30$).
14. The distribution of the difference between two sample means is approximately normal with variance, $\dfrac{\sigma_1^2}{n_1} + \dfrac{\sigma_2^2}{n_2}$, where n_1 and n_2 are the sample sizes from populations 1 and 2, respectively, and σ_1^2 and σ_2^2 are the respective variances, if the sample sizes are both greater than or equal to 30.
15. When testing for the difference between two population means, if the population variances are unknown and the sample sizes from the populations are both greater than or equal to 30, the associated test statistic is approximately a z score.
16. In making inferences on the difference between two population proportions, the calculated (pooled) proportion is given by $\hat{p} = \dfrac{x_1 + x_2}{n_1 + n_2}$, where x_1 and x_2 are the respective number of successes from populations 1 and 2, and n_1 and n_2 are the respective sample sizes.
17. If the null hypothesis is rejected, this means that the null hypothesis is not true.
18. When performing hypothesis tests on two population means, it is necessary to assume that the populations are normally distributed.
19. The *P*-value of a hypothesis test can be computed without the value of the test statistic.
20. The *P*-value of a hypothesis test is the smallest level of significance at which the null hypothesis can be rejected.
21. In hypothesis testing, the alternative hypothesis is assumed to be true.
22. In hypothesis testing, if the null hypothesis is rejected, the alternative hypothesis must also be rejected.

Completion Questions

1. The two broad areas of statistical inference are hypothesis testing and (point, interval) _____ estimation.
2. Rejecting a true null hypothesis is classified as a (type I, type II) _____ error.
3. Failing to reject a false null hypothesis is classified as a (type I, type II) _____ error.
4. In hypothesis testing, the cutoff values that define the rejection region are known as (*P*, critical, α) _____ values.
5. In a hypothesis test, if the computed *P*-value is less than 0.001, there is very strong evidence to (do not reject, reject) _____ the null hypothesis.
6. In a hypothesis test, if the computed *P*-value is greater than a specified level of significance, then we (reject, do not reject) _____ the null hypothesis.
7. The level of significance for a hypothesis test is equal to the probability of a (type I, type II) _____ error.
8. If we reject the (null, alternative) _____ hypothesis, the (null, alternative) _____ hypothesis may be accepted.
9. The point estimate for the difference between two population means $\mu_1 - \mu_2$ can be represented by $(\hat{p}_1 - \hat{p}_2, \bar{x}_1 - \bar{x}_2, \mu_1 - \mu_2)$ _____, where the subscripts will represent the corresponding populations.
10. In a hypothesis test for means, it is necessary to assume that the sample was selected from (any, a normal) _____ population.

11. The value of the level of significance lies between _____ and _____.
12. If a hypothesis test is performed at the 0.02 level of significance and the computed P-value is 0.01, you will (reject, not reject) _____ the null hypothesis.
13. The level of significance for a hypothesis test is the probability of rejecting a (true, false) _____ null hypothesis.
14. When conducting a hypothesis test for a single population mean, the test statistic is assumed to have a normal distribution if the sample size is (small, large) _____, when the population standard deviation is unknown.
15. The area under a curve that leads to rejection of the null hypothesis is also known as the (critical or rejection, do-not-reject) _____ region.
16. The number that separates the rejection region from the do-not-reject region is called a (critical, noncritical) _____ value of the test.
17. If we are performing a right-tailed test and the computed test statistic value $z = 2.99$, the P-value will be (0.0014, 0.0028) _____.
18. If we are performing a two-tailed test for the population mean when the population standard deviation is known, and if the test statistic value is 2.79, the P-value will be (0.0026, 0.0052) _____.
19. The P-value of a hypothesis test is the smallest level of significance at which the null hypothesis can (be rejected, not be rejected) _____.
20. In the P-value approach to hypothesis testing, if the P-value is less than a specified significance level α, then we (reject, do not reject) _____ the null hypothesis.

Multiple-Choice Questions

1. The calculated numerical value that is compared with a table value in a hypothesis test is called the
   (a) level of significance.
   (b) critical value.
   (c) population parameter.
   (d) test statistic.

2. A right-tailed test is conducted with $\alpha = 0.0582$. If the z tables are used, the critical value will be
   (a) -1.57.
   (b) 1.57.
   (c) -0.15.
   (d) 0.15.

3. A right-tailed test is performed with the test statistic having a standard normal distribution. If the computed test statistic is 3.00, the P-value for this test is
   (a) 0.4996.
   (b) 0.9996.
   (c) 0.0013.
   (d) 0.0500.

4. A new software is being integrated in the teaching of a course with the hope that it will help to improve the overall average score for this course. The historical average score for this course is 72. If a statistical test is done for this situation, the alternative hypothesis will be

    (a) $H_1: \mu \neq 72$.

    (b) $H_1: \mu < 72$.

    (c) $H_1: \mu = 72$.

    (d) $H_1: \mu > 72$.

5. Dr. J claims that 40 percent of his college algebra class (very large section) will drop his course by midterm. To test his claim, he selected 45 names at random and discovered that 20 of them had already dropped long before midterm. The test statistic value for his hypothesis test is

    (a) 0.6086.

    (b) 0.3704.

    (c) 8.3333.

    (d) 0.6847.

6. When testing a hypothesis, the hypothesis that is assumed to be true is

    (a) the alternative hypothesis.

    (b) the null hypothesis.

    (c) the null or alternative hypothesis.

    (d) neither the null nor the alternative hypothesis.

7. A type I error is defined to be the probability of

    (a) not rejecting a true null hypothesis.

    (b) not rejecting a false null hypothesis.

    (c) rejecting a false null hypothesis.

    (d) rejecting a true null hypothesis.

8. A type II error is defined to be the probability of

    (a) not rejecting a true null hypothesis.

    (b) not rejecting a false null hypothesis.

    (c) rejecting a false null hypothesis.

    (d) rejecting a true null hypothesis.

9. In hypothesis testing, the level of significance is the probability of

    (a) not rejecting a true null hypothesis.

    (b) not rejecting a false null hypothesis.

    (c) rejecting a false null hypothesis.

    (d) rejecting a true null hypothesis.

10. The level of significance can be any

    (a) z value.

    (b) parameter value.

    (c) any value between 0 and 1 inclusive.

    (d) α value.

11. If you do not reject the null hypothesis in the testing of a hypothesis, then

    (a) a type I error has definitely occurred.

    (b) a type II error has definitely occurred.

    (c) the computed test statistic is incorrect.

    (d) there is insufficient sample evidence to claim that the alternative hypothesis is true.

12. If we were testing the hypotheses H_0: $\mu = \mu_0$ versus H_1: $\mu > \mu_0$ (where μ_0 is a specified value of μ) at a given significance level of α, with large samples and unknown population variance, then H_0 will be rejected if the computed test statistic
    (a) $z > z_\alpha$.
    (b) $z < -z_\alpha$.
    (c) $z > z_{\alpha/2}$.
    (d) $z < -z_{\alpha/2}$.

13. Which of the following general guidelines is (are) used when using the P-value to perform hypothesis tests?
    (a) If the P-value > 0.1, there is little or no evidence to reject the null hypothesis
    (b) If $0.01 < P$-value ≤ 0.05, there is moderate evidence to reject the null hypothesis
    (c) If the P-value ≤ 0.001, there is very strong evidence to reject the null hypothesis
    (d) All the above

14. When the P-value is used in testing hypotheses, we will not reject the null hypothesis for a level of significance α when the
    (a) P-value $< \alpha$.
    (b) P-value $\geq \alpha$.
    (c) P-value $= \alpha$.
    (d) P-value $\neq \alpha$.

15. A real estate agent claims that the average price for homes in a certain subdivision is $150,000. You believe that the average price is lower. If you plan to test his claim by taking a random sample of the prices of the homes in the subdivision, the formulated set of hypotheses will be
    (a) H_0: $\mu \leq 150,000$ versus H_1: $\mu > 150,000$.
    (b) H_0: $\mu = 150,000$ versus H_1: $\mu \neq 150,000$.
    (c) H_0: $\mu < 150,000$ versus H_1: $\mu \geq 150,000$.
    (d) H_0: $\mu \geq 150,000$ versus H_1: $\mu < 150,000$.

16. A statistics student was not pleased with his final grade in his statistics course, so he decided to appeal his grade. He believes that the overall average percent for the course was less than 69, so he believes that the course examinations were unfair. He thinks that he should have made at least a grade of B in the course. He decided to test his claim about the course average. If he knows his "statistics," the correct set of hypothesis he will set up to test his claim is
    (a) H_0: $\mu \leq 69$ versus H_1: $\mu > 69$.
    (b) H_0: $\mu \geq 69$ versus H_1: $\mu < 69$.
    (c) H_0: $\mu = 69$ versus H_1: $\mu \neq 69$.
    (d) H_0: $\mu \neq 69$ versus H_1: $\mu = 69$.

17. An advertisement on the TV claims that a certain brand of tire has an average lifetime of 50,000 miles. Suppose that you plan to test this claim by taking a sample of tires and putting them on test. The correct set of hypotheses to set up is
    (a) H_0: $\mu \leq 50,000$ versus H_1: $\mu > 50,000$.
    (b) H_0: $\mu \geq 50,000$ versus H_1: $\mu < 50,000$.
    (c) H_0: $\mu = 50,000$ versus H_1: $\mu \neq 50,000$.
    (d) H_0: $\mu \neq 50,000$ versus H_1: $\mu = 50,000$.

18. The local newspaper reported that at least 25 percent of the population in a university community works at the university. You believe that the proportion is lower. If you selected a random sample to test this claim, the appropriate set of hypotheses would be
    (a) $H_0: p \leq 0.25$ versus $H_1: p > 0.25$.
    (b) $H_0: p = 0.25$ versus $H_1: p \neq 0.25$.
    (c) $H_0: p < 0.25$ versus $H_1: p \geq 0.25$.
    (d) $H_0: p \geq 0.25$ versus $H_1: p < 0.25$.

19. The local newspaper claims that 15 percent of the residents of its community play the state lottery. If you plan to test the claim by taking a random sample from the community, the appropriate set of hypotheses is
    (a) $H_0: p \geq 0.15$ versus $H_1: p < 0.15$.
    (b) $H_0: p \leq 0.15$ versus $H_1: p > 0.15$.
    (c) $H_0: p = 0.15$ versus $H_1: p \neq 0.15$.
    (d) $H_0: p \neq 0.15$ versus $H_1: p = 0.15$.

20. The local newspaper claims that no more than 5 percent of the residents of community are on welfare. If you plan to test the claim by taking a random sample from the community, the appropriate set of hypotheses is
    (a) $H_0: p \leq 0.05$ versus $H_1: p > 0.05$.
    (b) $H_0: p \geq 0.05$ versus $H_1: p < 0.05$.
    (c) $H_0: p = 0.05$ versus $H_1: p \neq 0.05$.
    (d) $H_0: p > 0.05$ versus $H_1: p \leq 0.05$.

21. For the following information:

$$n = 16 \qquad \mu = 15 \qquad \bar{x} = 16 \qquad \sigma^2 = 16$$

assume that the population is normal. Compute the test statistic if you were testing for a single population mean.

    (a) $z = 1$
    (b) $z = 0.25$
    (c) $z = 0$
    (d) $z = -1$

22. For the following information:

$$n = 16 \qquad \mu = 15 \qquad \bar{x} = 16 \qquad \sigma^2 = 16$$

assume that the population is normal. If you are performing a right-tailed test for a single population mean, then the

    (a) P-value $- 0.3413$.
    (b) P-value < 0.05.
    (c) P-value $= 0.1587$.
    (d) P-value $= 0.0794$.

23. For the following information:

$$n = 16 \qquad \mu = 15 \qquad \bar{x} = 16 \qquad \sigma^2 = 16$$

assume that the population is normal. If you are performing a right-tailed test for a single population mean, then you

(a) will reject the null hypothesis if $\alpha = 0.1$.
(b) will not reject the null hypothesis if $\alpha = 0.1$.
(c) will not be able to do the test because more information is needed.
(d) need the hypotheses to be given.

24. For the following information:

$$n = 16 \qquad \mu = 15 \qquad \bar{x} = 16 \qquad \sigma^2 = 16$$

assume that the population is normal. If you are performing a right-tailed test for a single population mean, then you

(a) will reject the null hypothesis if $\alpha = 0.2$.
(b) will not reject the null hypothesis if $\alpha = 0.2$.
(c) will not be able to do the test because more information is needed.
(d) need the hypotheses to be given.

25. If a null hypothesis is rejected at the 0.05 level of significance for a two-tailed test, you
(a) always will reject it at the 0.01 level of significance.
(b) always will reject it at the 0.10 level of significance.
(c) always will not reject it at the 0.01 level of significance.
(d) always will not reject it at the 0.04 level of significance.

26. If a null hypothesis is rejected at the 5 percent significance level for a right-tailed test, you
(a) always will reject it at the 0.1 level of significance.
(b) always will reject it at the 0.01 level of significance.
(c) always will not reject it at the 0.01 level of significance.
(d) always will reject it at the 0.03 level of significance.

27. For a left-tailed test concerning the population proportion with sample size 203 and $\alpha = 0.05$, the null hypothesis will be rejected if the computed test statistic is
(a) less than -1.96.
(b) less than -1.717.
(c) less than -1.645.
(d) less than -2.704.

28. It was reported that a certain population had a mean of 27. To test this claim, you selected a random sample of size 100. The computed sample mean and sample standard deviation were 25 and 7, respectively. The appropriate set of hypotheses for this test is
(a) H_0: $\mu \leq 27$ versus H_1: $\mu > 27$.
(b) H_0: $\mu = 27$ versus H_1: $\mu \neq 27$.
(c) H_0: $\mu \geq 25$ versus H_1: $\mu < 25$.
(d) H_0: $\mu \neq 25$ versus H_1: $\mu = 25$.

29. It was reported that a certain population had a mean of 27. To test this claim, you selected a random sample of size 100. The computed sample mean and sample standard deviation were 25 and 7, respectively. The computed test statistic for the appropriate set of hypotheses is
(a) -4.0816.
(b) -0.4082.

(c) −28.5714.

(d) −2.8571.

30. It was reported that a certain population had a mean of 27. To test this claim, you selected a random sample of size 100. The computed sample mean and sample standard deviation were 25 and 7, respectively. The *P*-value for the appropriate set of hypotheses is

(a) 0.0021.

(b) 0.9979.

(c) 0.0042.

(d) −0.4979.

31. It was reported that a certain population had a mean of 27. To test this claim, you selected a random sample of size 100. The computed sample mean and sample standard deviation were 25 and 7 respectively. At the 0.05 level of significance, you can claim that the average of this population is

(a) not equal to 25.

(b) equal to 25.

(c) not equal to 27.

(d) equal 27.

32. For a highly publicized murder trial, it was estimated that 25 percent of the population watched the proceedings on TV. A statistics student felt that this estimate was too small for his community and decided to do a hypothesis test. He selected a random sample of 100 residents from the university community where he lives and found that 32 of them actually watched at least three hours of the proceedings. The appropriate set of hypotheses for the test is

(a) $H_0: p \leq 0.32$ versus $H_1: p > 0.32$.

(b) $H_0: p \geq 0.25$ versus $H_1: p < 0.25$.

(c) $H_0: p \geq 0.32$ versus $H_1: p < 0.32$.

(d) $H_0: p \leq 0.25$ versus $H_1: p > 0.25$.

33. For a highly publicized murder trial, it was estimated that 25 percent of the population watched the proceedings on TV. A statistics student felt that this estimate was too small for his community and decided to do a hypothesis test. He selected a random sample of 100 residents from the university community where he lives and found that 32 of them actually watched at least three hours of the proceedings. The computed test statistic for the test is

(a) 1.6167.

(b) 1.5006.

(c) −1.6167.

(d) −1.5006.

34. For a highly publicized murder trial, it was estimated that 25 percent of the population watched the proceedings on TV. A statistics student felt that this estimate was too small for his community and decided to do a hypothesis test. He selected a random sample of 100 residents from the university community where he lives and found that 32 of them actually watched at least three hours of the proceedings. The *P*-value for the test is

(a) 0.4332.   (c) 0.0668.

(b) 0.0526.   (d) 0.4474.

35. For a highly publicized murder trial, it was estimated that 25 percent of the population watched the proceedings on TV. A statistics student felt that this estimate was too small for his community and decided to do a hypothesis test. He selected a random sample of 100 residents from the university community where he lives and found that 32 of them actually watched at least three hours the proceedings. At the 10 percent significance level, you can claim that the proportion of viewers in this community was
    (a) significantly greater than 32 percent.
    (b) significantly smaller than 32 percent.
    (c) significantly smaller than 25 percent.
    (d) significantly greater than 25 percent.

36. For a highly publicized murder trial, it was estimated that 25 percent of the population watched the proceedings on TV. A statistics student felt that this estimate was too small for his community and decided to do a hypothesis test. He selected a random sample of 100 residents from the university community where he lives and found that 32 of them actually watched at least three hours the proceedings. The standard deviation for the distribution of the sample proportion is
    (a) 0.19.   (c) 4.33.
    (b) 4.67.   (d) 0.23.

37. If two large samples are selected independently from two different populations, the sampling distribution of the difference of the sample means
    (a) has a mean that is the sum of the two population means.
    (b) has a variance that is the difference of the two variances for the two populations.
    (c) has a distribution that is approximately normal.
    (d) has mean and variance that are the average of the two population means and variances, respectively.

38. If we are trying to establish that the mean of population 1 is greater than the mean of population 2, the appropriate set of hypotheses is
    (a) $H_0: \mu_2 - \mu_1 \leq 0$ versus $H_1: \mu_2 - \mu_1 > 0$.
    (b) $H_0: \mu_1 - \mu_2 \geq 0$ versus $H_1: \mu_1 - \mu_2 < 0$.
    (c) $H_0: \mu_1 - \mu_2 = 0$ versus $H_1: \mu_1 - \mu_2 \neq 0$.
    (d) $H_0: \mu_1 - \mu_2 \leq 0$ versus $H_1: \mu_1 - \mu_2 > 0$.

39. If we are trying to establish that the mean of population 1 is not the same as the mean of population 2, the appropriate set of hypotheses is
    (a) $H_0: \mu_1 - \mu_2 \neq 0$ versus $H_1: \mu_1 - \mu_2 = 0$.
    (b) $H_0: \mu_1 - \mu_2 = 0$ versus $H_1: \mu_1 - \mu_2 \neq 0$.
    (c) $H_0: \mu_1 - \mu_2 \geq 0$ versus $H_1: \mu_1 - \mu_2 < 0$.
    (d) $H_0: \mu_1 - \mu_2 \leq 0$ versus $H_1: \mu_1 - \mu_2 > 0$.

40. In performing hypothesis tests for the difference between two population proportions, if n_1 and n_2 are the respective sample sizes and x_1 and x_2 are the respective successes, then the pooled estimate of the difference of the population proportions is given by

    (a) $\dfrac{x_1 - x_2}{n_1 + n_2}$.

(b) $\dfrac{x_1-x_2}{n_1-n_2}$.

(c) $\dfrac{x_1+x_2}{n_1+n_2}$.

(d) $\dfrac{x_1+x_2}{n_1-n_2}$.

Use the following information for Problems 41 to 46:

Two machines are used to fill 50-pound bags of dog food. Sample information for these two machines is given in the following table:

	MACHINE A	MACHINE B
Sample size	81	64
Sample mean (pounds)	51	48
Sample variance	16	12

41. The point estimate for the difference between the two population means ($\mu_A - \mu_B$) is
   (a) 17.
   (b) 3.
   (c) 4.
   (d) −4.

42. The standard deviation (standard error) for the distribution of differences between sample means ($\bar{x}_A - \bar{x}_B$) is
   (a) 0.6205.
   (b) 0.1931.
   (c) 0.3850.
   (d) 0.3217.

43. If you are to conduct a test to determine whether the average amount dispensed by machine A is significantly more than the average amount dispensed by machine B, the appropriate set of hypotheses is
   (a) $H_0: \mu_B - \mu_A \le 0$ versus $H_1: \mu_B - \mu_A > 0$.
   (b) $H_0: \mu_A - \mu_B = 0$ versus $H_1: \mu_A - \mu_B \ne 0$.
   (c) $H_0: \mu_A - \mu_B \ge 0$ versus $H_1: \mu_A - \mu_B < 0$.
   (d) $H_0: \mu_A - \mu_B \le 0$ versus $H_1: \mu_A - \mu_B > 0$.

44. If you are to conduct a test to determine whether the average amount dispensed by machine A is significantly more than the average amount dispensed by machine B, the computed test statistic for this test is
   (a) 7.7918.
   (b) −7.7918.
   (c) 4.8348.
   (d) 2.1988.

45. If you are to conduct a test to determine whether the average amount dispensed by machine A is significantly more than the average amount dispensed by machine B, the *P*-value for the test is

(a) approximately 0.5.

(b) approximately 0.0.

(c) approximately 1.0.

(d) none of the above answers.

46. If you are to conduct a test at the 0.01 significance level to determine whether the average amount dispensed by machine A is significantly more than the average amount dispensed by machine B, the correct decision is

(a) do not reject the null hypothesis.

(b) reject the null hypothesis.

(c) reject the alternative hypothesis.

(d) do not reject the alternative hypothesis.

Use the following information for Problems 47 to 52:

A study was conducted to determine whether remediation in mathematics enabled students to be more successful in an elementary statistics course. Success here means that a student received a grade of C or better, and remediation was for one year (students took an equivalent of one year of high school algebra). The following table shows the results of this study:

	REMEDIAL	NONREMEDIAL
Sample size	$n_1 = 34$	$n_2 = 150$
No. of successes	$x_1 = 20$	$x_2 = 104$

47. If we assume that the two population proportions are both equal to p, then a point estimate for p is

(a) 0.4565.

(b) 0.6739.

(c) 0.4078.

(d) 0.7241.

48. If we assume that the two population proportions are both equal to p, then an estimate for the standard deviation for the distribution of differences between sample proportions is approximately

(a) 0.0079.

(b) 0.1898.

(c) 0.0360.

(d) 0.0890.

49. If p_r and p_n are the population proportions for the remedial and nonremedial groups, respectively, the appropriate set of hypotheses for this situation is

(a) $H_0: p_r - p_n > 0$ versus $H_0: p_r - p_n \leq 0$.

(b) $H_0: p_r - p_n = 0$ versus $H_0: p_r - p_n \neq 0$.

(c) $H_0: p_r - p_n \geq 0$ versus $H_0: p_r - p_n < 0$.

(d) $H_0: p_r - p_n \leq 0$ versus $H_0: p_r - p_n > 0$.

50. If p_r and p_n are the population proportions for the remedial and nonremedial groups, respectively, the computed test statistic for the appropriate test is

(a) 3.6426.

(b) −1.1803.

(c) −13.2685.

(d) 1.3931.

51. If p_r and p_n are the population proportions for the remedial and nonremedial groups, respectively, the *P*-value for the appropriate test is

(a) −0.1190.

(b) 0.1190.

(c) 0.8810.

(d) 0.3810.

52. If p_r and p_n are the population proportions for the remedial and nonremedial groups, respectively, the correct decision for the appropriate test at the 10 percent level of significance is

(a) do not reject the null hypothesis.

(b) reject the null hypothesis.

(c) reject the alternative hypothesis.

(d) do not reject the alternative hypothesis.

Further Exercises

If possible, you could use any technology help available to solve the following questions.

1. A new shampoo is being test marketed. A large number of 16-ounce bottles were mailed out at random to potential customers with the hope that the customers would return an enclosed questionnaire. Of the 1,000 returned questionnaires, 575 indicated that they like the shampoo and will consider buying it when it becomes available on the market. Perform a hypothesis test to determine if the proportion of potential customers is at most 50 percent. Use a level of significance of 0.05.

2. In a test to compare the performance of two models of cars, the Bullet and the Speeding Bullet, 75 cars of each model were driven on the same speedway with a full tank of gas in each car (same size tanks). The mean number of miles for the Bullet was 540 miles with a standard deviation of 20 miles; the mean number of miles for the Speeding Bullet was 600 with a standard deviation of 38.

(a) What is the point estimate of the difference between the means for the populations (the Speeding Bullet − the Bullet)?

(b) At the 2 percent level of significance, are the two models of cars significantly different with respect to gas consumption?

3. A local politician ran on the issue of whether alcohol should be sold on Sundays in two adjoining counties. The following results were obtained by his staff:

COUNTY	SURVEYED VOTERS	VOTERS FAVORING THE PROPOSAL
1	600	220
2	400	160

(a) What is the point estimate for the difference between the population proportions for those who favor the proposal for county 1 and county 2?

(b) At the 5 percent level of significance, test the hypothesis that the proportions of voters favoring the proposal were the same in both counties.

(c) What is the P-value for the test in (b)?

4. For a highly publicized murder trial, a CNN poll showed that 68 of every 100 whites surveyed said that the defendant was guilty, whereas 15 of every 100 blacks surveyed said that the defendant was guilty.

(a) Compute the point estimate for the difference between the two population proportions for those who thought that the defendant was guilty (whites − blacks).

(b) At the 5 percent level of significance, can you conclude that the proportion of whites who thought that the defendant was guilty was significantly greater than the proportion of blacks who thought that the defendant was guilty?

(c) Compute a P-value for the test in part (b).

ANSWER KEY

True/False Questions

1. T   2. T   3. F   4. T   5. F   6. T   7. T   8. F   9. F   10. F   11. T
12. T   13. T   14. T   15. T   16. F   17. F   18. T   19. F   20. T   21. F   22. F

Completion Questions

1. interval   2. type I   3. type II   4. critical   5. reject   6. do not reject   7. type I
8. null, alternative   9. $\bar{x}_1 - \bar{x}_2$ 10. a normal   11. zero (0), one (1)   12. reject
13. false   14. large   15. critical or rejection   16. critical   17. 0.0014   18. 0.0052
19. be rejected   20. reject

Multiple-Choice Questions

1. (d)   2. (b)   3. (c)   4. (d)   5. (a)   6. (b)   7. (d)   8. (b)   9. (d)
10. (c)   11. (d)   12. (a)   13. (d)   14. (b)   15. (d)   16. (b)   17. (c)   18. (d)
19. (c)   20. (a)   21. (a)   22. (c)   23. (b)   24. (a)   25. (b)   26. (a)   27. (c)
28. (b)   29. (d)   30. (c)   31. (c)   32. (d)   33. (a)   34. (b)   35. (d)   36. (c)
37. (c)   38. (d)   39. (b)   40. (c)   41. (b)   42. (a)   43. (d)   44. (c)   45. (b)
46. (b)   47. (b)   48. (d)   49. (d)   50. (b)   51. (c)   52. (a)

Further Exercises

1. $H_0: p \leq 0.5$ versus $H_1: p > 0.5$; T.S.: $z = 4.74$; P-value $= 0.00$; $\alpha = 0.05$; $z_\alpha = 1.645$; decision: Reject H_0.

2. (a) $(600 - 540) = 60$; (b) $H_0: \mu_1 = \mu_2$ versus $H_1: \mu_1 \neq \mu_2$; T.S: $z = 12.1004$; P-value $= 0$; $\alpha = 0.02$; $z_{\alpha/2} = 2.33$; decision: Reject H_0.

3. (a) $(220/600 - 160/400) = -0.0333$; (b) $H_0: p_1 = p_2$ versus $H_1: p_1 \neq p_2$; T.S.: $z = -1.06$; P-value $= 0.287$; $\alpha = 0.05$; $z_{\alpha/2} = 1.96$; decision: Do not reject H_0; (c)P-value $= 0.287$.

4. (a) $(15/100 - 68/100) = 0.53$; (b) $H_0: p_1 \leq p_2$ versus $H_1: p_1 > p_2$; T.S.: $z = 7.61$; P-value $= 0.00$; $\alpha = 0.05$; $z_\alpha = 1.645$; decision: Reject H_0; (c) P-value $= 0.00$.

CHAPTER 13

Confidence Intervals and Hypothesis Tests: Small Samples

Get Started

Here we will focus on small-sample confidence intervals and hypothesis tests for the mean. We will consider both single- and two-population confidence intervals and hypothesis tests for the mean. In addition, for the two-population case we will consider both independent and dependent samples.

13-1 The *t* Distribution

Recall that for the confidence interval for the mean we assumed that the population standard deviation was known, or when it was unknown, we assumed that the sample size was large ($n \geq 30$). In the latter case, we replaced the population standard deviation with the sample standard deviation. In both cases, the standard normal distribution was used to find the confidence interval for the mean, and the variable of interest was assumed to be normally distributed. In many cases, however, the population standard deviation is unknown, and the sample size is small ($n < 30$). Again, we can replace the population standard deviation with the sample standard deviation, but in this case we use the ***t* distribution** and not the standard normal distribution.

The *t* distribution has some properties that are similar to and some that are different from the properties of the standard normal distribution. Properties of the *t* distribution are listed below.

Properties That Are Similar to Those of the *z* Distribution

- It is bell-shaped.
- It is symmetrical about the mean.
- The mean, median, and the mode are all equal to zero.
- The curve never touches the *x* axis (horizontal axis).

Properties That Are Different from Those of the *z* Distribution

- The variance is greater than 1.
- The shape of the distribution depends on the sample size or on the concept of degrees of freedom, *df*.
- As the sample size gets larger, the *t* distribution converges to the *z* distribution.

Note: The **degrees of freedom,** *df,* are the number of values that are free to vary after a statistic is computed from a set of data values. They tell us which *t* distribution we should use. For example, if the mean of 10 values is 3, then 9 of the 10 values are free to vary. However, once 9 values are selected, the tenth value must be a specific number. It must be the number such that the sum of all the numbers is $10 \times 3 = 30$. Thus the degrees of freedom are $10 - 1 = 9$. This tells us which *t* distribution to use. **Figure 13-1** displays some of these properties.

Figure 13-1: Comparison between the standard normal distribution and the *t* distribution with *df* = 3

Note: The middle curve in **Figure 13-1** is a *t* distribution with 25 degrees of freedom. Observe that it is almost the same as the *z* distribution.

In order to state formulas that can be used to compute the small-sample confidence intervals and hypothesis tests for a population mean, we need to be familiar with the notation $t_{\alpha, n-1}$ (read as "*t* sub alpha with $n - 1$ degrees of freedom").

Explanation of the notation—$t_{\alpha, n-1}$: $t_{\alpha, n-1}$ is a *t* score with $n - 1$ degrees of freedom such that an area of size α is to the right of the *t*-score value.

The diagram in **Figure 13-2** explains this notation.

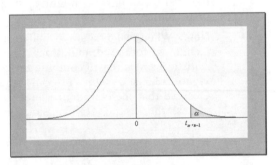

Figure 13-2: Diagram explaining the notation $t_{\alpha, n-1}$

Values for *t* scores with the appropriate degrees of freedom can be obtained from the *t* tables in the **Appendix**.

Example 13-1: What is the value of $t_{0.05, 10}$?

Solution: From the table in the **Appendix**, $t_{0.05, 10} = 1.812$.

Example 13-2: What is the value of $t_{0.9, 16}$?

Solution: Since the *t* distribution is symmetrical about zero, and based on the definition of $t_{\alpha, n-1}$, the value of $t_{0.9, 16}$ is equivalent to $- t_{0.1, 16}$. From the table in the **Appendix** we have $t_{0.9, 16} = - 1.337$.

13-2 Small-Sample Confidence Interval for a Population Mean

The general equation used in constructing a $(1 - \alpha) \times 100$ percent confidence interval for the population mean when the population standard deviation is unknown and the sample size $n < 30$ is given by

$$\bar{x} \pm t_{\alpha/2, n-1} \frac{s}{\sqrt{n}}$$

Note: The margin of error is given by $E = \pm\, t_{\alpha/2, n-1} \frac{s}{\sqrt{n}}$.

Example 13-3: A random sample of 16 public school teachers in a particular state has a mean salary of \$33,000 with a standard deviation of \$1,000. Construct a 99 percent confidence interval estimate for the true mean salary for public school teachers for the given state.

Solution: We are given that $\alpha = 0.01$ (1 percent), $\alpha/2 = 0.005$, $n = 16$, $df = 16 - 1 = 15$, $t_{0.005, 15} = 2.947$, $\bar{x} = 33,000$, $s = 1,000$, and $\frac{s}{\sqrt{n}} = 250$. Thus the 99 percent confidence interval estimate for the mean salary is $33{,}000 \pm 2.947 \times 250 = 33{,}000 \pm 736.75$. That is, we are 99 percent confident that the average salary for public school teachers for the given state will lie between \$32,263.25 and \$33,736.75.

Example 13-4: The president of a small community college wishes to estimate the average distance commuting students travel to the campus. A sample of 12 students was randomly selected and yielded the following distances in miles: 27, 35, 33, 30, 39, 25, 38, 22, 27, 37, 33, and 40. Construct a 95 percent confidence interval estimate for the true mean distance commuting students travel to the campus.

Solution: Since raw data are given, we need to find the sample mean and the sample standard deviation. These values are $\bar{x} = 32.1667$, and $s = 5.9365$. (Verify that these values are correct.) Also, we are given $\alpha = 0.05$, $\alpha/2 = 0.025$, $n = 12$, $df = 12 - 1 = 11$, $t_{0.025,\,11} = 2.201$, and $\dfrac{s}{\sqrt{n}} = 1.7137$. Thus the 95 percent confidence interval estimate for the mean distance is $32.1667 \pm 2.201 \times 1.7137 = 32.1667 \pm 3.7719$. That is, we are 95 percent confident that the average distance commuting students travel to the campus will lie between 28.3948 miles and 35.9386 miles.

Note: When real data are available, as in **Example 13-4**, you also may use the appropriate technology for the computations. Some technologies such as the TI-83/84 or the MINITAB statistical software will compute the confidence interval with both summary and raw data. **Figure 13-3** shows the TI–83/84 and MINITAB outputs with the confidence results. Observe that the confidence interval in the TI-83/84 output is correct to three decimal places, whereas the MINITAB output gives the exact values to four decimal places.

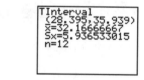

```
TInterval
 (28.395,35.939)
 x̄=32.16666667
 Sx=5.936533015
 n=12
```

One-Sample T: Miles

Variable	N	Mean	StDev	SE Mean	95% CI
Miles	12	32.1667	5.9365	1.7137	(28.3948, 35.9386)

Figure 13-3: TI-83/84 and MINITAB outputs for Example 13-3

13-3 Small-Sample Test for a Population Mean

We refer to tests based on the statistic $t = \dfrac{\bar{x} - \mu_0}{s/\sqrt{n}}$ as **small-sample tests** because we are assuming that the sampling distribution for the sample means has a t distribution. The test requires that the sample size $n < 30$ and requires that the population standard deviation be unknown. We also assume that the sampling distribution is normal.

Following is a summary of the tests for a population mean under these conditions.

Summary of Hypothesis Tests

1. One-tailed (right-tailed)

H_0: $\mu \le \mu_0$ (where μ_0 is a specified value of the population mean)

H_1: $\mu > \mu_0$

T.S.: $t = \dfrac{\bar{x} - \mu_0}{s/\sqrt{n}}$, for σ unknown and $n < 30$

D.R.: For a specified significance level α, reject the null hypothesis if the computed test statistic value t is greater than $+t_{\alpha, n-1}$.

Conclusion:

Note: This is a right-tailed test because the direction of the inequality sign in the alternative hypothesis is to the right.

2. One-tailed (left-tailed)

H_0: $\mu \geq \mu_0$ (where μ_0 is a specified value of the population mean)

H_1: $\mu < \mu_0$

T.S.: $t = \dfrac{\bar{x} - \mu_0}{s/\sqrt{n}}$, for σ unknown and $n < 30$

D.R.: For a specified significance level α, reject the null hypothesis if the computed test statistic value t is less than $-t_{\alpha, n-1}$.

Conclusion:

Note: This is a left-tailed test because the direction of the inequality sign in the alternative hypothesis is to the left.

3. Two-tailed

H_0: $\mu = \mu_0$ (where μ_0 is a specified value of the population mean)

H_1: $\mu \neq \mu_0$

T.S.: $t = \dfrac{\bar{x} - \mu_0}{s/\sqrt{n}}$, for σ unknown and $n < 30$

D.R.: For a specified significance level α, reject the null hypothesis if the computed test statistic value t is less than $-t_{\alpha/2, n-1}$ or if it is greater than $+t_{\alpha/2, n-1}$.

Conclusion:

Note: This is a two-tailed test because of the not-equal-to symbol in the alternative hypothesis. Also note that the level of significance is shared equally when finding the critical t value $(t_{\alpha/2, n-1})$.

Example 13-5: A teachers' union would like to establish that the average salary for high school teachers in a particular state is less than \$35,500. A random sample of 25 public high school teachers in the particular state has a mean salary of \$34,578 with a standard deviation of \$910. Test to establish whether the union's claim is correct at the 5 percent level of significance.

Solution: This is a left-tailed test. Why? We are given that $\alpha = 0.05$, $n = 25$, $df = 25 - 1$

$= 24$, $t_{0.05, 24} = 1.711$, $\bar{x} = 34{,}578$, $s = 910$, $\mu_0 = 35{,}500$, and $\dfrac{s}{\sqrt{n}} = \dfrac{910}{25} = 182$. Thus

H_0: $\mu \geq 35{,}500$

H_1: $\mu < 35{,}500$

T.S.: $t = \dfrac{\bar{x} - \mu_0}{s/\sqrt{n}} = \dfrac{34578 - 35500}{182} = -5.0659$

D.R.: For a significance level of $\alpha = 0.05$, reject the null hypothesis if the computed test statistic value $t = -5.0659 < -t_{0.05, 24} = -1.711$.

Conclusion: Since $-5.0659 < -1.711$, reject H_0. There is sufficient sample evidence to support the claim that the average salary for high school teachers in the state is less than \$35,500 at the 5 percent level of significance. That is, there is a significant difference between the sample mean and the postulated value of the population mean of \$35,500.

Figure 13-4 depicts the rejection region.

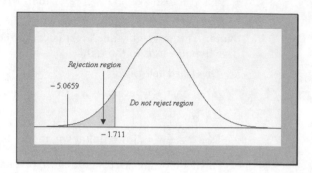

Figure 13-4: Diagram depicting the rejection region for Example 13-5

Example 13-6: The coach of a very popular male college basketball team claims that the average distance the fans travel to the campus to watch a game is 35 miles. The team members feel otherwise. A sample of 16 fans who travel to the games was randomly selected and yielded a mean of 36 miles and a standard deviation of 5 miles. Test the coach's claim at the 5 percent level of significance.

Solution: This is a two-tailed test because the team members do not believe the coach's claim. Note that the basketball players are not concerned whether the average distance traveled is less than 35 miles or more than 35 miles. We are given that $\alpha = 0.05$, $\alpha/2 = 0.025$, $n = 16$, $t_{0.025, 15} = 2.131$, $\bar{x} = 36$, $s = 5$, $\mu_0 = 35$, and $\dfrac{s}{\sqrt{n}} = 1.25$. Thus

H_0: $\mu = 35$

H_1: $\mu \neq 35$

T.S.: $t = \dfrac{\bar{x} - \mu_0}{s/\sqrt{n}} = \dfrac{36 - 35}{1.25} = 0.8$

D.R.: For a significance level $\alpha = 0.05$, reject the null hypothesis if the computed test statistic value $t = 0.8 < -t_{0.025, 15} = -2.131$ or if $t = 0.8 > t_{0.025, 15} = 2.131$.

Conclusion: Since neither of the conditions is satisfied, do not reject H_0. There is insufficient sample evidence to refute the coach's claim at the 5 percent level of significance. That is, there is not a significant difference between the sample mean and the postulated value of the population mean of 35 miles.

Figure 13-5 depicts the rejection region.

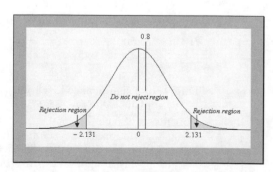

Figure 13-5: Diagram depicting the rejection region for Example 13-6

13-4 Independent Small-Sample Confidence Interval for the Difference between Two Population Means

When we have independent samples, there is a procedure that we can use to construct confidence intervals for the difference between two population means when the sample sizes are small and the population variances are unknown. Here the procedure assumes that the **samples are obtained from normal populations** and that the **populations have equal variances**. Let the equal variances be denoted by σ^2. Thus we have that the distribution of the differences of the sample means will have a standard deviation

$$\sigma_{\bar{x}_1 - \bar{x}_2} = \sqrt{\frac{\sigma_1^2}{n_1} + \frac{\sigma_2^2}{n_2}} = \sqrt{\frac{\sigma^2}{n_1} + \frac{\sigma^2}{n_2}} = \sigma\sqrt{\frac{1}{n_1} + \frac{1}{n_2}}$$

Since σ is unknown, the question is: With what should we estimate it? We use the pooled standard deviation s_p as the estimate for σ. The equation for the pooled variance is given by

$$s_p^2 = \frac{(n_1 - 1)s_1^2 + (n_2 - 1)s_2^2}{n_1 + n_2 - 2}$$

Note that the subscripts refer to the populations. Thus we can write

$$\sigma_{\bar{x}_1 - \bar{x}_2} \approx \sqrt{\frac{(n_1 - 1)s_1^2 + (n_2 - 1)s_2^2}{n_1 + n_2 - 2}} \times \sqrt{\frac{1}{n_1} + \frac{1}{n_2}}$$

The degrees of freedom for this situation are $df = n_1 + n_2 - 2$.

These properties can aid us in the construction of a $(1 - \alpha) \times 100$ percent confidence interval for the difference between two population means. The general equation used in constructing a $(1 - \alpha) \times 100$ percent confidence interval for the difference between two population means for small samples is given by

$$\boxed{(\bar{x}_1 - \bar{x}_2) \pm t_{\alpha/2, df} \times s_p \sqrt{\frac{1}{n_1} + \frac{1}{n_2}}}$$

Example 13-7: Two methods were used to teach a biostatistics course for a nurse-practitioner program. A sample of 16 scores was selected for method 1, and a sample of 25 scores was selected for method 2, with the summary results given in **Table 13-1**.

Table 13-1: Summary Information for Example 13-7

	METHOD 1	METHOD 2
Sample size	16	25
Sample mean	88	81
Sample standard deviation	2.5	1.8

Construct a 99 percent confidence interval for the difference in the mean scores (method 1 − method 2) for the two methods. Assume that the scores are normally distributed. Let subscript 1 represent the population for method 1 and let subscript 2 represent the population for method 2.

Solution: From the information given, we have $n_1 = 16$, $n_2 = 25$, $\bar{x}_1 = 88$, $\bar{x}_2 = 81$, $s_1 = 2.5$,

$$s_2 = 1.8, \ s_p^2 = \frac{(n_1 - 1)s_1^2 + (n_2 - 1)s_2^2}{n_1 + n_2 - 2} = \frac{(16-1) \times 2.5^2 + (25-1) \times 1.8^2}{16 + 25 - 2} = 4.3977, \ s_p = 2.0971, \ \alpha = $$

$$0.01, \ \alpha/2 = 0.005, \ df = 16 + 25 - 2 = 39, \ t_{0.005, \, 39} = 2.576, \text{ and } \sqrt{\frac{1}{n_1} + \frac{1}{n_2}} = \sqrt{\frac{1}{16} + \frac{1}{25}} = 0.3202$$

Thus the 99 percent confidence interval estimate for the difference of the means for the two methods (method 1 − method 2) is $(88 - 81) \pm 2.576 \times 2.0971 \times 0.3202 = 7 \pm 1.7298$. That is, we are 99 percent confident that the difference between the mean scores for the two teaching methods will lie between 5.2702 and 8.7298. Since both limits are positive, one may conclude that method 1 seems to be the better of the two methods. Thus we also can say that the average score for method 1 will be between 5.2702 and 8.7298 more than that of method 2.

Figure 13-6 shows a partial TI-83/84 output for the confidence interval.

Figure 13-6: Partial TI-83/84 output for Example 13-7

Note: The results are slightly different because the TI–83/84 calculator uses the exact t value in the formula, whereas an approximate z value was used from the table in the **Appendix** for the computations in the text.

Example 13-8: A male instructor claims that male and female instructors in his department, on average, wait the same amount of time for promotion to full professor. He collected data on 10 males and 10 female instructors. The number of years to be promoted to a full professor is given in **Table 13-2**.

Table 13-2: Time to Promotion to Full Professor

Male	11	17	14	10	13	11	17	10	19	14
Female	10	13	12	12	18	14	14	17	17	10

Construct a 95 percent confidence interval for the difference in the mean time (male − female) for promotion to full professor. Assume that the years to promotion are normally distributed. Let subscript 1 represent the male population and let subscript 2 represent the female population.

Solution: Since raw data are given, we will have to compute the sample means and sample variances. From the information given, we have $n_1 = 10$, $n_2 = 10$, $\bar{x}_1 = 13.6$, $\bar{x}_2 = 13.7$, $s_1 = 3.2$, $s_2 = 2.869$, $\alpha = 0.05$, $\alpha/2 = 0.025$, $df = 10 + 10 - 2 = 18$, $t_{0.025, 18} = 2.101$,

$$s_p^2 = \frac{(n_1-1)s_1^2 + (n_2-1)s_2^2}{n_1+n_2-2} = \frac{(10-1)\times 3.2^2 + (10-1)\times 2.869^2}{10+10-2} = 9.2356, \; s_p = 3.0390, \text{ and}$$

$$\sqrt{\frac{1}{n_1}+\frac{1}{n_2}} = \sqrt{\frac{1}{10}+\frac{1}{10}} = 0.4472. \text{ Thus the 95 percent confidence interval estimate for the}$$

difference of the means for the waiting times to be promoted to full professor is $(13.6 - 13.7) \pm 2.101 \times 3.0390 \times 0.4472 = -0.1 \pm 2.8553$. That is, we are 95 percent confident that the difference between the mean waiting times to full professor for male and female instructors in the given department will lie between −2.95534 and 2.7553. Observe that the lower limit is negative, whereas the upper limit is positive. Thus zero is included in the interval. This would imply that we cannot say that the means are different. That is, based on the confidence interval, we cannot refute the instructor's claim.

13-5 Independent Small-Sample Tests for the Difference between Two Population Means

There may be problems in which one must decide whether the observed difference between two small-sample means is due to chance or to the fact that the corresponding population means are not the same. Here we will discuss such problems.

Below is a summary of the tests for the difference between two population means when the samples are small, the population variances are unknown but **equal**, and the sampling populations are normally distributed.

Summary of Hypothesis Tests

1. **One-tailed (right-tailed)**

H_0: $\mu_1 \le \mu_2$

H_1: $\mu_1 > \mu_2$

T.S.: $t = \dfrac{\bar{x}_1 - \bar{x}_2}{s_p\sqrt{\dfrac{1}{n_1} + \dfrac{1}{n_2}}}$, where s_p is the pooled standard deviation.

D.R.: For a specified significance level α, reject the null hypothesis if the computed test statistic value t is greater than $+t_{\alpha, df}$, where $df = n_1 + n_2 - 2$.

Conclusion:

Note: This is a right-tailed test because the direction of the inequality sign in the alternative hypothesis is to the right.

2. **One-tailed (left-tailed)**

H_0: $\mu_1 \ge \mu_2$

H_1: $\mu_1 < \mu_2$

T.S.: $t = \dfrac{\bar{x}_1 - \bar{x}_2}{s_p\sqrt{\dfrac{1}{n_1} + \dfrac{1}{n_2}}}$, where s_p is the pooled standard deviation.

D.R.: For a specified significance level α, reject the null hypothesis if the computed test statistic value t is less than $-t_{\alpha, df}$, where $df = n_1 + n_2 - 2$.

Conclusion:

Note: This is a left-tailed test because the direction of the inequality sign in the alternative hypothesis is to the left.

3. **Two-tailed**

H_0: $\mu_1 = \mu_2$

H_1: $\mu_1 \ne \mu_2$

T.S.: $t = \dfrac{\bar{x}_1 - \bar{x}_2}{s_p\sqrt{\dfrac{1}{n_1} + \dfrac{1}{n_2}}}$, where s_p is the pooled standard deviation.

D.R.: For a specified significance level α, reject the null hypothesis if the computed test statistic value t is less than $-t_{\alpha/2, df}$, or if it is greater than $+t_{\alpha/2, df}$, where $df = n_1 + n_2 - 2$.

Conclusion:

Note: This is a two-tailed test because of the not-equal-to symbol in the alternative hypothesis. Also note that the level of significance is shared equally when finding the critical t value $(t_{\alpha/2, df})$.

Example 13-9: A researcher claims that the starting salary for male physician assistants is more than that for female physician assistants. A random sample of 12 male and 9 female physician assistants yielded the information given in **Table 13-3**. Is there enough sample evidence to support the researcher's claim? Test at the 1 percent level of significance.

Table 13-3: Summary Information for Example 13-9

	MALE	FEMALE
Sample size	12	9
Sample mean	$71,000	$69,500
Sample standard deviation	$1,000	$1,500

Solution: This is a right-tailed test. Why? Let subscript 1 represent the male population and subscript 2 represent the female population. From the information given, we have $n_1 = 12$, $n_2 = 9$, $\bar{x}_1 = 71,000$, $\bar{x}_2 = 69,500$, $s_1 = 1,000$, $s_2 = 1,500$, $\alpha = 0.01$, $df = 12 + 9 - 2 = 19$,

$$t_{0.01, 19} = 2.539,\ s_p^2 = \frac{(n_1-1)s_1^2 + (n_2-1)s_2^2}{n_1+n_2-2} = \frac{(12-1)\times 1,000^2 + (9-1)\times 1500^2}{12+9-2} = 1,526,315.789$$

$s_p = 1,235.4415$, and $\sqrt{\dfrac{1}{n_1}+\dfrac{1}{n_2}} = \sqrt{\dfrac{1}{12}+\dfrac{1}{9}} = 0.4410$. Thus

H_0: $\mu_1 \le \mu_2$

H_1: $\mu_1 > \mu_2$

T.S.: $t = \dfrac{\bar{x}_1 - \bar{x}_2}{s_p\sqrt{\dfrac{1}{n_1}+\dfrac{1}{n_2}}} = \dfrac{71,000 - 69500}{1235.4415 \times 0.4410} = 2.7532$

D.R.: For a significance level $\alpha = 0.01$, reject the null hypothesis if the computed test statistic value $t = 2.7532 > t_{0.01,19} = 2.539$.

Conclusion: Since $2.7532 > 2.539$, reject the null hypothesis. At the 1 percent significance level, we can conclude that the average starting salary for male physician assistants is greater than that for the female physician assistants. That is, the difference of the sample means is significantly different from zero.

Figure 13-7 shows a MINITAB output for the data in **Example 13-9.**

```
Two-Sample T-Test and CI

Sample   N    Mean   StDev   SE Mean
1        12   71000  1000    289
2        9    69500  1500    500


Difference = mu (1) - mu (2)
Estimate for difference:  1500.00
99% lower bound for difference:  116.54
T-Test of difference = 0 (vs >): T-Value = 2.75  P-Value = 0.006  DF = 19
Both use Pooled StDev = 1235.4415
```

Figure 13-7: MINITAB output for Example 13-9

Example 13-10: Use the information from **Figure 13-7** to write up the test in **Example 13-9** from a *P*-value standpoint.

H_0: $\mu_1 \le \mu_2$

H_1: $\mu_1 > \mu_2$

T.S.: *P*-value $= 0.006$

D.R. For a significance level $\alpha = 0.01$, reject the null hypothesis if the computed *P*-value $= 0.006 <$ the significance level $\alpha = 0.01$.

Conclusion: Since $0.006 < 0.01$, reject the null hypothesis. Thus, at the 1 percent significance level, we can conclude that the average starting salary for male physician assistants is greater than that for the female physician assistants. That is, the difference of the sample means is significantly different from zero.

13-6 Dependent Small-Sample Confidence Interval for the Difference between Two Population Means

In this section the *t* test is used when the samples are **dependent**. Samples are considered to be dependent when they are paired or matched in some way. For example, an instructor may give a test at the beginning of the semester to determine the basic math skill levels of the students in a course. At the end of the semester, the instructor will give the same test to determine the basic math skill levels of the students again. Although we have two different sets of data, they were obtained from the same set of students (for the students who remained in the course). Thus we say that the data are **dependent** because the same experimental units (students) were used. Another situation in which we may have dependent samples is, for example, when patients are matched or paired according to some variable of interest. Patients then may be assigned to two different groups. For instance, patients may be paired according to their age (blood pressure, etc.). That is, two patients with the same age will be paired, and then one will be assigned to one sample group and the other to another sample group. Caution should be taken when matching experimental units. In this example we matched by age, but this does not eliminate the influence of other variables.

In constructing confidence intervals for dependent data, we use the difference between the values before and after or the difference between the values of the matched pairs. By doing this, we will have a single sample of differences with which to construct a confidence interval.

The general equation used in constructing a $(1 - \alpha) \times 100$ percent confidence interval for the differences is given by

$$\overline{d} \pm t_{\alpha/2,n-1} \frac{s_d}{\sqrt{n}}$$

Here, $\overline{d}$ is the mean of the sample differences, s_d is the standard deviation of the differences, n is the number of pairs, and the df for the t distribution is $n - 1$.

Note: The margin of error is given by $E = \pm t_{\alpha/2,n-1} \dfrac{s_d}{\sqrt{n}}$

Example 13-11: An instructor wanted to measure the basic math skills of her students before and after her college algebra course. A skills test was administered at the beginning of the semester, and the scores were recorded. At the end of the semester, the instructor administered the same test and recorded the scores. **Table 13-4** shows the before and after scores for the test for the students who remained in the course until the end of the semester. The maximum possible score on the test was 100 points.

Table 13-4: Before and After Scores for Example 13-11

STUDENT #	1	2	3	4	5	6	7	8	9
Before	61	58	79	69	62	71	25	48	53
After	68	62	83	65	62	74	31	52	51

Construct a 95 percent confidence interval for this set of dependent data. Use (after − before) to compute the differences.

Solution: First, we need to find the differences (after − before) and use these differences as the raw data. The differences are given in **Table 13-5**.

Table 13-5: (After − Before) Differences for **Example 13-11**

STUDENT #	1	2	3	4	5	6	7	8	9
Differences	7	4	4	−4	0	3	6	4	−2

For the differences, we have $\overline{d} = 2.4444$, $s_d = 3.6780$, and $n = 9$. Also, $\alpha = 0.05$, $\alpha/2 = 0.025$, $df = 9 - 1 = 8$, $t_{0.025,8} = 2.306$, and $\dfrac{s_d}{\sqrt{n}} = 1.226$. Thus the 95 percent confidence interval for the differences is $2.4444 \pm 2.306 \times 1.226$ or 2.4444 ± 2.8272. That is, we are 95 percent confident that the true mean difference will lie between -0.3828 and 5.2716. Since 0 is contained in the interval, we cannot say that the course significantly improved the basic math skills of the students at this significance level ($\alpha = 0.05$).

Figure 13-8 shows a MINITAB output for the data in **Example 13-11**.

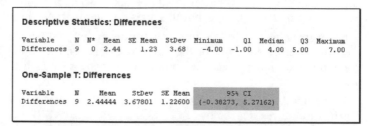

Figure 13-8: MINITAB output for Example 13-11

13-7 Dependent Small-Sample Tests for the Difference between Two Population Means

We refer to tests based on the statistic $t = \dfrac{\bar{d} - \mu_d}{s_d/\sqrt{n}}$ as **small-sample tests** because we are assuming that the sampling distribution for the sample means of the differences has a t distribution and where μ_d is the mean of the population of differences. The test requires that the population standard deviation of the differences be unknown and that the sampling distribution of the differences be normal.

Below is a summary of the tests for a population mean.

Summary of Hypothesis Tests

1. One-tailed (right-tailed)

H_0: $\mu_d \leq 0$

H_1: $\mu_d > 0$

T.S.: $t = \dfrac{\bar{d} - \mu_d}{s_d/\sqrt{n}}$

D.R.: For a specified significance level α, reject the null hypothesis if the computed test statistic value t is greater than $+t_{\alpha,\, n-1}$.

Conclusion:

Note: This is a right-tailed test because the direction of the inequality sign in the alternative hypothesis is to the right.

2. One-tailed (left-tailed)

H_0: $\mu_d \geq 0$

H_1: $\mu_d < 0$

T.S: $t = \dfrac{\bar{d} - \mu_d}{s_d/\sqrt{n}}$

D.R.: For a specified significance level α, reject the null hypothesis if the computed test statistic value t is less than $-t_{\alpha,\, n-1}$.

Conclusion:

Note: This is a left-tailed test because the direction of the inequality sign in the alternative hypothesis is to the left.

3. Two-tailed

H_0: $\mu_d = 0$

H_1: $\mu_d \neq 0$

T.S.: $t = \dfrac{\bar{d} - \mu_d}{s_d/\sqrt{n}}$

D.R.: For a specified significance level α, reject the null hypothesis if the computed test statistic value t is less than $-t_{\alpha/2, n-1}$ or if it is greater than $+t_{\alpha/2, n-1}$.

Conclusion:

Note: This is a two-tailed test because of the not-equal-to symbol in the alternative hypothesis. Also note that the level of significance is shared equally when finding the critical t value $(t_{\alpha/2, n-1})$.

Example 13-12: Test at the 5 percent level of significance if the college algebra course in **Example 13-11** improved the basic math skills of the students.

Solution: We will use the information given in **Example 13-11.** In order for the course to improve the basic math skills of the students, the after scores should be significantly greater than the before scores. That is, we would like to establish whether the average of the difference (after − before) is greater than zero. Thus

H_0: $\mu_d \le 0$

H_1: $\mu_d > 0$

T.S.: $t = \dfrac{\bar{d} - \mu_d}{s_d/\sqrt{n}} = \dfrac{2.4444}{3.6780/\sqrt{9}} = 1.9938$

D.R.: For a significance level of $\alpha = 0.05$, reject the null hypothesis if the computed test statistic value $t = 1.9938 > t_{0.05,8} = 1.86$.

Conclusion: Since $1.9938 > 1.86$, reject the null hypothesis and claim at the 5 percent level of significance that the average of the differences is greater than zero. That is, the average of the after scores is significantly larger than the average of the before scores. Thus one can conclude that the course indeed improved the basic math skills of the students who took it.

Figure 13-9 shows a TI-83/84 output for **Example 13-12**.

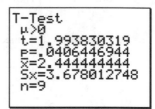

Figure 13-9: TI-83/84 output for Example 13-12

Example 13-13: Use the *P*-value in **Figure 13-9** to redo **Example 13-12** using the *P*-value approach.

Solution: Following is the *P*-value solution.

H_0: $\mu_d \le 0$

H_1: $\mu_d > 0$

T.S.: *P*-value = 0.0406

D.R.: For a significance level of $\alpha = 0.05$, reject the null hypothesis if the computed *P*-value = $0.0406 < \alpha = 0.05$.

Conclusion: Since $0.0406 < 0.05$, reject the null hypothesis and claim at the 5 percent level of significance that the average of the differences is greater than zero. That is, the average of the after scores is significantly larger than the average of the before scores. Thus one can conclude that the course indeed improved the basic math skills of the students who took it.

Figure 13-10 shows the EXCEL output for **Example 13-12**. It gives the *t* test statistic value, and the critical (table) and *P*-values for both the one-tail and two-tail tests.

	A	B	C
1	t-Test: Paired Two Sample for Means		
2			
3		*After*	*Before*
4	Mean	60.88888889	58.44444444
5	Variance	225.1111111	246.0277778
6	Observations	9	9
7	Pearson Correlation	0.972245692	
8	Hypothesized Mean Difference	0	
9	df	8	
10	t Stat	1.993830319	
11	P(T<=t) one-tail	0.040644695	
12	t Critical one-tail	1.859548033	
13	P(T<=t) two-tail	0.081289391	
14	t Critical two-tail	2.306004133	

Figure 13-10: EXCEL output for Example 13-12

Quick Tip

The *P*-value approach can be used for all the hypothesis tests discussed in this chapter.

Technology

Technology Corner

All the concepts discussed in this chapter can be computed and illustrated through most statistical software packages. All scientific and graphical calculators can be used for the computations. In addition, some of the newer calculators, such as the TI-83/84, will allow you to compute the confidence intervals and do the test directly on the calculator. If you own a calculator, you should consult the owner's manual to determine what statistical features are included.

Throughout this chapter, both the MINITAB software and the TI-83/84 calculator were integrated to help with the solutions of some of the problems. Care always should be taken when using the formulas for computations in hypothesis testing. One can use other appropriate technologies to help with the solutions to the problems presented in this chapter.

Here we considered small-sample confidence intervals and small-sample hypothesis tests for a single mean. We also addressed independent small-sample confidence intervals and independent small-sample hypothesis tests for the difference between two means. In addition, dependent small-sample confidence intervals and dependent small-sample hypothesis tests for the difference between two means were considered. These concepts were presented through

✓ Formulas

✓ Examples

✓ Use of technology

True/False Questions

1. If the sample size n is less than 30, a z score always will be associated with any hypothesis that deals with the mean.
2. In the P-value approach to hypothesis testing, if the P-value is less than any specified significance level α, then the null hypothesis will be rejected.
3. In making inferences about the difference between two population means, if the variances of the two populations are assumed to be equal, then the distribution of the differences between the sample means will follow a t distribution with degrees of freedom $n_1 + n_2 - 2$, for n_1 and/or n_2 <30.
4. When testing the difference between two population means, the pooled standard deviation (variance) is used when the underlying populations have unequal variances.
5. The matched-paired t test is used to test the difference between two means when the two selected samples are independent.
6. When performing hypothesis tests on two population means using small samples, it is necessary to assume that the populations from which the samples are obtained are normally distributed.
7. The P-value of a hypothesis test can be computed without the value of the test statistic.
8. The t distribution is used in the construction of confidence intervals for the population mean when the population standard deviation is unknown, the sample size is small, and the sampling population is normal.
9. When data are obtained from matching or pairing, one should use the z distribution in making inferences for the appropriate population parameter(s).
10. The mean and the variance for the z distribution and the t distribution are the same.

Completion Questions

1. The point estimate for the difference between two population means $\mu_1 - \mu_2$ is $(\hat{p}_1 - \hat{p}_2, \bar{x}_1 - \bar{x}_2, \mu_1 - \mu_2)$ _____, where the subscripts represent the corresponding populations.
2. If a small sample size is used in a hypothesis test for the mean, it is necessary to assume that the sample was selected from a (normal, t) _____ distribution.
3. When testing for the difference between two population means with small sample sizes, if we assume that the two population variances are equal and the populations are approximately normally distributed, the distribution of the test statistic will follow a (normal, t) _____ distribution.
4. We use a matched-paired t test when the samples are (independent, dependent) _____.
5. When conducting a hypothesis test for a single population mean, the test statistic will be assumed to have a standard normal distribution if the sample size is (small, large) _____.
6. In computing the confidence interval estimate for the difference between two population means, the t distribution (is, is not) _____ restricted to small samples.
7. In testing for the difference between two population means, when the sample variances of the two independent samples have to be combined, the resulting variance is called the _____ estimator of the variance.
8. When constructing a confidence interval for the population mean μ when the population standard deviation σ is known, the correct distribution to use is the (z, t) _____ distribution.

9. When using the pooled variance for inferences on the difference between two population means, we assume that the variances for the populations are (equal, not equal)
_____.

10. The variance for the *t* distribution is (less than, equal to, greater than) _____ 1.

Multiple-Choice Questions

1. Which of the following is true? The *t* distribution should be used to help make inferences
when
   (a) the sampling population is nonnormal.
   (b) the sampling population is unimodal.
   (c) the population standard deviation is unknown, the sample size is small, and the
   sampling distribution is normal.
   (d) the population standard deviation is known.

2. When we use the *t* distribution to construct a confidence interval for a single population
mean with sample size *n*, the degrees of freedom used are
   (a) $n \geq 30$.
   (b) $n < 30$.
   (c) n.
   (d) $n - 1$.

3. Suppose that a sample of size 15 is selected from a population with unknown variance. If
this information is used to construct a confidence interval for a single population mean,
which of the following statements is true?
   (a) The sample must be normally distributed.
   (b) The sampling population is assumed to be normally distributed.
   (c) The standard normal distribution table must be used to construct the interval.
   (d) The sample standard deviation cannot be used to estimate the population standard
   deviation because the sample size is small.

4. Construct a 98 percent confidence interval for the population mean μ given the following random sample: 8 10 20 18.
   (a) 7.1407 to 20.8593
   (b) 7.9650 to 20.0350
   (c) 2.9692 to 25.0308
   (d) 0.6317 to 27.3683

5. Suppose that the heights of the population of basketball players at a certain college, over
the past 30 years, are normally distributed. A random sample of 16 players is selected
from this population of players and yields an average height 6.2 feet and a standard deviation of 4 feet. Then the 90 percent confidence interval for the mean height of the population of basketball players is
   (a) 5.324 to 7.077.
   (b) 4.447 to 7.953.
   (c) 3.253 to 9.147.
   (d) 4.727 to 7.673.

6. The length of time it takes a worker to assemble a large product is assumed to be normally distributed. A random sample of 25 workers was selected, and their times to

assemble the product were recorded. The mean and variance for this sample were 3 and 0.5 hours, respectively. The 95 percent confidence interval for the mean length of time (in hours) it takes a worker to assemble the product is

(a) 2.7936 to 3.2064 hours.
(b) 2.7081 to 3.2919 hours.
(c) 2.8289 to 3.1711 hours.
(d) 2.7580 to 3.2919 hours.

7. The secretary in a statistics department would like to estimate how much coffee to brew per day such that there is enough fresh coffee for the consumers in the department. She decides to take a random sample of 10 of the coffee drinkers in the department and asks them to indicate the number of cups of coffee they consume per day when they are in the department. The results of her study are given below:

$$3 \quad 4 \quad 4 \quad 6 \quad 4 \quad 6 \quad 5 \quad 2 \quad 5 \quad 3$$

The 95 percent confidence interval for the average number of cups of coffee consumed per day by the consumers in this department is

(a) 3.2582 to 5.1418.
(b) 3.4368 to 4.9632.
(c) 2.8470 to 5.5530.
(d) 3.0253 to 5.3747.

8. The number of student riders on a campus bus that transports students from the parking lot to the campus on 12 randomly chosen trips yielded an average and standard deviation of 54.4167 and 7.2420 riders, respectively. What is the 90 percent confidence interval for the daily average number of students who ride the campus bus from the parking lot?

(a) 48.734 to 60.099
(b) 47.924 to 60.91
(c) 50.662 to 58.171
(d) 52.376 to 56.457

9. Which of the following statements is correct?
(a) The t distribution is exactly equal to the standard normal distribution when the sample size is equal to 30.
(b) The t distribution is approximately equal to the standard normal distribution when the sample size is 150.
(c) The t distribution is exactly equal to the standard normal distribution when the sample size is less than 30.
(d) The t distribution is approximately equal to the standard normal distribution when the sample size is less than 30.

10. Commuter students at a certain college claim that the average distance they have to commute to campus is 26 miles per day. A random sample of 16 commuter students was surveyed and yielded an average distance of 31 miles and a standard deviation of 8 miles. The test statistic for this test is

(a) $z = -2.5$.
(b) $z = 0.0394$.

(c) $t = 2.5$.

(d) $t = 1.25$.

11. For a small-sample left-tailed test for the population mean, the sample size was 18 and $\alpha = 0.01$. The critical (table) value for this test is

(a) -2.878.

(b) -2.552.

(c) 2.878.

(d) -2.567.

12. For the following information:

$$n = 16 \qquad \mu_0 = 15 \qquad \bar{x} = 16 \qquad s^2 = 16$$

assume that the population is normal. Compute the test statistic if you were testing for a population mean.

(a) $z = 1$

(b) $z = 0.25$

(c) $t = 1$

(d) $t = 0.25$

13. For the following information:

$$n = 16 \qquad \mu_0 = 14.247 \qquad \bar{x} = 16 \qquad s^2 = 16$$

assume that the population is normal. If you were performing a right-tailed test for the population mean, then the

(a) P-value < 0.25.

(b) P-value $= 0.05$.

(c) P-value < 0.04.

(d) P-value < 0.025.

14. An advertising agency would like to create an advertisement for a fast-food restaurant claiming that the average waiting time from ordering to receiving your order at the restaurant is less than 5 minutes. The agency measured the time from ordering to delivery of order for 25 customers and found that the average time was 4.7 minutes with a standard deviation of 0.6 minute. The test statistic that would be computed is

(a) -4.2.

(b) -12.5.

(c) -2.5.

(d) -20.8.

15. An advertising agency would like to create an advertisement for a fast food restaurant claiming that the average waiting time from ordering to receiving your order at the restaurant is less than 5 minutes. The agency measured the time from ordering to delivery of order for 25 customers and found that the average time was 4.7 minutes with a standard deviation of 0.6 minute. The P-value for this test would be

(a) 0.100.

(b) 0.050.

(c) 0.025.

(d) 0.010.

16. An advertising agency would like to create an advertisement for a fast-food restaurant claiming that the average waiting time from ordering to receiving your order at the restaurant is less than 5 minutes. The agency measured the time from ordering to delivery of order for 25 customers and found that the average time was 4.7 minutes with a standard deviation of 0.6 minute. The appropriate set of hypotheses to be tested is
    (a) H_0: $\mu \leq 4.7$ versus H_1: $\mu > 4.7$
    (b) H_0: $\mu \geq 4.7$ versus H_1: $\mu < 4.7$
    (c) H_0: $\mu \geq 5$ versus H_1: $\mu < 5$
    (d) H_0: $\mu \leq 5$ versus H_1: $\mu > 5$

17. An advertising agency would like to create an advertisement for a fast-food restaurant claiming that the average waiting time from ordering to receiving your order at the restaurant is less than 5 minutes. The agency measured the time from ordering to delivery of order for 25 customers and found that the average time was 4.7 minutes with a standard deviation of 0.6 minute. At the 5 percent level of significance, we can claim that the average time between ordering and receiving the order is
    (a) significantly greater than 4.7 minutes.
    (b) significantly smaller than 4.7 minutes.
    (c) significantly greater than 5 minutes.
    (d) significantly smaller than 5 minutes.

18. If two small samples are selected independently from two different normal populations with equal variances, the distribution of the test statistic used in testing for the difference between the population means
    (a) has a mean that is the difference between the two sample means.
    (b) has a variance that is the difference between the two variances for the two populations.
    (c) has a distribution that is normal.
    (d) has a t distribution.

19. If two small samples are selected independently from two different populations with equal variances, the combined variance that is associated with this situation is called
    (a) an estimate for the sample variance for the distribution of the differences.
    (b) the pooled estimate for the sample variance for the distribution of the differences.
    (c) the pooled estimate for the equal variances of the sampling populations.
    (d) none of the above.

20. If we are testing for the difference between two population means, the pooled variance is appropriate if
    (a) the populations are normally distributed.
    (b) the samples are small.
    (c) the population variances are unknown but assumed to be equal.
    (d) all the above are true.

21. In constructing a confidence interval for the difference between two population means with the assumptions that the sample sizes n_1 and n_2 are small and the populations are normally distributed with equal variances, the degrees of freedom for the associated t distribution is
    (a) $n_1 + n_2 - 1$.
    (b) $n_1 + n_2 - 2$.

(c) $n_1 + n_2 + 1$.

(d) $n_1 + n_2 + 2$.

22. In performing a large-sample test for the difference between two population means with known population variances, which of the following is not correct?

(a) The test statistic has a t distribution with $n_1 + n_2 - 2$ degrees of freedom.

(b) The test statistic has a standard normal distribution.

(c) Both the sample sizes need not be greater than 30.

(d) The population variances need not be equal to each other.

23. The matched-pair t test is appropriate

(a) when the samples are independent.

(b) only when the population variances are equal.

(c) when the samples are dependent.

(d) in none of the above cases.

24. Two machines are used to fill 50-pound bags of dog food. Sample information for these two machines are given below:

	MACHINE A	MACHINE B
Sample size	81	64
Sample mean (pounds)	51	48
Sample variance	16	12

The 90 percent confidence interval for the difference between the two population means $(\mu_A - \mu_B)$ is

(a) 3 ± 0.3850.

(b) 3 ± 0.0310.

(c) 3 ± 1.0207.

(d) 3 ± 1.4458.

25. A mathematics professor wants to determine whether there is a difference in final averages between the past two semesters (semester I and semester II) of his business statistics classes. For a random sample of 16 students from semester I, the mean of the final averages was 75 with a standard deviation of 4. For a random sample of 9 students from semester II, the mean was 73 with a standard deviation of 6. If the final averages from semesters I and II are assumed to be normally distributed with equal variances, the point estimate for the difference between the means of the two population (semester I − semester II) is

(a) −2.

(b) 2.

(c) 3.

(d) 7.

26. A mathematics professor wants to determine whether there is a difference in the final averages between the past two semesters (semester I and semester II) of his business statistics classes. For a random sample of 16 students from semester I, the mean of the final averages was 75 with a standard deviation of 4. For a random sample of 9 students

from semester II, the mean was 73 with a standard deviation of 6. If the final averages from semesters I and II are assumed to be normally distributed with equal variances, the appropriate set of hypotheses is

(a) H_0: $\mu_I - \mu_{II} \neq 0$ versus H_1: $\mu_I - \mu_I = 0$.

(b) H_0: $\mu_I - \mu_{II} = 0$ versus H_1: $\mu_I - \mu_{II} \neq 0$.

(c) H_0: $\mu_I - \mu_{II} \geq 0$ versus H_1: $\mu_I - \mu_{II} < 0$.

(d) H_0: $\mu_I - \mu_{II} \leq 0$ versus H_1: $\mu_I - \mu_{II} > 0$.

27. A mathematics professor wants to determine whether there is a difference in the final averages between the past two semesters (semester I and semester II) of his business statistics classes. For a random sample of 16 students from semester I, the mean of the final averages was 75 with a standard deviation of 4. For a random sample of 9 students from semester II, the mean was 73 with a standard deviation of 6. If the final averages from semesters I and II are assumed to be normally distributed with equal variances, the computed test statistic for the appropriate test is

(a) $z = 1.9964$.

(b) $t = 0.5009$.

(c) $t = 1.0018$.

(d) $z = 0.5009$.

28. A mathematics professor wants to determine whether there is a difference in the final averages between the past two semesters (semester I and semester II) of his business statistics classes. For a random sample of 16 students from semester I, the mean of the final averages was 75 with a standard deviation of 4. For a random sample of 9 students from semester II, the mean was 73 with a standard deviation of 6. If the final averages from semesters I and II are assumed to be normally distributed with equal variances, an appropriate range for the P-value for the appropriate test is

(a) $0.3 < P\text{-value} < 0.4$.

(b) $0.4 < P\text{-value} < 0.5$.

(c) $0.2 < P\text{-value} < 0.3$.

(d) $0.1 < P\text{-value} < 0.2$.

29. A mathematics professor wants to determine whether there is a difference in the final averages between the past two semesters (semester I and semester II) of his business statistics classes. For a random sample of 16 students from semester I, the mean of the final averages was 75 with a standard deviation of 4. For a random sample of 9 students from semester II, the mean was 73 with a standard deviation of 6. If the final averages from semesters I and II are assumed to be normally distributed with equal variances, the correct decision for the appropriate test at a 0.05 level of significance when the population variances are assumed to be equal is

(a) do not reject the null hypothesis.

(b) reject the null hypothesis.

(c) reject the alternative hypothesis.

(d) do not reject the alternative hypothesis.

30. A mathematics professor wants to determine whether there is a difference in the final averages between the past two semesters (semester I and semester II) of his business statistics classes. For a random sample of 16 students from semester I, the mean of the final averages was 75 with a standard deviation of 4. For a random sample of 9 students from semester II, the mean was 73 with a standard deviation of 6. If the final averages from semesters I and II are assumed to be normally distributed with equal variances,

the 90 percent confidence interval for the difference of the means (semester I − semester II) when the population variances are assumed to be equal is
(a) −1.4218 to 5.4218.
(b) −4.8313 to 8.8313.
(c) −2.991 to 6.991.
(d) −7.9640 to 11.9640.

31. A mathematics professor wants to determine whether there is a difference in the final averages between the past two semesters (semester I and semester II) of his business statistics classes. For a random sample of 16 students from semester I, the mean of the final averages was 75 with a standard deviation of 4. For a random sample of 9 students from semester II, the mean was 73 with a standard deviation of 6. If the final averages from semesters I and II are assumed to be normally distributed with equal variances, the standard error for the distribution of the differences of the sample means is
(a) 4.9910.
(b) 1.9964.
(c) 3.9856.
(d) 3.4737.

32. A mathematics professor wants to determine whether there is a difference in the final averages between the past two semesters (semester I and semester II) of his business statistics classes. For a random sample of 16 students from semester I, the mean of the final averages was 75 with a standard deviation of 4. For a random sample of 9 students from semester II, the mean was 73 with a standard deviation of 6. If the final averages from semesters I and II are assumed to be normally distributed with equal variances, the degrees of freedom for the appropriate test at a 0.05 level of significance are
(a) 25.
(b) 26.
(c) 24.
(d) 23.

33. A group of foreign students who would like to study in the United States registered for a special TOEFL (Test of English as a Foreign Language) preparatory course offered in their home country. They took a sample examination on the first day of classes and then retook it at the end of the course. The results for six of the students are given below:

STUDENT	1	2	3	4	5	6
Before	325	495	525	480	525	480
After	375	520	510	515	550	490

Such sample data would be considered to be
(a) independent data.
(b) dependent data.
(c) not large enough data.
(d) none of the above.

34. A group of foreign students who would like to study in the United States registered for a special TOEFL (Test of English as a Foreign Language) preparatory course offered

in their home country. They took a sample examination on the first day of classes and then retook it at the end of the course. The results for six of the students are given below:

STUDENT	1	2	3	4	5	6
Before	325	495	525	480	525	480
After	375	520	510	515	550	490

Let μ_d represent the mean of the population of differences (after score $-$ before score). If you want to determine whether the course helped to improve the students' scores, the appropriate set of hypotheses would be

(a) H_0: $\mu_d > 0$ versus H_1: $\mu_d \leq 0$.
(b) H_0: $\mu_d = 0$ versus H_1: $\mu_d \neq 0$.
(c) H_0: $\mu_d \geq 0$ versus H_1: $\mu_d < 0$.
(d) H_0: $\mu_d \leq 0$ versus H_1: $\mu_d > 0$.

35. A group of foreign students who would like to study in the United States registered for a special TOEFL (Test of English as a Foreign Language) preparatory course offered in their home country. They took a sample examination on the first day of classes and then retook it at the end of the course. The results for six of the students are given below:

STUDENT	1	2	3	4	5	6
Before	325	495	525	480	525	480
After	375	520	510	515	550	490

If you want to determine whether the course helped to improve the students' scores, the computed test statistic for the appropriate test is

(a) $z = 2.3814$.
(b) $t = 0.0169$.
(c) $z = -0.0169$.
(d) $t = 2.3814$.

36. A group of foreign students who would like to study in the United States registered for a special TOEFL (Test of English as a Foreign Language) preparatory course offered in their home country. They took a sample examination on the first day of classes and then retook it at the end of the course. The results for six of the students are given below:

STUDENT	1	2	3	4	5	6
Before	325	495	525	480	525	480
After	375	520	510	515	550	490

If you want to determine whether the course helped to improve the students' scores, the computed P-value for the appropriate hypothesis test is

(a) P-value > 0.05.
(b) $0.025 < P$-value < 0.05.
(c) P-value < 0.025.
(d) P-value $= 0.1$.

37. A group of foreign students who would like to study in the United States registered for a special TOEFL (Test of English as a Foreign Language) preparatory course offered in their home country. They took a sample examination on the first day of classes and then retook it at the end of the course. The results for six of the students are given below:

STUDENT	1	2	3	4	5	6
Before	325	495	525	480	525	480
After	375	520	510	515	550	490

If you want to determine whether the course helped to improve the students' scores, the appropriate degrees of freedom for the appropriate test is

(a) 6.
(b) 7.
(c) 5.
(d) 4.

38. A group of foreign students who would like to study in the United States registered for a special TOEFL (Test of English as a Foreign Language) preparatory course offered in their home country. They took a sample examination on the first day of classes and then retook it at the end of the course. The results for six of the students' are given below:

STUDENT	1	2	3	4	5	6
Before	325	495	525	480	525	480
After	375	520	510	515	550	490

If you want to determine whether the course helped to improve the students' scores, the correct decision at the 5 percent level of significance is

(a) do not reject the null hypothesis.
(b) reject the null hypothesis.
(c) reject the alternative hypothesis.
(d) do not reject the alternative hypothesis.

39. A group of foreign students who would like to study in the United States registered for a special TOEFL (Test of English as a Foreign Language) preparatory course offered in their home country. They took a sample examination on the first day of classes and then retook it at the end of the course. The results for six of the students are given below:

STUDENT	1	2	3	4	5	6
Before	325	495	525	480	525	480
After	375	520	510	515	550	490

The 99 percent confidence interval for the difference of the means (after − before) is

(a) −15.0173 to 58.3507.
(b) 6.6950 to 36.6429
(c) −58.3507 to 15.0173.
(d) −36.6429 to −6.6950.

40. Independent random samples are taken to test the difference between two means. The sample sizes are 50 and 60. The distribution for the test statistic used in testing for the difference between the population means has a(an)
   (a) *t* distribution with 110 degrees of freedom.
   (b) *t* distribution with 108 degrees of freedom.
   (c) exact normal distribution.
   (d) *t* distribution with 112 degrees of freedom.

Further Exercises

If possible, you can use any technology help to solve the following questions.

1. You are given the following random sample from a normal population:

$$25 \quad 39 \quad 59 \quad 32 \quad 46 \quad 49$$

   (a) Construct a 99 percent confidence interval for the population mean.
   (b) Test the hypothesis that the mean of the population is at most 50 at the 0.05 level of significance.

2. In a test to compare the performance of two models of cars, the Arrow and the Sparrow, 10 cars of each model were driven on the same speedway with a full tank of gas in each car (same size tanks). The mean number of miles for the Arrow was 550 miles with a standard deviation of 15 miles; the mean number of miles for the Sparrow was 600 with a standard deviation of 18.

   (a) What is the point estimate of the difference between the means for the populations (the Sparrow − the Arrow)?
   (b) Construct a 95 percent confidence interval for the difference between the two means (the Sparrow − the Arrow).
   (c) At the 2 percent level of significance, are the two models of cars significantly different with respect to average gas mileage?

3. To investigate whether one teaching method (method I) will yield better averages than the traditional method (method II) of teaching a specific course, two sections of the same course using the two teaching methods were offered by the same instructor. The following table gives a summary of some of the results:

	METHOD I	METHOD II
Sample size	15	13
Mean	88.9	82.9
Standard deviation	32	20

Assume that the two population (methods I and II) variances are equal and that the population of scores is normally distributed.

   (a) What is the point estimate for the difference between the two population means (method I − method II)?
   (b) Construct a 95 percent confidence for the difference between the means (method I − method II).
   (c) Can you conclude that method I has improved the overall scores of the students? Test at the 5 percent level of significance.

4. In a manufacturing company, a specific group of workers is responsible for assembling a certain component of an item. The floor manager was not satisfied with the rate at which they worked, so he decided to offer an incentive. The following is the number of components assembled per hour by five workers before and after the incentive was offered:

WORKER	BEFORE	AFTER
1	6	9
2	10	11
3	9	10
4	7	11
5	6	8

At the 5 percent level of significance, test to see whether the incentive improved production.

ANSWER KEY
True/False Questions
1. F 2. T 3. T 4. F 5. F 6. T 7. F 8. T 9. F 10. F

Completion Questions
1. $\bar{x}_1 - \bar{x}_2$ 2. normal 3. t 4. dependent 5. large 6. is 7. pooled 8. z
9. equal 10. greater than

Multiple-Choice Questions
1. (c) 2. (d) 3. (b) 4. (d) 5. (b) 6. (b) 7. (a) 8. (c) 9. (b)
10. (c) 11. (d) 12. (c) 13. (b) 14. (c) 15. (d) 16. (c) 17. (d) 18. (d)
19. (c) 20. (d) 21. (b) 22. (a) 23. (c) 24. (c) 25. (b) 26. (b) 27. (c)
28. (a) 29. (a) 30. (a) 31. (b) 32. (d) 33. (b) 34. (d) 35. (d) 36. (b)
37. (c) 38. (b) 39. (a) 40. (b)

Further Exercises
1. (a) 21.488 to 61.845; (b) H_0: $\mu \leq 50$ versus H_1: $\mu > 50$, T.S. $t = -1.6652$, P-value = 0.9216, $\alpha = 0.05$. Since P-value = 0.9216 > $\alpha = 0.05$, do not reject H_0.

2. (a) 50; (b) 34.433 to 65.567; (c) H_0: $\mu_s - \mu_A = 0$ versus H_1: $\mu_s - \mu_A \neq 0$, T.S. $t = 6.7481$, P-value = 0.000, $\alpha = 0.02$. Since P-value = 0.000 < $\alpha = 0.02$, reject H_0. There is a significant difference between the average gas mileages for the two models.

3. (a) 6; (b) -15.13 to 27.131; (c) H_0: $\mu_I - \mu_{II} \leq 0$ versus H_1: $\mu_I - \mu_{II} > 0$, T.S. $t = 0.5836$, P-value = 0.2822, $\alpha = 0.05$. Since P-value = 0.2822 > $\alpha = 0.05$, do not reject H_0. That is, there is not sufficient sample evidence to conclude that method I yielded a better average than method II.

4. H_0: $\mu_d \leq 0$ versus H_1: $\mu_d > 0$, T.S. $t = 3.773$, P-value = 0.0098, $\alpha = 0.05$. Since P-value = 0.0098 < $\alpha = 0.05$, reject H_0. That is, the incentive has improved production.

CHAPTER 14

Chi-Square Procedures

Do I Need to Read This Chapter?

You should read this chapter if you need to review or to learn about

→ Properties of the chi-square distribution

→ The chi-square test for goodness-of-fit

→ The chi-square test for independence

→ Benford's Law

Get Started

Here we will focus on the chi-square distribution and how it is used to test for goodness-of-fit and independence.

14-1 The Chi-Square Distribution

Here we will present some properties of the chi-square (χ^2) distribution.

Properties of the χ^2 Distribution

- It is a continuous distribution.
- It is not symmetrical.

- It is skewed to the right.
- The distribution depends on the degrees of freedom $df = n - 1$, where n is the sample size.
- The value of a χ^2 random variable is always nonnegative.
- There are infinitely many χ^2 distributions because each is uniquely defined by its degrees of freedom.
- For small sample size, the χ^2 distribution is much skewed to the right.
- As n increases, the χ^2 distribution becomes more and more symmetrical.

Figure 14-1 displays some of the properties for the χ^2 distribution.

Figure 14-1: Diagram with a family of χ^2 distributions

Since we will be using the χ^2 distribution for the tests in this chapter, we will need to be able to find critical values associated with the distribution.

Quick Tip

Extensive tables of critical χ^2 values are available for use in solving confidence intervals and hypothesis testing problems that are associated with the χ^2 distribution.

In order for us to perform hypothesis tests in this chapter, we need to be familiar with the notation $\chi^2_{\alpha, n-1}$ (read as "chi-square sub alpha with $n - 1$ degrees of freedom").

Explanation of the notation—$\chi^2_{\alpha, n-1}$: $\chi^2_{\alpha, n-1}$ is a value with $n - 1$ degrees of freedom such that area α is to the right of the corresponding χ^2 value.

The diagram in **Figure 14-2** shows a picture that explains the notation of $\chi^2_{\alpha, n-1}$.

Figure 14-2: Diagram explaining the notation $\chi^2_{\alpha, n-1}$

Values for the χ^2 random variable with the appropriate degrees of freedom can be obtained from the χ^2 tables in the **Appendix**.

Example 14-1: What is the value of $\chi^2_{0.05, 10}$?

Solution: From **Table 4** in the **Appendix**, $\chi^2_{0.05, 10} = 18.307$. (Verify.)

Example 14-2: What is the value of $\chi^2_{0.95, 20}$?

Solution: From **Table 4** in the **Appendix**, $\chi^2_{0.95, 20} = 10.851$. (Verify.)

14-2 The Chi-Square Test for Goodness-of-Fit

Have you ever wondered whether a sample of observed data (frequency distribution or proportions) fits some pattern or distribution? We should not expect the pattern to exactly fit a given distribution, so we can look for differences and make conclusions as to the **goodness-of-fit** of the data. For example, in **Figure 14-3**, you can see clearly that the pattern of the sample data does not quite follow the distribution of the population. As a matter of fact, the sample data deviate quite severely from the population distribution. Hence you may conclude intuitively in this case that the sample data did not come from the population

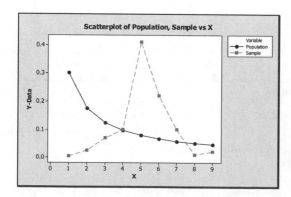

Figure 14-3: Display of sample distribution severely deviating from the population distribution

to which they are compared because of the large deviations from the sample distribution to the population distribution. In **Figure 14-4**, you can observe that the sample distribution follows the population distribution quite closely. In this case, you may conclude intuitively that the sample data did come from the population to which they are compared because of the very small deviation of the sample distribution from the population distribution.

Figure 14-4: Display of sample distribution closely following the population distribution

Generally, we can assume that a good fit exists. That is, we can propose a hypothesis that a specified theoretical distribution is appropriate to model the pattern. This, of course, will be your null hypothesis. Since this sample is one of the many possible samples, we can investigate the chance of obtaining this sample with the differences when we assume that the null hypothesis is true. If the chance is small, we can reject the null hypothesis and claim that the fit is not appropriate.

How should one go about deciding the significance of the observed differences? To do this, we use a statistic composed of the weighted differences of the frequencies. This statistic has a chi-square distribution with $n - 1$ degrees of freedom, where n is the number of (frequency) categories, and is given by

$$\chi^2 = \Sigma \frac{(\text{observed} - \text{expected})^2}{\text{expected}}$$

In this equation, *observed* represents the observed frequencies, and *expected* represents the expected frequencies.

Below is a summary of the tests for goodness-of-fit.

Summary of Hypothesis Test

H_0: (Statement indicating that the observed data fit some pattern or distribution.)

H_1: (Statement indicating that the observed data do not fit the pattern or distribution indicated in the null hypothesis.)

T.S.: $\chi^2 = \Sigma \dfrac{(\text{observed} - \text{expected})^2}{\text{expected}}$

D.R.: For a specified significance level α, reject the null hypothesis if the computed test statistic value χ^2 is greater than. $\chi^2_{\alpha,\,n-1}$.

Conclusion:

Example 14-3: At an international student organization function, the president of the organization believed that the students who were present consisted of 10 percent Africans, 25 percent Indians, 40 percent Asians, and 25 percent Americans. The students present consisted of 25 Africans, 15 Indians, 80 Asians, and 20 Americans. At the 5 percent level of significance, test the president's belief.

Solution: We are given that $\alpha = 0.05$, $n = 4$ (number of categories), $df = 4 - 1 = 3$, and $\chi^2_{0.05, 3} = 7.815$. Observe that there is a total of 140 students. The expected values then will be $0.10 \times 140 = 14$, $0.25 \times 140 = 35$, $0.40 \times 140 = 56$ and $0.25 \times 140 = 35$. The observed and expected frequencies are given in **Table 14-1**.

Table 14-1: Table with Observed and Expected Frequencies for Example 14-3

Observed	25	15	80	20
Expected	14	35	56	35

From the table,

$$\chi^2 = \frac{(25-14)^2}{14} + \frac{(15-35)^2}{35} + \frac{(80-56)^2}{56} + \frac{(20-35)^2}{35} = 36.7857$$

Thus we can write up the test as

H_0: The composition of the students at the function was of 10 percent Africans, 25 percent Indians, 40 percent Asians, and 25 percent Americans.

H_1: The distribution is different from the one stated in the null hypothesis.

T.S.: $\chi^2 = \sum \dfrac{(\text{observed} - \text{expected})^2}{\text{expected}} = 36.7857$

D.R.: For a significance level of 0.05, reject the null hypothesis if the computed test statistic value $\chi^2 = 36.7857 > \chi^2_{0.05, 3} = 7.815$.

Conclusion: Since $36.7857 > 7.815$, reject the null hypothesis. That is, at the 5 percent level of significance, there is enough sample evidence to reject the belief of the president with regard to the makeup of the international student organization.

Figure 14-5 depicts the rejection region.

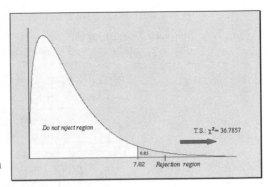

Figure 14-5: Diagram depicting the rejection region for Example 14-3

Example 14-4: There are four TV sets located in the student center of a large university. At a particular time each day, four different soap operas (1, 2, 3, and 4) are viewed on these TV sets. The percentages of the audience captured by these shows during one semester were 25, 30, 25, and 20 percent, respectively. During the first week of the following semester, 300 students are surveyed.

(a) If the viewing pattern has not changed, what number of students is expected to watch each soap opera?

Solution: Based on the information, the expected values will be $0.25 \times 300 = 75, 0.30 \times 300 = 90, 0.25 \times 300 = 75$, and $0.20 \times 300 = 60$. These expected values are shown **Table 14-2.**

Table 14-2: Expected Frequencies for Example 14-4(a)

	SOAP OPERA			
	1	2	3	4
Expected number	75	90	75	60

(b) Suppose that the actual observed numbers of students viewing the soap operas are given in **Table 14-3**.

Table 14-3: Observed Frequencies for Example 14-4(b)

	SOAP OPERA			
	1	2	3	4
Observed number	80	88	79	53

Test whether these numbers indicate a change at the 1 percent level of significance.

Solution: We are given that $\alpha = 0.01$, $n = 4$, $df = 4 - 1 = 3$, and $\chi^2_{0.01, 3} = 11.345$. The observed and expected frequencies are given in **Table 14-4**.

Table 14-4: Observed and Expected Frequencies for Example 14-4(b)

	SOAP OPERA			
	1	2	3	4
Observed frequencies	80	88	79	53
Expected frequencies	75	90	75	60

From **Table 14-4**,

$$\chi^2 = \frac{(80-75)^2}{75} + \frac{(88-90)^2}{90} + \frac{(79-75)^2}{75} + \frac{(53-60)^2}{60} = 1.4978$$

Thus we can write up the test as

H_0: The proportion of students who watched the soap operas (1, 2, 3, and 4) were 25, 30, 25, and 20 percent, respectively.

H_1: The distribution stated in the null hypothesis is not correct.

T.S.: $\chi^2 = \sum \dfrac{(\text{observed}-\text{expected})^2}{\text{expected}} = 1.4978$

D.R.: For a significance level of 0.01, reject the null hypothesis if the computed test statistic value $\chi^2 = 1.4978 > \chi^2_{0.01, 3} = 11.345$.

Conclusion: Since $1.4978 < 11.345$, do not reject the null hypothesis. That is, at the 1 percent level of significance, there is not enough sample evidence to reject the postulated distribution of students who watch the four soap operas.

Figure 14-6 depicts the rejection region.

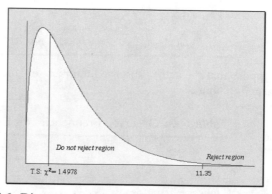

Figure 14-6: Diagram depicting the rejection region for Example 14-4

14-3 The Chi-Square Test for Independence

The chi-square **independence test** can be used to test for the independence between two variables.

Example 14-5: A survey was done by a car manufacturer concerning a particular make and model. A group of 500 potential customers was asked whether they purchased their current car because of its appearance, its performance rating, or its fixed price (no negotiating). The results, broken down by gender responses, are given in **Table 14-5**.

Table 14-5: Summary Data for **Example 14-5**

	OBSERVED FREQUENCIES		
	APPEARANCE	PERFORMANCE	COST
Male	100	50	35
Female	80	170	65

Question: Do females feel differently than males about the three different criteria used in choosing a car, or do they feel basically the same?

One way of answering this question is to determine whether the criterion used in buying a car is independent of gender. That is, we can do a test for independence. Thus the null hypothesis will be that the criterion used is independent of gender, whereas the alternative hypothesis will be that the criterion used is dependent on gender.

When data are arranged in tabular form for the chi-square independence test, the table is called a **contingency table**. Here, **Table 14-5** has two rows and three columns, so we say we have a **2 by 3 (2 × 3) contingency table.** The degrees of freedom for any contingency table is given by **(number of rows − 1) × (number of columns − 1)**. In this example, $df = (2 − 1) × (3 − 1) = 2$.

In order to test for independence using the chi-square independence test, we must compute expected values under the assumption that the null hypothesis is true. To find these expected values, we need to compute the row totals and the column totals. **Table 14-6** shows the observed frequencies with the row and column totals. These row and column totals are called **marginal totals**.

Table 14-6: Observed Frequencies with Marginal Totals for Example 14-5

	APPEARANCE	PERFORMANCE	COST	TOTAL
Male	100	50	35	185
Female	80	170	65	315
Total	180	220	100	Grand total = 500

The total for the first row (**Male**) is 185, and the total for the first column (**Appearance**) is 180. The expected value for the cell in the table where the first row (**Male**) and first column (**Appearance**) intersect will be $\frac{185 \times 180}{500} = 66.6$. Recall that the grand total of the observed values was 500. The expected value for the cell corresponding to the intersection of the second row (**Female**) and the third column (**Cost**) is $\dfrac{315 \times 100}{500} = 63$. We can continue in this manner to obtain the expected values for the rest of the cells. **Table 14-7** gives the expected frequencies. Check to see that the entries are correct.

Table 14-7: Expected Frequencies with Marginal Totals for Example 14-5

	APPEARANCE	PERFORMANCE	COST	TOTAL
Male	66.6	81.4	37	185
Female	113.4	138.6	63	315
Total	180	220	100	Grand total = 500

The χ^2 test statistic is computed in the same manner as we did when we did the goodness-of-fit test. A test for this situation is given next.

Solution: Let us use $\alpha = 0.01$. Thus $df = (2-1)(3-1) = 2$ and $\chi^2_{0.01, 2} = 9.210$. From the previous computations,

$$\chi^2 = \frac{(100-66.6)^2}{66.6} + \frac{(50-81.4)^2}{81.4} + \frac{(35-37)^2}{37} + \frac{(80-113.4)^2}{113.4}$$

$$+ \frac{(170-138.6)^2}{138.6} + \frac{(65-63)^2}{63} = 45.9536$$

Thus we can write up the test as

H_0: The criterion used in purchasing a car is independent of gender.

H_1: The criterion or criteria used in purchasing a car is dependent on gender.

T.S.: $\chi^2 = \sum \dfrac{(\text{observed} - \text{expected})^2}{\text{expected}} = 45.9536$

D.R.: For a significance level of 0.01, reject the null hypothesis if the computed test statistic value $\chi^2 = 45.9536 > \chi^2_{0.01, 2} = 9.210$.

Conclusion: Since $45.9536 > 9.210$, reject the null hypothesis. That is, at the 1 percent level of significance, there is enough sample evidence to claim that the criterion used in purchasing a car is dependent on gender.

Figure 14-7 depicts the rejection region.

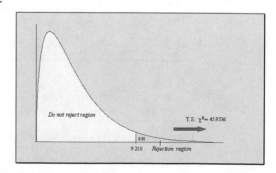

Figure 14-7: Diagram depicting the rejection region for Example 14-5

14-4 Benford's Law

Frank Benford, in the 1930s, noticed that logarithm tables (these were used by scientists long before the common use of computers and calculators) tended to be worn out on the early pages where the numbers started with the digit 1. Based on this observation and many others, he discovered that more numbers in the real world started with the digit 1 than with 2 and that more started with the digit 2 than with 3, and so on. He later published a formula that describes the proportion of times a number will begin with the digits 1, 2, 3, etc. This formula is now called **Benford's law. Table 14-8** shows the distribution of the proportions, to three decimal places, for the leading digits of numbers based on Benford's law.

Table 14-8: Distribution of Leading Digits Using Benford's Law

DIGIT	1	2	3	4	5	6	7	8	9
Proportion	0.301	0.176	0.125	0.097	0.079	0.067	0.058	0.051	0.046

In addition, **Figure 14-8** depicts the distribution graphically.

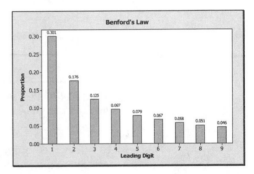

Figure 14-8: Bar chart depicting Benford's law

Benford's law has been used as a method of detecting fraudulent accounting data by looking at the first significant digit of each data entry and comparing the actual frequency of occurrence with the predicted or expected frequency. Most white-collar criminals are unaware of Benford's law and usually will use each digit about 10 percent of the time.

Example 14-6: Students who attend college and apply for student loans must submit a FAFSA (Free Application for Federal Student Aid) form. Part of the information that is required is the annual income of the parent or parents. A total of 3,633 forms was sampled from college records, and the proportions, to three decimal places, of the leading digits for the total annual incomes for the parents were recorded. This information is presented in **Table 14-9**.

Table 14-9: Distribution of Leading Digits for Reported Total Incomes for Parents on the FAFSA Form

DIGIT	1	2	3	4	5	6	7	8	9
Frequency	680	477	469	429	423	421	346	231	157
Proportion	0.187	0.131	0.129	0.118	0.116	0.116	0.095	0.064	0.043

Test at the 5 percent significance level whether the distributions of the first digits for the reported total salaries for the parents follow Benford's law.

Solution: Plots of the proportions of the leading digits for both Benford's law and the parents' salaries are shown in **Figure 14-9**. One may observe that the distributions seem different from each other. The objective is to determine statistically whether they are significantly different from each other. In other words, we need to check on the goodness-of-fit of the distributions of the proportions of the leading digits for the salaries of the parents with respect to the proportions specified by Benford's law.

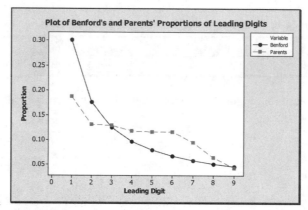

Figure 14-9: Plot of proportions of leading digits for Benford's law and the salaries for the parents

Table 14-10 shows the computations needed to compute the χ^2 test statistic. The value of the test statistic is equal to 507.527. To obtain the expected frequencies based on Benford's law, one should multiply the total of 3,633 by Benford's proportions. For example, from the table, the expected frequency value of 639.408 is obtained from $3,633 \times 0.176 = 639.408$, etc.

Table 14-10: Table with Computations to Obtain the Test Statistic Value $\chi^2 = 507.527$

DIGIT	OBSERVED FREQUENCY	EXPECTED FREQUENCY BASED ON BENFORD'S LAW	(OBSERVED − EXPECTED)²/ EXPECTED
1	680	1093.533	156.383
2	477	639.408	41.251
3	469	454.125	0.487
4	429	352.401	16.650
5	423	287.007	64.438
6	421	243.411	129.566
7	346	210.714	86.859
8	231	185.283	11.280
9	157	167.118	0.613
	Total = 3633		Total = 507.527

Note that the degrees of freedom for the test $df = 9 - 1 = 8$, $\alpha = 0.05$, and $\chi^2_{0.05, 8} = 15.507$. Using this information for the test, we have

H_0: The distribution of the proportions of the leading digits for the parents' salaries is the distribution described by Benford's law. That is, $p_1 = 0.301$, $p_2 = 0.179$, $p_3 = 0.125$, $p_4 = 0.301$, $p_5 = 0.079$, $p_6 = 0.067$, $p_7 = 0.058$, $p_8 = 0.051$, and $p_9 = 0.046$.

H_1: At least one of the proportions of the leading digits for the parents' salaries specified by Benford's law is different.

T.S.: $\chi^2 = 507.527$

D.R.: For a level of significance $\alpha = 0.05$, reject H_0 if the computed test statistic $\chi^2 = 507.527 > \chi^2_{0.05, 8} = 15.507$.

Conclusion: Since $507.527 > 15.507$, reject H_0. That is, there is sufficient evidence to support the claim that there is a significant discrepancy between the proportions of the leading digits expected from Benford's law and that observed for the reported salaries for the parents on the FAFSA forms. Hence the data for the parents' salaries reported on the forms may be suspect.

Figure 14-10 displays the rejection region.

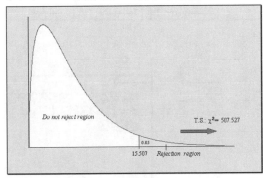

Figure 14-10: Diagram depicting the rejection region for Example 14-6

Technology Corner

All the concepts discussed in this chapter can be computed and illustrated through most statistical software packages. All scientific and graphical calculators can be used for the computations. In addition, some of the newer calculators, such as the TI-83/84 (all versions), will allow you to do the test directly on the calculator. If you own a calculator, you should consult the owner's manual to determine what statistical features are included.

Illustration: **Figure 14-11** shows the output computed by the MINITAB software for **Example 14-5**. You can extract the information from the output to help in writing up the test. Note that the output also gives the P-value for the test. **Figure 14-12** shows the output computed by the TI-83/84 calculator for **Example 14-5**. The P-values provided by both the MINITAB and TI-83/84 outputs can be used to write up the conclusion for the test. Care always should be taken when using the formulas for computations in hypothesis testing. One can use other features of the technologies to illustrate other concepts discussed in this chapter.

```
Worksheet size: 100000 cells

Chi-Square Test -- Example 14-5


Expected counts are printed below observed counts

            C1        C2        C3      Total
    1      100        50        35       185
           66.60     81.40     37.00

    2       80       170        65       315
          113.40    138.60     63.00

Total      180       220       100       500

Chi-Sq = 16.750 + 12.113 +  0.108 +
          9.837 +  7.114 +  0.063 = 45.985
DF = 2, P-Value = 0.000
```

Figure 14-11: MINITAB output for Example 14-5

```
X²-Test
 X²=45.98537932
 P=1.033717E⁻¹⁰
 df=2
```

Figure 14-12: TI-83/84 output for Example 14-5

Example 14-7: Use the information in **Example 14-5** and the P-value from **Figure 14-11** to write up an appropriate test.

H_0: The criterion used in purchasing a car is independent of gender.

H_1: The criterion or criteria used in purchasing a car is dependent on gender.

T.S.: P-value $= 0.00$

D.R.: For a significance level of 0.01, reject the null hypothesis if the computed P-value $= 0.00 <$ the level of significance $\alpha = 0.01$.

Conclusion: Since P-value $= 0.00 < \alpha = 0.01$, reject the null hypothesis. That is, at the 1 percent level of significance, there is enough sample evidence to claim that the criterion used in purchasing a car is dependent on gender.

Here, the focus was on chi-square tests for goodness-of-fit and for independence between two variables. Sometimes these tests are called **nonparametric tests** because no assumptions are made about the distribution of the sampling populations. The concepts in the chapter were illustrated through

✓ Formulas

✓ Examples

✓ Use of technology

True/False Questions

1. The goodness-of-fit test provides us with a procedure for determining whether a set of data is a good fit to a theoretical model.
2. In general, the number of degrees of freedom for any goodness-of-fit test is given by (number of frequency categories − 1).
3. The expected frequencies in a contingency table are the actual numbers observed or recorded in each cell of the table.
4. The observed frequencies in a contingency table represent the theoretical expected outcomes assuming that the null hypothesis is true.
5. In a contingency table, the expected frequency for any cell is computed from (row total + column total)/(grand total).
6. The degrees of freedom for an $r \times c$ contingency table is given by $(r - 1)(c - 1)$, where r represents the number of rows and c represents the number of columns.
7. The χ^2 random variable sometimes can assume negative values.
8. The sampling distribution for a goodness-of-fit test is the χ^2 distribution.
9. The χ^2 goodness-of-fit test is always demonstrated as a left-tailed test.
10. The number of degrees of freedom for a contingency table with 12 rows and 12 columns is 144.
11. One of the criteria used when performing the χ^2 goodness-of-fit test is that the expected frequency in each cell be less than 5.
12. The shape of the χ^2 distribution depends on the sample size.
13. The χ^2 distribution is used to test hypotheses concerning the population mean.
14. The χ^2 goodness-of-fit test is always a right-tailed test.
15. In a contingency table, you should pool categories whenever the observed frequency in any cell is less than 5.
16. The difference between the observed and expected frequencies in a contingency table is measured by a χ^2 statistic.
17. Benford's law is used to determine whether a distribution of leading digits is uniform.
18. Benford's law is sometimes used to determine whether financial data are suspect.

Completion Questions

1. The χ^2 goodness-of-fit test is always a (left, right, two) _____ -tailed test.
2. In an $r \times c$ contingency table, where r is the number of rows and c is the number of columns, the degrees of freedom will be $[(r - 1)(c + 1), (r - 1)(c - 1), (r + 1)(c - 1)]$ _____.
3. The χ^2 random variable can never assume (negative, positive, zero) _____ values.

4. The number of degrees of freedom for a χ^2 goodness-of-fit test is the (number of categories, sample size, total expected frequency) _____ − 1.

5. When doing tests that involve contingency tables and the χ^2 distribution, it is recommended that the expected frequencies in each cell be greater than or equal to (two, five, ten, n) _____.

6. In a χ^2 goodness-of-fit test, the expected values for the cells in the contingency table are computed by assuming that the null hypothesis is (true, false) _____.

7. In a 5 × 7 contingency table, the degrees of freedom are (35, 28, 30, 24) _____.

8. For the χ^2 goodness-of-fit test, the P-value will be the area to the (right, left) _____ of the computed χ^2 test statistic with the appropriate degrees of freedom.

9. A cross-classification of values in tabular form is called a(n) _____.

10. The number of cells that will result in a cross-classification of the two variables grade (A, B, C, D, E) and number of days absent from class (1, 2, 3, 4, 5) is (20, 16, 25) _____.

11. If the computed test statistic for the χ^2 goodness-of-fit test is large, this will tend to support the (null, alternative) _____ hypothesis.

12. In a contingency table, the expected cell frequency is computed by multiplying the row total and the column total and dividing by the (row, column, grand) _____ total.

13. Frequencies obtained from a sample are called (observed, expected) _____ frequencies.

14. The χ^2 procedure is defined for testing how well frequencies of categories in a sample represent frequencies of categories in the (sample, population) _____.

15. Benford's law is used to determine whether a distribution of leading digits in a data set (is uniform, is normal, follows Benford's distribution) _____.

16. Benford's law is sometimes used to determine whether financial data are (uniform, normal, fraudulent) _____.

Multiple-Choice Questions

1. The number of cells for a 5 × 7 contingency table is
   (a) 35.
   (b) 24.
   (c) 48.
   (d) 28.

2. A cross-classification of two categorical variables in tabular form is called a
   (a) frequency distribution table.
   (b) probability distribution table.
   (c) rows and columns table.
   (d) contingency table.

Use the following information to solve Problems 3 to 10:

Consider the table below, formed by cross-classifying age group and brand of cola consumed:

	UNDER AGE 15	AGES 15 AND UNDER 25	AGES 25 AND UNDER 35
Cola 1	150	100	200
Cola 2	300	125	200
Cola 3	300	200	300

3. The **under age 15** relative frequency is
   (a) 0.4000.
   (b) 0.2400.
   (c) 0.3733.
   (d) 0.4267.

4. The observed cell frequency for **ages 15 and under 25 cola 3** consumers is
   (a) 300.
   (b) 200.
   (c) 125.
   (d) 100.

5. The expected cell frequency for **ages 15 and under 25 cola 3** consumers is
   (a) 180.
   (b) 250.
   (c) 320.
   (d) 750.

6. If you were to test whether there is any difference in the proportions of people consuming the different brands based on age, the test statistic would be
   (a) 31.029.
   (b) 26.035.
   (c) 30.996.
   (d) 31.035.

7. If you were to test whether there is any difference in the proportions of people consuming the different brands based on age, the degrees of freedom for the distribution of the test statistic would be
   (a) 4.
   (b) 9.
   (c) 16.
   (d) 12.

8. If you were to test at the 5 percent level of significance whether there is any difference in the proportions of people consuming the different brands based on age, the rejection region will be
   (a) $\chi^2 > 16.919$.
   (b) $\chi^2 > 9.488$.
   (c) $\chi^2 > 26.296$.
   (d) $\chi^2 > 21.026$.

9. If you were to test at the 5 percent level of significance whether there is any difference in the proportions of people consuming the different brands based on age, the appropriate null hypothesis for the test would be

(a) there is some difference among the proportions of people consuming the different brands of cola based on age.
(b) there is a small difference among the proportions of people consuming the different brands of cola based on age.
(c) there is no difference among the proportions of people consuming the different brands of cola based on age.
(d) there is a large difference among the proportions of people consuming the different brands of cola based on age.

10. If you were to test at the 5 percent level of significance whether there is any difference in the proportions of people consuming the different brands based on age, the decision for the test would be
(a) do not reject the null hypothesis.
(b) reject the alternative hypothesis.
(c) do not reject the alternative hypothesis.
(d) reject the null hypothesis.

Use the following information to solve Problems 11 to 18:

A fair six-sided die with faces numbered 1, 2, . . . , 6 is rolled 300 times with the following outcomes:

OUTCOME	1	2	3	4	5	6
Observed frequencies	44	48	47	53	52	56

11. For an outcome of 4, the relative frequency is
(a) 53 percent
(b) 17.67 percent.
(c) 50 percent.
(d) 14.2857 percent.

12. The observed frequency for the outcome value of 5 is
(a) 260.
(b) 52/300.
(c) 52/5.
(d) 52.

13. The expected frequency for the outcome value of 5 is
(a) 52.
(b) 0.1733.
(c) 50.
(d) 5.

(*Hint:* The expected value for each category will be the same because the probability is 1/6 of observing a 1, 2, 3, 4, 5, or 6.)

14. If you were to test whether the die is fair, the alternative hypothesis would be that
(a) the die is fair.
(b) the die is not fair.
(c) the die is sometimes fair.
(d) the die is almost never fair.

15. If you were to test whether the die is fair, the computed test statistic will be
    (a) 1.96.
    (b) 1.80.
    (c) 1.76.
    (d) 2.00.

16. If you were to test whether the die is fair, the degrees of freedom for the distribution of the test statistic would be
    (a) 6.
    (b) 12.
    (c) 7.
    (d) 5.

17. If you were to test at the 5 percent level of significance whether the die is fair, the rejection region would be
    (a) $\chi^2 > 12.597$.
    (b) $\chi^2 > 11.070$.
    (c) $\chi^2 > 21.026$.
    (d) $\chi^2 > 14.067$.

18. If you were to test at the 5 percent level of significance whether the die is fair, your decision would be
    (a) do not reject the null hypothesis.
    (b) reject the alternative hypothesis.
    (c) do not reject the alternative hypothesis.
    (d) reject the null hypothesis.

Use this information for Questions 19 to 22:

The following table gives the frequency counts and proportions (to three decimal places) for the first digits for a set of observed numbers:

FIRST DIGIT	1	2	3	4	5	6	7	8	9
Frequency	30	17	12	11	14	7	8	10	5
Proportions	0.263	0.149	0.105	0.097	0.123	0.061	0.070	0.088	0.044

19. A plot of side-by-side bar graphs of these proportions along with the proportions specified by Benford's law is presented below.

Do you think from the graphical presentation of the distribution for the proportions that the observed proportions can be approximated by Benford's law?
(a) Disagree
(b) Agree
(c) Strongly disagree
(d) None of the above

20. If you were testing at the 5 percent level of significance to determine whether the observed proportions follow Benford's law, then the critical value for the test would be
(a) 16.919.
(b) 15.507.
(c) 19.023.
(d) 17.535.

21. If you were testing at the 5 percent level of significance to determine whether the observed proportions follow Benford's law, then the computed test statistic value for the test would be
(a) 4.46.
(b) 4.69.
(c) 6.41.
(d) 7.43.

22. If you were testing at the 5 percent level of significance to determine whether the observed proportions follow Benford's law, then your decision for the test would be
(a) reject the null hypothesis that the distribution follows Benford's law.
(b) reject the alternative hypothesis that the distribution follows Benford's law.
(c) do not reject the null hypothesis that the distribution follows Benford's law.
(d) do not reject the alternative hypothesis that the distribution follows Benford's law.

Further Exercises

If possible, you could use any technology help to solve the following questions.

1. A survey was done by a car manufacturer concerning a particular make and model. A group of 500 individuals was asked whether they purchased their car because of its appearance, its performance ratings, or its fixed price (no negotiating). The results are given in the following table:

OWNER/CRITERIA	APPEARANCE	PERFORMANCE	COST
Male	100	50	35
Female	80	170	65

(a) Compute the expected frequency for each entry.
(b) State the null and alternative hypotheses if you were to test whether there is any difference in the proportions using the three different criterian to purchase the given car based on gender.
(c) Compute the test statistic for the goodness-of-fit test.
(d) If you were testing at the 5 percent level of significance, what would be the rejection region?
(e) Perform a goodness-of-fit test at the 5 percent level of significance for the hypotheses stated in part (b).

(f) Estimate the *P*-value for this test.

2. A regular fair six-sided die was tossed 440 times, and the individual outcomes were recorded in the table below:

OUTCOME	1	2	3	4	5	6
Observed frequencies	61	83	57	64	85	90

Test at the 5 percent level of significance to determine whether the die is fair.

3. Consider the following sequence of numbers:

$$0, 1, 1, 2, 3, 5, 8, 13, 21, 34, 55, 89, 144, 233, 377, 610, 987, \ldots$$

Observe that such a sequence can be obtained by adding two consecutive numbers to get the next number in the sequence. Such a sequence is called a **Fibonacci sequence**. The following table gives the frequency distribution of the first digits for the first 1,000,000 numbers in the Fibonacci sequence.

FIRST DIGIT	1	2	3	4	5	6	7	8	9
Frequency	301031	176092	124939	96908	79182	66947	57992	51151	45758
Proportions	0.30	0.18	0.12	0.10	0.08	0.07	0.06	0.05	0.05

Test at the 5 percent level whether the distribution of the proportions follow Benford's law.

4. The following table gives the frequency counts for the first digits for the number of verses per chapter for the Bible. Test at the 1 percent level whether the distribution of the first digits follow Benford's law.

FIRST DIGIT	1	2	3	4	5	6	7	8	9
Frequency	314	408	242	93	55	23	17	20	17

ANSWER KEY
True/False Questions
1. T 2. T 3. F 4. F 5. F 6. T 7. F 8. T 9. F 10. F 11. F
12. T 13. F 14. T 15. F 16. T 17. F 18. T

Completion Questions
1. right 2. $(r-1)(c-1)$ 3. negative 4. number of categories 5. five 6. true
7. 24 8. right 9. contingency table 10. 25 11. alternative 12. grand
13. observed 14. population 15. follows Benford's distribution 16. fraudulent

Multiple-Choice Questions
1. (a) 2. (d) 3. (a) 4. (b) 5. (c) 6. (d) 7. (a) 8. (b) 9. (c)
10. (d) 11. (b) 12. (d) 13. (c) 14. (b) 15. (a) 16. (d) 17. (b) 18. (a)
19. (b) 20. (b) 21. (d) 22. (c)

Further Exercises

1. Below is a MINITAB output for the problem.

```
Chi-Square Test: Appearance, Performace, Cost

Expected counts are printed below observed counts
Chi-Square contributions are printed below expected counts

                  Appearance  Performace    Cost    Total
    Male                 100          50      35      185
                       66.60       81.40   37.00
                      16.750      12.113   0.108

    Female                80         170      65      315
                      113.40      138.60   63.00
                       9.837       7.114   0.063

    Total                180         220     100      500

Chi-Sq = 45.985, DF = 2, P-Value = 0.000
```

(a) The expected frequencies are highlighted in the output. Refer to Section 14-3.

(b) H_0: The criterion used in purchasing a car is independent of gender. H_1: The criterion or criteria used in purchasing a car is dependent on gender.

(c) T.S.: $\chi^2 = 45.9859$ (from the MINITAB output)

(d) $\alpha = 0.05$, $df = 2$, and $\chi^2_{0.05, 2} = 5.991$, so reject if T.S.: $\chi^2 > 5.991$.

(e) Since T.S.: $\chi^2 = 45.9859 > \chi^2_{0.05, 2} = 5.991$, reject H_0 from part (b).

(f) P-value $= 0.000$ (from MINITAB output)

2. $\alpha = 0.05$, $df = 5$, $\chi^2_{0.05, 5} = 11.070$; T.S.: $\chi^2 > 5.991$.

   H_0: The die is fair versus H_1: The die is unfair; T.S.: $\chi^2 = 13.8182$; D.R.: Reject H_0 if T.S.: $\chi^2 = 13.8182 > \chi^2_{0.05, 5} = 11.070$; Conclusion: Since $13.8182 > 11.070$, reject H_0 and conclude that the die is not fair.

3. $\alpha = 0.05$, $\chi^2 = 2.3508$, $\chi^2_{0.05, 8} = 15.507$; do not reject H_0 (as given in **Example 14-6**).

4. $\alpha = 0.01$, $\chi^2 = 405.9131$, $\chi^2_{0.01, 8} = 20.09$; reject H_0 (as given in **Example 14-6**).

CHAPTER 15

One-Way Analysis of Variance

Do I Need to Read This Chapter?

Y ou should read this chapter if you need to review or to learn about

➡ Comparing population means graphically

➡ Some terminology associated with analysis of variance (ANOVA)

➡ The F distribution

➡ One-way or single-factor ANOVA *F* tests

➡ Technology integration for one-way ANOVA

Get Started

There are many situations where we may want to compare several population means. For example, a chairperson of a statistics department may want to compare the final grade averages for the same course taught by different professors. A physician may want to compare the average time it takes a certain level of a migraine headache to subside for different dosages of the same medication. A farmer may want to compare the average yield of his corn crop using different fertilizers.

These are just a few examples where we may need to compare several means. These comparisons can be achieved by using a procedure called analysis of variance (ANOVA).

15-1 Comparing Population Means Graphically

The objective in comparing several population means is to determine whether there is a statistically significant difference between them. Thus, when random samples are obtained from these populations, the respective sample means can be computed to help determine whether there is a significant difference between the population means. If the sample means are very different, then it is likely that the true or population means will be different. The question is: "How large a difference is needed to conclude that there is a statistically significant difference between the population means?" Also, we need to determine whether the differences are due to random variation in the sample data or if there really are differences between the population means.

One simple way of looking at differences of population means is to display the data through box plots

Example 15-1: A random sample of students on a college campus was asked to count the number of pennies, nickels, dimes, and quarters they had on their person. The summary information is shown in **Table 15-1**.

Table 15-1: Summary of the Number of Different Coins that Were Sampled

PENNIES	NICKELS	DIMES	QUARTERS
9	3	2	4
7	5	6	3
10	8	4	2
14	6	3	6
5	4	2	5
8	3	8	2
12	2	1	1
19	3		3
15	6		
6			

Note: We can consider each of the four data sets as samples from their respective populations of pennies, nickels, dimes, and quarters.

Compute the sample means, and display the data using box plots. Are there any differences in the means of the potential populations from which these samples were obtained? If the sample means are different, are the differences large enough to conclude that the means of the populations from which these samples were obtained are significantly different? That is, if the average numbers of the types of coins computed from the data are very different, does this tell us that the average numbers of these different types of coins for the entire student population are expected to be different?

Solution: The sample means for the pennies, nickels, dimes, and quarters are, respectively, 10.36, 4.444, 3.714, and 3.25. Observe that the average number of pennies seem to be an outlying value relative to the values of the other means. Is this difference large enough to infer that the corresponding population mean for the number of pennies is significantly different (in this case greater) than the population means for the numbers of nickels, dimes, and quarters for the entire student population for that particular campus? Further discussions will help to answer this question.

The box plots and confidence intervals are shown in **Figures 15-1** and **15-2**, respectively. The box plots can give some insight as to whether these differences are significant. Observe that the box in the box plot for the number of pennies does not overlap with the boxes in the plots for the numbers of nickels, dimes, and quarters. Another way to observe this difference is to compute the one-sample confidence intervals. The confidence intervals for the number of coins are pennies: (7.5091, 13.2182); nickels: (2.95042, 5.93847); dimes: (1.40437, 6.02420); and quarters: (1.85464, 4.64536). From the confidence intervals, we see that the interval for the number of pennies does not overlap with the others. Both these observations would indicate that the population average for the number of pennies carried by the students is significantly different from the rest of the denominations of coins. Thus it is unlikely that the difference in the sample averages is due to sample variation. That is, we can say that the variability between the sample averages is large when compared with the variability within the samples.

Based on the preceding discussion, we can safely say that there is no significant difference between the averages for the populations of the numbers of nickels, dimes, and quarters. This can be further reinforced by observing that both the box plots and the confidence intervals overlap for these variables. Observe **Figure 15-1** and **Figure 15-2**.

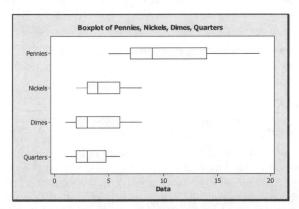

Figure 15-1: Box-plot display for the different denominations of coins

Figure 15-2: Confidence interval display for the different denominations of coins

Example 15-2: **Figure 15-3** shows random samples obtained from three different normal distributions. Discuss whether you think that the means of these populations are significantly different based on the samples.

Solution: Based on the display, we would expect the sample means to be nearly equal, as in this illustration. We also would expect the variation among the sample means (between

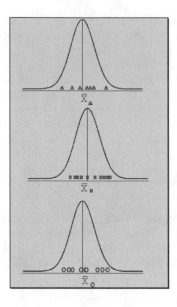

Figure 15-3: Samples from normal populations with almost equal means

samples) to be small relative to the variation found around the individual sample means (within samples). Thus one may infer that there would not be a significant difference between the population means.

Example 15-3: **Figure 15-4** shows random samples obtained from three different normal distributions. Discuss whether you think that the means of these populations are significantly different based on the samples.

Solution: Based on the display, we would expect the sample means to be significantly different, as in this illustration. We also would expect the variation among the sample means (between samples) to be large relative to the variation found around the individual sample means (within samples). Thus one may infer that there would be a significant difference between the population means.

These three examples provide us with a sense of whether or not there is a significant difference among the population means. However, they cannot help us to evaluate how likely it is that any observed difference is due to sampling variation or variations in the sample data. In this chapter we will present procedures that will help us to determine how likely it is that the observed differences among the sample means are due to sampling error. Such procedures are called **analysis of variance (ANOVA)**.

Figure 15-4: Samples from normal populations with significantly different means

15-2 Some Terminology Associated with Analysis of Variance (ANOVA)

In this section you will be introduced to some terminology used frequently in analysis of variance.

In **Example 15-1**, if we assume that these are four samples from four potential populations of pennies, nickels, dimes, and quarters, then the statistical method used to compare the four population means is called **analysis of variance**. This method is often referred to by the acronym **ANOVA**. This technique of analysis of variance will enable us to determine whether any observed differences among the sample means are due to sampling error.

Explanation of the term—ANOVA: ANOVA is a statistical method for determining the "existence" of the differences among several population means.

Suppose that a researcher would like to determine the effectiveness of three different drugs of equal dosage on migraine headaches. We can consider this as an **experiment**.

Explanation of the term—experiment: The term **experiment** in ANOVA is a statement of the problem to be solved.

Quick Tip

A careful statement of the problem to be solved goes a long way toward its solution.

Example 15-4: A researcher would like to determine whether there is a difference in the average mileages for three different brands of gasoline. What is the experiment in this case?

Solution: The problem to be solved in this example is to determine whether there is a difference in the average mileages for the three different brands of gasoline. Hence this is the experiment.

Example 15-5: What is the experiment in **Example 15-1**?

Solution: The problem to be solved in **Example 15-1** is to determine whether there was a statistically significant difference between the average numbers of coins for the different denominations for the students on a particular campus.

Suppose that a researcher is interested in determining the effectiveness of four teaching methods for a given course. In such an experiment, the researcher would be interested in the final averages for each student in the course for the different methods of teaching. Here we refer to the students as the **experimental units** and the final averages as the values for the **response variable**.

Explanation of the term—experimental units: Individuals or objects on which the experiment is performed are called **experimental units**.

Explanation of the term—response variable: A **response variable** in an experiment is a characteristic of an experimental unit on which information is to be obtained.

In the preceding example where the researcher may be interested in the time it takes for the migraine headache to subside, then the variable of **time** will be the response variable.

Note: The **response variable** may be **qualitative**, such as whether or not you suffer from migraine headaches, or **quantitative**, such as the time it takes for your migraine to subside from a certain pain level.

Many experimental variables that we can control are called **independent variables** or **factors**. Values of the factor are called **levels** of the factor.

Note: Factors may be **qualitative** or **quantitative**.

Explanation of the term—qualitative factor: A **qualitative factor** is a factor that has levels that may vary by category rather than by numerical values.

Explanation of the term—quantitative factor: A **quantitative factor** is a factor that has levels that may be counts or measurements.

In the example where we used different teaching methods, we refer to these different methods as the **treatments** or **levels** of the factor of teaching. In the example where the researcher wanted to determine whether there were differences in mileages for the different brands of gasoline, then these different brands of gasoline will be the treatments or levels of the experiment. In the case where the researcher wanted to determine the effectiveness of three different drugs of equal dosage on migraine headaches, then these different drugs will be the treatments or levels of that experiment. In the example about the migraine headaches, suppose that the researcher did another experiment where a single drug was used with five different dosages. Then the different dosages would be the treatment levels of the factor (single drug) for the experiment. Thus one can infer that ANOVA is designed to detect differences among means from populations subject to different treatments.

Note: Sometimes the word **treatment** is used interchangeably with the term **level** or may be combined as **treatment level**.

Explanation of the term—treatment (level) of a factor: An experimental condition that is applied to the experimental units is called a **treatment (level)** of the factor.

Note: The term **treatment** also can refer to the populations that are being analyzed. For example, if we are comparing the average incomes for four different counties in a particular state, we may refer to the four populations (counties) as four treatments.

Example 15-6: A farmer would like to determine whether there is a difference in the average yield per acre for his corn crop for equal amounts of five different fertilizers. In this experiment, assume that there were equal amounts of corn plants per acre. Identify the factor, treatment levels, experimental units, and response variable of the experiment.

Solution: Factor $\Rightarrow$ fertilizer; treatment levels $\Rightarrow$ the five different fertilizers; experimental units $\Rightarrow$ corn plants; response variable $\Rightarrow$ yield per acre.

Note: So far, all the examples deal with a single factor. In this text we will restrict our discussions to only one-factor analysis. That is, we will only discuss **one-factor** or **one-way ANOVA**.

Explanation of the term—one-factor or one-way ANOVA: A **one-factor** or **one-way ANOVA** deals with experiments that involve a single factor with different levels. These levels could be quantitative or qualitative.

15-3 The Hypothesis Test of One-Way Analysis of Variance

Suppose that we have a single-factor experiment in which there are r levels. Thus we will be sampling from r populations or treatments. We will select an independent random sample from each of these r populations. Let the size of the sample from population i for i, $= 1, 2, 3, ..., r$, be equal to n_i, and the total sample size is $n = n_1 + n_2 + n_3 + \cdots + n_r$.

Figure 15-5 shows the r populations from which the independent samples are selected. Observe that each population has its own mean, and the respective sample means are computed for the samples. Also indicated in the figure are the respective sample sizes.

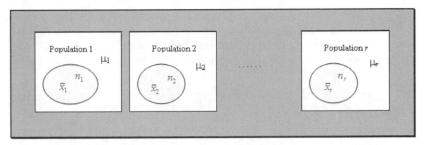

Figure 15-5: Display of the r populations from which samples are taken

The hypotheses that are associated with the one-way analysis of variance are given below.

The Null and Alternative Hypotheses for the One-Way Analysis of Variance

$$H_0: \mu_1 = \mu_2 = \mu_3 = \cdots = \mu_r$$
$$H_1: \text{Not all the population means are equal}$$

From these r samples, several different quantities will be computed that will help in calculating the test statistic when we assume that the null hypothesis is true. From the value of the test statistic and the critical value for a given level of significance, we will be able to determine whether to reject the null hypothesis or not. That is, we will be able to determine whether we can conclude that there is no difference between the population means or a significant difference between them.

Quick Tips

- When using the ANOVA technique to test for equality of population means, we usually would want $r > 2$.
- If $r = 2$, we can use the simpler two-sample t tests.
- The null hypothesis is called a *joint hypothesis* about the equality of several population means (parameters).
- It would not be efficient to compare two population means at a time to achieve what the ANOVA test will achieve.
- If we test two population means at a time to achieve what ANOVA will achieve, we will not be sure of the combined probability of a type I error for all the tests.
- By using the ANOVA technique to compare several population means at the same time, we will have control of the probability of a type I error.

Assumptions of a One-Way ANOVA

The required assumptions of a one-way ANOVA are

- The random samples from the r populations are independent.
- The r random samples are assumed to be selected from normal populations whose means may or may not be equal, but the populations have equal variances σ^2.

Suppose, for example, that we are comparing three population means μ_1, μ_2, and μ_3 and that we want to determine whether these means are equal. For this experiment, we will select separate independent random samples from each of the three populations that we assume to be normally distributed. **Figure 15-6** displays this situation.

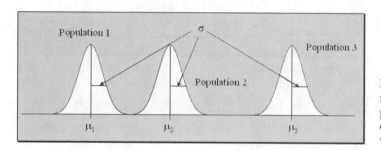

Figure 15-6: Three normally distributed populations with different means but with equal variance

How can we validate these assumptions when we test for the equality of means for a one-way ANOVA? There are several advanced procedures that you would encounter in most advanced texts about analysis of variance. These advanced techniques will not be discussed in this book. However, some simple graphical techniques will be used to help validate these assumptions.

Validating the Assumptions for a One-Way ANOVA

The assumptions for ANOVA should be validated before any inference is made about the population means. If these assumptions are not met, then the inference about the population means may not be reliable.

The assumptions are necessary in order for the test statistic used in the analysis to follow a certain probability distribution (discussed in the next section). If the populations are not exactly normally distributed but are approximately normally distributed, then the ANOVA procedure still will produce reliable results. If the distributions are highly skewed or very different from a normal distribution or the population variances are not equal or approximately equal, then ANOVA will not produce reliable results. In such cases, other tests, such as equivalent nonparametric tests, should be employed.

Two simple graphical techniques can be used to establish the assumptions for a one-way ANOVA. We can use the histogram with summary statistics to help establish the normality assumption, and we can use box plots to help establish the equal-variance assumption.

Example 15-7: Equal dosages of three drugs were used to ease a certain level of headache. Drug 1 was administered to 10 patients, and drugs 2 and 3 were administered to 9 patients each. The times, in minutes, for complete relief of the headache for the drugs are given in **Table 15-2**.

Table 15-2: Relief Time for Headache for the Three Groups of Patients

DRUG 1	DRUG 2	DRUG 3
6.0	4.5	9.0
7.0	6.0	8.5
5.5	5.5	10.0
8.0	4.0	7.0
6.5	6.0	6.5
9.5	5.0	6.0
6.5	6.5	5.0
7.5	7.0	8.0
8.5	7.5	7.0
5.0		

Before we use ANOVA to determine whether the average relieve times for the three drugs are the same, the validity of the ANOVA assumptions should be checked. This must be done so that the inference made about the population means will be reliable.

Solution: Graphical displays will be used to help check the validity of the ANOVA assumptions. **Figure 15-7** displays a histogram for the three data sets. **Figure 15-8** displays box plots for the three data sets.

By analyzing **Figure 15-7**, We can observe that the histograms for drugs 1, 2, and 3 all can be approximated by a normal distribution. Thus the assumption of normal populations has not been violated.

Next, let us look at **Figure 15-8** to help us determine whether the equal-variance assumption has been violated. By looking at these box plots, we can see that the spreads for the data sets are not the same. However, the spreads are **similar enough** for us to infer that it is likely that the observed differences in spread are due to sample variation. Thus we may assume that the equal-variance assumption has not been violated. Here, **similar enough** means that the range of values is approximately the same for the data sets. Also, the ranges for the middle 50 percent (length of the boxes) for the different data sets are approximately the same.

Figure 15-7: Histograms of the relief times for the three drugs

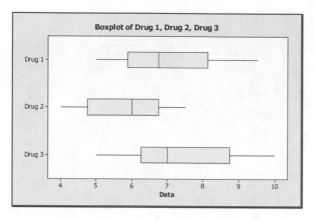

Figure 15-8: Box plots of the relief times for the three drugs

Since both the normality and the constant-variance assumptions have not been violated or severely violated, we can now proceed to test for equality of the population means using the analysis-of-variance procedure. This procedure will be covered in **Section 15-4**.

15-4 The Test Statistic and the *F* Distribution

The *F* **distribution** will enable us to compare different (at least three) population means statistically through the ANOVA procedure. Under the assumption that the null hypothesis given in **Section 15-3** is true for a one-way ANOVA, the test statistic of analysis of variance will follow an *F* **distribution**. The *F* distribution is obtained by taking the ratio of two chi-square distributions and thus has a numerator as well as a denominator degrees of freedom associated with it. The numerator degrees of freedom are $r - 1$, and the denominator degrees of freedom are $n - r$, where r is the number of populations or treatments and n is the combined sample size from these r populations (total data values).

Example 15-8: In **Example 15-1**, what are the numerator and denominator degrees of freedom if a one-way analysis of variance is run on the data.

Solution: From the information given in **Example 15-1**, the number of populations is $r = 4$, and the combined sample size is $n = 10 + 9 + 7 + 8 = 34$. Thus the numerator degrees of freedom are $r - 1 = 4 - 1 = 3$, and the denominator degrees of freedom are $n - r = 34 - 4 = 30$.

Note: The calculations leading to the *F* test statistic value will not be presented in this book. It will assume that the test statistic value is given.

The formulas associated with the computations are complex, and it is time-consuming to carry out the calculations by hand. Thus computational technology is indispensable in most situations involving ANOVA. Extensive use of technology will be integrated into the computations in this chapter. We will assume that the appropriate technology is available to compute the *F*-test statistic value for us. The one-way ANOVA test statistic is given by

$$\text{One-way ANOVA test statistic} \equiv F$$

We would have to compare this *F*-test statistic value with a critical *F* value from a table with $r - 1$ and $n - r$ degrees of freedom and a given level of significance α. Some *F* values are given in **Table 5** in the **Appendix** of this text for various numerator and denominator degrees of freedom.

Quick Tips

• The *F* statistic is usually computed from

$$F = \frac{\text{estimate of the variance based on the } r \text{ sample means}}{\text{estimate of the variance based on all sample observations}}$$

• Observe that the *F* value is computed from the ratio of two estimates for the sample variance—hence the acronym *ANOVA*.

• Note that the distribution of the sample variance is based on the chi-square distribution; hence the *F* statistic will be the ratio of two chi-square distributions.

The general decision rule to reject the null hypothesis H_0: $\mu_1 = \mu_2 = \mu_3 = \cdots = \mu_r$ for a given significance level α is given by

---

Reject H_0 if the computed test statistic *F* value is greater than the *F* critical value.

$$\Rightarrow \text{Reject } H_0 \text{ if } F > F_{r-1, \, n-r, \, \alpha}$$

Because we are comparing an *F* statistic value with an *F* critical value in the decision rule, we will refer to this test as an **F test**.

A general critical or rejection region for the *F* test is shown in **Figure 15-9**.

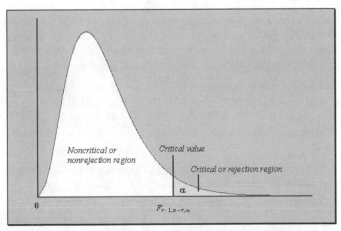

Figure 15-9: Diagram depicting the critical and noncritical regions for the *F* distribution

Note: If we use the *P*-value approach to hypothesis testing for the one-way ANOVA, we will reject H_0 if the *P*-value $< \alpha$.

Example 15-9: For the data given in **Example 15-1**, if an *F* test were conducted at the 5 percent significance level to determine whether there was a significant difference between the average numbers of pennies, nickels, dimes, and quarters, what would be the F critical value for the test?

Solution: From the information given, $r = 4$, $n = 34$, and $\alpha = 0.05$. Now, since the numerator degrees of freedom $= r - 1$, this value will be $4 - 1 = 3$. Also, since the denominator degrees of freedom $= n - r$, this value will be $34 - 4 = 30$. From the F table in the **Appendix** of this text, we have $F_{3, 30, 0.05} = 2.92$. Thus the F critical value for the test will be 2.92.

At this juncture we also may implement an appropriate form of technology to help with the solution of **Example 15-9** We apply the MINITAB software to help in finding the F critical value. We use the **Inverse Cumulative Distribution Function** feature for the F distribution in MINITAB to determine the F critical value. The result is shown in **Figure 15-10**. Observe that the value in the output matches the table value to two decimal places. To obtain this value with the MINITAB software, select the **CALC** menu, select **PROBABILITY DISTRIBUTIONS**, select F, and enter the appropriate entries in the dialog box. Note, that the input constant would be 0.95 ($= 1 - \alpha = 1 - 0.5$).

```
Inverse Cumulative Distribution Function

F distribution with 3 DF in numerator and 30 DF in denominator

P( X <= x )       x
      0.95   2.92228
```

Figure 15-10: MINITAB output with F critical value for Example 15-9

Example 15-10: For the data given in **Example 15-7**, if an F test were conducted for the one-way ANOVA at the 1 percent significance level to determine whether there was a significant difference between the average times for complete relief of the headache using the three drugs, what would be the F critical value for the test?

Solution: From the information given, $r = 3$, $n = 28$, and $\alpha = 0.01$. Now, since the numerator degrees of freedom $= r - 1$, this value will be $3 - 1 = 2$. Also, since the denominator degrees of freedom $= n - r$, this value will be $28 - 3 = 25$. From the F table in the **Appendix** of this text, we have $F_{2, 28, 0.01} = 5.45$. Thus the F critical value for the test will be 5.45.

The MINITAB solution is shown in **Figure 15-11**. Observe that the value in the output is equal to the table value to two decimal places.

```
Inverse Cumulative Distribution Function

F distribution with 2 DF in numerator and 28 DF in denominator

P( X <= x )        x
      0.99   5.45294
```

Figure 15-11: MINITAB output with F critical value for Example 15-10

15-5 One-Way or Single-Factor ANOVA Tests

So far in all the previous examples we had a single factor with different levels of the treatments. In this section we will present the F test for these single-factor experiments. We sometimes refer to this single-factor F test as **one-way ANOVA F test**.

Summary of the One-Way ANOVA Hypothesis F Test Using the Classical Approach

If the **classical** (or critical region) approach to hypothesis testing is used, then use the following steps to test for equality of r population means.

H_0: $\mu_1 = \mu_2 = \mu_3 = \cdots = \mu_r$

H_1: Not all the population means are equal.

T.S.:

$$F = \frac{\text{estimate of variance based on means from the } r \text{ sample}}{\text{estimate of variance based on all sample observations}}$$

D.R.: For a specified significance level α, reject the null hypothesis if the computed test statistic value F is greater than the critical value $F_{r-1, n-r, \alpha}$.

Conclusion:

Quick Tip

The F test is a right-tailed test.

Example 15-11: Perform a one-way ANOVA F test for the information given in **Example 15-1**. That is, test whether there is a significant difference in the population averages for the numbers of pennies, nickels, dimes, and quarters for the student population at that particular campus. Test at a significance level of 0.05, and use the classical approach to hypothesis testing.

Solution: As mentioned earlier, because of the complexity of the formulas for the F test, appropriate technology will be integrated into the solution of this problem. The MINITAB statistical software was used for the computations, and the output is shown in **Figure 15-12.**

Observe that the F-test statistic value from the output is 12.04. The numerator degrees of freedom are $r - 1 = 4 - 1 = 3$, and the denominator degrees of freedom are $n - r = 34 - 4 = 30$. Thus the F critical value obtained from the F table is $F_{3, 30, 0.05} = 2.92$.

Note: From the MINITAB output, the numerator degrees of freedom are the **Factor** degrees of freedom (DF), and the denominator degrees of freedom are the **Error** degrees of freedom.

Using the information from the output, as well as the information obtained from the tables, we can now present the hypothesis test:

H_0: $\mu_1 = \mu_2 = \mu_3 = \mu_4$

H_1: Not all the population means are equal.

T.S.: $F = 12.04$

D.R.: For a given significance level of 0.05, reject the null hypothesis if the computed test statistic value of $12.04 > F_{3, 30, 0.05} = 2.92$.

Conclusion: Since $12.04 > 2.92$, reject H_0. That is, at the 5 percent significance level, there is a significant difference between the population means for the four different denominations of coins.

```
One-way ANOVA: Pennies, Nickels, Dimes, Quarters

Source  DF       SS      MS      F      P
Factor   3   319.91  106.64  12.04  0.000
Error   30   265.65    8.86
Total   33   585.56

S = 2.976   R-Sq = 54.63%   R-Sq(adj) = 50.10%


                            Individual 95% CIs For Mean Based on
                            Pooled StDev
Level       N    Mean  StDev  ------+---------+---------+---------+---
Pennies    10  10.500  4.453                             (-----*-----)
Nickels     9   4.444  1.944      (-------*------)
Dimes       7   3.714  2.498   (------*-------)
Quarters    8   3.250  1.669  (------*------)
                              ------+---------+---------+---------+---
                                 3.0       6.0       9.0      12.0
```

Figure 15-12: MINITAB one-way ANOVA output for Example 15-1

Note: From the MINITAB output in **Figure 15-12**,

- The first part of the MINITAB output (i.e., excluding the confidence intervals) is usually referred to as the **one-way ANOVA table**. This involves information on the factor (between information) and the error (within information).

- The F-test statistic value of 12.04 is obtained by dividing 106.64 by 8.86 ($\equiv$ MS Factor/MS Error)

- The source due to **Factor** is the contribution from the between samples, that is, the contribution when comparing the variability for the four samples means. This is associated with the numerator in the test statistic F value.

- The source due to **Error** is the contribution from the within samples, that is, the contribution when comparing the variability for all the sample data. This is associated with the denominator in the test statistic F value.

Since the null hypothesis was rejected and we concluded that there is a significant difference between the population averages, then the question is: Which of the means are different from the others? We can use **multiple comparisons** to answer this question.

Multiple Comparisons

One way to visualize which population means are significantly different from the others is to compute the confidence intervals using the sample information. The MINITAB output in **Figure 15-12** shows plots of the 95 percent confidence intervals. Observe that the confidence intervals for the average numbers of nickels, dimes, and quarters all overlap. This would indicate that there is not a significant difference between these averages. On the other hand, the confidence interval for the average number of pennies does not overlap with any of the other confidence intervals. This would indicate that the average number of pennies is significantly different from the average numbers of nickels, dimes, and quarters. In particular, since the confidence interval for the average number of pennies is to the right of the other intervals, we can conclude that this population average is significantly greater than the other population means.

Generally, when performing a one-way ANOVA, you should follow the procedure depicted in **Figure 15-13**.

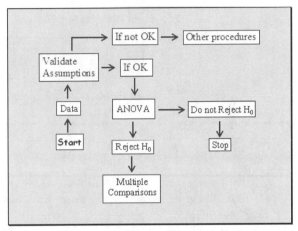

Figure 15-13: The ANOVA process

When the one-way ANOVA is analyzed using an appropriate statistical software, such as MINITAB, or if other appropriate technologies are used, one of the values usually computed is the *P*-value for the test. We can use this number to make a decision as to whether the null hypothesis should be rejected or not. Following is the *P*-value approach to the hypothesis test.

Using the *P*-Value Approach to a One-Way ANOVA Hypothesis Test

If we use the *P*-value approach to perform the test, then we can present the test for **Example 15-11** in the following manner.

H_0: $\mu_1 = \mu_2 = \mu_3 = \mu_4$

H_1: Not all the population means are equal.

T.S.: *P*-value = 0.00 (obtained from the MINITAB output in **Figure 15-12**).

D.R.: For a given significance level of 0.05, reject the null hypothesis if the computed *P*-value of 0.00 is less than the significance level of 0.05.

Conclusion: Since $0.00 < 0.05$, reject H_0. That is, at the 5 percent significance level, there is a significant difference between the population means for the four different denominations of coins.

Note: In the preceding test, the test statistic is the *P*-value not the *F* value. Hence we have the same conclusion.

Figure 15-14 depicts the rejection region.

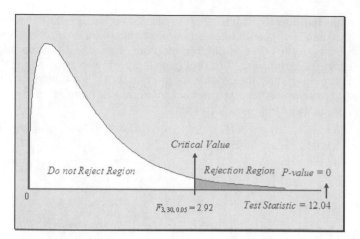

Figure 15-14: Diagram depicting the rejection region for Example 15-11

Quick Tips

- You need to first check the *F*-test assumptions before proceeding with the test.
- Severe deviations from the assumptions result in unreliable results.

Technology

Technology Corner

As illustrated in **Example 15-11**, the F test for one-way or one-factor ANOVA can be performed using the MINITAB software. There are a host of other statistical software tools that will perform the same test. Microsoft Excel has a Data Analysis option in the Tools menu that you can use to do one-way ANOVA. Some graphical calculators such as the TI-83/84 (all versions) will aid directly in computations for one-way ANOVA.

Illustration using the TI-83/84: Use the TI-83/84 to help with the computations for **Example 15-11**. Input the values for pennies, nickels, dimes, and quarters in lists **L1, L2, L3**, and **L4**, respectively. Select the **STAT** button, and choose **TESTS**. Scroll down to **F: ANOVA**, and press **ENTER**. Input the lists **L1, L2, L3**, and **L4**, and press **ENTER**. The **one-way ANOVA** computations will be displayed. You will need to scroll down to view all the output. The output is shown on two screens in **Figure 15-15**.

```
One-way ANOVA
 F=12.04242703
 p=2.4089811E-5
 Factor
  df=3
  SS=319.90803
↓ MS=106.63601
```

```
One-way ANOVA
↑ MS=106.63601
 Error
  df=30
  SS=265.650794
  MS=8.85502646
 Sxp=2.97573965
```

Figure 15-15: TI-83/84 one-way ANOVA output for Example 15-11

Observe that the *F*-test statistic value (12.04, to two decimal places) is the same as that produced in the MINITAB output in **Figure 15-12**. Also, the *P*-value produced by the TI-83/84 is given as $P = 2.4089811E-5 \approx 0.00002 \approx 0$, just as in the MINITAB output.

Validating the Assumptions for a One-Way ANOVA (Revisited)

When validating the one-way ANOVA assumptions in the preceding section, we used box plots to help check the constant-variance assumption, and we used histograms to help check the normality assumptions. Because of the computer and readily available statistical software, it is easy to check these assumptions. Following are two MINITAB outputs that we can analyze to help establish these assumptions.

Normality Assumption: We can use MINITAB (and other technologies as well) to present a **normality plot** for the data and observe the *P*-value for the normality test. The hypotheses to test whether or not a data set was selected from a normal distribution are as follows:

H_0: The distribution from which the sample was drawn is normally distributed.

H_1: The distribution from which the sample was drawn is not normally distributed.

Figure 15-16 shows the normality plot for the headache relief time for the **Drug 1** data of **Example 15-7**.

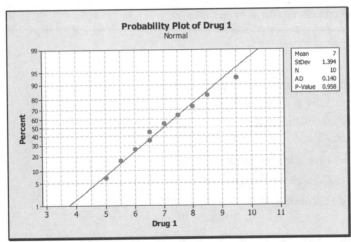

Figure 15-16: Normality plot and test for the headache relief time for **Drug 1** of Example 15-7

Observe that when the data reflect normality, they will follow a linear pattern, as displayed in the plot. Also observe that the *P*-value (0.958) for the normality test is very large, so *P*-values $< \alpha$ will not be true for any of the usual choices of a significance level. Thus one would not reject the null hypothesis of normality. We could analyze similarly for **Drug 2** and **Drug 3**.

Constant-Variance Assumption: Recall that in the ANOVA display shows 95 percent confidence intervals for the means. We can use MINITAB (or other appropriate technologies) similarly to construct confidence intervals for the standard deviations. **Figure 15-17** shows such a plot for **Example 15-7**. Also displayed are *P*-values for tests for equal variances.

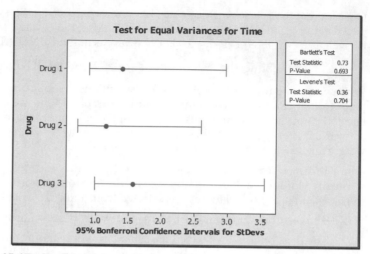

Figure 15-17: Confidence interval plots and constant variance tests for Example 15-7

Observe that the intervals overlap, and hence we can assume that the constant-variance assumption has not been violated. Also, the *P*-values (0.693 and 0.704) for equal variance are large, so *P*-values < α will not happen, which supports the overlapping confidence interval plots.

Analysis of variance concepts can be investigated through
✓ Graphical procedures
✓ *F* distribution
✓ *F* tests
✓ Multiple comparisons
✓ Confidence intervals
✓ Technology

Care always should be taken when doing the *F* test for the one-way analysis of variance. Caution should be relied on when the ANOVA assumptions have been violated.

True/False Questions
1. In a one-way ANOVA, the population variances are assumed to be equal.
2. The *F*-test for the one-way ANOVA procedure is always a right-tailed test.
3. In order to use the one-way ANOVA procedure, you must have more than three populations under consideration.
4. To have reliable results when using the one-way ANOVA procedure, the populations of interest must be normally distributed.
5. The one-way ANOVA procedure is a statistical procedure used to determine whether the means of three or more samples are equal.
6. The variable of interest in a one-way ANOVA procedure is called a level.

7. When performing a one-way ANOVA, the term **treatment** refers to the levels of a factor.
8. When performing a one-way ANOVA, the alternative hypothesis states that all the sample means are different.
9. If the response variable is weight loss and you are comparing the weight loss for three different diets, this would be an example of a three-way ANOVA.
10. The sampling distribution for the test statistic in a one-way ANOVA is the F distribution.
11. When performing a one-way ANOVA, all the sample sizes must be equal.
12. We can use the one-way ANOVA to test for the equality of several population proportions.

Completion Questions

1. If we were comparing the weight loss of six different fabrics using a one-way ANOVA procedure, the factor here would be _____.
2. If we were comparing the weight loss of five different diets using a one-way ANOVA procedure, then this problem has one (factor, level) _____ and five different (factors, levels) _____.
3. When a one-way ANOVA procedure is used, the population variances are assumed to be (equal, approximately equal, not equal) _____ to each other.
4. One assumption for the one-way ANOVA is that the samples are (independent of, dependent on) _____ each other.
5. In a one-way ANOVA, the term **treatment** refers to different (factors, levels) _____ for the experiment.
6. When performing a one-way ANOVA, the alternative hypothesis states that (all, none, not all) _____ of the population means are equal to each other.
7. The variable of interest in a one-way ANOVA procedure is called a (response, level, factor) _____ variable.
8. The one-way ANOVA procedure is a statistical procedure used to determine whether we can reject the null hypothesis of (equal, not equal) _____ population means.
9. In a one-way ANOVA, if the sample means differ significantly from each other, then the (between sample means, within sample) _____ variability will be large.
10. In a one-way ANOVA, the entity on which a response variable is measured is called the (experimental unit, level, factor) _____.

Multiple-Choice Questions

1. One-way ANOVA techniques are used to perform hypothesis tests for means when
   (a) there are exactly two populations.
   (b) there are at least two populations.
   (c) there are more than three populations.
   (d) there are at least three populations.
2. One-way ANOVA techniques are usually used to test
   (a) for the equality of two or more population variances.
   (b) a single population variance.

(c) for the equality of two or more population means.

(d) for the equality of three or more population means.

3. In using ANOVA,

(a) it is possible to determine exactly which population means differ from the others.

(b) it is assumed that the population distributions are not normal.

(c) it is assumed that the population variances are unknown but unequal.

(d) it is assumed that the samples are independent.

4. Which of the following is not true when applying one-factor ANOVA techniques?

(a) The population variances are not equal to each other

(b) The populations are normally distributed

(c) The selected samples are independent

(d) The sample sizes do not have to be equal to each other

5. In a one-factor ANOVA experiment, the independent variables are also called the

(a) factors of the experiment.

(b) treatments of the experiment.

(c) levels of the experiment.

(d) errors of the experiment.

6. Which of the following is true when applying one-factor ANOVA technique?

(a) It involves a one-tailed test

(b) The degrees of freedom equal the number of levels

(c) The between-samples sum of squares always will equal the within-samples sum of squares

(d) The variances of the populations are assumed to be different from each other

7. If there are five levels in a one-factor ANOVA, which of the following is the most appropriate alternative hypothesis?

(a) $H_1: \mu_1 = \mu_2 = \mu_3 = \mu_4 = \mu_5$.

(b) H_1: Not all the population means are equal.

(c) H_1: All the population means are different.

(d) $H_1: \mu_1 \neq \mu_2 \neq \mu_3 \neq \mu_4 \neq \mu_5$.

8. If there are five levels in a one-factor ANOVA and the null hypothesis is rejected, then the most appropriate conclusion will be that

(a) all five sample means are significantly different.

(b) at least four of the sample means are significantly different.

(c) not all the population means are equal.

(d) all five population means are equal.

9. The independent variable of interest in a one-factor ANOVA procedure is called

(a) a level.

(b) a factor.

(c) a treatment.

(d) an experimental unit.

10. The sampling distribution of the test statistic for a one-factor ANOVA is the

(a) normal distribution.

(b) t distribution.

(c) χ^2 distribution.

(d) F distribution.

11. If a one-factor ANOVA is carried out on five levels of the factor with eight observations per level, the degrees of freedom (numerator, denominator) for the distribution of the F-test statistic are

    (a) $(5, 40)$.

    (b) $(5, 8)$.

    (c) $(4, 40)$.

    (d) $(4, 35)$.

Use the following information to solve Problems 12 to 18:

The summary for a one-factor ANOVA is given below:

	SUM OF SQUARES	DEGREES OF FREEDOM	MEAN SQUARE	F RATIO
Between samples (factor)	800	3	266.6667	2
Within samples (combined samples)	1,600	12	133.3333	
Total	2,400	15		

12. How many levels are there for the factor?

    (a) 3

    (b) 4

    (c) 2

    (d) 15

13. How many values of the response variable are there for each level if it is assumed that each level of the factor has equal sample size?

    (a) 3

    (b) 5

    (c) 12

    (d) 4

14. A possible null hypothesis for this table is

    (a) $H_0: \mu_1 \neq \mu_2 = \mu_3 = \mu_4$.

    (b) $H_0: \mu_1 = \mu_2 = \mu_3 = \mu_4$.

    (c) $H_0: \mu_1 = \mu_2 = \mu_3$.

    (d) $H_0: \mu_1 \neq \mu_2 \neq \mu_3 \neq \mu_4$.

15. The test statistic value for this table is

    (a) 266.67.

    (b) 133.33.

    (c) 2.

    (d) 3.

16. The degrees of freedom (numerator, denominator) for the distribution of the F-test statistic are

    (a) $(3, 12)$.

    (b) $(3, 15)$.

(c) (12,15).

(d) (4, 12).

17. If you are to test at the 5 percent level of significance for equality of means, then the critical F value for the test is

(a) 2.

(b) 3.47.

(c) 8.74.

(d) 5.95.

18. If you are to test at the 5 percent level of significance for equality of means, your decision will be

(a) fail to reject the null hypothesis.

(b) reject the alternative hypothesis.

(c) fail to reject the alternative hypothesis.

(d) reject the null hypothesis.

The following information relates to Questions 19 through 30:

A farmer is testing the effects of four different fertilizers on the yields of a certain variety of tomato plants. The four fertilizers are applied to each of five different tomato plants, and the numbers of tomatoes produced by each plant are recorded. **Table 15-3** gives the actual data, and **Figure 15-18** shows the MINITAB output that gives the results of the one-way ANOVA analysis.

Table 15-3: Data for Problems 19 through 30

FERTILIZER A	FERTILIZER B	FERTILIZER C	FERTILIZER D
33	26	31	29
29	22	36	34
37	16	42	30
39	17	34	31
35	20	30	34

```
One-way ANOVA: Fertilizer A, Fertilizer B, Fertilizer C, Fertilizer D

 Source  DF    SS     MS      F      P
 Factor   3  703.4  234.5  15.87  0.000
 Error   16  236.4   14.8
 Total   19  939.8

 S = 3.844   R-Sq = 74.84%   R-Sq(adj) = 70.13%

                                Individual 95% CIs For Mean Based on
                                Pooled StDev
 Level         N    Mean  StDev  --+---------+---------+---------+------
 Fertilizer A  5  34.600  3.847                        (-----*-----)
 Fertilizer B  5  20.200  4.025  (-----*-----)
 Fertilizer C  5  34.600  4.775                        (-----*-----)
 Fertilizer D  5  31.600  2.302                   (-----*-----)
                                 --+---------+---------+---------+------
                                 18.0      24.0      30.0      36.0

 Pooled StDev = 3.844
```

Figure 15-18: MINITAB output for Problems 19 through 30

19. In the one-way ANOVA described for the fertilizers and tomato plants, what are the assumptions for the experiment?
    (a) The samples of tomato yields are random and independent within and between for the different fertilizers.
    (b) The sampling populations for the tomato yields are assumed to be normally distributed.
    (c) The variances for the populations for the tomato yields are assumed to be equal.
    (d) All the above.

20. The following box plots are for the yields for **Fertilizers A, B, C**, and **D**. Can you conclude, based on the plots, that the constant-variance assumption for the sampling populations has been severely violated?

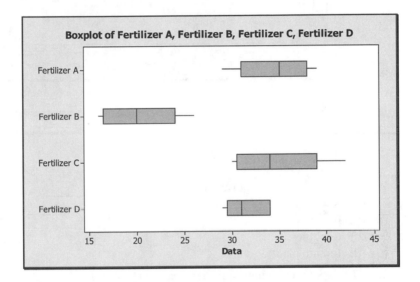

    (a) Yes
    (b) No
    (c) Maybe
    (d) None of the above

21. The following normal probability plot is for the yields for **Fertilizer A**. Can you conclude, based on the plot and the *P*-value, that the normality assumption for the sampling population for **Fertilizer A** has been severely violated? The *P*-value in the output is for the following test of normality:

    H_0: The distribution of the population from which the sample for **Fertilizer A** was selected **is** normally distributed.

    H_1: The distribution of the population from which the sample for **Fertilizer A** was selected **is not** normally distributed.

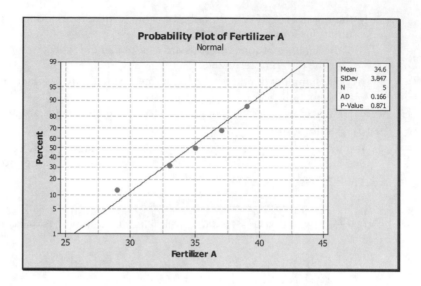

(a) Yes

(b) No

(c) Maybe

(d) None of the above

22. The factor for this experiment is (are)

(a) the farmer.

(b) fertilizer.

(c) tomatoes.

(d) tomato plants.

23. The experimental unit(s) for this experiment is (are)

(a) the farmer.

(b) fertilizers.

(c) tomatoes.

(d) tomato plants.

24. The factor for this experiment is (are)

(a) the farmer.

(b) fertilizer.

(c) tomatoes.

(d) tomato plants.

25. If you were testing for equality of mean tomato yield, then the computed test statistic value would be (refer to the MINITAB output)

(a) 14.80.

(b) 15.87.

(c) 234.3.

(d) 12.32.

26. If you were testing for equality of average tomato yield, the degrees of freedom (numerator, denominator) for the distribution of the test statistic would be (refer to the MINITAB output)
    (a) $(16, 3)$.
    (b) $(3, 19)$.
    (c) $(3, 16)$.
    (d) $(16, 19)$.

27. If you were testing at the 5 percent level of significance for the equality of average tomato yield, the critical value for the test would be
    (a) 3.24.
    (b) 8.70.
    (c) 2.23.
    (d) 3.13.

28. If you were testing at the 5 percent level of significance for the equality of average tomato yield, the rejection region would be
    (a) $F > 3.13$.
    (b) $F > 8.70$.
    (c) $F > 2.23$.
    (d) $F > 3.24$.

29. If you were testing at the 5 percent level of significance for equality of average tomato yield, your decision would be
    (a) fail to reject the null hypothesis of equality of means.
    (b) reject the alternative hypothesis of at least two means is different.
    (c) fail to reject the alternative hypothesis of at least two means is different.
    (d) reject the null hypothesis of equality of means.

30. Based on the MINITAB output, one can conclude that
    (a) the average tomato yield using **Fertilizer A** is significantly different from the average yield using **Fertilizers C** and **D**.
    (b) the average tomato yield using **Fertilizer B** is significantly different from the average yield using **Fertilizers A, C**, and **D**.
    (c) the average tomato yield using **Fertilizer C** is significantly different from the average yield using **Fertilizers A** and **D**.
    (d) the average tomato yield using **Fertilizer D** is significantly different from the average yield using **Fertilizers A** and **C**.

The following information relates to Questions 31 through 42:

A statistics instructor wishes to determine whether there is any difference in the three methods (1, 2, or 3) of teaching an elementary statistics course with regard to the final averages. Students in three different sections of the course were taught using one of the methods. Assuming that all other variables remain fixed (e.g., common exams etc.), a preliminary sample of the overall course averages from the three sections is given in **Table 15-4**. The table gives the actual data, and **Figure 15-19** shows the MINITAB output that gives the results of the one-way ANOVA analysis.

Table 15-4: Data for Problems 31 through 42

METHOD 1	METHOD 2	METHOD 3
80	71	68
92	81	76
87	79	70
84	73	72

```
One-way ANOVA: Method 1, Method 2, Method 3

Source    DF    SS     MS      F      P
Factor     2   424.5  212.3  10.63  0.004
Error      9   179.8   20.0
Total     11   604.3


S = 4.469   R-Sq = 70.25%   R-Sq(adj) = 63.64%


                                  Individual 95% CIs For Mean Based on
                                  Pooled StDev
Level      N    Mean   StDev   -----+---------+---------+---------+----
Method 1   4   85.750  5.058                       (------*-------)
Method 2   4   76.000  4.761        (-------*------)
Method 3   4   71.500  3.416   (------*------)
                                  -----+---------+---------+---------+----
                                    70.0      77.0      84.0      91.0

Pooled StDev = 4.469
```

Figure 15-19: MINITAB output for Problems 31 through 42

31. The following are confidence interval plots for the standard deviations for the data for **Methods 1, 2,** and **3** and *P*-values for equal-variance tests. The equal-variance tests (Bartlett's and Levene's) test the null hypothesis $H_0: \sigma^2_1 = \sigma^2_2 = \sigma^2_3$ against the alternative of H_1: Not all the population variances are the same. Can you conclude, based on the plots and the *P*-values for the tests, that the constant-variance assumption for the sampling populations has been severely violated?

(a) Yes
(b) No
(c) Maybe
(d) None of the above

32. The following normal probability plot is for the data for **Method 3**. Can you conclude, based on the plot and the P-value, that the normality assumption for the sampling population for **Method 3** has been severely violated? The P-value in the output is for the following test of normality:

H_0: The distribution of the population from which the sample for **Method 3** was selected **is** normally distributed.

H_1: The distribution of the population from which the sample for **Method 3** was selected **is not** normally distributed.

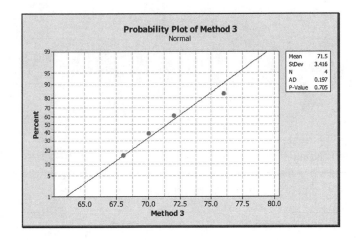

(a) Yes
(b) No
(c) Maybe
(d) None of the above

33. The factor for this experiment is
    (a) teaching method.
    (b) methods 1, 2, and 3.
    (c) students in this elementary statistics course.
    (d) overall average.

34. The following box plots are for the data for **Methods 1, 2**, and **3**. Can you conclude, based on the plots, that the constant-variance assumption for the sampling populations has been severely violated?

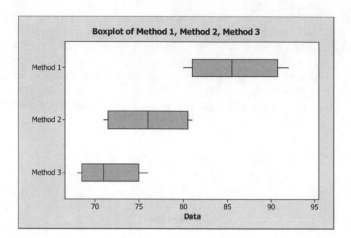

(a) Yes

(b) No

(c) Maybe

(d) None of the above

35. The single-factor degrees of freedom (degrees of freedom for the numerator in the F-test statistic (or the between degrees of freedom) are

(a) 2.

(b) 9.

(c) 3.

(d) 4.

36. The degrees of freedom for the denominator in the F-test statistic (or the within degrees of freedom) are

(a) 2.

(b) 9.

(c) 11.

(d) 3.

37. If you were using a one-way ANOVA to test for the equality of the means for the three different methods, the computed test statistic would be

(a) 179.8.

(b) 20.00.

(c) 10.63.

(d) 54.93.

38. The degrees of freedom (numerator, denominator) for the distribution of the test statistic are

(a) (9, 11).

(b) (11, 9).

(c) (2, 11).

(d) (2, 9).

39. If you were testing at the 1 percent level of significance for the equality of the means for the different methods, the rejection region would be

(a) $F > 7.21$.
(b) $F > 4.63$.
(c) $F > 8.02$.
(d) $F > 5.11$.

40. If you were testing at the 1 percent level of significance for the equality of the means for the different methods, your decision would be
   (a) fail to reject the null hypothesis of equality of means.
   (b) reject the alternative hypothesis of at least two of the means being different.
   (c) fail to reject the alternative hypothesis of at least two of the means being different.
   (d) reject the null hypothesis of equality of means.

41. Based on the MINITAB output, one can conclude that
   (a) the final average using **Method 1** is significantly different from the final averages using **Methods 2** and **3**.
   (b) the final average using **Method 2** is significantly different from the final averages using **Methods 1** and **3**.
   (c) the final average using **Method 3** is significantly different from the final averages using **Methods 1** and **2**.
   (d) the final average using **Method 1** is significantly different from the final average using **Method 3**.

42. If you were testing at the 1 percent level of significance for the equality of the means for the different methods and the *P*-value approach is used, your decision would be
   (a) fail to reject the null hypothesis of equality of means.
   (b) reject the alternative hypothesis of at least two of the means being different.
   (c) fail to reject the alternative hypothesis of at least two of the means being different.
   (d) reject the null hypothesis of equality of means.

ANSWER KEY

True/False Questions

1. T   2. T   3. F   4. T   5. F   6. F   7. T   8. F   9. F   10. T   11. F   12. F

Completion Questions

1. fabric   2. factor, levels   3. equal   4. independent of   5. levels   6. not all
7. response   8. equal   9. between sample means   10. experimental unit

Multiple-Choice Questions

1. (d)   2. (d)   3. (d)   4. (a)   5. (a)   6. (a)   7. (b)   8. (c)   9. (b)
10. (d)   11. (d)   12. (b)   13. (d)   14. (b)   15. (c)   16. (a)   17. (b)   18. (a)
19. (d)   20. (b)   21. (b)   22. (b)   23. (d)   24. (b)   25. (b)   26. (c)   27. (a)
28. (d)   29. (d)   30. (b)   31. (b)   32. (b)   33. (a)   34. (b)   35. (a)   36. (b)
37. (c)   38. (d)   39. (c)   40. (d)   41. (d)   42. (d)

Appendix

✓ Table 1–The Binomial Distribution
✓ Table 2–The Standard Normal Distribution
✓ Table 3–The *t* Distribution
✓ Table 4–Critical Values for the Chi-square Distribution
✓ Table 5–Critical Values of the *F* Distribution

Table 1–The Binomial Distribution

		p										
n	x	0.05	0.1	0.2	0.3	0.4	0.5	0.6	0.7	0.8	0.9	0.95
2	0	0.9025	0.81	0.64	0.49	0.36	0.25	0.16	0.09	0.04	0.01	0.002
	1	0.0950	0.18	0.32	0.42	0.48	0.50	0.48	0.42	0.32	0.18	0.095
	2	0.0025	0.01	0.04	0.09	0.16	0.25	0.36	0.49	0.64	0.81	0.902
3	0	0.857	0.729	0.512	0.343	0.216	0.125	0.064	0.027	0.008	0.001	0.000
	1	0.135	0.243	0.384	0.441	0.432	0.375	0.288	0.189	0.096	0.027	0.007
	2	0.007	0.027	0.096	0.189	0.288	0.375	0.432	0.441	0.384	0.243	0.135
	3	0.000	0.001	0.008	0.027	0.064	0.125	0.216	0.343	0.512	0.729	0.857
4	0	0.815	0.656	0.410	0.240	0.130	0.063	0.026	0.008	0.002	0.000	0.000
	1	0.171	0.292	0.410	0.412	0.346	0.250	0.154	0.076	0.026	0.004	0.000
	2	0.014	0.049	0.154	0.265	0.346	0.375	0.346	0.265	0.154	0.049	0.014
	3	0.000	0.004	0.026	0.076	0.154	0.250	0.346	0.412	0.410	0.292	0.171
	4	0.000	0.000	0.002	0.008	0.026	0.063	0.130	0.240	0.410	0.656	0.815

399

Table 1 *(continued)*–**The Binomial Distribution**

							p					
n	*x*	0.05	0.1	0.2	0.3	0.4	0.5	0.6	0.7	0.8	0.9	0.95
5	0	0.774	0.590	0.328	0.168	0.078	0.031	0.010	0.002	0.000	0.000	0.000
	1	0.204	0.328	0.410	0.360	0.259	0.156	0.077	0.028	0.006	0.000	0.000
	2	0.021	0.073	0.205	0.309	0.346	0.313	0.230	0.132	0.051	0.008	0.001
	3	0.001	0.008	0.051	0.132	0.230	0.313	0.346	0.309	0.205	0.073	0.021
	4	0.000	0.000	0.006	0.028	0.077	0.156	0.259	0.360	0.410	0.328	0.204
	5	0.000	0.000	0.000	0.002	0.010	0.031	0.078	0.168	0.328	0.590	0.774
6	0	0.735	0.531	0.262	0.118	0.047	0.016	0.004	0.001	0.000	0.000	0.000
	1	0.232	0.354	0.393	0.303	0.187	0.094	0.037	0.010	0.002	0.000	0.000
	2	0.031	0.098	0.246	0.324	0.311	0.234	0.138	0.060	0.015	0.001	0.000
	3	0.002	0.015	0.082	0.185	0.276	0.313	0.276	0.185	0.082	0.015	0.002
	4	0.000	0.001	0.015	0.060	0.138	0.234	0.311	0.324	0.246	0.098	0.031
	5	0.000	0.000	0.002	0.010	0.037	0.094	0.187	0.303	0.393	0.354	0.232
	6	0.000	0.000	0.000	0.001	0.004	0.016	0.047	0.118	0.262	0.531	0.735
7	0	0.698	0.478	0.210	0.082	0.028	0.008	0.002	0.000	0.000	0.000	0.000
	1	0.257	0.372	0.367	0.247	0.131	0.055	0.017	0.004	0.000	0.000	0.000
	2	0.041	0.124	0.275	0.318	0.261	0.164	0.077	0.025	0.004	0.000	0.000
	3	0.004	0.023	0.115	0.227	0.290	0.273	0.194	0.097	0.029	0.003	0.000
	4	0.000	0.003	0.029	0.097	0.194	0.273	0.290	0.227	0.115	0.023	0.004
	5	0.000	0.000	0.004	0.025	0.077	0.164	0.261	0.318	0.275	0.124	0.041
	6	0.000	0.000	0.000	0.004	0.017	0.055	0.131	0.247	0.367	0.372	0.257
	7	0.000	0.000	0.000	0.000	0.002	0.008	0.028	0.082	0.210	0.478	0.698
8	0	0.663	0.430	0.168	0.058	0.017	0.004	0.001	0.000	0.000	0.000	0.000
	1	0.279	0.383	0.336	0.198	0.090	0.031	0.008	0.001	0.000	0.000	0.000
	2	0.051	0.149	0.294	0.296	0.209	0.109	0.041	0.010	0.001	0.000	0.000
	3	0.005	0.033	0.147	0.254	0.279	0.219	0.124	0.047	0.009	0.000	0.000
	4	0.000	0.005	0.046	0.136	0.232	0.273	0.232	0.136	0.046	0.005	0.000
	5	0.000	0.000	0.009	0.047	0.124	0.219	0.279	0.254	0.147	0.033	0.005
	6	0.000	0.000	0.001	0.010	0.041	0.109	0.209	0.296	0.294	0.149	0.051
	7	0.000	0.000	0.000	0.001	0.008	0.031	0.090	0.198	0.336	0.383	0.279
	8	0.000	0.000	0.000	0.000	0.001	0.004	0.017	0.058	0.168	0.430	0.663
9	0	0.630	0.387	0.134	0.040	0.010	0.002	0.000	0.000	0.000	0.000	0.000
	1	0.299	0.387	0.302	0.156	0.060	0.018	0.004	0.000	0.000	0.000	0.000
	2	0.063	0.172	0.302	0.267	0.161	0.070	0.021	0.004	0.000	0.000	0.000
	3	0.008	0.045	0.176	0.267	0.251	0.164	0.074	0.021	0.003	0.000	0.000
	4	0.001	0.007	0.066	0.172	0.251	0.246	0.167	0.074	0.017	0.001	0.000
	5	0.000	0.001	0.017	0.074	0.167	0.246	0.251	0.172	0.066	0.007	0.001
	6	0.000	0.000	0.003	0.021	0.074	0.164	0.251	0.267	0.176	0.045	0.008
	7	0.000	0.000	0.000	0.004	0.021	0.070	0.161	0.267	0.302	0.172	0.063
	8	0.000	0.000	0.000	0.000	0.004	0.018	0.060	0.156	0.302	0.387	0.299
	9	0.000	0.000	0.000	0.000	0.000	0.002	0.010	0.040	0.134	0.387	0.630

						p						
n	*x*	0.05	0.1	0.2	0.3	0.4	0.5	0.6	0.7	0.8	0.9	0.95
10	0	0.599	0.349	0.107	0.028	0.006	0.001	0.000	0.000	0.000	0.000	0.000
	1	0.315	0.387	0.268	0.121	0.040	0.010	0.002	0.000	0.000	0.000	0.000
	2	0.075	0.194	0.302	0.233	0.121	0.044	0.011	0.001	0.000	0.000	0.000
	3	0.010	0.057	0.201	0.267	0.215	0.117	0.042	0.009	0.001	0.000	0.000
	4	0.001	0.011	0.088	0.200	0.251	0.205	0.111	0.037	0.006	0.000	0.000
	5	0.000	0.001	0.026	0.103	0.201	0.246	0.201	0.103	0.026	0.001	0.000
	6	0.000	0.000	0.006	0.037	0.111	0.205	0.251	0.200	0.088	0.011	0.001
	7	0.000	0.000	0.001	0.009	0.042	0.117	0.215	0.267	0.201	0.057	0.010
	8	0.000	0.000	0.000	0.001	0.011	0.044	0.121	0.233	0.302	0.194	0.075
	9	0.000	0.000	0.000	0.000	0.002	0.010	0.040	0.121	0.268	0.387	0.315
	10	0.000	0.000	0.000	0.000	0.000	0.001	0.006	0.028	0.107	0.349	0.599
11	0	0.569	0.314	0.086	0.020	0.004	0.000	0.000	0.000	0.000	0.000	0.000
	1	0.329	0.384	0.236	0.093	0.027	0.005	0.001	0.000	0.000	0.000	0.000
	2	0.087	0.213	0.295	0.200	0.089	0.027	0.005	0.001	0.000	0.000	0.000
	3	0.014	0.071	0.221	0.257	0.177	0.081	0.023	0.004	0.000	0.000	0.000
	4	0.001	0.016	0.111	0.220	0.236	0.161	0.070	0.017	0.002	0.000	0.000
	5	0.000	0.002	0.039	0.132	0.221	0.226	0.147	0.057	0.010	0.000	0.000
	6	0.000	0.000	0.010	0.057	0.147	0.226	0.221	0.132	0.039	0.002	0.000
	7	0.000	0.000	0.002	0.017	0.070	0.161	0.236	0.220	0.111	0.016	0.001
	8	0.000	0.000	0.000	0.004	0.023	0.081	0.177	0.257	0.221	0.071	0.014
	9	0.000	0.000	0.000	0.001	0.005	0.027	0.089	0.200	0.295	0.213	0.087
	10	0.000	0.000	0.000	0.000	0.001	0.005	0.027	0.093	0.236	0.384	0.329
	11	0.000	0.000	0.000	0.000	0.000	0.000	0.004	0.020	0.086	0.314	0.569
12	0	0.540	0.282	0.069	0.014	0.002	0.000	0.000	0.000	0.000	0.000	0.000
	1	0.341	0.377	0.206	0.071	0.017	0.003	0.000	0.000	0.000	0.000	0.000
	2	0.099	0.230	0.283	0.168	0.064	0.016	0.002	0.000	0.000	0.000	0.000
	3	0.017	0.085	0.236	0.240	0.142	0.054	0.012	0.001	0.000	0.000	0.000
	4	0.002	0.021	0.133	0.231	0.213	0.121	0.042	0.008	0.001	0.000	0.000
	5	0.000	0.004	0.053	0.158	0.227	0.193	0.101	0.029	0.003	0.000	0.000
	6	0.000	0.000	0.016	0.079	0.177	0.226	0.177	0.079	0.016	0.000	0.000
	7	0.000	0.000	0.003	0.029	0.101	0.193	0.227	0.158	0.053	0.004	0.000
	8	0.000	0.000	0.001	0.008	0.042	0.121	0.213	0.231	0.133	0.021	0.002
	9	0.000	0.000	0.000	0.001	0.012	0.054	0.142	0.240	0.236	0.085	0.017
	10	0.000	0.000	0.000	0.000	0.002	0.016	0.064	0.168	0.283	0.230	0.099
	11	0.000	0.000	0.000	0.000	0.000	0.003	0.017	0.071	0.206	0.377	0.341
	12	0.000	0.000	0.000	0.000	0.000	0.000	0.002	0.014	0.069	0.282	0.540
13	0	0.513	0.254	0.055	0.010	0.001	0.000	0.000	0.000	0.000	0.000	0.000
	1	0.351	0.367	0.179	0.054	0.011	0.002	0.000	0.000	0.000	0.000	0.000
	2	0.111	0.245	0.268	0.139	0.045	0.010	0.001	0.000	0.000	0.000	0.000
	3	0.021	0.100	0.246	0.218	0.111	0.035	0.006	0.001	0.000	0.000	0.000
	4	0.003	0.028	0.154	0.234	0.184	0.087	0.024	0.003	0.000	0.000	0.000
	5	0.000	0.006	0.069	0.180	0.221	0.157	0.066	0.014	0.001	0.000	0.000

Table 1 *(continued)*–**The Binomial Distribution**

							p					
n	*x*	**0.05**	**0.1**	**0.2**	**0.3**	**0.4**	**0.5**	**0.6**	**0.7**	**0.8**	**0.9**	**0.95**
	6	0.000	0.001	0.023	0.103	0.197	0.209	0.131	0.044	0.006	0.000	0.000
	7	0.000	0.000	0.006	0.044	0.131	0.209	0.197	0.103	0.023	0.001	0.000
	8	0.000	0.000	0.001	0.014	0.066	0.157	0.221	0.180	0.069	0.006	0.000
	9	0.000	0.000	0.000	0.003	0.024	0.087	0.184	0.234	0.154	0.028	0.003
	10	0.000	0.000	0.000	0.001	0.006	0.035	0.111	0.218	0.246	0.100	0.021
	11	0.000	0.000	0.000	0.000	0.001	0.010	0.045	0.139	0.268	0.245	0.111
	12	0.000	0.000	0.000	0.000	0.000	0.002	0.011	0.054	0.179	0.367	0.351
	13	0.000	0.000	0.000	0.000	0.000	0.000	0.001	0.010	0.055	0.254	0.513
14	0	0.488	0.229	0.044	0.007	0.001	0.000	0.000	0.000	0.000	0.000	0.000
	1	0.359	0.356	0.154	0.041	0.007	0.001	0.000	0.000	0.000	0.000	0.000
	2	0.123	0.257	0.250	0.113	0.032	0.006	0.001	0.000	0.000	0.000	0.000
	3	0.026	0.114	0.250	0.194	0.085	0.022	0.003	0.000	0.000	0.000	0.000
	4	0.004	0.035	0.172	0.229	0.155	0.061	0.014	0.001	0.000	0.000	0.000
	5	0.000	0.008	0.086	0.196	0.207	0.122	0.041	0.007	0.000	0.000	0.000
	6	0.000	0.001	0.032	0.126	0.207	0.183	0.092	0.023	0.002	0.000	0.000
	7	0.000	0.000	0.009	0.062	0.157	0.209	0.157	0.062	0.009	0.000	0.000
	8	0.000	0.000	0.002	0.023	0.092	0.183	0.207	0.126	0.032	0.001	0.000
	9	0.000	0.000	0.000	0.007	0.041	0.122	0.207	0.196	0.086	0.008	0.000
	10	0.000	0.000	0.000	0.001	0.014	0.061	0.155	0.229	0.172	0.035	0.004
	11	0.000	0.000	0.000	0.000	0.003	0.022	0.085	0.194	0.250	0.114	0.026
	12	0.000	0.000	0.000	0.000	0.001	0.006	0.032	0.113	0.250	0.257	0.123
	13	0.000	0.000	0.000	0.000	0.000	0.001	0.007	0.041	0.154	0.356	0.359
	14	0.000	0.000	0.000	0.000	0.000	0.000	0.001	0.007	0.044	0.229	0.488
15	0	0.463	0.206	0.035	0.005	0.000	0.000	0.000	0.000	0.000	0.000	0.000
	1	0.366	0.343	0.132	0.031	0.005	0.000	0.000	0.000	0.000	0.000	0.000
	2	0.135	0.267	0.231	0.092	0.022	0.003	0.000	0.000	0.000	0.000	0.000
	3	0.031	0.129	0.250	0.170	0.063	0.014	0.002	0.000	0.000	0.000	0.000
	4	0.005	0.043	0.188	0.219	0.127	0.042	0.007	0.001	0.000	0.000	0.000
	5	0.001	0.010	0.103	0.206	0.186	0.092	0.024	0.003	0.000	0.000	0.000
	6	0.000	0.002	0.043	0.147	0.207	0.153	0.061	0.012	0.001	0.000	0.000
	7	0.000	0.000	0.014	0.081	0.177	0.196	0.118	0.035	0.003	0.000	0.000
	8	0.000	0.000	0.003	0.035	0.118	0.196	0.177	0.081	0.014	0.000	0.000
	9	0.000	0.000	0.001	0.012	0.061	0.153	0.207	0.147	0.043	0.002	0.000
	10	0.000	0.000	0.000	0.003	0.024	0.092	0.186	0.206	0.103	0.010	0.001
	11	0.000	0.000	0.000	0.001	0.007	0.042	0.127	0.219	0.188	0.043	0.005
	12	0.000	0.000	0.000	0.000	0.002	0.014	0.063	0.170	0.250	0.129	0.031
	13	0.000	0.000	0.000	0.000	0.000	0.003	0.022	0.092	0.231	0.267	0.135
	14	0.000	0.000	0.000	0.000	0.000	0.000	0.005	0.031	0.132	0.343	0.366
	15	0.000	0.000	0.000	0.000	0.000	0.000	0.000	0.005	0.035	0.206	0.463
16	0	0.440	0.185	0.028	0.003	0.000	0.000	0.000	0.000	0.000	0.000	0.000
	1	0.371	0.329	0.113	0.023	0.003	0.000	0.000	0.000	0.000	0.000	0.000
	2	0.146	0.275	0.211	0.073	0.015	0.002	0.000	0.000	0.000	0.000	0.000
	3	0.036	0.142	0.246	0.146	0.047	0.009	0.001	0.000	0.000	0.000	0.000
	4	0.006	0.051	0.200	0.204	0.101	0.028	0.004	0.000	0.000	0.000	0.000
	5	0.001	0.014	0.120	0.210	0.162	0.067	0.014	0.001	0.000	0.000	0.000

n	x	0.05	0.1	0.2	0.3	0.4	0.5	0.6	0.7	0.8	0.9	0.95
	6	0.000	0.003	0.055	0.165	0.198	0.122	0.039	0.006	0.000	0.000	0.000
	7	0.000	0.000	0.020	0.101	0.189	0.175	0.084	0.019	0.001	0.000	0.000
	8	0.000	0.000	0.006	0.049	0.142	0.196	0.142	0.049	0.006	0.000	0.000
	9	0.000	0.000	0.001	0.019	0.084	0.175	0.189	0.101	0.020	0.000	0.000
	10	0.000	0.000	0.000	0.006	0.039	0.122	0.198	0.165	0.055	0.003	0.000
	11	0.000	0.000	0.000	0.001	0.014	0.067	0.162	0.210	0.120	0.014	0.001
	12	0.000	0.000	0.000	0.000	0.004	0.028	0.101	0.204	0.200	0.051	0.006
	13	0.000	0.000	0.000	0.000	0.001	0.009	0.047	0.146	0.246	0.142	0.036
	14	0.000	0.000	0.000	0.000	0.000	0.002	0.015	0.073	0.211	0.275	0.146
	15	0.000	0.000	0.000	0.000	0.000	0.000	0.003	0.023	0.113	0.329	0.371
	16	0.000	0.000	0.000	0.000	0.000	0.000	0.000	0.003	0.028	0.185	0.440
17	0	0.418	0.167	0.023	0.002	0.000	0.000	0.000	0.000	0.000	0.000	0.000
	1	0.374	0.315	0.096	0.017	0.002	0.000	0.000	0.000	0.000	0.000	0.000
	2	0.158	0.280	0.191	0.058	0.010	0.001	0.000	0.000	0.000	0.000	0.000
	3	0.041	0.156	0.239	0.125	0.034	0.005	0.000	0.000	0.000	0.000	0.000
	4	0.008	0.060	0.209	0.187	0.080	0.018	0.002	0.000	0.000	0.000	0.000
	5	0.001	0.017	0.136	0.208	0.138	0.047	0.008	0.001	0.000	0.000	0.000
	6	0.000	0.004	0.068	0.178	0.184	0.094	0.024	0.003	0.000	0.000	0.000
	7	0.000	0.001	0.027	0.120	0.193	0.148	0.057	0.009	0.000	0.000	0.000
	8	0.000	0.000	0.008	0.064	0.161	0.185	0.107	0.028	0.002	0.000	0.000
	9	0.000	0.000	0.002	0.028	0.107	0.185	0.161	0.064	0.008	0.000	0.000
	10	0.000	0.000	0.000	0.009	0.057	0.148	0.193	0.120	0.027	0.001	0.000
	11	0.000	0.000	0.000	0.003	0.024	0.094	0.184	0.178	0.068	0.004	0.000
	12	0.000	0.000	0.000	0.001	0.008	0.047	0.138	0.208	0.136	0.017	0.001
	13	0.000	0.000	0.000	0.000	0.002	0.018	0.080	0.187	0.209	0.060	0.008
	14	0.000	0.000	0.000	0.000	0.000	0.005	0.034	0.125	0.239	0.156	0.041
	15	0.000	0.000	0.000	0.000	0.000	0.001	0.010	0.058	0.191	0.280	0.158
	16	0.000	0.000	0.000	0.000	0.000	0.000	0.002	0.017	0.096	0.315	0.374
	17	0.000	0.000	0.000	0.000	0.000	0.000	0.000	0.002	0.023	0.167	0.418
18	0	0.397	0.150	0.018	0.002	0.000	0.000	0.000	0.000	0.000	0.000	0.000
	1	0.376	0.300	0.081	0.013	0.001	0.000	0.000	0.000	0.000	0.000	0.000
	2	0.168	0.284	0.172	0.046	0.007	0.001	0.000	0.000	0.000	0.000	0.000
	3	0.047	0.168	0.230	0.105	0.025	0.003	0.000	0.000	0.000	0.000	0.000
	4	0.009	0.070	0.215	0.168	0.061	0.012	0.001	0.000	0.000	0.000	0.000
	5	0.001	0.022	0.151	0.202	0.115	0.033	0.004	0.000	0.000	0.000	0.000
	6	0.000	0.005	0.082	0.187	0.166	0.071	0.015	0.001	0.000	0.000	0.000
	7	0.000	0.001	0.035	0.138	0.189	0.121	0.037	0.005	0.000	0.000	0.000
	8	0.000	0.000	0.012	0.081	0.173	0.167	0.077	0.015	0.001	0.000	0.000
	9	0.000	0.000	0.003	0.039	0.128	0.185	0.128	0.039	0.003	0.000	0.000
	10	0.000	0.000	0.001	0.015	0.077	0.167	0.173	0.081	0.012	0.000	0.000
	11	0.000	0.000	0.000	0.005	0.037	0.121	0.189	0.138	0.035	0.001	0.000
	12	0.000	0.000	0.000	0.001	0.015	0.071	0.166	0.187	0.082	0.005	0.000
	13	0.000	0.000	0.000	0.000	0.004	0.033	0.115	0.202	0.151	0.022	0.001
	14	0.000	0.000	0.000	0.000	0.001	0.012	0.061	0.168	0.215	0.070	0.009
	15	0.000	0.000	0.000	0.000	0.000	0.003	0.025	0.105	0.230	0.168	0.047
	16	0.000	0.000	0.000	0.000	0.000	0.001	0.007	0.046	0.172	0.284	0.168

Table 1 *(continued)*–**The Binomial Distribution**

n	x	p										
		0.05	0.1	0.2	0.3	0.4	0.5	0.6	0.7	0.8	0.9	0.95
	17	0.000	0.000	0.000	0.000	0.000	0.000	0.001	0.013	0.081	0.300	0.376
	18	0.000	0.000	0.000	0.000	0.000	0.000	0.000	0.002	0.018	0.150	0.397
19	0	0.377	0.135	0.014	0.001	0.000	0.000	0.000	0.000	0.000	0.000	0.000
	1	0.377	0.285	0.068	0.009	0.001	0.000	0.000	0.000	0.000	0.000	0.000
	2	0.179	0.285	0.154	0.036	0.005	0.000	0.000	0.000	0.000	0.000	0.000
	3	0.053	0.180	0.218	0.087	0.017	0.002	0.000	0.000	0.000	0.000	0.000
	4	0.011	0.080	0.218	0.149	0.047	0.007	0.001	0.000	0.000	0.000	0.000
	5	0.002	0.027	0.164	0.192	0.093	0.022	0.002	0.000	0.000	0.000	0.000
	6	0.000	0.007	0.095	0.192	0.145	0.052	0.008	0.001	0.000	0.000	0.000
	7	0.000	0.001	0.044	0.153	0.180	0.096	0.024	0.002	0.000	0.000	0.000
	8	0.000	0.000	0.017	0.098	0.180	0.144	0.053	0.008	0.000	0.000	0.000
	9	0.000	0.000	0.005	0.051	0.146	0.176	0.098	0.022	0.001	0.000	0.000
	10	0.000	0.000	0.001	0.022	0.098	0.176	0.146	0.051	0.005	0.000	0.000
	11	0.000	0.000	0.000	0.008	0.053	0.144	0.180	0.098	0.017	0.000	0.000
	12	0.000	0.000	0.000	0.002	0.024	0.096	0.180	0.153	0.044	0.001	0.000
	13	0.000	0.000	0.000	0.001	0.008	0.052	0.145	0.192	0.095	0.007	0.000
	14	0.000	0.000	0.000	0.000	0.002	0.022	0.093	0.192	0.164	0.027	0.002
	15	0.000	0.000	0.000	0.000	0.001	0.007	0.047	0.149	0.218	0.080	0.011
	16	0.000	0.000	0.000	0.000	0.000	0.002	0.017	0.087	0.218	0.180	0.053
	17	0.000	0.000	0.000	0.000	0.000	0.000	0.005	0.036	0.154	0.285	0.179
	18	0.000	0.000	0.000	0.000	0.000	0.000	0.001	0.009	0.068	0.285	0.377
	19	0.000	0.000	0.000	0.000	0.000	0.000	0.000	0.001	0.014	0.135	0.377
20	0	0.358	0.122	0.012	0.001	0.000	0.000	0.000	0.000	0.000	0.000	0.000
	1	0.377	0.270	0.058	0.007	0.000	0.000	0.000	0.000	0.000	0.000	0.000
	2	0.189	0.285	0.137	0.028	0.003	0.000	0.000	0.000	0.000	0.000	0.000
	3	0.060	0.190	0.205	0.072	0.012	0.001	0.000	0.000	0.000	0.000	0.000
	4	0.013	0.090	0.218	0.130	0.035	0.005	0.000	0.000	0.000	0.000	0.000
	5	0.002	0.032	0.175	0.179	0.075	0.015	0.001	0.000	0.000	0.000	0.000
	6	0.000	0.009	0.109	0.192	0.124	0.037	0.005	0.000	0.000	0.000	0.000
	7	0.000	0.002	0.055	0.164	0.166	0.074	0.015	0.001	0.000	0.000	0.000
	8	0.000	0.000	0.022	0.114	0.180	0.120	0.035	0.004	0.000	0.000	0.000
	9	0.000	0.000	0.007	0.065	0.160	0.160	0.071	0.012	0.000	0.000	0.000
	10	0.000	0.000	0.002	0.031	0.117	0.176	0.117	0.031	0.002	0.000	0.000
	11	0.000	0.000	0.000	0.012	0.071	0.160	0.160	0.065	0.007	0.000	0.000
	12	0.000	0.000	0.000	0.004	0.035	0.120	0.180	0.114	0.022	0.000	0.000
	13	0.000	0.000	0.000	0.001	0.015	0.074	0.166	0.164	0.055	0.002	0.000
	14	0.000	0.000	0.000	0.000	0.005	0.037	0.124	0.192	0.109	0.009	0.000
	15	0.000	0.000	0.000	0.000	0.001	0.015	0.075	0.179	0.175	0.032	0.002
	16	0.000	0.000	0.000	0.000	0.000	0.005	0.035	0.130	0.218	0.090	0.013
	17	0.000	0.000	0.000	0.000	0.000	0.001	0.012	0.072	0.205	0.190	0.060
	18	0.000	0.000	0.000	0.000	0.000	0.000	0.003	0.028	0.137	0.285	0.189
	19	0.000	0.000	0.000	0.000	0.000	0.000	0.000	0.007	0.058	0.270	0.377
	20	0.000	0.000	0.000	0.000	0.000	0.000	0.000	0.001	0.012	0.122	0.358

Table 2–The Standard Normal Distribution

z	0.00	0.01	0.02	0.03	0.04	0.05	0.06	0.07	0.08	0.09
0.0	0.0000	0.0040	0.0080	0.0120	0.0160	0.0199	0.0239	0.0279	0.0319	0.0359
0.1	0.0398	0.0438	0.0478	0.0517	0.0557	0.0596	0.0636	0.0675	0.0714	0.0753
0.2	0.0793	0.0832	0.0871	0.0910	0.0948	0.0987	0.1026	0.1064	0.1103	0.1141
0.3	0.1179	0.1217	0.1255	0.1293	0.1331	0.1368	0.1406	0.1443	0.1480	0.1517
0.4	0.1554	0.1591	0.1628	0.1664	0.1700	0.1736	0.1772	0.1808	0.1844	0.1879
0.5	0.1915	0.1950	0.1985	0.2019	0.2054	0.2088	0.2123	0.2157	0.2190	0.2224
0.6	0.2257	0.2291	0.2324	0.2357	0.2389	0.2422	0.2454	0.2486	0.2517	0.2549
0.7	0.2580	0.2611	0.2642	0.2673	0.2703	0.2734	0.2764	0.2794	0.2823	0.2852
0.8	0.2881	0.2910	0.2939	0.2967	0.2995	0.3023	0.3051	0.3078	0.3106	0.3133
0.9	0.3159	0.3186	0.3212	0.3238	0.3264	0.3289	0.3315	0.3340	0.3365	0.3389
1.0	0.3413	0.3438	0.3461	0.3485	0.3508	0.3531	0.3554	0.3577	0.3599	0.3621
1.1	0.3643	0.3665	0.3686	0.3708	0.3729	0.3749	0.3770	0.3790	0.3810	0.3830
1.2	0.3849	0.3869	0.3888	0.3907	0.3925	0.3944	0.3962	0.3980	0.3997	0.4015
1.3	0.4032	0.4049	0.4066	0.4082	0.4099	0.4115	0.4131	0.4147	0.4162	0.4177
1.4	0.4192	0.4207	0.4222	0.4236	0.4251	0.4265	0.4279	0.4292	0.4306	0.4319
1.5	0.4332	0.4345	0.4357	0.4370	0.4382	0.4394	0.4406	0.4418	0.4429	0.4441
1.6	0.4452	0.4463	0.4474	0.4484	0.4495	0.4505	0.4515	0.4525	0.4535	0.4545
1.7	0.4554	0.4564	0.4573	0.4582	0.4591	0.4599	0.4608	0.4616	0.4625	0.4633
1.8	0.4641	0.4649	0.4656	0.4664	0.4671	0.4678	0.4686	0.4693	0.4699	0.4706
1.9	0.4713	0.4719	0.4726	0.4732	0.4738	0.4744	0.4750	0.4756	0.4761	0.4767
2.0	0.4772	0.4778	0.4783	0.4788	0.4793	0.4798	0.4803	0.4808	0.4812	0.4817
2.1	0.4821	0.4826	0.4830	0.4834	0.4838	0.4842	0.4846	0.4850	0.4854	0.4857
2.2	0.4861	0.4864	0.4868	0.4871	0.4875	0.4878	0.4881	0.4884	0.4887	0.4890
2.3	0.4893	0.4896	0.4898	0.4901	0.4904	0.4906	0.4909	0.4911	0.4913	0.4916
2.4	0.4918	0.4920	0.4922	0.4925	0.4927	0.4929	0.4931	0.4932	0.4934	0.4936
2.5	0.4938	0.4940	0.4941	0.4943	0.4945	0.4946	0.4948	0.4949	0.4951	0.4952
2.6	0.4953	0.4955	0.4956	0.4957	0.4959	0.4960	0.4961	0.4962	0.4963	0.4964
2.7	0.4965	0.4966	0.4967	0.4968	0.4969	0.4970	0.4971	0.4972	0.4973	0.4974
2.8	0.4974	0.4975	0.4976	0.4977	0.4977	0.4978	0.4979	0.4979	0.4980	0.4981
2.9	0.4981	0.4982	0.4982	0.4983	0.4984	0.4984	0.4985	0.4985	0.4986	0.4986
3.0	0.4987	0.4987	0.4987	0.4988	0.4988	0.4989	0.4989	0.4989	0.4990	0.4990

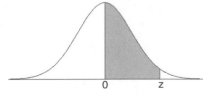

Numerical entries represent the probability that a standard normal random variable is between 0 and z.

Table 3–The *t* Distribution

	Confidence Intervals	80%	90%	95%	98%	99%
	One-Tail, α	0.10	0.05	0.025	0.01	0.005
df	Two-Tail, α	0.20	0.10	0.05	0.02	0.01
1		3.078	6.314	12.706	31.821	63.657
2		1.886	2.920	4.303	6.965	9.925
3		1.638	2.353	3.182	4.541	5.841
4		1.533	2.132	2.776	3.747	4.604
5		1.476	2.015	2.571	3.365	4.032
6		1.440	1.943	2.447	3.143	3.707
7		1.415	1.895	2.365	2.998	3.499
8		1.397	1.860	2.306	2.896	3.355
9		1.383	1.833	2.262	2.821	3.250
10		1.372	1.812	2.228	2.764	3.169
11		1.363	1.796	2.201	2.718	3.106
12		1.356	1.782	2.179	2.681	3.055
13		1.350	1.771	2.160	2.650	3.012
14		1.345	1.761	2.145	2.624	2.977
15		1.341	1.753	2.131	2.602	2.947
16		1.337	1.746	2.120	2.583	2.921
17		1.333	1.740	2.110	2.567	2.898
18		1.330	1.734	2.101	2.552	2.878
19		1.328	1.729	2.093	2.539	2.861
20		1.325	1.725	2.086	2.528	2.845
21		1.323	1.721	2.080	2.518	2.831
22		1.321	1.717	2.074	2.508	2.819
23		1.319	1.714	2.069	2.500	2.807
24		1.318	1.711	2.064	2.492	2.797
25		1.316	1.708	2.060	2.485	2.787
26		1.315	1.706	2.056	2.479	2.779
27		1.314	1.703	2.052	2.473	2.771
28		1.313	1.701	2.048	2.467	2.763
(z) ∞		1.282[a]	1.645	1.960	2.326[b]	2.576[c]

[a] $1.282 \approx 1.28$
[b] $2.326 \approx 2.33$
[c] $2.576 \approx 2.58$

Table 4–Critical Values for the Chi-square Distribution

DEGREES OF FREEDOM					α					
	0.005	0.01	0.025	0.05	0.1	0.9	0.95	0.975	0.99	0.995
1	7.879	6.635	5.024	3.841	2.706	0.016	0.004	0.001	0.000	0.000
2	10.597	9.210	7.378	5.991	4.605	0.211	0.103	0.051	0.020	0.010
3	12.838	11.345	9.348	7.815	6.251	0.584	0.352	0.216	0.115	0.072
4	14.860	13.277	11.143	9.488	7.779	1.064	0.711	0.484	0.297	0.207
5	16.750	15.086	12.833	11.070	9.236	1.610	1.145	0.831	0.554	0.412
6	18.548	16.812	14.449	12.592	10.645	2.204	1.635	1.237	0.872	0.676
7	20.278	18.475	16.013	14.067	12.017	2.833	2.167	1.690	1.239	0.989
8	21.955	20.090	17.535	15.507	13.362	3.490	2.733	2.180	1.646	1.344
9	23.589	21.666	19.023	16.919	14.684	4.168	3.325	2.700	2.088	1.735
10	25.188	23.209	20.483	18.307	15.987	4.865	3.940	3.247	2.558	2.156
11	26.757	24.725	21.920	19.675	17.275	5.578	4.575	3.816	3.053	2.603
12	28.300	26.217	23.337	21.026	18.549	6.304	5.226	4.404	3.571	3.074
13	29.819	27.688	24.736	22.362	19.812	7.042	5.892	5.009	4.107	3.565
14	31.319	29.141	26.119	23.685	21.064	7.790	6.571	5.629	4.660	4.075
15	32.801	30.578	27.488	24.996	22.307	8.547	7.261	6.262	5.229	4.601
16	34.267	32.000	28.845	26.296	23.542	9.312	7.962	6.908	5.812	5.142
17	35.718	33.409	30.191	27.587	24.769	10.085	8.672	7.564	6.408	5.697
18	37.156	34.805	31.526	28.869	25.989	10.865	9.390	8.231	7.015	6.265
19	38.582	36.191	32.852	30.144	27.204	11.651	10.117	8.907	7.633	6.844
20	39.997	37.566	34.170	31.410	28.412	12.443	10.851	9.591	8.260	7.434
21	41.401	38.932	35.479	32.671	29.615	13.240	11.591	10.283	8.897	8.034
22	42.796	40.289	36.781	33.924	30.813	14.041	12.338	10.982	9.542	8.643
23	44.181	41.638	38.076	35.172	32.007	14.848	13.091	11.689	10.196	9.260
24	45.559	42.980	39.364	36.415	33.196	15.659	13.848	12.401	10.856	9.886
25	46.928	44.314	40.646	37.652	34.382	16.473	14.611	13.120	11.524	10.520
26	48.290	45.642	41.923	38.885	35.563	17.292	15.379	13.844	12.198	11.160
27	49.645	46.963	43.195	40.113	36.741	18.114	16.151	14.573	12.879	11.808
28	50.993	48.278	44.461	41.337	37.916	18.939	16.928	15.308	13.565	12.461
29	52.336	49.588	45.722	42.557	39.087	19.768	17.708	16.047	14.256	13.121
30	53.672	50.892	46.979	43.773	40.256	20.599	18.493	16.791	14.953	13.787
40	66.766	63.691	59.342	55.758	51.805	29.051	26.509	24.433	22.164	20.707
50	79.490	76.154	71.420	67.505	63.167	37.689	34.764	32.357	29.707	27.991
60	91.952	88.379	83.298	79.082	74.397	46.459	43.188	40.482	37.485	35.534
70	104.215	100.425	95.023	90.531	85.527	55.329	51.739	48.758	45.442	43.275
80	116.321	112.329	106.629	101.879	96.578	64.278	60.391	57.153	53.540	51.172
90	128.299	124.116	118.136	113.145	107.565	73.291	69.126	65.647	61.754	59.196
100	140.169	135.807	129.561	124.342	118.498	82.358	77.929	74.222	70.065	67.328

Table 5–Critical Values of the *F* Distribution ($\alpha = 0.1$)

		NUMERATOR DEGREES OF FREEDOM								
		1	2	3	4	5	6	7	8	9
	1	39.86	49.50	53.59	55.83	57.24	58.20	58.91	59.44	59.86
D	2	8.53	9.00	9.16	9.24	9.29	9.33	9.35	9.37	9.38
e	3	5.54	5.46	5.39	5.34	5.31	5.28	5.27	5.25	5.24
n	4	4.54	4.32	4.19	4.11	4.05	4.01	3.98	3.95	3.94
o	5	4.06	3.78	3.62	3.52	3.45	3.40	3.37	3.34	3.32
m	6	3.78	3.46	3.29	3.18	3.11	3.05	3.01	2.98	2.96
i	7	3.59	3.26	3.07	2.96	2.88	2.83	2.78	2.75	2.72
n	8	3.46	3.11	2.92	2.81	2.73	2.67	2.62	2.59	2.56
a	9	3.36	3.01	2.81	2.69	2.61	2.55	2.51	2.47	2.44
t	10	3.29	2.92	2.73	2.61	2.52	2.46	2.41	2.38	2.35
o	11	3.23	2.86	2.66	2.54	2.45	2.39	2.34	2.30	2.27
r	12	3.18	2.81	2.61	2.48	2.39	2.33	2.28	2.24	2.21
D	13	3.14	2.76	2.56	2.43	2.35	2.28	2.23	2.20	2.16
e	14	3.10	2.73	2.52	2.39	2.31	2.24	2.19	2,15	2.12
g	15	3.07	2.70	2.49	2.36	2.27	2.21	2.16	2.12	2.09
r	16	3.05	2.67	2.46	2.33	2.24	2.18	2.13	2.09	2.06
e	17	3.03	2.64	2.44	2.31	2.22	2.15	2.10	2.06	2.03
e	18	3.01	2.62	2.42	2.29	2.20	2.13	2.08	2.04	2.00
s	19	2.99	2.61	2.40	2.27	2.18	2.11	2.06	2.02	1.98
	20	2.97	2.59	2.38	2.25	2.16	2.09	2.04	2.00	1.96
o	21	2.96	2.57	2.36	2.23	2.14	2.08	2.02	1.98	1.95
f	22	2.95	2.56	2.35	2.22	2.13	2.06	2.01	1.97	1.93
F	23	2.94	2.55	2.34	2.21	2.11	2.05	1.99	1.95	1.92
r	24	2.93	2.54	2.33	2.19	2.10	2.04	1.98	1.94	1.91
e	25	2.92	2.53	2.32	2.18	2.09	2.02	1.97	1.93	1.89
e	26	2.91	2.52	2.31	2.17	2.08	2.01	1.96	1.92	1.88
d	27	2.90	2.51	2.30	2.17	2.07	2.00	1.95	1.91	1.87
o	28	2.89	2.50	2.29	2.16	2.06	2.00	1.94	1.90	1.87
m	29	2.89	2.50	2.28	2.15	2.06	1.99	1,93	1.89	1.86
	30	2.88	2.49	2.28	2.14	2.05	1.98	1.93	1.88	1.85
	40	2.84	2.44	2.23	2.09	2.00	1.93	1.87	1.83	1.79
	60	2.79	2.39	2.18	2.04	1.95	1.87	1.82	1.77	1.74
	120	2.75	2.35	2.13	1.99	1.90	1.82	1.77	1.72	1.68
	∞	2.71	2.30	2.08	1.94	1.85	1.77	1.72	1.67	1.63

		NUMERATOR DEGREES OF FREEDOM								
		10	12	15	20	24	30	40	60	120
D	1	60.19	60.71	61.22	61.74	62.00	62.26	62.53	62.79	63.06
e	2	9.39	9.41	9.42	9.44	9.45	9.46	9.47	9.47	9.48
n	3	5.23	5.22	5.20	5.18	5.18	5.17	5.16	5.15	5.14
o	4	3.92	3.90	3.87	3.84	3.83	3.82	3.80	3.79	3.78
m	5	3.30	3.27	3.24	3.21	3.19	3.17	3.16	3.14	3.12
i	6	2.94	2.90	2.87	2.84	2.82	2.80	2.78	2.76	2.74
n	7	2.70	2.67	2.63	2.59	2.58	2.56	2.54	2.51	2.49
a	8	2.54	2.50	2.46	2.42	2.40	2.38	2.36	2.34	2.32
t	9	2.42	2.38	2.34	2.30	2.28	2.25	2.23	2.21	2.18
o	10	2.32	2.28	2.24	2.20	2.18	2.16	2.13	2.11	2.08
r	11	2.25	2.21	2.17	2.12	2.10	2.08	2.05	2.03	2.00
	12	2.19	2.15	2.10	2.06	2.04	2.01	1.99	1.96	1.93
D	13	2.14	2.10	2.05	2.01	1.98	1.96	1.93	1.90	1.88
e	14	2.10	2.05	2.01	1.96	1.94	1.91	1.89	1.86	1.83
g	15	2.06	2.02	1.97	1.92	1.90	1.87	1.85	1.82	1.79
r	16	2.03	1.99	1.94	1.89	1.87	1.84	1.81	1.78	1.75
e	17	2.00	1.96	1.91	1.86	1.84	1.81	1.78	1.75	1.72
e	18	1.98	1.93	1.89	1.84	1.81	1.78	1.75	1.72	1.69
s	19	1.96	1.91	1.86	1.81	1.79	1.76	1.73	1.70	1.67
o	20	1.94	1.89	1.84	1.79	1.77	1.74	1.71	1.68	1.64
f	21	1.92	1.87	1.83	1.78	1.75	1.72	1.69	1.66	1.62
	22	1.90	1.86	1.81	1.76	1.73	1.70	1.67	1.64	1.60
F	23	1.89	1.84	1.80	1.74	1.72	1.69	1.66	1.62	1.59
r	24	1.88	1.83	1.78	1.73	1.70	1.67	1.64	1.61	1.57
e	25	1.87	1.82	1.77	1.72	1.69	1.66	1.63	1.59	1.56
e	26	1.86	1.81	1.76	1.71	1.68	1.65	1.61	1.58	1.54
d	27	1.85	1.80	1.75	1.70	1.67	1.64	1.60	1.57	1.53
o	28	1.84	1.79	1.74	1.69	1.66	1.63	1.59	1.56	1.52
m	29	1.83	1.78	1.73	1.68	1.65	1.62	1.58	1.55	1.51
	30	1.82	1.77	1.72	1.67	1.64	1.61	1.57	1.54	1.50
	40	1.76	1.71	1.66	1.61	1.57	1.54	1.51	1.47	1.42
	60	1.71	1.66	1.60	1.54	1.51	1.48	1.44	1.40	1.35
	120	1.65	1.60	1.55	1.48	1.45	1.41	1.37	1.32	1.26
	∞	1.60	1.55	1.49	1.42	1.38	1.34	1.30	1.24	1.17

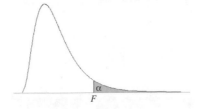

Table 5 *(continued)*–**Critical Values of the *F* Distribution ($\alpha = 0.05$)**

		1	2	3	4	5	6	7	8	9
		\multicolumn{9}{c}{NUMERATOR DEGREES OF FREEDOM}							
D	1	161.45	199.5	215.7	224.58	230.1	233.99	236.7	238.8	240.5
e	2	18.51	19.00	19.16	19.25	19.30	19.33	19.35	19.37	19.38
n	3	10.13	9.55	9.28	9.12	9.01	8.94	8.89	8.85	8.81
o	4	7.71	6.94	6.59	6.39	6.26	6.16	6.09	6.04	6.00
m	5	6.61	5.79	5.41	5.19	5.05	4.95	4.88	4.82	4.77
i	6	5.99	5.14	4.76	4.53	4.39	4.28	4.21	4.15	4.10
n	7	5.59	4.74	4.35	4.12	3.97	3.87	3.79	3.73	3.68
a	8	5.32	4.46	4.07	3.84	3.69	3.58	3.50	3.44	3.39
t	9	5.12	4.26	3.86	3.63	3.48	3.37	3.29	3.23	3.18
o	10	4.96	4.10	3.71	3.48	3.33	3.22	3.14	3.07	3.02
r	11	4.84	3.98	3.59	3.36	3.20	3.09	3.01	2.95	2.90
	12	4.75	3.89	3.49	3.26	3.11	3.00	2.91	2.85	2.80
D	13	4.67	3.81	3.41	3.18	3.03	2.92	2.83	2.77	2.71
e	14	4.60	3.74	3.34	3.11	2.96	2.85	2.76	2.70	2.65
g	15	4.54	3.68	3.29	3.06	2.90	2.79	2.71	2.64	2.59
r	16	4.49	3.63	3.24	3.01	2.85	2.74	2.66	2.59	2.54
e	17	4.45	3.59	3.20	2.96	2.81	2.70	2.61	2.55	2.49
e	18	4.41	3.55	3.16	2.93	2.77	2.66	2.58	2.51	2.46
s	19	4.38	3.52	3.13	2.90	2.74	2.63	2.54	2.48	2.42
o	20	4.35	3.49	3.10	2.87	2.71	2.60	2.51	2.45	2.39
f	21	4.32	3.47	3.07	2.84	2.68	2.57	2.49	2.42	2.37
	22	4.30	3.44	3.05	2.82	2.66	2.55	2.46	2.40	2.34
F	23	4.28	3.42	3.03	2.80	2.64	2.53	2.44	2.37	2.32
r	24	4.26	3.40	3.01	2.78	2.62	2.51	2.42	2.36	2.30
e	25	4.24	3.39	2.99	2.76	2.60	2.49	2.40	2.34	2.28
e	26	4.23	3.37	2.98	2.74	2.59	2.47	2.39	2.32	2.27
d	27	4.21	3.35	2.96	2.73	2.57	2.46	2.37	2.31	2.25
o	28	4.20	3.34	2.95	2.71	2.56	2.45	2.36	2.29	2.24
m	29	4.18	3.33	2.93	2.70	2.55	2.43	2.35	2.28	2.22
	30	4.17	3.32	2.92	2.69	2.53	2.42	2.33	2.27	2.21
	40	4.08	3.23	2.84	2.61	2.45	2.34	2.25	2.18	2.12
	60	4.00	3.15	2.76	2.53	2.37	2.25	2.17	2.10	2.04
	120	3.92	3.07	2.68	2.45	2.29	2.18	2.09	2.02	1.96
	∞	3.84	3.00	2.60	2.37	2.21	2.10	2.01	1.94	1.88

		NUMERATOR DEGREES OF FREEDOM							
		10	12	15	20	24	30	40	60	120
	1	241.88	243.90	245.9	248.0	249.0	250.1	251.1	252.2	253.2
D	2	19.40	19.41	19.43	19.45	19.45	19.46	19.47	19.48	19.49
e	3	8.79	8.74	8.70	8.66	8.64	8.62	8.59	8.57	8.55
n	4	5.96	5.91	5.86	5.80	5.77	5.75	5.72	5.69	5.66
o	5	4.74	4.68	4.62	4.56	4.53	4.50	4.46	4.43	4.40
m	6	4.06	4.00	3.94	3.87	3.84	3.81	3.77	3.74	3.70
i	7	3.64	3.57	3.51	3.44	3.41	3.38	3.34	3.30	3.27
n	8	3.35	3.28	3.22	3.15	3.12	3.08	3.04	3.01	2.97
a	9	3.14	3.07	3.01	2.94	2.90	2.86	2.83	2.79	2.75
t	10	2.98	2.91	2.85	2.77	2.74	2.70	2.66	2.62	2.58
o	11	2.85	2.79	2.72	2.65	2.61	2.57	2.53	2.49	2.45
r	12	2.75	2.69	2.62	2.54	2.51	2.47	2.43	2.38	2.34
D	13	2.67	2.60	2.53	2.46	2.42	2.38	2.34	2.30	2.25
e	14	2.60	2.53	2.46	2.39	2.35	2.31	2.27	2.22	2.18
g	15	2.54	2.48	2.40	2.33	2.29	2.25	2.20	2.16	2.11
r	16	2.49	2.42	2.35	2.28	2.24	2.19	2.15	2.11	2.06
e	17	2.45	2.38	2.31	2.23	2.19	2.15	2.10	2.06	2.01
e	18	2.41	2.34	2.27	2.19	2.15	2.11	2.06	2.02	1.97
s	19	2.38	2.31	2.23	2.16	2.11	2.07	2.03	1.98	1.93
	20	2.35	2.28	2.20	2.12	2.08	2.04	1.99	1.95	1.90
o	21	2.32	2.25	2.18	2.10	2.05	2.01	1.96	1.92	1.87
f	22	2.30	2.23	2.15	2.07	2.03	1.98	1.94	1.89	1.84
F	23	2.27	2.20	2.13	2.05	2.01	1.96	1.91	1.86	1.81
r	24	2.25	2.18	2.11	2.03	1.98	1.94	1.89	1.84	1.79
e	25	2.24	2.16	2.09	2.01	1.96	1.92	1.87	1.82	1.77
e	26	2.22	2.15	2.07	1.99	1.95	1.90	1.85	1.80	1.75
d	27	2.20	2.13	2.06	1.97	1.93	1.88	1.84	1.79	1.73
o	28	2.19	2.12	2.04	1.96	1.91	1.87	1.82	1.77	1.71
m	29	2.18	2.10	2.03	1.94	1.90	1.85	1.81	1.75	1.70
	30	2.16	2.09	2.01	1.93	1.89	1.84	1.79	1.74	1.68
	40	2.08	2.00	1.92	1.84	1.79	1.74	1.69	1.64	1.58
	60	1.99	1.92	1.84	1.75	1.70	1.65	1.59	1.53	1.47
	120	1.91	1.83	1.75	1.66	1.61	1.55	1.50	1.43	1.35
	∞	1.83	1.75	1.67	1.57	1.52	1.46	1.39	1.32	1.22

Table 5 *(continued)*–**Critical Values of the *F* Distribution** ($\alpha = 0.025$)

		1	2	3	4	5	6	7	8	9
					NUMERATOR DEGREES OF FREEDOM					
	1	647.79	799.4	864.1	899.6	921.83	937.1	948.20	956.6	963.2
D	2	38.51	39.00	39.17	39.25	39.30	39.33	39.36	39.37	39.39
e	3	17.44	16.04	15.44	15.10	14.88	14.73	14.62	14.54	14.47
n	4	12.22	10.65	9.98	9.60	9.36	9.20	9.07	8.98	8.90
o	5	10.01	8.43	7.76	7.39	7.15	6.98	6.85	6.76	6.68
m	6	8.81	7.26	6.60	6.23	5.99	5.82	5.70	5.60	5.52
i	7	8.07	6.54	5.89	5.52	5.29	5.12	4.99	4.90	4.82
n	8	7.57	6.06	5.42	5.05	4.82	4.65	4.53	4.43	4.36
a	9	7.21	5.71	5.08	4.72	4.48	4.32	4.20	4.10	4.03
t	10	6.94	5.46	4.83	4.47	4.24	4.07	3.95	3.85	3.78
o	11	6.72	5.26	4.63	4.28	4.04	3.88	3.76	3.66	3.59
r	12	6.55	5.10	4.47	4.12	3.89	3.73	3.61	3.51	3.44
D	13	6.41	4.97	4.35	4.00	3.77	3.60	3.48	3.39	3.31
e	14	6.30	4.86	4.24	3.89	3.66	3.50	3.38	3.29	3.21
g	15	6.20	4.77	4.15	3.80	3.58	3.41	3.29	3.20	3.12
r	16	6.12	4.69	4.08	3.73	3.50	3.34	3.22	3.12	3.05
e	17	6.04	4.62	4.01	3.66	3.44	3.28	3.16	3.06	2.98
e	18	5.98	4.56	3.95	3.61	3.38	3.22	3.10	3.01	2.93
s	19	5.92	4.51	3.90	3.56	3.33	3.17	3.05	2.96	2.88
	20	5.87	4.46	3.86	3.51	3.29	3.13	3.01	2.91	2.84
o	21	5.83	4.42	3.82	3.48	3.25	3.09	2.97	2.87	2.80
f	22	5.79	4.38	3.78	3.44	3.22	3.05	2.93	2.84	2.76
F	23	5.75	4.35	3.75	3.41	3.18	3.02	2.90	2.81	2.73
r	24	5.72	4.32	3.72	3.38	3.15	2.99	2.87	2.78	2.70
e	25	5.69	4.29	3.69	3.35	3.13	2.97	2.85	2.75	2.68
e	26	5.66	4.27	3.67	3.33	3.10	2.94	2.82	2.73	2.65
d	27	5.63	4.24	3.65	3.31	3.08	2.92	2.80	2.71	2.63
o	28	5.61	4.22	3.63	3.29	3.06	2.90	2.78	2.69	2.61
m	29	5.59	4.20	3.61	3.27	3.04	2.88	2.76	2.67	2.59
	30	5.57	4.18	3.59	3.25	3.03	2.87	2.75	2.65	2.57
	40	5.42	4.05	3.46	3.13	2.90	2.74	2.62	2.53	2.45
	60	5.29	3.93	3.34	3.01	2.79	2.63	2.51	2.41	2.33
	120	5.15	3.80	3.23	2.89	2.67	2.52	2.39	2.30	2.22
	∞	5.02	3.69	3.12	2.79	2.57	2.41	2.29	2.19	2.11

NUMERATOR DEGREES OF FREEDOM									
	10	12	15	20	24	30	40	60	120
1	968.63	976.72	984.87	993.08	997.27	1001.40	1005.60	1009.79	1014.04
2	39.40	39.41	39.43	39.45	39.46	39.46	39.47	39.48	39.49
3	14.42	14.34	14.25	14.17	14.12	14.08	14.04	13.99	13.95
4	8.84	8.75	8.66	8.56	8.51	8.46	8.41	8.36	8.31
5	6.62	6.52	6.43	6.33	6.28	6.23	6.18	6.12	6.07
6	5.46	5.37	5.27	5.17	5.12	5.07	5.01	4.96	4.90
7	4.76	4.67	4.57	4.47	4.42	4.36	4.31	4.25	4.20
8	4.30	4.20	4.10	4.00	3.95	3.89	3.84	3.78	3.73
9	3.96	3.87	3.77	3.67	3.61	3.56	3.51	3.45	3.39
10	3.72	3.62	3.52	3.42	3.37	3.31	3.26	3.20	3.14
11	3.53	3.43	3.33	3.23	3.17	3.12	3.06	3.00	2.94
12	3.37	3.28	3.18	3.07	3.02	2.96	2.91	2.85	2.79
13	3.25	3.15	3.05	2.95	2.89	2.84	2.78	2.72	2.66
14	3.15	3.05	2.95	2.84	2.79	2.73	2.67	2.61	2.55
15	3.06	2.96	2.86	2.76	2.70	2.64	2.59	2.52	2.46
16	2.99	2.89	2.79	2.68	2.63	2.57	2.51	2.45	2.38
17	2.92	2.82	2.72	2.62	2.56	2.50	2.44	2.38	2.32
18	2.87	2.77	2.67	2.56	2.50	2.44	2.38	2.32	2.26
19	2.82	2.72	2.62	2.51	2.45	2.39	2.33	2.27	2.20
20	2.77	2.68	2.57	2.46	2.41	2.35	2.29	2.22	2.16
21	2.73	2.64	2.53	2.42	2.37	2.31	2.25	2.18	2.11
22	2.70	2.60	2.50	2.39	2.33	2.27	2.21	2.14	2.08
23	2.67	2.57	2.47	2.36	2.30	2.24	2.18	2.11	2.04
24	2.64	2.54	2.44	2.33	2.27	2.21	2.15	2.08	2.01
25	2.61	2.51	2.41	2.30	2.24	2.18	2.12	2.05	1.98
26	2.59	2.49	2.39	2.28	2.22	2.16	2.09	2.03	1.95
27	2.57	2.47	2.36	2.25	2.19	2.13	2.07	2.00	1.93
28	2.55	2.45	2.34	2.23	2.17	2.11	2.05	1.98	1.91
29	2.53	2.43	2.32	2.21	2.15	2.09	2.03	1.96	1.89
30	2.51	2.41	2.31	2.20	2.14	2.07	2.01	1.94	1.87
40	2.39	2.29	2.18	2.07	2.01	1.94	1.88	1.80	1.72
60	2.27	2.17	2.06	1.94	1.88	1.82	1.74	1.67	1.58
120	2.16	2.05	1.94	1.82	1.76	1.69	1.61	1.53	1.43
∞	2.05	1.94	1.83	1.71	1.64	1.57	1.48	1.39	1.27

Denominator Degrees of Freedom

Table 5 *(continued)*–**Critical Values of the *F* Distribution ($\alpha = 0.01$)**

		NUMERATOR DEGREES OF FREEDOM							
		1	2	3	4	5	6	7	8	9
	1	4052.18	4999.34	5403.53	5624.26	5763.96	5858.95	5928.33	5980.95	6022.40
D	2	98.50	99.00	99.16	99.25	99.30	99.33	99.36	99.38	99.39
e	3	34.12	30.82	29.46	28.71	28.24	27.91	27.67	27.49	27.34
n	4	21.20	18.00	16.69	15.98	15.52	15.21	14.98	14.80	14.66
o	5	16.26	13.27	12.06	11.39	10.97	10.67	10.46	10.29	10.16
m	6	13.75	10.92	9.78	9.15	8.75	8.47	8.26	8.10	7.98
i	7	12.25	9.55	8.45	7.85	7.46	7.19	6.99	6,84	6.72
n	8	11.26	8.65	7.59	7.01	6.63	6.37	6.18	6.03	5.91
a	9	10.56	8.02	6.99	6.42	6.06	5.80	5.61	5.47	5.35
t	10	10.04	7.56	6.55	5.99	5.64	5.39	5.20	5.06	4.94
o	11	9.65	7,21	6.22	5.67	5.32	5.07	4.89	4.74	4.63
r	12	9.33	6.93	5.95	5.41	5.06	4.82	4.64	4.50	4.39
D	13	9.07	6.70	5.74	5.21	4.86	4.62	4.44	4.30	4.19
e	14	8.86	6.51	5.56	5.04	4.69	4.46	4.28	4.14	4.03
g	15	8.68	6.36	5.42	4.89	4.56	4.32	4.14	4.00	3.89
r	16	8.53	6.23	5.29	4.77	4.44	4.20	4.03	3.89	3.78
e	17	8.40	6.11	5.19	4.67	4.34	4.10	3.93	3.79	3.68
e	18	8.29	6.01	5.09	4.58	4.25	4.01	3,84	3.71	3.60
s	19	8.18	5.93	5.01	4.50	4.17	3.94	3.77	3.63	3.52
	20	8.10	5.85	4.94	4.43	4.10	3.87	3.70	3.56	3.46
o	21	8.02	5.78	4.87	4.37	4.04	3.81	3.64	3.51	3.40
f	22	7.95	5.72	4.82	4.31	3.99	3.76	3.59	3.45	3.35
F	23	7.88	5.66	4.76	4.26	3.94	3.71	3.54	3.41	3.30
r	24	7.82	5.61	4.72	4.22	3.90	3.67	3.50	3.36	3.26
e	25	7.77	5.57	4.68	4.18	3.85	3.63	3.46	3.32	3.22
e	26	7.72	5.53	4.64	4.14	3.82	3.59	3.42	3.29	3.18
d	27	7.68	5.49	4.60	4.11	3.78	3.56	3.39	3.26	3.15
o	28	7.64	5.45	4.57	4.07	3.75	3.53	3.36	3.23	3.12
m	29	7.60	5.42	4.54	4.04	3.73	3.50	3.33	3.20	3.09
	30	7.56	5.39	4.51	4.02	3.70	3.47	3.30	3.17	3.07
	40	7.31	5.18	4.31	3.83	3.51	3.29	3.12	2.99	2.89
	60	7.08	4.98	4.13	3.65	3.34	3.12	2.95	2.82	2.72
	120	6.85	4.79	3.95	3.48	3.17	2.96	2.79	2.66	2.56
	∞	6.63	4.61	3.78	3.32	3.02	2.80	2.64	2.51	2.41

		NUMERATOR DEGREES OF FREEDOM								
		10	12	15	20	24	30	40	60	120
D	1	6055.93	6106.68	6156.97	6208.66	6234.27	6260.35	6286.43	6312.97	6
e	2	99.40	99.42	99.43	99.45	99.46	99.47	99.48	99.48	99.49
n	3	27.23	27.05	26.87	26.69	26.60	26.50	26.41	26.32	26.22
o	4	14.55	14.37	14.20	14.02	13.93	13.84	13.75	13.65	13.56
m	5	10.05	9.89	9.72	9.55	9.47	9.38	9.29	9.20	9.11
i	6	7.87	7.72	7.56	7.40	7.31	7.23	7.14	7.06	6.97
n	7	6.62	6.47	6.31	6.16	6.07	5.99	5.91	5.82	5.74
a	8	5.81	5.67	5.52	5.36	5.28	5.20	5.12	5.03	4.95
t	9	5.26	5.11	4.96	4.81	4.73	4.65	4.57	4.48	4.40
o	10	4.85	4.71	4.56	4.41	4.33	4.25	4.17	4.08	4.00
r	11	4.54	4.40	4.25	4.10	4.02	3.94	3.86	3.78	3.69
	12	4.30	4.16	4.01	3.86	3.78	3.70	3.62	3.54	3.45
D	13	4.10	3.96	3.82	3.66	3.59	3.51	3.43	3.34	3.25
e	14	3.94	3.80	3.66	3.51	3.43	3.35	3.27	3.18	3.09
g	15	3.80	3.67	3.52	3.37	3.29	3.21	3.13	3.05	2.96
r	16	3.69	3.55	3.41	3.26	3.18	3.10	3.02	2.93	2.84
e	17	3.59	3.46	3.31	3.16	3.08	3.00	2.92	2.83	2.75
e	18	3.51	3.37	3.23	3.08	3.00	2.92	2.84	2.75	2.66
s	19	3.43	3.30	3.15	3.00	2.92	2.84	2.76	2.67	2.58
	20	3.37	3.23	3.09	2.94	2.86	2.78	2.69	2.61	2.52
o	21	3.31	3.17	3.03	2.88	2.80	2.72	2.64	2.55	2.46
f	22	3.26	3.12	2.98	2.83	2.75	2.67	2.58	2.50	2.40
F	23	3.21	3.07	2.93	2.78	2.70	2.62	2.54	2.45	2.35
r	24	3.17	3.03	2.89	2.74	2.66	2.58	2.49	2.40	2.31
e	25	3.13	2.99	2.85	2.70	2.62	2.54	2.45	2.36	2.27
e	26	3.09	2.96	2.81	2.66	2.58	2.50	2.42	2.33	2.23
d	27	3.06	2.93	2.78	2.63	2.55	2.47	2.38	2.29	2.20
o	28	3.03	2.90	2.75	2.60	2.52	2.44	2.35	2.26	2.17
m	29	3.00	2.87	2.73	2.57	2.49	2.41	2.33	2.23	2.14
	30	2.98	2.84	2.70	2.55	2.47	2.39	2.30	2.21	2.11
	40	2.80	2.66	2.52	2.37	2.29	2.20	2.11	2.02	1.92
	60	2.63	2.50	2.35	2.20	2.12	2.03	1.94	1.84	1.73
	120	2.47	2.34	2.19	2.03	1.95	1.86	1.76	1.66	1.53
	∞	2.32	2.18	2.04	1.88	1.79	1.70	1.59	1.47	1.32

Index